CAMBRIDGE STUDIES IN LINGUISTICS

Functional syntax and universal grammar

In this series

*Issued in hard covers and as a paperback

FUNCTIONAL SYNTAX AND UNIVERSAL GRAMMAR

WILLIAM A. FOLEY

Australian National University

ROBERT D. VAN VALIN, Jr

University of California, Davis

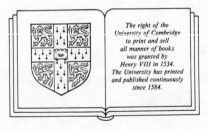

The right of the
University of Cambridge
to print and sell
all manner of books
was granted by
Henry VIII in 1534.
The University has printed
and published continuously
since 1584.

CAMBRIDGE UNIVERSITY PRESS

CAMBRIDGE

LONDON   NEW YORK   NEW ROCHELLE

MELBOURNE   SYDNEY

Published by the Press Syndicate of the University of Cambridge
The Pitt Building, Trumpington Street, Cambridge CB2 1RP
32 East 57th Street, New York, NY 10022, USA
296 Beaconsfield Parade, Middle Park, Melbourne 3206, Australia

First published 1984

Printed in Great Britain at the University Press, Cambridge

Library of Congress catalogue card number: 83–23949

British Library Cataloguing in Publication Data
Foley, William A.
    Functional syntax and universal grammar. –
    (Cambridge studies in linguistics, ISSN 0068–676x; 38)
    1. Grammar, comparative and general – Syntax
    2. Functionalism (Linguistics)
    I. Title II. Van Valin, Robert D., Jr
    415   P291

ISBN 0 521 25956 8
ISBN 0 521 26904 0

NP

Contents

List of tables

List of figures

Preface

This book is the result of a collaborative effort over a number of years to develop a non-derivational, functionally-based theory of grammar. We have attempted to construct a rigorous yet flexible theory which describes coherently a wide range of typologically varied languages. We do not regard the structure of one language type as prototypical and other types as deviations from this prototype, a position often associated with current alternative models of grammatical description such as Government and Binding Theory. Data from 'exotic' languages, such as Austronesian, Papuan, Australian, and American Indian languages, have played decisive roles in the formulation of many of our basic theoretical concepts. We feel that the foregrounding of data from such 'exotic' languages is now crucially important, as much current and recent theorizing has depended too heavily on English and familiar European languages, with this result that this theorizing has been biased in favor of languages of essentially one grammatical type (Whorf's *Standard Average European*). The actual richness of human language types has been ignored, and we believe that much of current grammatical theory has been impoverished as a consequence. Familiar languages such as English have not been ignored in our work, but they have also not been accorded primacy. It is a measure of the descriptive power of our analytical concepts that although usually developed independently, they offer new insights into English grammar. This book is only a first step in the development of a fully articulated functional theory of grammar, but the initial results of the approach are encouraging indeed.

We owe much to many people for support and stimulation over the years that this work has matured. Our greatest single debt is to Michael Silverstein, who has provided continuous encouragement and perspicacious commentary on earlier papers and drafts of this book. His work has provided much of the basic framework as well as substantive concepts for a functional theory of grammar. We also owe a great debt to Michael Olson, whose pioneering work on interclausal relations in this Ph.D. dissertation at the Australian National University provided a basis and stimulus for the theory of interclausal relations presented here in Chapters 5–7. Other people who have played important roles in the development of our thought are: Alton Becker, R.M.W. Dixon, Charles Fillmore, John Gumperz, Jeffery Heath, Johanna Nichols, Anna Wierzbicka, and David Wilkins. In addition, we would like to thank the following people for comments on earlier drafts of this book: Avery Andrews, Edith Bavin, Carolyn Coleman, Alan Dench, Mark Durie, Bronwyn Eather, Cliff Goddard, Ian Green, Mark Harvey, Jeri Jaeger, Harold Koch, Tim Shopen, Charles Walton, Kenneth Whistler, and an anonymous referee. We wish to extend our most sincere and special thanks to Mrs Ellalene Seymour, who did a valiant job of typing the draft chapters, usually from very untidy handwritten manuscripts, a joyless task no doubt but one which she dispatched with cheerful determination. We would also like to thank Penny Carter at Cambridge University Press for her help in getting the manuscript to press.

For institutional support, our primary debt is to the Australian National University. It generously offered a two-year research fellowship to Van Valin so that the co-authors could work together and finish this book. The facilities of the Australian National University must certainly be among the very best in the world, and without its support this book would have been much more difficult and time consuming to complete. In addition, W.A. Foley wishes to thank the Australian Research Grants Scheme for its continuing support of his research into the Yimas languages of Papua New Guinea. Some of the results of this study figure prominantly in our analyses. Foley wishes to take the opportunity here to publicly thank the Yimas people for their many kindnesses during the years in which this research has proceeded.

The order of authors' names is strictly alphabetical. This book is a fully collaborative effort over five years, to which each author has contributed in important and equal ways. However, much of the actual writing was done separately, according to the following schedule: Chapter 1 is by Van Valin. Chapter 2 is also by Van

Valin, except 2.7 which is by Foley. Chapter 3 contains joint work, but is primarily by Van Valin. Chapter 4 is a joint effort. Chapter 5 is by Foley. The first third of Chapter 6 is joint work, but the last two-thirds is by Van Valin. The first half of Chapter 7 is by Foley, the last half by Van Valin. In general, sections dealing with African, Southeast Asian and Pacific (Austronesian and Papuan) languages are by Foley; those discussing European, Australian and American Indian languages are by Van Valin.

September, 1983   W.A. Foley,
                                                  Canberra, Australia.

                                                  R.D. Van Valin, Jr,
                                                  Davis, California, USA

Abbreviations

A	actor	ERG	ergative
ABL	ablative	excl	exclusive
ABS	absolutive	EXH	exhortative
ACC	accusative	FACT	factitive
ACT	active	F	feminine, focus
AF	actor focus	FUT	future
ALL	allative	GER	gerund
ANT	anterior	HAB	habitual
ANTI	antipassive	HUM	human
AOR	aorist	IF	illocutionary
ART	article		force
AUG	augment	IMM	immediate
AUX	auxiliary	IMP	imperative
BF	benefactive	IMPF	imperfective
	focus	IN	instrument
C	core	INAN	inanimate
CAS	casual	INDEF	indefinite
CL	classifier	INDIC	indicative
CM	clause marker	INF	infinitive,
CNJ	conjunct mode		instrument focus
COM	comitative	INTENS	intensive
COMP	complementizer	INTR	intransitive
CONJ	conjunction	INV	inverse
DAT	dative	invol	involuntary
DECL	declarative	IP	inner periphery
DEF	definite	IRH	interclausal
DEM	demonstrative		relations
DEP	dependent		hierarchy
DIFF	different	IRR	irrealis
DIR	directional,	L	locative
	direct (Cree)	LD	left dislocation
dl	dual	LF	locative focus
DR	different	LIG	ligature
	referent	LINK	linker
DUR	durative	M	masculine

MOD	modality	PP	prepositional
N	nucleus, neuter		phrase
NCD	noun-classified	PST	past
	deletion	PTC	proposed topic
NP	noun phrase		construction
NEG	negative	PURP	purposive
NOM	nominative	PVT	pivot
NMZ	nominalizer	Q	question
NPST	non-past	REFL	reflexive
O	object	REL	relativizer
OBL	oblique	REMPAST	remote past
OBV	obviative	REP	repetitive
OF	object focus	S	intransitive
P	periphery,		subject
	patient	SEQ	sequential
p	person	sg/SG	singular
PASS	passive	SIM	simultaneous
PASTPART	past participle	SmP	semantic pivot
PF	patient focus	SPEC	specific
pl/PL	plural	SR	same referent
PERF	perfective	SUFF	suffix
PN	proper noun	TH	theme
POSS	possessive	THF	theme focus
PRED	predicate	TNS	tense
PREF	prefix	TOP	topic
PRES	present	TR	transitive
PRESEQ	presequentive	U	undergoer
PROG	progressive	UF	undergoer focus
PROX	proximate	vol	voluntary
PrP	pragmatic pivot	X	non-core

1 *Theoretical preliminaries*

1.0 Introduction

When human beings communicate with each other linguistically, they do not do so in isolated simple sentences. Rather, discourse is constituted by complex expressions made up of a number of clauses linked together in various ways. A necessary precondition for intelligible discourse is cohesion among these expressions, and a very important aspect of this cohesion involves the tracking of participants across clause sequences. When talking about sequences of situations in which the same participants are involved, it is necessary to refer to them in each clause in such a way that they can be identified as being the same as or different from the participants referred to in previous clauses. Moreover, speakers need to signal the temporal relations between situations, e.g. whether the situations occurred at the same time, whether one immediately followed the other, or whether one followed the other after an interval. Languages provide speakers with the means to indicate who is doing what to whom not only in simple sentences, but also across the chains of sentences of which discourse is composed.

In this book we will investigate these means in a variety of languages with the goal of uncovering some important aspects of the interaction between syntax and certain discourse processes. We will focus in particular on the relationship of clause-internal morphosyntax to clause linkage and cross-clause reference-tracking mechanisms. Our goal is to demonstrate that crucial features of clause structure such as case marking and voice options are intimately tied up with these interclausal phenomena and accordingly can be fully understood only with reference to them. Hence the analysis of the morphosyntax of the clause must, on this view, proceed from an interclausal and ultimately discourse perspective.

It is necessary to clarify what is meant by 'discourse' in this context. Human beings engage in a variety of speech activities, e.g. chatting, discussing, arguing, lecturing, storytelling, etc. (see e.g. Gumperz 1982), and these activities may be grouped together into different types of discourse or speech genres, e.g. conversation, narrative, ritual speech, etc. (see e.g. Hymes 1974). We will limit the scope of this inquiry to narrative discourse, for several reasons. First, the problem to be investigated, the tracking of events and participants across clauses, shows up most clearly in this type of discourse. Secondly, many of the morphosyntactic phenomena which have traditionally been at the center of linguistic investigation, e.g. case marking, grammatical relations, and clause linkage, are crucially involved in reference and predication and therefore play fundamental roles in discourse tracking. Consequently by examining them from the point of view of their potential discourse functions we will provide more explanatory analyses of these phenomena. Thirdly, narrative texts are often the only kind of discourse data available on many languages. This amounts to a practical rather than a theoretical limitation. At present, data on other discourse genres, particularly conversation, are obtainable for only a very few languages, and therefore if one wishes to study the interaction of syntax and discourse in a wide range of languages, then one is forced to concentrate on narrative texts. Thus when we speak of the 'discourse function' of a particular form or construction, it must be kept in mind that we are talking about its function *in a particular discourse type*. It is entirely possible and indeed probable that the function of a form or construction could vary across different discourse genres, and such possible variation will be a significant area of future research, assuming that the necessary data become available. In this study, however, the focus is on narrative discourse.

This investigation will be carried out within the theory of Role and Reference Grammar [RRG]. A preliminary sketch of the theory appeared in Van Valin & Foley (1980), and aspects of RRG are discussed in a number of other works.[1] We assume no acquaintance with the theory in this presentation, and accordingly we will introduce and develop the theoretical constructs of RRG throughout this inquiry.

1.1 Functional syntax

The title of this book contains two terms, *functional syntax* and *universal grammar*, which require elucidation in order to situate this discussion firmly in the context of current linguistic theory. In this and the following section we will explicate these two notions from an RRG perspective.

Current theorizing in linguistics may be divided into two broad schools of thought which we will label *formal* versus *functional* orientations. Within each orientation there are a number of competing theories; the dominant formal theory is of course transformational generative grammar, but there is no comparable dominant theory among the functionalists. We will attempt to characterize the differences between these two points of view by comparing their positions on a number of fundamental issues.[2]

Perhaps the most fundamental issue of all concerns the nature of the object of linguistic inquiry. From a formal point of view, a language is 'a set of structural descriptions of sentences, where a full structural description determines (in particular) the sound and meaning of a linguistic expression' (Chomsky 1977:81). A structural description accomplishes this task by including (1) a representation of the sound of the expression in terms of a system of phonological units and their phonetic realizations, (2) a specification of the meaning-bearing grammatical units (morphemes), (3) a representation of the structural arrangements of the grammatical units, and finally (4) a representation of the meaning of the utterance (in a restricted sense) as derived from the meaning of the units and their configuration. A structural description of a sentence is thus a formal object composed of a number of formal representations, and a language is a (potentially infinite) set of these representations. Since the constituent elements of the structural description of a sentence make up what has traditionally been considered to be the grammar of the language, 'language', as a general concept, is in effect reduced to 'grammar', and accordingly linguistics, the study of language, is reduced to the study of grammar. 'The study of generative grammar in the modern sense ... was marked by a significant shift in focus in the study of language. To put it briefly, the focus of attention was shifted from "language" to "grammar"' (Chomsky 1981a:4). Thus the definition of a language as a set of structural descriptions of sentences entails a change in the object of inquiry from language to grammar.

The shift has important consequences for both the scope and goals of linguistic inquiry. Because linguistics is the study of the structural descriptions of sentences, only those areas of linguistic analysis which relate to the linking of sound and meaning – phonology, morphology, syntax, and semantics – fall into the proper domain of linguistic investigation. This limitation of the scope of linguistics is not unique to contemporary formal theories; both Saussure and Bloomfield proposed similar delimitations of the field. Chomsky's motivation is the same as Bloomfield's: to apply the methodology of the natural sciences to the study of 'language' (cf. Bloomfield 1926, 1936): 'The shift of focus from language (an obscure and I believe ultimately unimportant notion) to grammar is essential if we are to proceed towards assimilating the study of language to the natural sciences' (Chomsky 1981a:7). Another parallel to Bloomfieldian theory in current Chomskyan theory is the exclusion of non-linguistic semantics from the domain of inquiry. Bloomfield's defining away of semantics is well known (see 1933:139–44), and Chomsky now takes the position that the only aspects of semantics which are within the scope of linguistic analysis are those which constitute the 'logical form' of a sentence, i.e. 'those aspects of semantic representation which are strictly determined by grammar' (1977:5), e.g. interpretation of bound anaphora, scope of negation and quantifiers, and thematic relations (see also 1975:105). The meaning of words and the full semantic interpretation of expressions involves real-world knowledge and other not-strictly linguistic factors, and consequently they are excluded from consideration in both Bloomfieldian and Chomskyan theory. This is not true of all formal theories, however; Montague grammar is a notable exception.

The definition of a language as a set of structural descriptions of sentences is logically independent of the psychological orientation of a theory, but if it professes to make psychological claims, then this definition shapes the nature of those claims in certain respects. Chomsky's main concern is a speaker's knowledge of grammar, or linguistic competence, and for him 'the fundamental empirical problem of linguistics is to explain how a person can acquire knowledge of language' (1977:81). What does 'knowledge of language' consist of? Because a language is a potentially infinite set of structural descriptions of sentences, and because human beings have a finite set of cognitive resources at their disposal, speakers must have internalized a finite set of rules which specify (generate) the structural descriptions. Thus the question concerning knowledge of language becomes one of knowledge of a set of rules specifying a potentially infinite set of formal objects. The next step is to ask how a person comes to know these highly complex formal rules, and we arrive at the 'fundamental empirical problem of linguistics' for Chomsky.

There are a variety of solutions that can be offered to this problem, none of which are supported by any strong psycholinguistic evidence. Chomsky's proposal, that the abstract outlines of the rule systems are part of a human being's genetic endowment (e.g. 1975, 1977, 1980b), is based on the apparent inability of current learning theories to account for the speed and ease of acquisition as well as for the richness and complexity of the resulting cognitive structures. The primary argument which is made in support of this view is the argument from the poverty of the stimulus. In *Reflections on Language*, for example, Chomsky argues that the structure-dependent nature of syntactic rules is not learned through experience and therefore must be a precondition for language learning and a feature of our innate language capacity. All claims that a given theoretical construct in generative grammar is innate are based solely on arguments such as this.[3]

Particularly relevant to these questions is the issue of the nature of this innate language faculty and its relation to other aspects of human cognition. Indeed, as Chomsky (1975:13, 33) points out, this is *the* crucial issue. No one doubts that human beings are born to talk and that there are in-built predispositions to language learning; consequently the fundamental issue is whether the genetically determined structures which make language acquisition possible are uniquely linguistic and independent of all other human capacities, or whether they are part of a general human learning schema which underlies linguistic and non-linguistic learning alike. Chomsky's position is directly related to the notion of language which he assumes. The catalogue of innate linguistic principles includes such things as the X-bar schema for constituent structure, and conditions on rules and the interpretation of bound anaphora, and these are purely linguistic in application; they in no way relate to any aspect of human ability or cognition outside of language. Accordingly, it is not surprising that Chomsky describes these innate linguistic structures as an independent 'module' or 'organ' in the mind (see e.g. 1975, 1977, 1980b) which interacts with other mental modules or organs only in the actual use of language in concrete situations.

The goal of linguistics (at least for Chomsky) is thus to explain how human beings acquire their first language, and the strategy for accomplishing this goal is to characterize the innate language faculty (or language acquisition device) which makes this acquisition possible. This has definite consequences for linguistic theory and analysis. In light of this goal, the concept of explanation in the theory is directly tied to the problem of language acquisition, so that an analysis is considered to be explanatory only insofar as it contributes to the solution of this problem (see Chomsky 1965, Lightfoot 1980, Hornstein & Lightfoot 1981). In practice explanatory analyses take one of two forms: (1) showing that a given phenomenon can be subsumed under or derived from a principle or rule which has already been hypothesized to be part of the innate mental organ of language, or (2) demonstrating that a particular rule, constraint, etc. must be part of the innate mental structures. The methods of gathering data for these analyses is naturally influenced by the linguist's ultimate goal. Since it is to uncover knowledge and not to analyze actual verbal behavior, naturally occurring speech, which is at best only an indirect reflection of underlying knowledge, is not the focus of analysis. Rather, the most direct means for getting at a speaker's unconscious knowledge of language (grammar) would seem to be to present the speaker with sentences illustrating the theoretical construct(s) under consideration in order to elicit judgments of grammaticality of the sentences. From the judgments of grammaticality and (non-)synonymy the linguist is able to infer the principles underlying the sentences and to construct a model of the speaker's grammatical knowledge. Since the knowledge consists of a set of generative rules capable of specifying an infinite set of structural descriptions of sentences, analysis is concentrated on deriving these structural descriptions from the hypothesized rules rather than on describing systematic oppositions among phonological, morphological, and syntactic categories (see Nichols 1979a).

It must be noted that not all formal theories have the psychological orientation and goals of transformational generative grammar; Montague grammar (Dowty 1979) and corepresentational grammar (Kac 1980) are two such formal theories. Relational grammar is oriented towards universals: 'The basic question of linguistic theory can be stated very simply: what ways do natural languages differ, and what ways are they all alike?' (Perlmutter 1980:195). Answering this question will accomplish the three primary goals of linguistic theory: (1) providing 'a satisfactory characterization of the notion "natural language" that makes explicit the class of natural languages' (*ibid.*); (2) providing explanations for the facts of particular languages; and (3) providing 'adequate and insightful' grammars of individual languages. We will discuss this set of goals for linguistic theory in more detail in 1.2 below, where we will see that this conception of the goals of linguistic theory is much less different from Chomsky's than it appears at first glance.

In this discussion we have attempted to characterize the views of formal linguistic theories on a number of major issues. These views follow either directly or indirectly from the assumption that a language is a potentially infinite set of structural descriptions of sentences. We now turn to functionally oriented linguistic theories, and we will likewise describe their stands on the issues in relation to the conception of language that underlies them.

The theme unifying the various functional approaches is the belief that language must be studied in relation to its role in human communication. Language is thus viewed as a system of human communication, rather than as an infinite set of structural descriptions of sentences. Inherent in this conception of language is a claim about its primary function, namely, that it is an instrument of verbal interaction among human beings. Chomsky explicitly denies that communication is a necessary or even important function of language (see 1975:56–7, 1980b:229–30); rather, for him 'human language is a system for free expression of thought, essentially independent of stimulus control, need-satisfaction or instrumental purpose' (1980b:239). This 'creative aspect' has always been considered to be an essential feature of language by Chomsky (see e.g. 1965:6, 1975:56), and this creativity is the ability of native speakers to produce and understand an (in principle) infinite number of sentences. This, of course, takes us right back to Chomsky's definition of a language, and here again we find a direct relationship between it and a major theoretical claim.

It is important to clarify what is meant by 'human communication'. Human beings do not communicate with each other in a vacuum but rather in socioculturally defined activities and situations in which the participants take on socially defined roles and statuses. There is, then, a significant sociocultural aspect to communication. Communication is often construed in a narrow sense to mean 'conveying propositional information from one person to another', and within such a view linguistic behavior consists primarily of referring and predicating about situations in the world, all other types of verbal behavior, e.g. asking questions or giving commands, being derivative of it. Silverstein (1976a, 1977, 1980a) has cogently argued that such a view is fundamentally mistaken and that referring-and-predicating is only one of the many socially constituted functions of language and not a privileged one at that. Hence in talking about communication, we do not mean this narrow sense but rather a concept encompassing the wide range of speech events found in a society, only one of which is reference and predication in the service of passing propositional information between interlocutors. In looking at communication in this way, we investigate 'the purposes of speech to achieve particular socially recognized goals in terms of socially constituted role relations – in short, speech organized as an elaborate system of types of discourse events' (Silverstein 1977:140). Thus the assumption that language is a system of human communication treats language as a crucial component of human social interaction and takes linguistic behavior, e.g. asserting, asking, promising, commanding, wishing and requesting, and the larger-scale speech activities which they constitute, to be social behavior. It would therefore be more accurate to say that language is a form of social action, in particular, a form of communicative social action.

This emphasis on the role of language in verbal social interaction does not entail the extreme view that every use of language must reduce to an instance of communication. This is the straw man that Chomsky attacks in his discussions of the function of language (see references cited above). There may well be instances of verbal behavior which are non-communicative, but this in no way undermines the fundamental functionalist tenet that an understanding of language structure requires an understanding of the functions language can serve, communication being the primary one (see Martinet 1964 for some discussion). This position is analogous to claiming that in order to understand the structure of hammers it is necessary to know that they are used primarily for driving nails, even though they may also be employed as doorstops or paperweights or for tapping the ashes out of a pipe. Indeed, it would be difficult to account for the fact that the head of a hammer is always heavy metal and the handle wood or plastic and never vice versa, if one ignores its primary function, since a hammer could easily be a doorstop, paperweight, or pipetapper with a plastic head and a metal handle. Languages are much more complex than hammers, both structurally and functionally, but in both cases one cannot understand form independent of function.[4] It must be noted that this emphasis on communication does not deny or de-emphasize the significance of the native speaker's ability to use language creatively. Rather, it examines this creativity in terms of the variety of speech activities in which it manifests itself.

We saw clearly in our discussion of formal theories that the definition of language relates directly to the delineation of the proper domain of linguistic inquiry. Since functional theories assume a broader notion of language than formal theories, the scope of linguistic investigation is correspondingly wider. The core areas of linguistic analysis – phonology, morphology, syntax, and semantics – are naturally included, but their focus is different. If one is concerned with the role of language in social interaction, then aspects of linguistic structure which serve to signal social as opposed to purely referential meaning share center stage with the purely referential elements, rather than being shunted off into the wastebasket of performance. Sociolinguistic research has shown that social cues can be found in the phonological, morphological, and syntactic systems in a language (see e.g. Gumperz 1971, 1982, Labov 1972, Hymes 1974, Silverstein 1976a, Sankoff 1980), and accordingly, linguists working within this orientation have adopted what we may call the *dependency hypothesis*, adapted from Duranti (1981): 'Any aspect of linguistic structure can depend upon, interact with or create (some aspect) of social context.'[5] Thus rather than analyzing linguistic structures in context-independent terms, functional analysis directs its attention to the context-dependent nature of linguistic units.

But this is only half of the story. The study of language in its sociocultural context requires not only an analysis of linguistic forms but also an analysis of speech events, speech activities, and the sociocultural situations that define them. The characterization of speech events such as asserting, asking a question, ordering, promising, and requesting has been attempted by some philosophers of language and linguists working in pragmatics (see e.g. J. Austin 1962, Searle 1969, Cole & Morgan 1975). Ethnographers of speaking have concentrated on describing speech activities in different societies and cultures (see e.g. Gumperz 1971, Gumperz & Hymes 1972, Hymes 1974, Bauman & Sherzer 1974). Up to now this work has been considered to be outside of 'straight' or 'unhyphenated' linguistics and to be in some sense an addendum to supplement the purely formal work on phonology, morphology, and syntax.[6] Within the conception of functionalist linguistic theory we are sketching, such work is directly relevant to linguistic inquiry, and moreover it is important, indeed crucial, for the analysis of these areas of linguistic form because of the dependency hypothesis. Silverstein (1980a) sums up the issue of the scope of analysis:

> This functionalism sees the problem of language structure as a reflection of how speech is effectively or ineffectively used in social action, as an instrument for transforming participants' understanding of specific, socially-defined situations. Thus, if such a theory is to be general, there must be some notion of the recurrence of socially-defined situations, implying, in turn, an analysis of such situations, relevant to linguistic use ... And there must be a general analysis of formal features of language so as to relate them directly to their uses in context, to explain them by their 'function' in context. (1980a:5–6)

Functionalists are concerned with language rather than just grammar, and the goal of understanding human language rather than one particular aspect of it distinguishes them clearly from formalists. This investigation of language includes two particularly important questions, which may appear at first glance to be indistinguishable from those of the formal linguistic theories:

(1) What is the nature of the native speaker's knowledge of language and how is it acquired?
(2) In what ways do natural languages differ, and in what ways are they alike?

These questions are of course precisely the ones posed by Chomsky and Perlmutter and discussed in detail above. However, when the functionalist conception of language is considered, the answers to them take on a radically different form. A native speaker's knowledge of language from a formalist perspective is grammatical competence, the knowledge of a set of rules which can specify an infinite set of structural descriptions of sentences. Linguistic creativity is important for functionalists too, as mentioned above, but for them there is more to a speaker's knowledge of language than the ability to generate structural descriptions of sentences. Halliday (1976) comments in this regard that 'the speaker's command of his *langue* includes an awareness of the difference between text and non-text – lists of words or random sets of sentences' (p. 28). Thus a speaker's linguistic knowledge goes beyond individual sentences to encompass judgments about whether or not a given string of sentences constitutes a text or not. Since, as pointed out in 1.0, people normally communicate with each other in utterances composed of more than a simple sentence, this 'textual competence' relates directly to the communicative functions of language. Furthermore, because speaking is a form of social behavior and the different activities in which speaking plays a role are governed by sociocultural norms and conventions, a speaker's knowledge of language also includes knowledge of these social constraints. Hence what the functionalist seeks to characterize is what Hymes (1971, 1974) calls a speaker's *communicative competence*, a notion which subsumes Chomsky's concept of grammatical competence and which explicitly involves both linguistic and social knowledge.

Any theory which concerns itself with acquired knowledge in some domain of human behavior inevitably runs up against the question of how that knowledge is acquired by individuals. As Chomsky correctly points out, the real question is not innate structures versus *tabula rasa* but rather the nature of our innate learning capacities. The formalist answer is that the cognitive structures which make language acquisition possible are uniquely linguistic and independent of all other cognitive structures. This, as we argued above, follows from the formalist definition of language. In this view, communicative competence would be factored into two independent components, grammatical and pragmatic competence (Chomsky 1977, 1980b, 1981b), with linguistic theory concerned only about the former. Such a conception is incompatible with a functional view of language which is concerned with grammatical aspects of language use and pragmatic influences on and interactions with clause-level morphosyntax. Moreover, since what the child acquires is not simply knowledge of grammar but also knowledge of the norms and conventions governing appropriate use of language in social interaction (see e.g. Halliday 1973), the most reasonable working hypothesis would be that the same general learning structures underlie the acquisition of both (see Macnamara 1972). This is an empirical hypothesis, and consequently it must be evaluated with respect to both internal, i.e. linguistic, and external, i.e. psychological and neurological, evidence.[7]

The answer to the second question will also be very different from a functional perspective. If the formalist view of language is assumed, then the focus is on inventories of formal rules and principles governing their application. The features common to all languages will be found in the rules generating the structural descriptions of the sentences of the languages. If, on the other hand, the functionalist conception of language is adopted, then the question becomes 'in what ways are human linguistic communication systems alike and how do they differ?', and a satisfactory answer to it involves more than lists of rules and principles. Morphosyntactic universals are only one part of the picture; discourse and sociolinguistic universals (e.g. Grice 1975, Brown & Levinson 1978, Wenger 1982) complement them and ultimately will be shown to interact with them, yielding universals concerning the interplay of form and (communicative) function in human language.

Even though functional theories of language may seek to uncover a speaker's communicative competence and to explain its acquisition, functional explanation is not primarily psychologically oriented as is explanation in the Chomskyan framework. Indeed, because the functionalist working hypothesis about innate linguistic abilities is that they are part of a more general cognitive-learning schema, the avenue of 'explaining' some phenomenon by declaring the rule describing it to be innate is not available; there is no uniquely linguistic cognitive component of which it would be a part, on this view. Consequently, functional explanations for morphosyntactic phenomena relate not only to such things as markedness relations among linguistic forms but also to pragmatic principles, and discourse and sociolinguistic universals, which themselves must be related to necessary properties of communication systems in general and human perceptual mechanisms and social interaction in particular (see 1.2 below). A meaningful explanation is one which not only accounts for the phenomena under consideration but also raises new questions and moves the investigation to a new level. Explaining a fact about the grammatical structure of human language by claiming it to be innate terminates the discussion; 'why is this feature and not some other innate?' is not a question that can be answered, since it involves speculations about the evolution of language which can never be empirically grounded.[8] On the other hand, explaining some grammatical phenomenon in terms of recurrent discourse patterns in human language is not a dead end, for it raises a whole new set of questions, e.g. Why is this particular discourse pattern universal? Does it relate to the structure and functioning of our speech production and comprehension faculties? To the nature of human social interaction? To both? The first explanation generates new questions and ultimately more and deeper answers.

With respect to methodological issues, it is obvious (or at least it should be) that a speaker's communicative competence cannot be fully uncovered by eliciting judgments about grammaticality and synonymy by presenting speakers with context-free individual sentences. Rather, the crucial data come from analysis of actual language use in social interaction, as well as from narrative texts and other forms of discourse. Direct elicitation is not ruled out as a source of data in functional analysis; since crucial forms for deciding between two grammatical analyses may not occur in the stretches of speech under study, elicitation may be used to get

the necessary data. However, in functional linguistic analysis elicitation is only one of a number of sources of data, and it has no
privileged status.

The final point of comparison between formal and functional
theories concerns the nature of linguistic description itself. It was
mentioned at the end of our discussion of formal theories that
the foci of analysis are the sets of rules which specify the structural
descriptions of sentences and the interaction of these rules in their
derivation. These are consonant with the formal conception of
language. If, however, the object to be described is a system of
communication rather than a set of structural descriptions, then
the analytic foci will be the components of the communication
system and their interaction. We may provisionally identify four
major components: (1) a system of verbal semantics and argument
functions; (2) a morphosyntactic system; (3) a pragmatic system
including notions such as illocutionary force, presupposition,
topicality, and definiteness; and (4) a system of social norms
governing different kinds of speech events and activities. In
analyzing a language from a functional perspective, a linguist seeks
to uncover (a) what the constituent elements or concepts of each
of these systems are and what their contrastive and combinatory
properties are, and (b) how these different components interact.
Although this characterization has been phrased in terms of 'components', it is important not to misconstrue this to mean 'autonomous formal components' as in generative grammar. These components are separate but not autonomous. Indeed, one of the basic
principles of functional linguistics is that clause-internal morphosyntax can only be understood with reference to the semantic and
pragmatic functions of its constituent units, and consequently the
major task is to describe the complex interaction of form and
function in language. Sapir (1921) showed with respect to the
morphological realizations of grammatical functions that a given
form can have a number of functions, and a given function can be
expressed through a variety of forms; the same holds true for the
interaction of morphosyntactic forms with semantic, pragmatic,
and social functions. An example of the interaction of components
can be seen in the notions of speaker and addressee, which are part
of the pragmatic component but which are in fact ultimately
socially defined roles (Silverstein 1977). Accordingly, a full

description of the first and second person pronouns in a language must involve three components: morphosyntax, pragmatics, and social norms. The interaction of the components in a given linguistic system is perhaps the most important topic of functional linguistic analysis, for it is here that the functions of linguistic elements are revealed. Thus the very nature of linguistic analysis and description can be said to differ significantly between formal (primarily generative grammar) and functional orientations.

It must be emphasized that functional theories are *not* performance theories. That is, they seek to describe language in terms of the *types* of speech activities in which language is used as well as the *types* of constructions which are used in speech activities. They do not attempt to predict the actual *tokens* of speech events. In other words, the theories seek to describe the interaction of syntax, semantics, and pragmatics in types of speech activities; they do not try to predict the occurrence of particular constructions in actual speech events. They are theories of systems, not of actual behavior.

Role and reference grammar [RRG] is a functional theory of language; its functional orientation is clear from the topic to be investigated in this book which was laid out in 1.0. The major theoretical assumptions and goals of RRG have been presented above, but several points need to be made before we proceed to the discussion of universal grammar. Unlike transformational grammar, which posits multiple levels of analysis (D-structure, S-structure, logical form, and surface structure), RRG postulates only two: a semantic 'logical structure' in which the predicate of a clause and its arguments are represented, and the actual morphosyntactic form of the utterance. There are no abstract syntactic structures akin to D- or S-structures. Consequently, there are no syntactic derivations from a more abstract to a less abstract level of syntactic representation. Instead of deriving a family of sentences from an abstract underlying form, analysis in RRG concentrates on uncovering the contextual dependencies, both linguistic and social, of the utterances with the same 'meaning', i.e. which denote the same situation (see the dependency hypothesis on pp. 9–10). Since morphosyntactic structure exhibits these contextual dependencies as well as expressing the fundamental semantics of the predicate and its argument(s), the interplay of these semantic, pragmatic, and sociolinguistic factors has a dominant role in shaping the morphosyntactic structure of an utterance. Indeed, the name of the theory derives from the emphasis on the interaction of role (semantic) and referential (pragmatic) factors in grammatical systems. While they are the primary determinants, they are not the only ones. Most of the formal morphosyntactic features of a language, e.g. word order, type of adpositions, and structure of relative clauses, are the result of the diachronic development of the language and are not therefore attributable to any direct functional influences. However, given the formal resources of a language, it is the interaction of the other three functional components which strongly constrains the morphosyntactic structure of an utterance. Previous work in RRG (Foley & Van Valin 1977, Van Valin 1980b, 1981a, Van Valin & Foley 1980) has shown that the interaction of syntax, semantics, and pragmatics is not the same in all languages, and one of the most significant areas in the functional analysis of a language concerns the nature of this interaction.[9] Thus RRG seeks to analyze language with reference to its role in human communication and hence to analyze languages with respect to how morphosyntactic form and communicative function interact.[10]

1.2 Universal grammar

Having elucidated the notion of functional syntax, we now turn our attention to the related concept of universal grammar [UG]. Here again we will discuss this notion from both formal and functional perspectives.

Chomskyan generative grammar is vitally concerned with the problem of language acquisition, and the solution proposed within this theory is the postulation of an innate language-specific cognitive mechanism which makes acquisition possible. The mechanism, a 'mental organ' of language (Chomsky 1975:36), has been hypothesized primarily on the basis of analyses of English syntax. However, since a child can learn any language it is exposed to with equal facility, this innate language acquisition device cannot be structured in such a way as to be oriented toward the grammar of any particular language. Thus the principles and rules it contains must be of universal application, and accordingly the language acquisition device is a theory of U G. Chomsky summarizes this concept of U G as follows:

Let us define 'universal grammar' (U G) as the system of principles, conditions, and rules that are elements or properties of all human languages not merely by accident but by necessity – of course, I mean biological, not logical necessity. Thus U G can be taken as expressing the 'essence of human language'. U G will be invariant among humans. U G will specify what language learning must achieve, if it takes place successfully ... Each language will conform to U G; languages will differ in other, accidental properties. (1975:29)

The notion of 'biological necessity' is important, because Chomsky claims that U G is a 'species-specific, genetically determined property' of the human mind (1975:79). Any theory of U G must meet two basic conditions:

On the one hand, it must be compatible with the diversity of existing (indeed, possible) grammars. At the same time, U G must be sufficiently rich and restrictive in structure so as to provide an account for the fact that each of the grammars can develop in the mind on the basis of quite limited evidence. (1981d:123)

The actual content of the theory has changed considerably over the past two decades, and many of the changes have been in response to the first condition resulting from the extension of detailed generative analysis to languages other than English.

In Chomsky (1965) it was hypothesized that U G is composed of two types of universals: *substantive* universals which specify that 'items of a particular kind in any language must be drawn from a fixed class of items' (p. 28), and *formal* universals which stipulate 'the character of the rules that appear in grammars and the ways in which they can be interconnected' (p. 29). Examples of substantive universals include Jakobsonian phonological distinctive features and parts of speech such as noun, verb, and adposition. They represent the range of variation in such areas as phonetics and grammatical categories, and they are arrived at inductively from the analysis of many languages. More important for the Chomskyan conception of U G are formal universals, e.g. Ross's (1967) island constraints, the transformational component, *X*-bar syntax. These are constraints on the form and organization of grammars of human languages, and they are the 'biologically necessary' 'elements or properties of all human languages'. Thus even though Chomsky (1965:30) says that both kinds of universals are relevant to the problem of language acquisition, formal universals have priority in the theory, because the notions subsumed under substantive universals are learned by the child from experience, whereas formal universals are not. The language learner cannot know *a priori* which of the Jakobsonian distinctive features are employed in the language to be acquired, whether verbs and adjectives are separate parts of speech, or whether the adpositions in the language are prepositional or postpositional. All of this must be induced from the linguistic forms to which the child is exposed. Such is not the case with formal universals: they are part of U G precisely because they cannot be inferred on the basis of experience. On this view children do not learn that the syntax of a language is autonomous and divided up into categorial and transformational components, that rules in the transformational and phonological components apply in a cyclical fashion, or that it is impossible to extract an N P out of a relative clause; all of this is part of their genetic endowment. Formal universals thus form the part of U G most essential for language acquisition.

This conception of U G was developed on the basis of the detailed analysis of English syntax together with the argument from the poverty of the stimulus (see p. 5). It was seriously undermined, however, by the analysis of Warlpiri reported by Hale (1979). Hale argues that Warlpiri has no phrase-structure rules of the type found in English and no transformational rules of any kind. These conclusions have profound consequences for the *Aspects* conception of U G, for they show that phrase-structure and transformational rules are not necessary features of all human languages. If they are not found in every language, then children must infer their existence in a language from linguistic experience; such rules cease to be formal universals and must be considered substantive universals at best. Moreover, if phrase-structure and transformational rules are not formal universals, then neither are the constraints which govern their application and interaction, e.g. island constraints. The entire syntactic component of U G (and the language acquisition device) collapses as a result of Hale's analysis of Warlpiri, since it can no longer be claimed that the general outline of a generative grammar is innate and a precondition for language acquisition (see n. 3).

The obvious solution to this dilemma is to abolish the distinction between formal and substantive universals and to postulate that U G consists of a system of factors, each containing one or more variables which must be determined on the basis of exposure to linguistic data. Once a factor is so determined, then a whole complex of innate structures is set which then plays the crucial role in language acquisition. Let us assume that the existence of phrase-structure rules in a language entails that of transformational rules, and vice versa. They together would constitute one complex factor which would also include the principles and constraints governing their form and application. Thus all the language learner would have to induce would be that the language has phrase-structure or transformational rules, and all of the rest follows: if it does have them, then the child has determined not only their existence but also their form and the constraints on their application, yielding a 'configurational' language; if it does not have them, then none of this complex becomes part of the child's internal grammar, yielding a 'non-configurational' language. Such a conception of U G is compatible with languages like English (configurational) and Warlpiri (non-configurational).

Such a view of U G has been proposed in Chomsky's writings since 1980. U G consists of a set of 'parameters' which must be fixed by experience (1981a:8–9, 1981b:38, 1981c:4–6, 1981d:124–5); they delineate a restricted class of possible grammars and constrain their form. (See Macken & Ferguson in press, for some critical discussion.) Among the parameters which Chomsky discusses are configurational versus non-configurational syntax (1981b:42) and bounding nodes for subjacency (1981b:52–3). There is only a finite set of parameters with a finite set of values for each, and there are markedness relations holding among them. For example, the unmarked value for the parameter concerning bounding nodes for subjacency is {NP, S̄, S}; in Italian, however, only {NP, S̄} serve as bounding nodes, yielding a marked value for this parameter. When the parameters have all been fixed, the result is not the grammar of the language being acquired but rather something more restricted, a 'core grammar'. The full grammar of a language contains constructions which are not derivable from the parameters of U G and have to be learned from experience. An example of such a 'marked' construction is the English accusative-plus-infinitive construction (*John believed him to have won the race*), which involves (on Chomsky's analysis) 'exceptional case marking' (e.g. 1980a:30, 1981b:61). Markedness is also invoked here to distinguish structures generated by the core grammar (unmarked) from those that are not (marked). The situation may be summarized as follows:

[UG] provides a highly restricted system of 'core grammar', which represents in effect the 'unmarked case'. Fixing the parameters of core grammar and adding more marked constructions that make use of richer descriptive resources, the language learner develops a full grammar representing grammatical competence. (1980a:3)

The inductive burden on the language learner is much greater in this theory of U G, since he or she must not only infer the patterns in the data to set the parameters, but also induce the rules governing the marked constructions which are not derivable from U G.

Not all formal theories assume this psychological concept of U G. It was noted in the previous section that relational grammar has a universals-oriented goal: to ascertain how human languages differ and how they are alike. This goal is often expressed in terms of an attempt to characterize the notion of 'possible human language'. In relational grammar a number of formal universal 'laws' are proposed, together with an inventory of the possible rules found in natural languages (see Perlmutter 1980). This would appear to be a different conception of U G from Chomsky's, but the main difference is simply that relational grammar does not reify U G as a cognitive construct. Because it must account for the acquisition of any human language, innate U G must contain a characterization of the notion of possible human language; the conditions, principles, and rules which are biologically necessary features of all human languages delimit the range of variation of human language, thereby constituting the desired characterization. Relational grammar strives toward this same goal but without concern for the problem of language acquisition. It is not surprising, then, that formal constraints and principles ('laws') occupy such an important position in both theories of U G.

The functionally oriented study of U G is in its infancy compared to the formalist study, but nevertheless enough work has been done to permit a comparison with the formal theories. One major difference between the two conceptions is that none of the functional theories of U G thus far proposed are primarily concerned with explaining language acquisition, and accordingly they are not psychological theories. As noted several times in 1.1, functional analysis focuses on the interaction of linguistic forms and communicative functions, and there are two general types of universals which may be postulated with regard to this interaction. First, one could identify a particular functional domain, e.g. signaling coreference across clause sequences, and then investigate the various formal means which languages employ in this domain (see Heath 1975, 1978; Chapter 7 below). Secondly, one could concentrate on a particular formal construction, e.g. the passive construction, and investigate the various functions it can carry out, e.g. cross-clause coreference, signaling politeness, or an evidential indicator (see Silverstein 1978, 1980a; Chapter 4 below), both in a single language and cross-linguistically. In both cases generalizations about both form and function are necessary, for 'there is no such thing as a formal universal without a substantive assumption (i.e., universal also implied); there is no such thing as a functional or substantive universal without assumptions about the forms that have these functions or substance' (Silverstein 1980b:2–3). Both types of formal–functional universals have a component that is primarily formal or primarily functional. Establishing and characterizing a particular functional domain as in the first example involves formulating generalizations with respect to the relevant phenomena so that cross-linguistic variation in the domain itself is accounted for and the domain can be identified and delineated. That accomplished, the investigation of the formal devices functioning in the domain can begin. Similarly, if the functional variability of a particular form is to be examined, then it is necessary to be able to identify it cross-linguistically before the various functions it serves can be studied. Thus functional universals or formal universals are insufficient by themselves; each must be linked to the other in order to produce significant generalizations about human languages.

Based upon these formal–functional universals, a functional theory of UG aims to characterize the notion of 'possible human linguistic communication system', in which the facts of particular languages are to be grounded but not rigidly determined. As in formal theories of UG, particular languages must be compatible with its functional principles and generalizations, but are not completely derivable from them (Silverstein 1980b, 1981). Since the relationship between U G and particular languages is the same in both formal and functional theories, the primary difference between them lies in the nature of the universals which constitute the respective theories of U G.[11] Moreover, functional theories are concerned not only to establish a theory of U G but also to provide the analytic tools for the description of particular languages within the boundaries set down by it.

As should be manifest from the discussion in this and the previous section, R R G differs from transformational generative grammar on most major theoretical points, and, in the context of this comparison on views of U G, there is one difference which deserves particular attention. In talking about changes in Chomsky's theory of U G we mentioned the contrast between configurational and non-configurational languages, a contrast which is captured in U G by making it a parameter with two values to be fixed by experience. Although it is never explicitly stated, within the markedness theory which specifies the marked and un-marked values for each parameter it is clear that configurationality, i.e. the presence of hierarchical phrase structure and the trans-formational rule 'Move α', is the unmarked choice, non-configura-tionality the marked one. This is evident from the fact that all principles and conditions on rules are stated in configurational terms and then adapted, where necessary, to non-configurational languages. In analytic terms, this position assumes that a language is configurational until proven otherwise. R R G makes a very different assumption: R R G assumes a notion of clause structure which is independent of the configurationality parameter (see Chapters 3, 5), and which therefore applies equally to both types of languages. This radical shift in orientation has a number of important consequences for both description and explanation. It facilitates comparisons which are difficult in a theory which represents clauses in the two types of languages in radically dif-ferent ways. Consider the sentences in (1.1) and (1.2).

(1.1)   *What did you see the man who bought?
(1.2)   Wičhaša wã taku   ophethũ ki he wãlaka   he.[12]
        man   a   WH/smthg 3sg-buy the that 2sg-see-3sg Q

        'Did you see the man who bought something?'
        *'What did you see the man who bought?'

Example (1.1) from English illustrates the well-known impossibility of extraction out of a relative clause; in Ross (1967) this is accounted for by the complex noun phrase constraint [CNPC], and in Chomsky (1973) and subsequent writings by the principle of subjacency. These accounts are both stated in terms of the impossibility of moving an NP out of a certain syntactic configuration which is described in terms of constituent structure, the defining feature of configurational languages. Example (1.2) is from Lakhota (Teton Dakota), a Siouan language; it is a non-configurational language (Van Valin in press), and therefore has no rule of Move α to move (in this case) the WH-word to clause-initial position in a WH-question (Chomsky 1981a, c). Hence Lakhota lacks both the constituent structure in terms of which CNPC or subjacency can be stated, and the movement rule which these principles are meant to constrain. Nevertheless, something akin to CNPC or subjacency is involved in this sentence, because it is impossible to interpret *taku* 'WH-something' as a question word in (1.2); that is, (1.2) cannot be interpreted with *taku* as the focus of the question analogous to *what* in (1.1), but only with the non-interrogative meaning 'something' in the relative clause, while the main clause is understood as a yes–no question. What is significant about (1.2) is that something is preventing it from having the same reading as (1.1), thereby ruling out the expression of (1.1) in Lakhota. Thus in neither language is it possible to construct a question such that the question word functions as an argument of the verb in a relative clause.

The explanation for the ungrammaticality of (1.1) is stated in terms of constituent structure and the movement of an NP, and consequently it is not applicable to (1.2), since there is neither constituent structure analogous to that in (1.1) nor any NP movement. A transformational grammarian faced with this situation would appear to have two options. On the one hand he or she could claim that there are different things going on in (1.1) and (1.2), and therefore that the explanation for (1.1) should not be extended to deal with (1.2), which requires a separate analysis and explanation. This is not a very satisfactory solution, because there is a fundamental similarity between the two sentences. The other option would be to claim that in Lakhota the relevant constraint holds not at the level of S-structure or surface structure, but rather at the level of logical form; moreover, English and Lakhota do not differ appreciably at this level, so it is possible to transform the surface structure in (1.2) into a logical form that looks like (1.1), yielding a constituent structure tree with a moved NP so that the constraint can take effect (see Huang 1981). This 'solves' the problem, but it does so by notational fiat rather than by uncovering any kind of similarity between the two sentences which would explain (in a meaningful sense) these facts. Indeed, this would seem to be linguistic engineering at its best, changing a language with no WH-movement into one with it. This analysis obliterates what is interesting about (1.1) and (1.2), namely, that they exhibit the same constraint despite the striking formal differences between them. From an RRG perspective, on the other hand, the problem is not to make English look like Lakhota, or vice versa, but rather to answer the question 'Why is it impossible in both English and Lakhota to form a WH-question when the WH-word functions as an argument of the verb in a relative clause?'. Note that this question is not phrased in terms of constituent structure or NP movement, features not found in all of the languages which exhibit the phenomenon under consideration. No attempt will be made here to answer this question; the point of this discussion is not the ultimate explanation of (1.1) and (1.2), but rather the consequences of the markedness assumptions a theory makes regarding configurationality. If English is assumed to represent the unmarked type, then the explanation devised for English must be adapted to fit Lakhota (or perhaps more accurately, Lakhota must be adapted to fit the solution for English). If, on the other hand, one looks at the problem independent of configurationality, then it is readily apparent from a comparison of (1.1) and (1.2) that the peculiar formal properties of a configurational language like English are at best only indirectly related to the problem at hand. From a functional point of view, we have a well-defined functional domain (asking WH-questions), and two languages which, despite very different formal means for carrying out this function, exhibit the same phenomenon. The explanation for this phenomenon must be found in common functional considerations and not in the formal disparities between them. The way is thus open for an explanation encompassing both configurational and non-configurational languages.

1.3 Outline of the discussion

The topic to be investigated in this book concerns the means which languages use to code participants and situations in discourse. We will focus especially on one particular aspect of this problem, the tracking of participants across clause sequences. We will show how all major aspects of clause-internal morphosyntax are involved in the signaling of same or different referents in discourse. We approach this task in a rather traditional fashion, starting with predicate semantics and working up to discourse. Chapter 2 deals with predicate semantics and the semantic relations holding between a predicate and its argument(s). The system of predicate semantics to be presented draws heavily on the work of Dowty (1979). In Chapter 3 we explore the morphosyntactic coding of the relations proposed in Chapter 2, following the general outline of Silverstein's (1976b, 1980b, 1981) theory of case marking. In this chapter the notion of clause structure which underlies all subsequent discussion – the layered structure of the clause – is introduced. Chapter 4 is concerned with two major features of clause-internal syntax, passivization and antipassivization. The discussion of complex sentences commences in Chapter 5 with analyses of the semantic operators which modify the various layers of clause structure and the joining of these layers in complex sentences. Chapter 6 continues the presentation of the theory of clause linkage with a discussion of nexus, the relations holding between clauses (or sub-clausal units) in complex sentences. The final chapter deals with reference tracking in discourse itself; it ties together the types of formal reference-tracking mechanisms with the nature of the linkage between clauses, clause-internal morphosyntax, and predication complexes of verbs and their arguments. In a sense this book was written backwards, as the most powerful way of demonstrating these functional relationships would be to start with discourse and work down to verbs.

It is worth reiterating the point made in 1.0, that the discussion in this book is limited to narrative discourse, and accordingly claims about the functions of particular forms are relative to the type of discourse under study. There are many important syntactic phenomena that we have left for future discussions. In 1.1 we sketched a program for functional linguistic analysis, and this book represents an exploration of one small but important area in the domain of functional linguistics.

2 *The semantic structure of the clause*

2.0 Introduction

One of the most fundamental problems in the analysis of clause structure is the characterization of predicates and the semantic relations which obtain between them and their arguments. Regardless of the type of discourse under consideration, the clauses which constitute the discourse are constructed around predications consisting of a predicate and its argument(s). In this chapter we will develop a system for capturing the semantic role structure of the clause. This system is based on an opposition between the notions of actor and undergoer, on the one hand, and a program of lexical decomposition of predicates into a set of primitive predicates and operators, on the other. Briefly, actor and undergoer are the two arguments in a transitive predication, either one of which may be the single argument of an intransitive verb. They are not equivalent to syntactic relations such as subject and direct object, nor to Fillmorean case roles such as agent and patient. These notions will be discussed in detail in 2.1. The system of lexical decomposition to be adopted is the one developed in Dowty (1979), which is based on a revised version of the verb classification presented in Vendler (1967). The decomposed predicate structures provide the basis for an account of the semantic (or thematic, following Gruber) relations holding between a predicate and its arguments. Thus, relations such as agent, patient, theme, or locative are not independently existing primitive relations which are assigned arbitrarily to verbs; rather, they are relations which are derived from the semantic structure of predicates themselves. This treatment of these relations is similar to that proposed in Gruber (1965) and Jackendoff (1976), but the system of decomposition and primitive predicates comes from Dowty (1979).

Throughout this chapter these concepts will be developed and illustrated primarily with reference to data from English. This is unavoidable, for two reasons. First, the major discussions of verb semantics which we will draw upon deal almost exclusively with English. Secondly, many of the tests for the verb classification require native-speaker judgments about particular constructions. Since we are native speakers of English and since the contructions needed for these tests are rarely explicitly discussed in descriptions of other languages, we are forced to make use of English as the primary data source. Nevertheless, we will endeavor to bring in relevant facts from other languages whenever possible.

The predominance of English in this chapter should *not* be interpreted as an implicit claim that the classification and concomitant analyses of English verbs presented herein are applicable without alteration to the verb system of any language. On the contrary, any proposed verb classification must be justified by the semantic contrasts which are found in the language under consideration (see Dowty 1979:72). However, it is assumed that the categories, primitive predicates, and operators employed in the analysis of English will be relevant to the analysis of other languages. These constructs have the same status as Jakobsonian distinctive features; languages employ different sets of them in a variety of ways, but they provide the basis for a unified description of aspects of phonological systems. Thus the concepts to be developed in this chapter should be considered etic categories out of which the analyst constructs emic analyses of the verb systems of particular languages.

2.1 The notions of actor and undergoer

The guiding insight of the work of Gruber (1965) and Fillmore (1968) is that in a clause there is a set of unvarying semantic relations which may have multiple syntactic manifestations. This is illustrated in (2.1), which has a transitive verb with two arguments.

(2.1) a. The hunter shot the bear.
      b. The bear was shot by the hunter.

It is a commonplace that in a passive construction the doer of the
action and the entity affected by the action are the same as in
the corresponding active construction, despite the different
choices of syntactic subject in the two forms. We introduce the
terms *actor* and *undergoer* to capture one aspect of the semantic
functions of *the hunter* and *the bear*, respectively, in this pair of
sentences. Provisionally we may characterize the actor as the
argument of a predicate which expresses the participant which
performs, effects, instigates, or controls the situation denoted by
the predicate, and the undergoer as the argument which expresses
the participant which does not perform, initiate, or control any
situation but rather is affected by it in some way. It is clear from
(2.1) that actor is not equivalent to syntactic subject, nor is undergoer equivalent to syntactic direct object. These non-equivalences
are reinforced when we look at single-argument predicates, some
of which have actors and some of which have undergoers as their
single argument, an argument which is always syntactically the
subject.

(2.2) a. John ran down the street.
      b. Mary swam for an hour.
      c. The boy went to the store.

(2.3) a. The janitor suddenly became ill.
      b. The door opened.
      c. Fritz was very unhappy.

All of the verbs in (2.2) involve actions effected by willful,
intending participants, and accordingly the single argument is in
each case an actor. In (2.3), on the other hand, the predicates
denote states or changes of states which the participant experiences
or undergoes; consequently the single argument is an undergoer
in these sentences. Here again syntactic subject cannot be equated
with actor, since there are intransitive predicates which have
undergoer subjects.

    Actor and undergoer are generalized semantic relations between
a predicate and its arguments, but they are NOT to be equated
with either Fillmorean case roles or Gruberian thematic relations

such as agent, patient, or theme. NPs bearing a number of different
case roles/thematic relations may be an actor, and the same is true
with respect to undergoer. The examples in (2.4) illustrate the
semantic possibilities of the actor, and in (2.5) those of the undergoer.

(2.4) a. *Colin* killed the taipan.   (Agent)
       b. *The rock* shattered the mirror.   (Instrument)
       c. *The lawyer* received a telegram.   (Recipient/Goal)
       d. *The dog* sensed the earthquake.   (Experiencer)
       e. *The sun* emits radiation.   (Source)
(2.5) a. Phil threw *the ball* to the umpire.   (Theme)
       b. The avalanche crushed *the cottage*.   (Patient)
       c. the arrow hit *the target*.   (Locative)
       d. The mugger robbed *Fred* of
           $50.00.   (Source)
       e. The announcer presented *Mary*
           with the award.   (Recipient/Goal)

The italicized NPs in (2.4) are all actors, but there is no identity
in terms of the case role/thematic relation which the actor bears
to the verb. *Colin* in (2.4a) is an agent, *the rock* in (b) is an
instrument, *the lawyer* in (c) is a recipient/goal, *the dog* in (d) is
an experiencer, and *the sun* in (e) is a source; yet they are all actors.
Similarly, the italicized NPs in (2.5) are all undergoers, even
though *the ball* in (a) is a theme, *the cottage* in (b) is a patient,
the target in (c) is a locative, *Fred* in (d) is a source, and *Mary*
in (e) is a recipient/goal. Actor and undergoer are thus *macroroles*
which subsume particular groups of Fillmorean case roles or
Gruberian thematic relations.

It is particularly striking that there is some overlap in the case
roles/thematic relations which occur with actor and undergoer;
NPs functioning as recipient/goal and source appear to be able
to be either actor or undergoer. However, the interpretation of
an actor–source differs considerably from that of an undergoer–
source, and likewise for the two kinds of recipient/goals. It is
significant that this difference is not a function of the syntactic
status of the argument, since it is invariant under syntactic
permutation.

(2.6) a. Radiation is emitted by the sun.   (cf. (2.4e))
      b. Fred was robbed of $50.00 by the
         mugger.   (cf. (2.5d))
      c. A telegram was received by the lawyer.   (cf. (2.4c))
      d. Mary was presented with the award by
         the announcer.   (cf. (2.5e))

Rather, the difference in interpretation follows from the semantic contrast between actor and undergoer: a source argument, for example, which is also the potential initiating and controlling participant versus one which is affected by the action. The semantics of actor and undergoer will be discussed in more detail in 2.2 below.

These notions have syntactic implications as well. In (2.4) the NPs functioning as agent, instrument, recipient/goal, experiencer and source all receive the same morphosyntactic treatment, and the same situation obtains in (2.5) with respect to theme, patient, locative, source, and recipient/goal NPs. Furthermore, the members of each group of case roles/thematic relations behave alike with respect to passivization, as the examples in (2.7) illustrate.

(2.7) a. The taipan was killed by Colin.
      b. The mirror was shattered by the rock.
      c. The earthquake was sensed by the dog.
      d. The ball was thrown to the umpire by Phil.
      e. The cottage was crushed by the avalanche.
      f. The target was hit by the arrow.

The notions of actor and undergoer simplify significantly the statement of the English active–passive opposition. Without them passive would have to be described as a construction in which the patient, theme, locative, recipient/goal, or source is the syntactic subject, and the agent, instrument, recipient/goal, source, or experiencer occurs as the object of the preposition *by*, if it occurs at all. Using actor and undergoer, one can state passive in terms of the undergoer occurring as syntactic subject and the actor as the object of *by*, if it occurs at all. We will see in subsequent chapters that these concepts, particularly actor, are of enormous importance in the grammar of many languages, and that in some languages the major grammatical processes are stated with respect to actor and undergoer rather than syntactic relations like subject and object.

Thus, actor and undergoer, the two arguments of a transitive predication, have both semantic and syntactic significance. In an important sense they constitute an interface between syntactic relations such as subject and semantic relations such as case roles or thematic relations. We assume actor and undergoer to be universal semantic relations, and as such part of the grammar of every language. We make no such assumption with respect to grammatical relations such as subject and direct object (see e.g. Foley & Van Valin 1977, Van Valin 1977b, 1981a). The status of grammatical relations within RRG is discussed in Chapter 4 (see also Van Valin & Foley 1980).

2.2 The token-specific semantics of actor and undergoer

One of the significant features of actor and undergoer discussed in the previous section is that they do not have a constant semantic content. While all actors have in common that they are potential initiators and/or controllers of the action of the predicate, their exact interpretation in any clause is a function of the nature of the predicate and, to a lesser extent, the inherent lexical content (Silverstein 1976b) of the NP argument serving as actor. Similar considerations apply to undergoer. In (2.4a), for example, *kill* means roughly that some action on the part of the actor brings it about that the undergoer dies. If the actor is animate, as in (2.4a), then the normal interpretation is that the actor's actions were volitional and under his control. It is also possible to have inanimate actors with *kill*, as in (2.8).

(2.8) a. An arrow through the heart killed Max.
       b. Malaria killed Nigel.

The actors in these sentences initiate some action or event which directly leads to the death of the undergoer, but their actions are not volitional or under their control, because they are inanimate and are incapable of volitional, controlled acts. Thus the interpretation of the actor of *kill* in these sentences is crucially affected by the animacy of the NP occuring as actor. With *sense* and *emit*, on the other hand, animacy is not so crucial, but for different reasons. *Sense*, by virtue of its meaning, requires an animate actor which refers to a sentient being. The animacy of the actor of *emit* is irrelevant, since it is impossible to emit anything willfully. Hence the actors in (2.4e) and (2.9) would be interpreted the same way, regardless of the difference in their inherent lexical content.

(2.9) Felix emits foul odors.

Thus the inherent lexical content of the actor NP plays an important role in its interpretation in some instances, but its importance is constrained by the semantics of the predicate itself.

The interpretation of the undergoer in a sentence is almost exclusively determined by the semantics of the predicate; inherent lexical content appears to be of lesser significance. *Kill*, by virtue of its meaning, requires an animate undergoer or one with somewhat animate-like properties, e.g. *light, fire*; but *throw, climb, hit*, and *rob* are indifferent to the animacy of the undergoer. The undergoer of *throw* changes its location, while that of *crush* and *kill* suffers a change of state. *The target* in (2.5c) with *hit* specifies the location of the contact which the arrow makes. *Fred* and *Mary* denote the participant from whom something is taken (*rob*) and to whom something is given (*present*), respectively. In each of these cases the interpretation of the undergoer follows from the lexical meaning of the predicate.

How can this token-specific aspect of the meaning of actor and undergoer be captured? By 'token-specific aspect of meaning' we mean the actual interpretation of actor and undergoer which depends upon the predicate with which they cooccur. Thus the question becomes, how does one account for the fact that the actor of one verb, e.g. *kill* in (2.4a), is an agent and the undergoer a patient, whereas with e.g. *receive* in (2.4c) the actor is a recipient/ goal and the undergoer a theme? We will consider two proposals, one deriving from the work on case grammar by Fillmore and the other from the work on lexical semantics by Gruber. (See Fillmore 1968, Gruber 1965.) In Fillmorean case grammar, a number of semantic case roles are posited, e.g., agent, instrument, object/patient, experiencer, and dative, and these are assigned to verbs in the form of case frames. A verb like *break* or *open*, for example, would be assigned the case roles agent, instrument, and patient because of sentences like (2.10).

(2.10) a.   Fred opened the door with the key.
       b.   The boy broke the vase with the hammer.

The case frame for these verbs would be [(Ag) P (I)], agent and instrument being in parenthesis because they are omissible. In this system, case roles constitute a universal set of semantic relations which exist independently of the actual predicates in any language. The assignment of roles to particular predicates results in a classification in terms of case frames, for example, *break*, *open*, *crack*, *shatter*, and *split* would fall together by virtue of their common case frame. This assignment is, in an important sense, somewhat arbitrary, since it does not follow directly from the semantic structure of the predicate, which is never explicitly represented in any way. Indeed, it is the presumed semantic structure of the predicate which is derived from the case-role assignment and represented in the case frame. This arbitrariness underlies many of the problems inherent in this approach to semantic relations; these are discussed in Fillmore (1977).

Although the thematic relations proposed by Gruber (1965) and elaborated by Jackendoff (1972, 1976) are often considered to be rough equivalents of Fillmorean case roles, they differ crucially from them in that they are derivative of the explicitly represented semantic structure of predicates. Formally, thematic relations are a function of the argument positions of abstract predicates such as CAUSE and GO. Jackendoff (1976) specifies CAUSE as a two argument predicate, CAUSE(x, e), where x is an individual and e an event. By virtue of its status as the first argument of CAUSE, x has the thematic relation *agent*. Hence if a verb contains CAUSE in its semantic structure, then the NP argument which is associated with x is the agent of that verb. Similar considerations apply to GO(x, y, z), which yields x = theme, y = source and z = goal; hence in a sentence like *the ball rolled from the door to the wall*, *ball* = x = theme, *door* = y = source, and *wall* = z = goal. The important question of how NPs in a clause are associated with the argument positions of abstract predicates will be addressed in detail in 2.6 and 3.3.1. Thus the Gruber–Jackendoff system of abstract predicates and derivative thematic relations offers a very plausible approach to expressing the semantics of actor and undergoer in any clause. Whether an undergoer is a theme or locative, for example, would depend upon which argument position of which abstract predicate in the semantic structure of its predicate it is construed with. The linking of the actor and undergoer arguments of the predicate to argument positions in the representation of the semantic structure of the predicate captures the token-specific aspects of the meaning of actor and undergoer in a straight-forward manner. The general approach adopted by Gruber and Jackendoff is that of lexical decomposition, and it is a lexical-decomposition-based analysis, albeit not that of Gruber and Jackendoff, that we will adopt here.

Theories of lexical decomposition may, for our purposes, be divided into two types: those which strive to represent all aspects of the meaning of predicates, on the one hand, and those which aim only to account for certain aspects of the meaning of predicates, in particular those aspects which are definitive of the class of the predicate. This distinction may be illustrated as in (2.11).

(2.11)

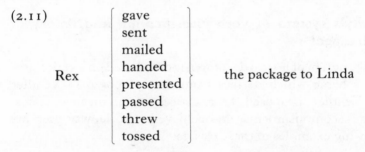

All of these verbs characterize the same basic event, namely the transfer of an object (the package) from one person (Rex) to another (Linda), but the exact nature of the transferring action differs from verb to verb. In theories of lexical decomposition which attempt to capture the 'entire meaning' of predicates, the representation of the semantic structure of these verbs will reflect not only their basic transfer meaning but also the idiosyncratic variations which differentiate them. A less ambitious theory would concentrate on making explicit the basic transfer aspect of their meaning: that one participant, acting volitionally, instigated a change of possession or location of a particular object such that it changes from the instigator's possession to that of another participant. Exactly how this is done, e.g. by direct hand-to-hand transfer or mediated through a governmental institution, is not specified. The difference between the two approaches to lexical decomposition revolves around the amount of detail to be represented.

The system of lexical decomposition in Dowty (1979) seeks to capture only the more general aspects of the meaning of predicates. With respect to (2.11), it would attempt to characterize the basic transfer meaning which allows us to determine that the actor, *Rex*, is the volitional instigator of the transfer and its point of origin, and that the undergoer, *the package*, undergoes a change of location and possession. The possible variations of how this transfer can be effected have no bearing on the semantics of the actor and undergoer in these sentences, and they are not represented in Dowty's schema. Accordingly, we will adopt the system of lexical decomposition based on Montague grammar developed in Dowty (1979).

2.3 Dowty's system of verb classification and theory of verb aspect

Dowty's program of lexical decomposition is based on a verb classification scheme which derives from that proposed in Vendler (1967). Vendler proposed four classes of predicates: states, activities, accomplishments, and achievements. Dowty presents the following examples of these classes.

(2.12)	*States*	*Activities*	*Accomplishments*	*Achievements*
	know	run	paint a picture	recognize
	believe	walk	make a chair	spot
	have	swim	deliver a sermon	find
	desire	push a cart	draw a circle	lose
	love	drive a car	recover from illness	die

The syntactic and semantic tests which are used to define these classes are summarized in Table 1, from Dowty (1979:60):

Table 1 *Syntactic and semantic tests for verb classification*

Criterion	States	Activities	Accomplishments	Achievements
1. meets non-stative tests	no	yes	yes	?
2. has habitual interpretation in simple present tense:	no	yes	yes	yes
3. ϕ *for an hour, spend an hour ϕing:*	OK	OK	OK	bad
4. ϕ *in an hour, take an hour to ϕ:*	bad	bad	OK	OK
5. ϕ *for an hour* entails ϕ *at all times in the hour:*	yes	yes	no	d.n.a.
6. *x is ϕing* entails *x has ϕed:*	d.n.a.	yes	no	d.n.a.
7. complement of *stop:*	OK	OK	OK	bad
8. complement of *finish:*	bad	bad	OK	bad
9. ambiguity with *almost:*	no	no	yes	no
10. *x ϕed in an hour* entails *x was ϕing during that hour:*	d.n.a.	d.n.a.	yes	no
11. occurs with *studiously, attentively, carefully*, etc.	bad	OK	OK	bad

OK = the sentence is grammatical, semantically normal
bad = the sentence is ungrammatical, semantically anomalous
d.n.a. = the test does not apply to verbs of this class.

In order to explain the properties of the verbs in these classes, Dowty makes the following proposal:

The idea is that the different aspectual properties of the various kinds of verbs can be explained by postulating a single homogeneous class of predicates – *stative predicates* – plus three or four sentential operatives and connectives. English stative verbs are supposed to correspond directly to these stative predicates in logical structure, while verbs of the other categories have logical structures that consist of one or more stative predicates embedded in complex sentences formed with these 'aspectual' connectives and operators (1979:71).[1]

The verbs in each of these classes would have the same semantic structure consisting of a stative predicate plus (for the non-state classes) one or more 'operators or connectives'. The meaning of each individual verb in a particular class would be primarily a function of the stative predicate(s) in its semantic structure. This proposal therefore involves lexical decomposition, but only to a limited degree; it seeks to capture only certain aspects of the meaning of English verbs. Achievement verbs offer the simplest example of this system, for they consist of a stative predicate plus the operator BECOME. *Die*, for example, would be BECOME NOT **alive′** (x),[2] *realize* would be BECOME **know′** (x,y), and *lose* would be BECOME NOT **have′** (x, y).[3] BECOME is an operator which Dowty (p. 76) defines as follows:

(2.13)   Where ϕ is any predicate formula and t is any time,
         BECOME ϕ is true at t if ϕ is true at t and false at t-1.[4]

Accomplishment verbs, on the other hand, have the logical structure ϕ CAUSE ψ, where ϕ and ψ are each logical structures. The most common patterns is for ϕ to be an activity predicate and ψ an achievement predicate. The most discussed accomplishment verb, *kill*, can be given the preliminary logical structure in (2.14); it is preliminary because we have not yet discussed activity predicates.

(2.14)   [x does something] CAUSE [BECOME NOT **alive′** (y)]

CAUSE here is not an abstract predicate but rather a sentential connective which relates the causing event to the caused event. Treating CAUSE in this way makes explicit an analysis of causation which treats it as a relationship between two events rather than between an individual and an event.[5] Accomplishment verbs, then, have complex logical structures consisting of two logical structures joined by the connective CAUSE.

The final class, activity verbs, are somewhat problematic for Dowty's scheme. It is difficult to imagine, for example, what kind of truly stative predicate could underlie verbs like *roll*, *fall*, *run*, and *walk*; the obvious candidate, something like **be in motion′**, is a rather suspicious stative predicate. Dowty concludes his discussion by proposing a model-theoretic characterization of this class of verb without being able to supply any 'atomic predicate' which could function as key semantic component of this class. He does, however, postulate an operator for some of the verbs in this class. It is DO, originally hypothesized in Ross (1972) as being part of the underlying structure of action sentences. In Dowty's framework, DO is treated as an operator, analogous to BECOME, which supplies the notion of agency. Thus, for example, the difference between *see* and *watch* would be that the logical structure of *watch*, but not *see*, contains DO. The precise characterization of the semantics of DO proposed by Dowty is that the state or actor is 'under the unmediated control of the agent' (1979:118). DO would play a role in accomplishment predicates as well, since the causing predicate (ϕ in ϕ CAUSE ψ) is often a volitional activity which would have DO as part of its logical structure.

This schema is summarized in Table 2.

Table 2 *Verb classes and logical structures*

Verb class	Logical structure
State	**predicate′** (x)
Achievement	BECOME **predicate′** (x)
Activity	DO (x, [**predicate′** (x)])
Accomplishment	ϕ CAUSE ψ
	(where ϕ is normally an activity
	verb and ψ an achievement verb)

There are a number of interrelations among the verb classes which are not easily expressed in the Vendler four-way classification in (2.12). For example, activity verbs may become accomplishment verbs if a definite goal is added, e.g. *walk* (activity) versus *walk to the store* (accomplishment). Conversely, some accomplishment verbs may become activity verbs if their object is a mass noun or generic, e.g. *eat a bag of popcorn* (accomplishment) verses *eat popcorn* (activity). These considerations, plus the adoption of an interval-based rather than a point-based temporal logic, led Dowty to the revised classification presented in Table 3 (1979:184). The main differences from the earlier classification are the agentive–non-agentive bifurcation of the classes, the division of state predicates into four types, and the splitting up of accomplishment predicates into three classes (6, 7, 8). The criteria for the classification are given below the classes.[6]

2.4 Application of Dowty's system to Lakhota

Dowty argues for the verb classification and the hypothesis about the logical structures underlying the verb classes (see Table 2)

Table 3 *Dowty's verb classification*

	Non-Agentive	Agentive
States	1a. *be asleep in the garden; love, know*	2a. possibly *be polite, be a hero*, etc. belong here, or in 4.
	1b. interval statives: *sit, stand, lie*	2b. interval statives: *sit, stand, lie* (with human subject)
Activities	3. *make noise, roll, rain*	4. *walk, laugh dance* (cf. 2a)
Single change of state	5. *notice, realize; ignite*	6. *kill point out* (*something to someone*)
Complex change of state	7. *flow from x to y dissolve*	8. *build* (*a house*), *walk from x to y, walk a mile*

I	*Momentary* (1a and 'habituals' in all classes) vs. *interval* predicates (1b, 2b, 3–8). Syntactic test: ability to occur in the progressive. (Note: 6 and especially 5 appear less readily in the progressive than other interval predicates.)
II	Predicates entailing *definite or indefinite change* 3–8 vs. those entailing *no change* (1 and 2). Syntactic test: ability to occur in *do* constructions (pseudo-clefts, *do so* reduction, etc.).
III	*Definite change of state* predicates (5–8) vs. *activity* predicates or indefinite change of state predicates (3 and 4). Syntactic test: Does *x was V-ing* (pragmatically) entail *x has V-ed*?
IV	*Singulary change* predicates (5–6) vs. *complex change* predicates (7–8). Syntactic test: Is *x finished V-ing* acceptable?
V	*Agentive* (2, 4, 6, 8) vs. *non-agentive* (1, 3, 5, 7) predicates. Syntactic test: ability to occur in agentive contexts like imperatives, *persuade x to V, do V deliberately*, etc.

solely on the basis of English phenomena. There are languages in which the principles governing the classification of its verbal system are more directly reflected in the morphology of the verbs. One such language is Lakhota (Teton Dakota), a Siouan language. We will briefly examine the organization of the Lakhota verbal system in this section. A qualification is in order. We are relying on published materials and are therefore unable to apply the syntactic tests (where these would be applicable) with native speakers. Accordingly, we will attempt only to sketch out the general features of the verb system. Nevertheless, Lakhota provides an interesting example of how features of the logical structures proposed by Dowty for verb classification may be made morphologically explicit by a language.

Boas & Deloria (1939: 1;23) summarize the Lakhota verbal system as follows:

> There is a fundamental distinction between verbs expressing states and those expressing actions. The two groups may be designated as neutral and active (p. 1) ... By far the majority of verbal stems are neutral. The concept of a condition extends over almost all inanimate objects that may be brought into a condition. 'To scratch' is not primarily an activity; the active verb is derived from the condition of a scratched surface. These stems can be made active only by adding instrumental prefixes which express the means by which the condition is brought about, or by locative elements which apply the condition to a certain object. Active verbs are almost exclusively those referring to bodily or mental activities, actions that can be performed by or on living beings only (p. 23).

Neutral and active verbs are distinguished by a number of formal criteria, e.g. rules of accentuation and patterns of reduplication, but more relevant for this discussion is the fact that the 'subjects' of the two classes are expressed by distinct pronominal forms, as illustrated in (2.15). (The data in this section are from Boas & Deloria (1939) and Buechel (1970).)[7]

(2.15) a. Wa-lowã. 'I sing.'   b. Ma-khuže. 'I am sick.'
          Ya-lowã. 'You sing.'   Ni-khuže. 'You are sick.'
          Ø-lowã. 'He sings.'   Ø-khuže. 'He is sick.'

The pronominal prefixes in (a) also serve to indicate the 'subject' of active transitive verbs, whose 'objects' are expressed by the prefixes in (b).

There are two classes of neutral verbs: those which may have either stative or inchoative meanings, and those which can be interpreted only as stative. Examples of each class are given below.

(2.16) a. t'a   'die, be dead'
          nit'e   'you are dead, you are dying'
       b. spaya   'be wet, get wet'
          maspaye   'I am wet, I am getting wet'
       c. čhãze   'be angry, get angry'
          mačhãze   'I am angry, I am getting angry'

        d. yazã   'feel pain, be sick'

          Ø-yazã   'He feels pain, he is sick, he is getting sick'

          yazãhĩgla   'become sick suddenly' (*-hĩgla* 'suddenly')

(2.17) a. -blaza   'be ripped open'

          blazahã   'it is rent, torn open'

        b. -blečha   'be shattered (said of brittle material)'

          blečhahã   'it is shattered'

        c. -wega   'be fractured (said of a long round object)'

          wegahã   'it (e.g. a pole) is broken'

        d. -khĩča   'be scraped'

          khĩčahã   'the outside is scraped off'

The verbs in these two classes differ both semantically and morphologically. Those in (2.16) may function as state predicates without any modification and they may be interpreted as either stative or inchoative. The verbs like those in (2.17) cannot, for the most part, occur directly as predicates; rather, they must take the suffix *-hã*, which serves to indicate continuing states, events, or actions. Boas & Deloria describe its use with these verbs as follows:

> Many neutral verbs are used as verbs only with instrumental prefixes or in reduplicated form. A considerable number have a neutral meaning when used without instrumental prefixes, but with the continuative suffix *hã*. All of these seem to express a state which is the permanent result of some action ... All those that express the effect of an action that has no permanent result cannot take the suffix *hã*. (1939:61)

Thus an inchoative meaning is precluded by virtue of their expressing a continuing result state. The verbs in (2.17) cannot normally take the person prefixes presented in (2.15b) because their single arguments are inanimate, and inanimate arguments are not cross-referenced on the Lakhota verb. There is at least one example of a verb stem of this type which may function like those in (2.16). Buechel (1970) gives the form *blečha* (first-person singular, *mablečha*) which has the apparently idiomatic meaning 'getting poorer and poorer as from sickness' (p. 110). It seems reasonable to assume that this form is related to the *-blečha* of (2.17b) by the metaphorical extension of talking about a person's situation being shattered by some catastrophic event like illness.

The way Lakhota most closely follows Dowty's decomposition scheme is in the derivation of transitive (accomplishment) verbs from neutral verbs via a process of causativization. There are two means of causativization, one involving the causative auxiliary *-ya* and the other instrumental prefixes. Verbs of the type given in (2.16) take *-ya* and the other instrument prefixes, with the exception of *t'a* which falls into both paradigms.

(2.18) a. t'e-ya   'cause to die, kill'
            Ø-t'e-wa-ye.   'I caused him/it to die.'
            3sgU-die-1sgA-CAUSE
        b. spaye-ya   'cause to be wet, moisten'
            Ø-spaye-ya-ye.   'You moistened it.'
            3sgU-wet-2sgA-CAUSE
        c. čhãze-ya   'cause to be angry, anger'
            Ma-čhãze-ya-ye.   'You made me angry.'
            1sgU-angry-2sgA-CAUSE
        d. yazã-ya   'cause to be sick, sicken'
            Ni-yazã-Ø-ye.   'He made you sick.'
            2sgU-sick-3sgA-CAUSE

Other verbs which pattern this way include *puza* 'be dry, become dry' versus *pusya* 'cause to be dry', *sapa* 'be black, become black' versus *sabya* 'blacken', and *iyokišiča* 'be sad' versus *iyokišilya* 'sadden, displease'.

The verbs in (2.17) are transitivized primarily by means of instrumental prefixes, with some verbs taking locative prefixes instead. The instrumental prefixes are given in (2.19), and examples of derived transitive verbs are found in (2.20).

(2.19) *ya-*   'with the mouth'
        wa-   'by a sawing motion, with a knife'
        wo-   'by action from a distance'
        yu-   'by pulling, with the hands'
        pa-   'by pushing along'
        ka-   'by sudden impact'
        na-   'with the foot or leg'
        na-   'by an inner force'

(2.20) a. yablaza   'tear open with the teeth'

          wablaza   'rip open lengthwise, as in butchering an animal'

          kablaza   'make rip open or burst by striking or throwing down'

          woblaza   'tear open by shooting, e.g. the bowels of an animal'

    b. yablečha   'break or crush with the teeth'

         yublečha   'break to pieces or crush by pressing with the hands'

         pablečha   'break or crush by pressing, pushing or sitting on'

         nablečha   'break by kicking or stepping on'

    c. yawega   'break, e.g. a stick with the mouth but not entirely off'

         yuwega   'break, e.g. a stick with the hands but not entirely off'

         kawega   'fracture by striking'

         wowega   'break, but not off, by shooting'

    d. yukhĩča   'scrape off with the hand or finger'

         kakhĩča   'scrape, e.g. hair from a hide'

         nakhĩča   'scrape off, e.g. hair with the foot'

These examples illustrate some, but not all, of the possible combinations of the verbs in (2.17) with the prefixes in (2.19). There are no purely inchoative forms for these verbs; they have either the result-state form with -*hã* in (2.17) or the transitive accomplishment form in (2.20). The closest Lakhota equivalent to an English clause like *the glass broke* would involve *nablečha* with *na-* being the 'by an inner force' prefix. This verb is formally identical to the other *nablečha* 'break with the foot', but due to the meaning of the prefix it cannot have an explicit actor.

(2.21) a. žãžãwakšiča   ki na-blečhe.
         drinking. glass the PREF-shatter
         'The drinking glass broke', or 'He broke the drinking glass with his foot.'

    b. žãžãwakšiča   ki wa-na-blečhe.
         drinking. glass the 1sgA-PREF-shatter
         'I broke the drinking glass (*by an inner force/with my foot).'

In (2.21b) *nablečha* can be interpreted only as 'break with the foot' because of the explicit first person singular actor inflection on the verb.

A number of neutral verbs of the first type also take instrumental prefixes. The most notable one is *t'a* 'be dead, die', which occurs with all except *na-* 'by an inner force' to derive verbs for various means of killing; it normally occurs with the prefixes rather than with *-ya*.

(2.22) a. yat'a   'bite to death'
        b. wat'a   'stab to death'
        c. wot'a   'shoot to death'
        d. yut'a   'strangle'
        e. pat'a   'crush to death'
        f. kat'a   'beat to death'
        g. nat'a   'kick to death'

Yu- in some cases has taken on the meaning of a 'general instrumental when no specific meaning is prominently implied' (Boas & Deloria 1939:49), and several neutral verbs have causative forms with both *-ya* and *yu-*.

(2.23) a. yučhãze   'make angry' (cf. (2.18c))
        b. wašte   'good'
           wašteya, yuwašte   'make good'
        c. šiča   'bad'
           šilya, yušiča   'spoil'

Less commonly, neutral verbs may be transitivized by means of one of the locative prefixes *a-* 'on' and *o-* 'in'.

(2.24) a. Ma-bleza.   'I am clear-minded.'
           A-wa-bleza.   'I notice, observe it.'
        b. Ma-chãze.   'I am angry.' (cf. (2.16c), (2.18c), (2.23a))
           A-∅-wa-chãze.   'I am angry at him.'
           PREF-3sgU-1sgA-be.angry
        c. Ma-Pemni.   'I am twisted.'
           O-wa-pemni.   'I wrap it up in it.'

The locative prefix adds an additional nominal argument,

increasing the valence of the verb. Because the verb is now transitive, it takes actor inflection for its 'subject'. It is interesting to note that *čhãze* 'be angry' transitivizes both ways; in causativization of the neutral verb the undergoer remains the same in both forms, whereas in transitivization with a locative prefix the undergoer of the neutral verb becomes the actor of the active verb. Transitivization by means of a locative prefix is thus distinct from causativization, and consequently the derivation of the transitive verbs in (2.24) is not accounted for within Dowty's system.

Thus in the derivation of transitive change-of-state (accomplishment) verbs from neutral (state and inchoative) verbs via causativization, Lakhota provides an example of a language in which one important part of Dowty's schema is realized explicitly in the verbal morphology. Activity verbs with controlling actors make up a large part of the basic active verbs in the language, e.g. *mani* 'walk', *nũwã* 'swim', *zo* 'whistle', *lowã* 'sing', *wačhi* 'dance', *kiya* 'fly', *psiča* 'jump', *ʔu* 'come', and *ya* 'go'. (See Boas & Deloria 1939:24–5.) Non-agentive activity predicates are neutral verbs, e.g. *hĩxpaya* 'fall' (*mahĩxpaya* 'I fall'), *hĩhã* 'fall as rain, snow' and *gmigma* 'go round like a wheel.' None of the agentive activity verbs is morphologically derived from a neutral verb. Achievement predicates have no consistent morphological treatment in Lakhota. Some are neutral verbs, e.g. *t'a* 'die' and *puza* 'become dry', some are active verbs, e.g. *uya* 'lose' and *hi* 'arrive', and some are derived transitive verbs, e.g. *ableza* 'notice' and *iyeya* 'find'.[8]

In this brief discussion of the Lakhota verbal system we have illustrated how Dowty's verb classification can be applied to a language radically different from English. We have seen that one aspect of his explanatory hypothesis about the verb classes, i.e. the claim that transitive accomplishment verbs are derived from stative and achievement predicates via causativization, is not only true of the language but also is directly reflected in the verbal derivational morphology. Just how many classes of verbs there are in Lakhota and the membership of each class cannot be ascertained without a detailed analysis, and it is unlikely that the result of such an investigation would be a table isomorphic with Table 3. This emphasizes the point made in 2.0 that it is our purpose here to set up a framework which provides linguists with the tools to analyze the grammatical systems of languages and not to propose analyses which are assumed to be valid in every detail for every language. Dowty's theory of verb semantics and classification is such a tool, and we are using it as a tool rather than as a straitjacket.

2.5 A system of logical structures and semantic relations

The verb classification in Table 3 and the logical structures in Table 2 are first steps toward a theory of semantic relations which derives them from the logical structures of predicates, because they specify that whole classes will have the same logical structure and what the general form of it will be. We are not yet, however, in a position to account fully for the semantic relations which contribute to the meaning of actor and undergoer in a given clause. If *see*, for example, is a state verb and we represent its logical structure as **see'** (x, y), what are the semantic relations of x and y, and which one will be the actor and which one the undergoer? The answer to this question has implications for the analysis of other verb classes, since *watch* (activity) would have the logical structure DO **see'** (x, y), *notice* (achievement) BECOME **see'** (x, y), and *show* (accomplishment) [...] CAUSE [BECOME **see'** (x, y)]. Because the stative predicates underlie the other classes, it is essential to provide a more detailed and explicit analysis of their semantic structure.

The simplest stative predicates are those expressing a state or condition of being, and location. Examples of the former include *be tall, be sick, be dead, be happy, be afraid*, and *be fat*. Locational states are expressed primarily by *be* plus a locative preposition, e.g. *be in, be at, be on, be under*, etc.; this is a two-place relation involving a located entity and its location. The logical structure of predicates of the first type can be represented simply as **predicate'** (x), e.g. **tall'** (x), **sick'** (x). Because these predicates express the state or condition of being of an entity, the semantic relation of x to the predicate is that of PATIENT. We thus define patient as being the semantic relation of the single argument of a one-place stative predicate. Predicates expressing location have in their logical structure the two-place abstract predicate **be-at'** (x, y); x is the located entity and is a THEME while y is the location and hence bears a LOCATIVE semantic relation to the predicate.[9] Accordingly, the sentences in (2.25) have the logical structures in (2.26).[10]

(2.25) a. The boy is sick.
       b. The cat is on the mat.
(2.26) a. **sick′** (the boy)
       b. **be-at′** (the cat, the mat)

In these sentences, both *the boy* and *the cat* are undergoers, and, in addition, *the boy* is a patient and *the cat* a theme; *the mat* is a locative. These semantic relations follow from the meaning of these predicates. **Be-at′** is also related to the logical structure of verbs of possession, e.g. *have*, which are stative. The locative aspect of alienable possession comes out in paraphrases of *have* such as *be in X's possession*, as in *John has the book = The book is in John's possession*. Indeed, in many languages, e.g. Russian, Tagalog, and Guugu Yimidhirr (Australia; Haviland 1979), there is no verb corresponding to English *have*, and explicitly locative constructions are used to express this kind of possession, e.g. *the book is at/to John*. Thus we will assume **have′**(John, the book) to be the logical structure of *John has the book*, when *John* is the locative argument and *the book* is the theme. **Have′** and **be-at′** differ only in the order of their arguments; with **be-at′** the first is theme and the second locative, whereas with **have′** the first is locative and the second theme.

Perception and cognition verbs are also state predicates, according to Dowty's criteria, and, as we saw above with *see*, they may be part of the logical structure of achievement and accomplishment verbs. Since they are stative semantically, it would be desirable for them to have logical structures which yield the same semantic relations as other statives. A consideration of what happens in a perceptual event yields a clue to the logical structure of perception verbs. In physical terms, a stimulus of some kind, e.g. visual, auditory, or tactile, comes into contact with a sense organ of the perceiver, and this sets off a complex chain of events in the nervous system of the perceiver. Since the crucial feature of this process is the contact between the stimulus and the sense organ, perception may be viewed as having an essential locational aspect, and accordingly we will analyze perception verbs as having a locative component to their meaning. (See Wierzbicka

1980 for detailed arguments in support of a locative analysis of perception verbs.) The semantic relations inherent in a locative relationship are theme and locative, and as the stimulus is in contact with the perceiver's sense organ, the stimulus would be a theme and the perceiver's sense organ a locative. We do not, however, normally speak of John's eyes seeing Mary's image or Mary's nose smelling John's odor, and consequently we will treat the source of the stimulus as the theme, and the person possessing the sense organ in question as the locative.

(2.27) a. John saw Mary.
       b. Mary smelled John.
(2.28) a. **see**′ (John, Mary)
       b. **smell**′ (Mary, John)

Thus in the logical structure of a perception verb, the first argument is a locative and the second a theme.[11]

Cognition and propositional attitude verbs such as *know*, *think*, and *believe* have explicitly stative paraphrases which reveal features of their logical structure.

(2.29) a. Fred believes/thinks that Ronald is a fool.
       b. Fred is of the opinion that Ronald is a fool.
       c. Fred holds the belief that Ronald is a fool.
(2.30) a. Barbara knows French cooking thoroughly.
       b. Barbara has a thorough knowledge of French cooking.
(2.31) a. Max knows that the world is round.
       b. It is known to Max that the world is round.

The paraphrases of the (a) sentences in these sets of examples reveal the stative nature of these verbs, especially (2.29b) and (2.31b), and the possessive or 'having' aspect of their meaning, as in (2.29c) and (2.30b). We argued above that alienable possession is at least in part a locational relationship, and consequently it appears that knowing and believing also have a locative component to their meaning. The location aspect of cognition is brought out even more clearly in the various metaphors we commonly use.[12]

(2.32) a. What are you thinking about?
       a′. What's *on* your mind?
       b. I can't think of anything except Mary.

b′ I can't get Mary *out of* my mind.
c. I was thinking the very same thing myself.
c′. That's just what I *had in* mind.

In these metaphors and many others thinking is characterized as having something in or on one's mind. Thus an important part of the meaning of cognition verbs is locational, and from the examples in (2.29)–(2.32) we may conclude that the thought, belief, or knowledge is located with respect to the thinker, believer, or knower's mind. This means that in the logical structure of, e.g. *believe*, **believe′** (x,y), the first argument (*x*) is the believer and a locative, and the second argument (*y*) is the belief and a theme. The two arguments of state verbs of cognition and propositional attitude are the same as those of verbs of perception and cognition. It must be emphasized that this analysis does not claim that all of these verbs have the same meaning. Rather, the claim being made is exactly analogous to the claim inherent in Dowty's analysis of achievement verbs as having logical structures containing BECOME plus a stative predicate: the verbs in this group have certain semantic features in common, and this is captured in the proposed logical structure. It is not a claim that all achievement verbs mean the same thing. Similarly, our contention that these two-argument state verbs all have locative and theme arguments is an attempt to capture what is common to them as state verbs. Indeed, the fact that they all fall into the same class can only be explained by characterizing their common semantic features.

As noted in 2.3, activity verbs are problematic in that there is no atomic predicate which can be said to underlie them or simple formula akin to the BECOME **stative′** of achievement verbs which expresses their logical structure. Dowty argues that activity verbs fall into two general types: those that take the operator DO, e.g. *walk*, *swim*, *talk*, and *ignore*, on the one hand, and those that may not take DO and necessarily involve motion or movement of some kind, e.g. *fall*, *roll*, *make noise*, and *rotate* (see Dowty 1979:163–5). With respect to the problem of agency and control, Dowty adopts the operator DO which was originally proposed in Ross (1972), giving it the rough meaning 'action is under the unmediated control of the agent'. The logical structure

of *John swam*, for example, would be DO (John, [**swim**′
(John)]), whereas that of *The stone fell* would be **fall**′ (stone).
There are verbs which are unmarked for agency, e.g. *smile*, which
can refer either to an involuntary reflex, as in (2.33a), or to an
intentional act, as in (2.33b).

(2.33) a. Max instinctively smiled at the laughing baby.
      b. Max intentionally smiled at the comely lass.

The logical structure of (a) includes **smile**′ (Max, baby), and that
of (b) DO (Max, [**smile**′ (Max, lass)]). The first argument of
DO is an AGENT, while the first argument of a non-motion
activity verb is an EFFECTOR.

The other group of activity verbs includes verbs which
necessarily involve motion or movement of some kind, either
internal or external. The simplest type of verb in this group is
that of pure physical motion, and Dowty proposes the following
truth conditions for a verb *move*(x): (L is a function which 'assigns
a place to each individual at each moment in time' (1979:169).)

(2.34) '*move*(x)' is true at interval *i* if there is a place *p* such that
      L(x) = p at the lower bound of *i* and L(x) ≠ p at the upper
      bound of *i*.

This can be expressed using the predicates and operators already
introduced in this chapter with the addition of a sentential connective & 'and then'.[13]

(2.35)   **be-at**′ (x, y) & BECOME NOT **be-at**′ (x, y)

The logical structure in (2.35) captures the essence of motion as
change of location over time. Verbs with this logical structure are
illustrated in (2.36).

(2.36) a. The vase fell off of the table.
      b. The ball rolled down the nature strip.

These two arguments of *fall* and *roll* have the semantic relations
of theme and locative, by virtue of their being arguments of **be-at**′
in (2.35). A theme is no longer simply the located entity but also
the entity which undergoes a change of location. Theme may
therefore be more broadly characterized as the entity whose
location is at issue. Like Dowty we have been unable to provide

a succinct logical formula to account for activity verbs, but we have presented significant aspects of the meaning of the various verb types in this class.

Accomplishment verbs require no special discussion, since they have complex logical structures consisting of other verb types linked by the sentential connective CAUSE. The most common case is for the first argument of CAUSE to be an activity predicate and the second argument an achievement predicate. As an example, let us consider the verb *break* in a sentence like *Joan broke the glass*. A first approximation of its logical structure would be (2.37).

(2.37) [Joan do something] CAUSE [BECOME **broken′** (glass)]

The second part of this logical structure is that of the inchoative achievement verb *break*, which by itself would represent the logical structure of the sentence *the glass broke*. The first part has been left vague, because its form depends upon whether the breaking was deliberate or accidental. There are three interpretations of *Joan broke the glass* with respect to the deliberateness of the breaking. First, Joan could have accidentally done something and not have intended to break the glass; this is represented in (2.38a). Secondly, she could have done something intentionally but not intended to break the glass; i.e. the doing something is deliberate but the breaking of the glass was an unintended side effect. This situation is represented in (2.38b). Thirdly, she could have done something intentionally and intended that it should break the glass; this is represented in (2.38c).

(2.38) a. [**do′** (Joan)] CAUSE [BECOME **broken′** (glass)]
      b. [DO (Joan, [**do′** (Joan)])] CAUSE [BECOME **broken′** (glass)]
      c. DO (Joan, [DO (Joan, [**do′** (Joan)])]) CAUSE [BECOME **broken′** (glass)])

(2.38a) is equivalent to (2.37), and the successive addition of DO operators in (b) and (c) indicate that Joan's doing is intentional in (b) and (c), and that the effect was intended in (c), in which the outermost DO has scope over the entire logical structure presented in (b). In a sentence like *Joan broke the glass* the causing event is not specified, and accordingly it is represented by the generalized activity predicate **do′** in (2.38). **Do′** is unmarked for agency, and therefore the operator DO must be used as in (b) and (c) to stipulate that the causing action is volitional. Given these logical structures, the semantic relations of the arguments can be determined. *Glass* in every case is the single argument of a stative predicate and hence is a patient. *Joan* is the single argument of **do′** in (2.38a) and accordingly is an effector. In (2.38b, c), however, **do′** is modified by the operator DO, and consequently *Joan* is an agent rather than an effector. The semantic relations of the arguments of accomplishment verbs are a function of their status as arguments of the constituent predicates.

The logical structures and concomitant semantic relations proposed in this section are summarized in Table 4.

Table 4 *Logical structures and semantic relations*

I	State Verbs		
	A. Locative	**be-at′** (x, y)	x = theme
			y = locative
	B. Non-locative		
	1. State or condition	**predicate′** (x)	x = patient
	2. Perception	**see′** (x, y)	x = locative
			y = theme
	3. Cognition	**believe′** (x, y)	x = locative
			y = theme
	4. Possession	**have′** (x, y)	x = locative
			y = theme
II	Activity verbs		
	A. Potentially controllable		
	1. Controlled	DO (x,(**predicate′** (x)])	x = agent
	2. Uncontrolled	**predicate′** (y)	y = effector
	B. Motional	**fall′** (x)	x = theme

2.6 The token-specific semantics of actor and undergoer revisited

Having laid out the fundamentals of a system of lexical decomposition and semantic relations derivative of the decomposed predicate structures, we are now in a position to address the problem of the token-specific semantics of actor and undergoer.

Actors may be agents, effectors, or locatives, depending primarily upon the verb it cooccurs with. In any given clause, although arguments bearing more than one of these semantic relations may be present, the actor may be interpreted as only one of them, and the possibilities for interpreting the actor, i.e. the linking of NPs with argument positions in the logical structure of the verb, always follow a strict hierarchy. Thus, in a clause with a verb like *break* which contains both an agent and an effector, the actor must be understood as the agent.

(2.39) a. Fred broke the vase with the rock.
   b. [[DO (Fred, [**do′** (Fred)])] CAUSE [**do′** (rock)]] CAUSE [BECOME **broken′** (vase)]][14]

Break in (2.39a) is an agentive accomplishment verb, and this is reflected in its ϕ CAUSE ψ logical structure, However, because the causing event is itself complex, i.e. Fred intentionally does something which causes the rock to do something, the ϕ argument of CAUSE is another ϕ CAUSE ψ logical structure. Therefore (2.39b) would be read: 'Fred intentionally does something which causes the rock to do something, and this causes the vase to become broken.' *Fred* is an agent, *rock* an effector, and *vase* a patient by virtue of the predicates of which they are arguments. Given such a logical structure, only the argument of DO may be the actor; if a verb takes both an agent and an effector and the actor is the effector, then the resulting sentence is ungrammatical.

(2.40) *The rock broke the vase by/with Fred.

The actor may be an effector only if there is no agent argument in the logical structure of the verb.

(2.41) a. The rock broke the vase.
   b. [**do′** (rock)] CAUSE [BECOME **broken′** (vase)]]

These data establish the hierarchy agent > effector for the interpretation of the actor.[15]

This relationship between NPs and argument positions in the logical structure of the verb may be viewed from two different perspectives. On the one hand, we may take an English sentence, e.g. (2.39a), as our starting point and ask how its NP arguments may be interpreted, i.e. linked to arguments in (2.39b). On the other hand, we may start from the logical structure in (2.39b) and investigate the possible ways the three arguments may be realized in actual sentences. Within the first perspective the agent $>$ effector hierarchy constrains interpretation; within the second it governs the possible realizations of the arguments in the logical structure of a verb. These two perspectives are two sides of the same coin, and throughout this discussion we will look at these phenomena from both points of view.

Achievement verbs like *receive*, perception verbs like *see*, and cognition verbs like *believe* all have locative actors. An example with *receive* is given in (2.42).

(2.42) a. Felicia received a package.
        b. BECOME **have**′ (Felicia, package)

Felicia is a locative (recipient) and *package* a theme, and only *Felicia* may be the actor. If a verb has both effector and locative arguments, the effector outranks the locative for actorhood.

(2.43) a. The cane hit the wall.
        b. [**do**′ (cane)] CAUSE [BECOME **be-at**′ (cane, wall)]

Cane here is both the effector and theme, and *wall* locative; only the effector–theme may be the actor.

(2.44) *The wall hit with the cane.

Thus the hierarchy of accessibility to (or interpretation of) actor-hood is agent $>$ effector $>$ locative, when more than one of the relations occurs in a clause.

The situation regarding undergoer is more complex, because a given verb with a single logical structure may allow two arguments bearing different semantic relations to be undergoer. There are no such variable choices for the actor. An example of variable undergoer assignment is presented in (2.45).

(2.45) a. John gave the book to Bill.
        b. John gave Bill the book.
        c. [DO (John, [**do**′ (John)])] CAUSE [BECOME **have**′ (Bill, book)]

In the logical structure in (2.45), *Bill*, the first argument of **have**′, is the locative, while *book*, the second argument of **have**′, is a theme. Both the theme *book* and the locative *Bill* are possible undergoers, as (2.45a–b) are equally grammatical.

However, this pattern of variation of accessibility to undergoer does not extend to all possible combinations of semantic relations in logical structures. A patient is always undergoer and therefore outranks all other relations; or, in other words, with certain verbs the undergoer must always be interpreted as a patient. Contrast (2.46a–b) with (2.45a–b).

(2.46)   a.   Fred broke the window with the teacup.
       b.   Fred broke the teacup against the window.

Unlike (2.45a–b), which have the same basic meaning, the sentences in (2.46) do not mean the same thing; in (a) the window gets broken, whereas in (b) the teacup breaks. In both it is the participant experiencing a change of state, i.e. the patient, which is the undergoer. The logical structures for these two sentences are given in (2.47).

(2.47)   a.   [[DO (Fred, [**do**′ (Fred)])] CAUSE [**do**′ (teacup)]] CAUSE [BECOME **broken**′ (window)]
       b.   [[DO (Fred, [**do**′ (Fred)])] CAUSE [BECOME **be-at**′ (teacup, window)]] CAUSE [BECOME **broken**′ (teacup)]

The logical structure in (2.47a) has already been discussed above. The logical structure in (b) differs from it in two ways; first, it specifies the fact that the teacup came into contact with the window, and second, that the teacup undergoes the change of state. It is the patient in each logical structure which appears as the undergoer in (2.46a–b).

Break contrasts with a verb like *hit* with respect to the possibility of different semantic relations being undergoers. Compare (2.46a–b) with (2.48a–b).

(2.48)   a.   The man hit the cane against the wall.
       b.   The man hit the wall with the cane.
       c.   [[DO(man,[**do**′ (man)])] CAUSE [**do**′ (cane)]] CAUSE [BECOME **be-at**′ (cane, wall)]

The logical structure of (2.48a–b) is represented by (2.48c), which, like (2.45a–b), have the same basic meaning; in both sentences *the cane* is an effector–theme because it is an argument of both **do′** and **be-at′**, and *the wall* is a locative. Either argument may be the undergoer. This pattern is the same as that of the well-known cases of verbs like *spray* and *load* discussed in Anderson (1971).

(2.49) a. Bill loaded (the) hay on the truck.
        b. Bill loaded the truck with (the) hay.
(2.50) a. Harry sprayed (the) paint on the wall.
        b. Harry sprayed the wall with (the) paint.
(2.51) [DO (x, [**do′** (x)])] CAUSE [BECOME **be-at′** (y, z)]

The logical structure of verbs like *spray* and *load* is given in (2.51),[16] and from it we can see that these verbs have theme and locative arguments, either of which may be the undergoer. The much-discussed difference in interpretation between each pair of sentences will be examined below.

Another group of verbs exhibiting an alternation between a locative and a theme undergoer includes verbs like *drain* and *empty*.

(2.52) a. John drained the water from the pool.
        b. John drained the pool of its water.
(2.53) a. Max emptied the contents from the box.
        b. Max emptied the box of its contents.
(2.54) [DO (x, [**do′** (x)])] CAUSE [BECOME NOT **be-at′** (y, z)]

Like *spray* and *hit*, these verbs have theme and locative arguments and both are possible undergoers, as the examples in (2.52) and 2.53) show. This pattern of alternation is also found lexicalized in the pair of English verbs *rob* and *steal*, both of which have the logical structure given in (2.54).

(2.55) a. Peter stole the valuable book from Sam.
        b. Peter stole Sam the valuable book. (≠ a)

(2.56) a. Peter robbed Sam of the valuable book.
        b. *Peter robbed the valuable book from Sam.

Neither of these verbs allows the theme–locative undergoer alternation characteristic of verbs alone like *hit*, *load*, and *drain*, but together they exhibit it, with each verb lexicalizing one of the choices.

Because arguments bearing different semantic relations may occur as undergoer with a given verb, no strict hierarchy of accessibility to undergoer analogous to that given above for actor is possible. However, with particular verbs there is a hierarchy of potential undergoers in that when the verb occurs with only an actor and an undergoer there is only one possible interpretation of the undergoer. This is illustrated in the following examples.

(2.57)   a.   John hit the cane against the wall.
        b.   John hit the cane.
        c.   John hit the wall.

(2.58)   a.   Max gave flowers to the girl.
        b.   Max gave flowers.
        c.   ?Max gave the girl.

(2.59)   a.   Herbert took the magazine from the vendor.
        b.   Herbert took the magazine.
        c.   Herbert took the vendor.

(2.60)   a.   John drained the water from the pool.
        b.   ?John drained the water.
        c.   John drained the pool.

(2.61)   a.   Fred loaded the hay.
        b.   Fred loaded the truck.

With *hit* the undergoer must be interpreted as a locative when it stands alone as in (2.57b–c). *Cane* in (2.57a) is an effector–theme, and these facts suggest that locative outranks effector–theme for undergoer status with *hit*. In (2.58) and (2.59) the theme appears to be higher ranking than the locative with *give* and *take*, as the undergoer in constructions like (2.58b) and (2.59b) must be understood as a theme and not as a locative. *Drain* appears to work just the opposite. *Load* seems to accept both possibilities. These preferences are confirmed by evidence from nominalizations. If there were a noun *canehitter* (analogous to *canecutter*) in English, it could only refer to a person who goes around striking canes, not to one who goes around hitting things with canes. With *give* we could have a *flowergiver* but not a **girlgiver*, in the sense of someone who gives things to girls. In the same way we could have *magazinetakers* but not **vendortakers*, but we do have *pooldrainers* instead of **waterdrainers*. Verbs like *load* and *spray* seem happy with both possibilities, as we have *paintsprayers* as well as *plantsprayers*.

Rather than propose a separate hierarchy or hierarchies for undergoers based on these rankings, we may combine the accessibility to actor hierarchy with these preferences for undergoerhood into a single cline, as represented in Figure 1, with the arrows indicating the increasing markedness of the choice.[17]

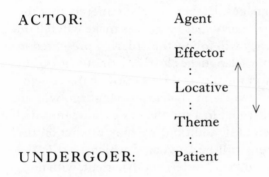

ACTOR: Agent
         :
         Effector
         :
         Locative
         :
         Theme
         :
UNDERGOER: Patient

Figure 1 Actor/Undergoer hierarchy

The actor hierarchy works from the top down and undergoer from the bottom up, with agent the primary choice for actor, patient the primary choice for undergoer, and all others falling between them. They overlap in the middle of the cline; there are verbs which have a locative actor, e.g. *see*, *believe*, and *receive*, and there are verbs which may have an effector–theme undergoer, e.g. *hit*. Effector–theme would fall between effector and locative on the cline. It is outranked for actorhood by effectors, but ranks higher than locative, which we saw with respect to (2.43). Conversely locative ranks higher than effector–theme for undergoerhood, as (2.57) illustrates. The facts regarding accessibility to actor and undergoer, respectively, complement each other exactly. In interpretive terms, Figure 1 signifies that the most natural or unmarked interpretation for the actor is agent and for the undergoer is patient, the other interpretations being progressively more marked.

In the cline in Figure 1, there are gaps between the labeled relations, and this is to signify that this represents a continuum of semantic relations between agent at one extreme and patient at the other, with effector, locative, and theme being major points in the continuum. We have already seen evidence of an additional important relation between locative and effector, i.e. effector–theme. Given this cline, we avoid having to postulate a fixed number of semantic relations and to claim that they are a feature of the grammar of all languages. Rather, we claim merely that the semantic distinctions which particular languages make will fall on this continuum and that they will follow the ordering presented in Figure 1; i.e. if, for example, a language clearly distinguishes agent from effector, the agent argument will always outrank the effector for actorhood. Moreover, we claim that in no language will an agent ever occur as an undergoer in a simple, basic clause, nor will a patient ever occur as actor. In addition, we may predict on the basis of Figure 1 that there will be languages which restrict the interpretation of actor to agent and undergoer to patient, with non-agent and non-patient arguments receiving different case marking from true agents and patients. In the middle part of the cline, some variation is likely. We have already seen that in English, verbs like *give* and *take* rank theme over locative for undergoer, whereas *drain* prefers the reverse order. Nevertheless the end points are clear, with the agent the unmarked choice for actor and patient for undergoer. Indeed, it follows from this that the prototypical actor is an agent and the prototypical undergoer a patient. In 2.1 we described actor and undergoer as the two arguments in a transitive predication, and in a 'cardinal transitive relationship' as defined by Hopper & Thompson (1980) they would be agent and patient semantically.

That the prototypical undergoer is a patient correlates with certain well-known facts of semantic interpretation concerning verbs which allows more than one NP as its undergoer. The examples given in (2.49) and (2.50) are repeated in (2.62) and (2.63).

(2.62) a. Bill loaded (the) hay on the truck.
       b. Bill loaded the truck with (the) hay.
(2.63) a. Harry sprayed (the) paint on the wall.
       b. Harry sprayed the wall with (the) paint.

These sentences have been discussed by numerous writers, e.g. Hall (1965), Anderson (1971), with respect to the interpretation of the locative arguments, *truck* in (2.62) and *wall* in (2.63). In the (a) sentences the locative can be interpreted as being partially affected by the action of the verb, whereas in the (b) sentences it can be understood as being totally affected (i.e. filled with hay or covered with paint). This reading of total affectedness correlates with the occurrence of the locative as undergoer. The same variation in interpretation holds for the theme arguments. The (a) examples imply that all of the theme underwent a change of location; that is, all of the hay was loaded on the truck in (2.62a), and all of the paint was sprayed on the wall in (2.63a). No such implication obtains in the (b) sentences. Notice that (2.62a) implies that all of the hay was loaded but not that the truck was full, whereas (2.62b) implies that the truck was full but not that all of the hay was loaded. This is a clear correlation between the occurrence of an argument as undergoer and a reading of total affectedness. This relates directly to the close link between undergoer and patient, since patients are arguments which suffer a change of state and are therefore thoroughly affected by the action of the verb, and since patients are prototypical undergoers. Affectedness is part of the inherent semantics of undergoer, and arguments other than patients occurring as undergoer acquire this semantic flavoring in addition to the meaning of their own semantic relation. Note that this additional meaning of affectedness is not due to their syntactic status as direct object, since the same reading obtains when the NP is in a different syntactic status but is still an undergoer.

(2.64) a. The truck was loaded with hay by John.
       b. The truck was easy to load with hay.
(2.65) a. The hay was loaded on the truck by John.
       b. The hay was difficult to load on the truck.

It must be noted that not all cases of theme–locative alternation exhibit this type of semantic difference. In the examples with *give* in (2.45) there is no difference in meaning akin to that in (2.62) and (2.63). Similarly in (2.48), repeated here as (2.66), the same pattern of syntactic and semantic relation variation is found as in (2.62) and (2.63), but there is no comparable difference in meaning.

(2.66) a. The man hit the cane against the wall.
        b. The man hit the wall with the cane.

There is likewise no variation in the interpretation of the locative due to the nature of the action: with an impact verb either there is impact or there is none, and consequently there can be no distinction between partial versus total affectedness. Note, however, that there is a difference in what Fillmore (1977) calls *perspective* in the examples with *give* and *hit*; in (2.66a) the cane is presented as the primary focus of the impact, whereas in (2.66b) the wall is so viewed. This is not a difference in affectedness in the sense of (2.62) – (2.63) but rather is a difference of which participant is treated as being primarily affected by the action.

    This can be seen clearly in the following sentences.

(2.67) a. Fred hit the door with his fist and broke/??hurt it.
        b. Fred hit his fist against the door and broke/hurt it.

In (2.67a) *it* in the second clause preferentially refers to *the door* and not to *his fist*, hence the oddity of *hurt it*. However, in (2.67b) the preferred interpretation of *it* is as coreferential to *his fist*, and consequently both second possibilities are fine. Thus even with *hit* there is a semantic difference relating to the choice of the undergoer, albeit more subtle than that with *load* and *spray*.

    In this section we have shown how the token-specific meanings of actor and undergoer are a function of the semantic relation of the argument which occurs as actor or undergoer. This semantic relation is derivative of the semantic structure of the predicate in the clause. Thus the actor is an agent if it occurs with a verb which has DO in its logical structure, an effector if the verb has a predicate like **do'** or **smile'** in its logical structure, or a locative if it is a stative verb of possession, cognition, or perception. Similarly, the undergoer is a patient if there is a stative predicate denoting a state or condition in the logical structure of the verb, and is a theme or locative if the verb contains a state predicate of location, possession, cognition, or perception (see table 4). There is a cline of semantic relations which expresses the accessibility of an argument bearing a given semantic relation to occurrence as actor or undergoer. The prototypical actor is an agent and the prototypical undergoer a patient, and this latter fact has consequences for the interpretation of non-patient undergoers.

2.7 The Tagalog verbal system: classification and logical structures

We will now apply the ideas developed (with respect to English) in this chapter to a language of a radically different type, Tagalog. Tagalog is a language with both nominal case marking and verbal cross-referencing. The nominal case-marking system makes use of two prepositional particles: *ng*, which marks actors, patients, and themes, and *sa*, which marks locative NPs. Tagalog is basically a verb-initial language, but word order among the full NPs following the verb is quite free. There is a further constraint in the Tagalog clause in that one of the NP arguments of the verb must be put *in focus*.[18] The case marker *ng* or *sa* which would normally precede the NP according to semantic role is replaced by the preposition *ang*, and its semantic relation is coded on the verb by means of an affix.

(2.68) a. B-*um*-ili ng isda sa bata ang lalake.
AF-buy TH fish L child F man
'The man bought some fish from the child.'

b. B-in-ili-∅   ng lalake sa bata ang isda.
PERF-buy-THF   A man L child F fish
'The man bought the fish from the child.'

c. B-in-ilh-*an* ng lalake ng isda ang bata.
PERF-buy-LF A man TH fish F child
'The man bought some fish from the child.'

In these examples we have standardized the nominal word-order for ease of comparison. Free permutation of the NPs is possible although there are some preferences. As in these examples, the NP in focus most commonly occurs in the clause-final position, and a non-focused actor in the immediately post-verbal position, but these are only tendencies, not rigid constraints. In all the sentences in (2.68), *lalake* 'man' is an agent and must therefore function as actor. Tagalog has the same rule of accessibility to actor as English: if an agent is present it must be the actor. Also, in (2.68), *isda* 'fish' is a theme, as it is transferred in an action, and *bata* 'child' is a locative–source, the original possessor.[19] The logical structure for all these examples would be [DO (lalake, [**do′** (lalake)])] CAUSE [BECOME NOT **be-at′** (isda, bata) & BECOME **be-at′** (isda, lalake)].

Any of these three NPs can be in focus. The (a) sentence is an example of a clause in which the actor NP is in focus, an actor–focus construction. The normal case-marker for actors, *ng*, is replaced by the focus particle *ang*, and the verb is affixed with the infix *-um-*, which encodes that an actor NP is the NP in focus. Sentence (2.68b) is the corresponding theme–focus construction. The undergoer *isda* 'fish', in this case a theme, is in focus, and its normal case marker *ng* is replaced by the focus particle *ang*. The verb takes a $\emptyset$ focus affix, which in the perfective is the marker for theme focus. Finally, (2.68c) is a sentence in which a source NP *bata* 'child' is in focus. Source NPs are normally case marked by *sa* (as in examples (a) and (b)), but when focused they are marked with the general focus particle *ang*. The verb appears with the suffix *-an*, which means that an NP of the locative group, including sources and goals, is in focus. Thus, what is common in all these constructions is that a single NP is chosen as the focused NP of the clause, marked by *ang*, and its function is indicated by affixation in the verb. These three constructions are the most basic focus types, but Tagalog does have a wide variety of secondary focus types which we will not discuss here. For a detailed analysis of Tagalog focus constructions and affixes see Schachter and Otanes (1972:284–355).

As is apparent from the discussion thus far, the primary burden of case marking in Tagalog falls on the system of verbal affixes, and we will center our discussion on these. From a careful analysis of the basic semantic distinctions made by the verbal affixes, a clear understanding of the basic system of semantic relations and functions in Tagalog can be gained. We will first discuss the verbal affixes and corresponding constructions associated with the actor.

Tagalog makes a sharp distinction between actions which are controlled and volitional, and those which are not. In other words, Tagalog distinguishes explicitly between logical structures which contain the abstract predicate DO and those which do not. This is a fundamental contrast in Tagalog grammar. All focus types have contrasting verbal affixes, one indicating a controlled volitional action, the other indicating an uncontrolled non-volitional action. In actor focus constructions, the volitional affixes are either *-um-* or *mag-*. Most verbs take one or the other, but some verbs may take both with a corresponding contrast in meaning, often along aspectual lines which will not concern us here. The affix *-um-* occurs widely with both transitive and intransitive verbs while *mag-* favors transitive verbs. Note these examples. (The perfective form of *mag-* is *nag-* which signals imperfective in conjunction with reduplication of the stem.)

(2.69) a. T-*um*-akbo sa   bahay ang lalake.
           AF-run   L   house F   man
           'The man ran to the house.'
    b. K-*um*-ain ng isda ang lalake.
           AF-eat   P   fish   F   man
           'The man ate fish.'
    c. *Um*-agaw ng bola sa bata ang lalake.
           AF-grab TH ball L child F   man
           'The man grabbed a ball from the child.'
    d. *Mag*-da-dala   ng kahon ang lalake.
           AF-REDUP-carry TH box   F   man
           'The man will carry a box.'
    e. *Nag*-bigay ng   libro sa bata ang lalake.
           AF-give   TH book L child F   man
           'The man gave a book to the child.'
    f. *Nag*-lu-luto   ng pagkain ang lalake.
           AF-REDUP-cook P   food   F   man
           'The man is cooking food.'

All of the verbs in these examples have logical structures containing the predicate DO. Verbs whose logical structures do not contain the component DO exhibit a variety of verbal affixes which differentiate the various semantic classes of verbs. We will discuss each of these classes and the associated verbal prefixes.

Stative verbs are those denoting states and have the logical structure **predicate′** (x). In Tagalog, such verbs are marked with either *ma-* or ∅: *ma-bigat* 'heavy', *ma-ganda* 'beautiful', *ma-bilis* 'fast', *ma-pait* 'bitter', *pagod* 'tired', *tulog* 'asleep', *basag* 'broken'. Some stative verb roots can occur with both *ma-* and ∅, but with a contrast in meaning: *ma-* denotes a relatively transitory state, while ∅ indicates a more permanent state.

(2.70) a. *Ma*-puti   ang bulaklak.
              -white F   flower
              'The flower is white' (it faded).
     b. ∅-puti   ang bulaklak.
              -white F   flower
              'The flower is (naturally) white.'
(2.71) a. *Ma*-bilog   ang buwan.
              -round F   moon
              'The moon is full.'
     b. ∅-bilog   ang buwan.
              -round F   moon
              'The moon is round.'

The examples in (2.70–2.71) sharply point up this contrast. When full, the moon is in a transitory state of roundness, whereas, of course, its shape as a heavenly body is inherently round.

Verbs specifying locations rather than states have the logical structure **be-at′** (a, b). In Tagalog, verbs of this class are also marked with the prefix *ma-* (perfective form *na-*).

(2.72) a. *Na*-upo sa sahig ang lalake.
              -sit L floor F   man
              'The man sat on the floor.'
     b. *Na*-sa kusina   ang lalake.
              -L kitchen F   man
              'The man is in the kitchen.'

Change of state or process achievement verbs have the logical structure BECOME **predicate′** (x). Tagalog uses the affixes *-um-* and *ma-* to indicate this class according to the following rule: if the corresponding stative form is marked with ∅, the change of state form is marked with *ma-*, while if the stative verb is marked with *ma-*, the corresponding process verb is marked with *-um-*.

Some examples are: *matay* 'dead', *ma-matay* 'die'; *pagod* 'tired', *ma-pagod* 'become tired'; *bingi* 'deaf', *ma-bingi* 'go deaf'; but *ma-buti* 'good', *b-um-uti* 'improve, become good'; *ma-laki* 'big', *l-um-aki* 'increase'; *ma-tanda* 'old', *t-um-anda* 'age, become older'. Also, in change of state verbs, there occurs the transitory versus permanent contrast discussed above with regard to stative verbs. If a change of state verb normally marked with *-um-* is viewed as denoting a transitory change of state in a certain instance, then it occurs with *maN-* (perfective *naN-*) rather than *-um-*.[20]

(2.73) a. P-um-ula ang dahon.
           -red F   leaf
          'The leaf turned red.'
      b. Nam-(p)ula ang lalake.
           -red   F   man
          'The man blushed.'

Ma- is also used with emotion achievement verbs when the experiencer of the emotion is in focus.

(2.74) a. *Na*-galit   ang lalake.
           -angry F   man
          'The man got angry.'
      b. *Na*-ligalig ang lalake.
           -upset F   man
          'The man became upset.'
      c. *Na*-hiya   ang lalake.
           -ashamed F   man
          'The man became ashamed.'

These verbs all have the logical structure BECOME **predicate′** (x). The man undergoes a change of state and the resulting state is that he is angry/upset/ashamed.

We now turn to transitive verbs which have an actor which may be an agent (controlled) or an effector (non-controlled). This contrast relates to the presence of DO in the logical structure of the verb. If a verb has DO in its logical structure, *ma-* may be used to cancel it, rendering the verb non-volitional. For example, the verb *hiwa* 'cut' has the logical structure of an accomplishment verb.

(2.75) a. H-*um*-iwa   ng lalake ng   kutsilyo ang babae.
            vol.AF-cut P man   EFF-TH knife   F   woman
            'The woman cut a man with the knife.'
        b. [[DO (babae, [**do**′ (babae)])] CAUSE [BECOME
            be-at′ (kutsilyo, lalake)]] CAUSE [BECOME **cut**′
            (lalake)]

Example (2.75) has an explicit agentive-component DO. This
component can be canceled by replacing the affix -*um*- by either
ma- (*na*-) to mark the patient in focus, or *maka*- (perfective *naka*-)
for the actor in focus.

(2.76) a. *Na*-hiwa   ng kutsilyo ang lalake.
            invol.PF-cut A knife   F   man
            'The man got cut on a/the knife.'
        b. *Naka*-hiwa   ng lalake ang kutsilyo.
            invol.AF-cut P man   F   knife
            'A man got cut on the knife.'

In contrast to (2.75b), these sentences have the logical structure

(2.77) [BECOME **be-at**′ (kutsilyo, lalake)] CAUSE
        [BECOME **cut**′ (lalake)]

in which the knife moves and effects a change of state but is not
intentionally manipulated by agents.[21] Thus, *ma-/maka*- simply
cancels the DO component.

   With other verbs of different logical structures the *ma-/maka*-
affixes likewise eliminate DO.

(2.78) a. *Nag*-alis   ng libro sa aklatan ang lalake.
            vol. AF-remove TH book L library F   man
            'The man removed a book from the library.'
        b. [DO (lalake, [**do**′ (lalake)])] CAUSE [BECOME
            NOT **be-at**′ (libro, aklatan)]
        c. *Naka*-alis   ng libro sa aklatan ang lalake.
            invol. AF-remove TH book L library F   man
            'The man accidentally removed a book from the
            library.'
        d. [**do**′ (lalake)] CAUSE [BECOME NOT **be-at**′
            (libro, aklatan)]
(2.79) a. T-*um*-anggap   ng gantimpala ang lalake.
            vol. AF-receive TH prize   F   man
            'The man accepted a prize.'

b. DO (lalake, [BECOME **have**′ (lalake, gantimpala)])
c. *Naka*-tanggap   ng   gantimpala ang lalake.
   invol. A F-receive TH prize   F   man
   'The man received a prize.'
d. BECOME **have**′ (lalake, gantimpala)

In these examples the DO component of the (a) sentence and (b) logical structures is eliminated when the affixes *mag-* or *-um-* are replaced by object-focus *ma-* or actor-focus *maka-*.

In 2.5 we argued that non-volitional perception verbs have the logical structure of a state verb, e.g. **see**′ (x, y) whereas volitional perception verbs like *watch*, *listen to*, etc. have the logical structure DO (x, [**see**′ (x, y)]). With *see* the actor NP is a locative, whereas with *watch* the actor is an agent, the argument of DO. Tagalog verbs of perception are divided into two classes, according to whether the perception is volitional or not. This distinction is generally lexicalized in different verb roots, e.g. *-kita* 'see', *-nood* 'watch'; and *-rinig* 'hear', *-kinig* 'listen to'. The distinction between volitional and non-volitional perception is also apparent in the focus affixes involved. Non-volitional perception verbs occur with *maka-* to mark the perceiver in focus and *ma-* to mark the perceived in focus, whereas volitional perception verbs use *ma-* to mark the perceiver in focus and *pa-* ... *-an* to mark the perceived in focus.

(2.80) a. *Naka*-rinig   ng   ingay ang lalake.
      PERCEIVER.F-hear TH noise F   man
      'The man heard a noise.'
   b. *Na*-rinig   ng lalake ang ingay.
      PERCEIVED.F-hear A man   F   noise.
      'The man heard the noise.'
   c. *Na*-kinig   ng   musik ang lalake.
      PERCEIVER.F-listen to TH music F   man
      'The man listened to music.'
   d. *P*-in-*a*-kinig-*an*   ng lalake ang musik.
      PERCEIVED.F-listen to A man   F   music
      'The man listened to the music.'

The verb *rinig* 'hear' in (a) and (b) is a non-volitional perception verb and occurs with *maka-* or *ma-*, while *kinig* 'listen to' in (c) and (d) is a volitional perception verb and occurs with *ma-* and *pa-* ... *-an*.

Let us try to systematize what we have discussed thus far. In Tagalog, as well as most western Austronesian languages, there is a fundamental distinction between actions which are volitional and those which are non-volitional, or, in our terms, between verbs whose logical structures contain DO and those whose logical structures do not contain DO. Volitional verbs always occur with either *-um-* or *mag-* in actor focus constructions, whereas non-volitional verbs occur with a range of verbal affixes, the most basic of which is *ma-*. *Ma-* occurs with a wide range of different verb classes, and some generalizations on its functions are called for.

In order to understand the function of *ma-* we need to elaborate on the structure of lexical entries for Tagalog verbs. Tagalog is much like Lakhota as discussed in 2.4 in that verbs involving a state or change of state are represented simply as states in the lexicon. Thus, verbs like *ma-buti* 'good', *ma-laki* 'big', $\emptyset$/*ma-pula* 'red', *basag* 'broken', and *puno* 'full', are all stative verbs and have the logical structure **predicate′** (x). This is the basic logical structure in the lexical entries for all these verbs. Some of these verbs obligatorily occur with *ma-* to indicate stativity, others optionally take it, and still others may never occur with it. The change of state (i.e. achievement) forms of these verbs with the logical structure BECOME **predicate′** (x) can be formed by a derivational process of verbal affixation: *b-um-uti* 'become good', *ma-basag* 'become broken', and *ma-puno* 'become full'. The inchoative form occurs with either *-um-* or *ma-*, generally according to whether the stative form is *ma-* or $\emptyset$.

The derivational process can be carried still further by adding an agentive DO component to the logical structure resulting in an accomplishment-verb logical structure, [DO (x, [**do′** (x)])] CAUSE [BECOME **predicate′** (y)]. This further step in a derivation is marked by the prefix *mag-* in combination with the causative prefix *pa-* with roots which have *ma-* statives and *-um-* change of state verbs: *mag-pa-buti* 'improve', *mag-pa-pula* 'redden', *mag-basag* 'break', and *mag-puno* 'fill'. Thus, with a verb like *basag* 'broken', *mag-* indicates the accomplishment-verb logical structure [DO (x, [**do**′ (x)])] CAUSE [BECOME **predicate**′ (y)], *ma-* the achievement-verb logical structure BECOME **predicate**′ (x), and ∅ the state-verb logical structure **predicate**′ (x); but the logical structure as entered in the lexicon is only **predicate**′ (x) as the other two are formed by a regular lexical derivational process.

This analysis aids in elucidating the functions of *ma-*. Note that there are two derivational patterns in the morphology. The first exhibited by *buti* 'good' has stative form *ma-*, change of state form *-um-*, and agentive form *mag-pa*, while the second pattern exhibited by *basag* 'broken', has stative form ∅, change of state form *ma-*, and agentive form *mag-*. Thus *ma-* indicates state or change of state depending on this verb type. Looking more closely at the semantics of the two classes, the roots of the first class with *ma*-statives are all qualities, properties which objects have inherently, like size or color, whereas roots of the second class with ∅ statives are states which result from the change of state of an object, and are more closely related to verbs. *Ma-* with this second class denotes the change of state which brought about the resulting state, a transitory succession of states which resulted in the final state. With the first class of roots which denotes inherent properties of objects, the *ma-* converts them into mutable qualities which are now susceptible to change, more transitory. Thus, *ma-* marks transitory states and a transitory sequence of states, i.e. a change of state. This transitory meaning of *ma-* was apparent with *bilog* 'round' as applied to the moon as discussed in (2.71): *bilog* with regard to the moon denotes its inherent round quality (permanent), while *ma-bilog* with regard to the moon denotes the roundness of a full moon (transitory).

The second function of *ma-* is with verbs whose basic logical structure contains the component DO. With such verbs *ma-* (actor focus *maka-*) operates as a DO canceler. It is this function of *ma/maka-* which explains their usage with non-volitional perception verbs, as in (2.80). These verbs lack the DO component in their logical structure, just as, e.g. (2.78) above, and, consequently, they are marked morphologically by *ma/maka-* in exactly the same way. The verb affixes discussed in this section are summarized in Table 5.

Table 5 *Tagalog verbal affixes*

State		Achievement		Accomplishment	
Ø- (Permanent)		*ma-*		*mag-*	(AF)
ma- (Transitory)		*-um-*, *maN-*		*mag + pa-* (AF)	
		Volitional		Non-volitional	
Perception		*ma-*	AF	*maka-* AF	
		pa-...-*an*	THF	*ma-*	P/THF
Non-perception		*-um-*/*mag-*	AF	*maka-* AF	
		-Ø/-*i*	P/THF	*ma-*	P/THF

It is quite clear from the discussion of the elaborate use of the verbal prefixes above that the concept of actor is a vital one in Tagalog grammar, and furthermore the distinction between a volitional actor, an agent, and a non-volitional one, an effector or locative, is a basic division in the morphological categories of verb affixation. This is in striking contrast to English, in which the distinctions among various types of actors are by and large covert and not indicated by any explicit morphological means like verbal affixation or case marking. However, in English, distinctions among various types of undergoers are elaborately and explicitly coded, usually in the form of the prepositions associated with the following oblique phrase (see 3.3.1). Thus, while we may say that in English the morphological coding of distinctions among types of actors is weakly developed, the coding of distinctions among types of undergoers is strongly developed. In English a wide range of semantic relations is accessible to undergoer, and the semantics of such choices is reflected in the choice of prepositions, as will be seen in the next chapter. In Tagalog, on the other hand, undergoer is quite weakly developed.

As we pointed out at the beginning of this section, Tagalog possesses a variety of verbal affixes which permit a wide range of non-actor semantic roles to be in focus: patients, themes, locatives, etc., and these semantic relations are coded explicitly in the verbal morphology.

(2.81)   a.   B-in-asag-Ø   ng lalake ang baso.   (Patient)
             PERF-break-PF A man   F   glass
             'The man broke the glass.'

         b.   *I*-b-in-igay   ng lalake sa bata ang   (Theme)
             THF-PERF-give A man   L child F
             libro.

book

'The man gave the book to a/the child.'

c. B-in-igy-*an*   ng lalake ng libro ang   (Locative–
PERF-give-LF A man TH book F   Goal)
bata.
child

'The man gave a book to the child.'

d. B-in-ilh-*an*   ng lalake ng libro ang (Locative–
PERF-buy-LF A man TH book F   Source)
bata.
child

'The man bought a book from the child.'

e. T-in-amn-*an*   ng lalake ang bukid.   (Locative)
PERF-plant-LF A man F   field

'The man planted in the field.'

f. *I*-p-in-utol   ng lilake ng tinapay ang (Effector–
THF-PERF-cut A man P bread F   Theme)
kutsilyo.
knife

'The man cut some bread with the knife.'

These data illustrate the following rules for the semantic roles of NP in focus: -∅ marks patients, -*an* marks locatives, whether simple locatives, locative–goals, or locative–sources, and *i*- marks themes, whether simple themes or effector–themes. The verbal morphology strictly marks the basic semantic relation of the argument in focus, rather than signaling 'undergoer in focus' and neutralizing these distinctions. This can be seen most clearly in the semantic contrasts in (2.82) and (2.83) below.

(2.82) a. Ni-linis-∅   ng lalake ang kotse.
            PERF-clean-PF A man F   car
            'The man cleaned the car.'

      b. P-in-unas-*an*   ng lalake ang mesa.
            PERF-wipe-LF A man F   table
            'The man wiped the table.'

(2.83) a. B-in-asa-∅   ng lalake ang damit.
            PERF-wet-PF A man F   clothes
            'The man drenched the clothes.'

b. W-in-isik-*an*   ng lalake ang damit.
   PERF-sprinkle-LF A man F   clothes
   'The man sprinkled the clothes.'

These examples are parallel to the *load hay on the truck* versus *load the truck with hay* (cf. (2.62), (2.63)) sentences. The focus affix associated with patients, -$\emptyset$, is used to mark more thoroughly affected NPs in contrast to less affected NPs which are marked by -*an*, the locative focus suffix. However, these Tagalog facts differ from English in that there are no clear cases of alternations. Which affix is used is associated with the particular semantics of each verb, and there do not seem to be any verb roots which can take both of the two affixes to exhibit just this contrast. Thus there appears to be no real evidence in Tagalog for the existence of undergoer as a macrorole distinct from the individual roles of patient, theme, and locative.[22]

Tagalog is an interesting contrast to English in its heavy use of verbal morphology to express what English either leaves covert or expresses through lexicalization or preposition choices. We have discussed the extensive morphology that the language employs to express the precise semantic roles of the participants in the logical structure. This applies equally to those roles belonging to the actor complex and those of the undergoer complex. While the language makes heavy use of the actor notion, both in marking alternations with a verb root between volitional and non-volitional causation, and in general syntactic constructions like reflexives (see Schachter 1976, 1977, and Foley & Van Valin 1977), the undergoer is very weakly developed, basically being equivalent to the semantic role patient, which is the prototypical undergoer in all languages.

3 *Case marking*

3.0 Introduction

In the previous chapter we presented a theory of the semantic relations which obtain between a predicate and its arguments. We now turn to the issue of how these relations are signaled in clauses, the issue of case marking. We understand this notion in its widest sense; i.e. we take it to encompass all of the various means by which languages indicate the grammatical functions of the nominal arguments in a clause, e.g. nominal inflection, verbal cross-referencing, word order. Our purpose is not to present a theory of case marking; rather we will work within the theory developed by Michael Silverstein in a series of papers (1976b, 1980b, 1981), and attempt to integrate into it the theory of the semantic structure of the clause developed in Chapter 2. We begin by outlining Silverstein's theory of case marking and then turn to an investigation of certain aspects of case marking in three typologically quite distinct languages: English, Eastern Pomo, and Dyirbal. In the final section we will take a look at case marking in causative constructions and propose an explanation for the general pattern of case marking in these constructions first noted in Comrie (1976b).

3.1 Silverstein's theory of case marking

Silverstein develops a 'functional morphosyntax' of case marking, concentrating on the grammatical cases, i.e. nominative, accusative, ergative, and dative, in his 1976(b) paper; the 1980(b) and 1981 papers are attempts at clarifying a number of the points made in the original presentation. The main feature of Silverstein's approach is that he treats case marking not as a means for the direct expression of some other, more abstract grammatical phenomenon, e.g. grammatical relations or semantic (thematic) relations, but rather as the expression of a complex set of interacting linguistic factors. Accordingly, in order to understand what it is that case marking marks, a variety of phenomena must be investigated. Silverstein summarizes his approach as follows. 'In such an approach, the morphosyntactic phenomenon of (surface) case marking is treated as a DEPENDENT VARIABLE, the various attested configurations of which are the results of the interaction of a number of INDEPENDENT VARIABLES of referential-and-predicational meaningfulness of ongoing linguistic discourse' (Silverstein 1981:228–9 (emphasis in original)). There are four independent variables: inherent lexical content of noun phrases, propositional function or case relations within a clause, the clause-linkage environment in which the clause occurs, and the type of discourse coreference system employed. Silverstein characterizes them in the following terms:

I. The inherent referential content of noun phrases, coded 'locally' in noun phrase categories, and organized by criteria of both pragmatic and semantic preferential markedness into a feature-space of categories of referring;
II. The case relations – 'Agent-of', 'Patient-of', 'Subject-of', 'Dative-of' (A, O, S, D) – that noun phrases bear within schemata of predicate argument relationships at the clause-level of analysis, however we wish to represent these;
III. The (logical) clause-linkage type connecting two (or more) clause-level structures in a complex or compound sentence, or in sequential discourse, forming a kind of hierarchy of tightness of linkage . . ., evidenced by greater and greater deformation of the full, plain surface structure of at least one, and sometimes both, of the linked clauses;
IV. The reference–maintenance relations of arguments of predicates (as expressed by noun phrases in non-linked clausal structures) across discourse-level structures, so-called anaphoric 'coreference' and 'switch reference' being names for specific types of formal-functional systems for indicating this (*ibid.*, 229–30).

Of these four variables, the only one not dealt with in detail in this book is I, inherent referential (or lexical) content. This is thoroughly discussed in Silverstein (1976b), and we have nothing to add to that presentation. Variable II, 'case relations' or 'clause-level propositionality' (Silverstein 1980b) was the topic of Chapter 2, and the main focus of this chapter is to show how the system developed there can be used in the explanation of certain case marking phenomena. Variables III and IV are considered in later chapters: clause linkage in Chapter 6 and reference maintenance in Chapter 7.

Because case marking is sensitive to all four of these factors, an investigation of any one of them necessarily involves an attempt to hold all of the others constant. We can eliminate III and IV by dealing with simple sentences out of context, but I will nevertheless still come into play, unless we use noun-phrase arguments of the same inherent lexical content in all examples. Since this is impossible, variable I cannot be factored out entirely.

3.2 The layered structure of the clause

Silverstein's theory seeks to provide an analysis of the 'central or grammatical cases' as noted above. Before turning to aspects of case marking in English, Eastern Pomo, and Dyirbal, we will now make precise this notion of 'central grammatical cases' in terms of the theory of clause structure which underlies all of the subsequent discussion and analysis in this book. This view of the clause takes it to be a layered structure, with the outer layers enclosing the inner layers. Each of these layers has its own set of constituents, and, as we will see in Chapter 5, its own set of operators. The innermost layer of the clause is the NUCLEUS, which contains the predicate. It is the heart of the clause. The nucleus may be complex and consist of more than one predicate; numerous examples of this will be given in Chapter 6. Surrounding the nucleus is the CORE of the clause, which consists of one or two arguments of the predicate, depending on its valence. Traditionally these two arguments have been called 'subject' and 'direct object';[1] in a simple active clause they are semantically the actor and undergoer. The arguments occurring in the core of the clause will henceforth be referred to as 'core arguments'. The outermost layer of the clause is the PERIPHERY, which contains arguments expressing the spatio-temporal setting of the event, as well as the secondary participants in the event, e.g. beneficiaries. The layered structure of the clause is represented in Figure 2.

The theory of the layered structure of the clause was originally developed in Olson (1981) and Foley & Olson (in press). The distinction between core and peripheral arguments is not unique to it. For example, Dixon (1977) employs a similar opposi-

[(NP) ... (NP) [NP (NP) [Predicate]]]

<u>NUCLEUS</u>

<u>CORE</u>

<u>PERIPHERY</u>

CLAUSE

Figure 2   The layered structure of the clause

tion in his description of Yidiɲ; Andrews (in press) proposes an
analogous distinction between 'core' and 'oblique' arguments in
his analysis of grammatical relations; tagmemic theory (Pike &
Pike 1982) makes a similar distinction between nucleus (= core)
and margin (= periphery); and Dik (1978) proposes a comparable
opposition between nuclear (= core) arguments and satellites
(= peripheral arguments). The layered structure of the clause, as
represented in Figure 2, is not based on nor does it express
constituent-structure relationships of the type captured in phrase-
structure rules. The distinction between nucleus, core, and
periphery is found in the grammars of all languages, regardless
of whether they have constituent structure in this sense or not
(see 3.3.1, 3.3.3). This is an important point, given the existence
of the so-called 'non-configurational' languages, which lack
constituent structure of the type characteristic of English (see Hale
1979, Chomsky 1981a, c; 1.2, 5.5). Accordingly any theory of
clause structure crucially based on immediate constituent analysis
will be inadequate in principle with respect to non-configurational
languages. In 'configurational' languages like English, phrase-
structure categories of the kind proposed in X-bar syntax (Jackendoff 1977) do not for the most part correspond directly to the
levels of the clause in Figure 2. Nucleus is equivalent to V in
most cases, but core is not equivalent to $\bar{V}$ (VP), because the core

includes the 'subject' as well as the 'direct object'; there is no phrase-structure category which includes just the 'subject', verb, and 'direct object' (see 6.5, esp. n. 12).

Each of these layers or levels of clause structure can be motivated by both intraclausal and interclausal morphosyntactic phenomena. We will thoroughly examine their importance for cross-clause syntax in Chapter 6. With respect to intraclausal criteria, the primary evidence in support of the nucleus as a distinct level from the core comes from the fact that the nucleus has its own operators, e.g. aspect, independent of the core and its arguments (see Chapter 5 for detailed discussion), and that it may be internally complex (see Chapter 6). There is evidence from both morphological coding and syntactic behavioral properties which substantiates the contrast between core and periphery. Since this chapter is concerned with case marking, we will discuss only the relevant coding phenomena in this section. The differential syntactic behavior of core versus peripheral arguments will be amply illustrated in subsequent chapters.

The main coding feature distinguishing core from peripheral arguments is that core arguments tend to occur in unmarked morphological or syntactic forms and peripheral arguments in marked, often adpositional, codings. This is the case, for example, in English, French, Indonesian, Barai (Olson 1981), Jacaltec and other Mayan languages (Craig 1977, Dayley 1981), Malagasy (Keenan 1976a), Tunica (Haas 1940), and Kinyarwanda and other Bantu languages (Kimenyi 1980). The two non-oblique core arguments of a transitive verb are very often distinguished by their ordering alone. Correlating with the unmarked morphological status of core arguments is the possibility of their being cross-referenced on the verb. In Jacaltec, Tunica, and Kinyarwanda only core arguments are cross-referenced on the verb, and peripheral arguments cannot be. In English the only argument which may trigger verb agreement is a core argument, the 'subject'. In languages with extensive nominal inflection, e.g. Warlpiri (Hale 1973), concomitant cross-referencing in the verbal complex (in Warlpiri, on the auxiliary) distinguishes core from peripheral arguments. A similar situation obtains in Basque (Brettschneider 1979). (See Andrews in press.)

There are languages in which coding properties alone are insufficient to distinguish core from peripheral arguments. In German, for example, it is obvious only that the nominative case NP is a core argument, by virtue of its unmarked morphological status and its triggering verb agreement. How does one determine whether either or both accusative and dative NPs (which are not objects of prepositions) are core arguments? Coding properties cannot be appealed to, since neither is morphologically unmarked or triggers verb agreement. In such an instance we must examine their syntactic behavior within the clause. A striking and crucial difference between accusative and dative arguments in German is that only the erstwhile accusative case-marked argument may be the nominative subject of a passive construction; the dative case-marked argument can never become the subject of a passive, even if it is the 'direct object' of a verb like *helfen* or *danken* which take dative objects (see 4.4). This shows that the accusative NP but not the dative NP is a core argument, for only the accusative NP can become the nominative subject of a passive. As we will show in Chapter 4, the ability to be 'subject' is a crucial property of core arguments.

It is impossible to give a single criterion that will enable one to differentiate core from peripheral arguments in all languages. Rather, there are several interacting criteria which are necessary, given the morpho-syntactic diversity of human languages. Nevertheless, the distinction is a clear one, particularly in complex sentences, as we will see in Chapters 5 and 6. The 'central or grammatical cases' which Silverstein's theory of case marking deals with are those expressing core arguments in a simple clause. The 'non-grammatical' or 'adverbial' cases are those of peripheral arguments. When we take all four of the case-marking variables into account in Chapters 6 and 7, it is the case marking of core arguments, not peripheral ones, which is affected.

3.3 Aspects of case marking in three languages

In the following sections we will investigate aspects of case marking in three languages, English, Eastern Pomo, and Dyirbal. These languages represent three distinct case-marking systems: nominative–accusative, split intransitive, and ergative–absolutive, respectively. (See Dixon 1979a for a detailed discussion of the typology of case-marking systems.)

3.3.1 English: preposition assignment There are two separate but related dimensions to English case marking: the ordering of core arguments and the assignment of prepositions to peripheral arguments. The layered structure of the English clause is given in (3.1), where P = periphery, C = core, and N = nucleus.

(3.1) ₚ[c[N P ₙ[Predicate]ₙ (N P)]c (P P) ... (P P)]ₚ

The pre-nuclear core argument has been traditionally called the 'subject', and the post-nuclear core argument has been called the 'direct object' (cf. n. 1). English verbs normally have no more than two core arguments.[2,3] With an active-voice transitive verb, the 'subject' is an actor and the 'direct object' an undergoer. With intransitive verbs the single argument may be either actor or undergoer, depending upon the nature of the verb, as we saw in 2.1. In a passive construction, the undergoer occurs as 'subject' and the actor as a peripheral argument, if at all (see Chapter 4 for more detailed discussion). Little more need be said about core arguments in English; their ordering is captured in (3.1), and their semantics is a function of the voice of the verb, its valence, and its semantic structure, as we saw in 2.2 and 2.6.

Prepositional case marking is much more complex. In some approaches it is accounted for by notational fiat. For example, in Jackendoff (1976) the prepositional arguments which may occur with a verb are simply listed in its lexical entry, as exemplified in (3.2).

(3.2) +[N P¹__N P²(from N P³) (to N P⁴) (with N P⁵)]

The superscript numbers index each argument to an argument position in the semantic representation of the verb, thereby linking prepositions to thematic relations. A more interesting and systematic analysis of English would be one in which prepositions did not have to be idiosyncratically specified with each verbal lexical entry but rather could be predicted by some general principles relating to the semantics of verbs and the assignment of arguments to morphosyntactic positions within the clause. The logical structures proposed in Chapter 2, together with the layered conception of the English clause and the notions of actor and undergoer, provide the means for formulating general rules of preposition assignment for English.

It is generally the case that the NP not functioning as undergoer is marked in English by a preposition. A number of examples are repeated here from the discussion in 2.6.

(3.3) a. The man hit the wall with the cane.   (= 2.48b)
       b. The man hit the cane against the wall.   (= 2.48a)
(3.4) a. Bill loaded (the) hay on the truck.   (= 2.49a)
       b. Bill loaded the truck with (the) hay.   (= 2.49b)
(3.5) a. John drained the water from the pool.   (= 2.52a)
       b. John drained the pool of its water.   (= 2.52b)
(3.6) a. The compere presented the award to Bert
           Newton.
       b. The compere presented Bert Newton
           with the award.

In (3.3a) the non-undergoer *cane* is marked by *with*, while in (3.3b) the non-undergoer *wall* occurs with *against*. In (3.4a) the non-undergoer takes *on*, in (3.4b) *with*. The non-undergoers in (3.5) are marked by *from* in (a) and *of* in (b), while in (3.6) they are marked by *to* and *with*.[4] It is obviously beyond the scope of this discussion to deal with all or even a majority of English prepositions. Accordingly we will concentrate on a select few: *with*, *of* (as in (3.5b)), and several locative prepositions.

With is perhaps the most interesting English preposition because of its variety of uses and apparent lack of direct correlation with any particular semantic relation. Fillmore (1977:78) noted that themes which are not undergoers are marked by *with*. Examples (3.3a), (3.4b), (3.6b) illustrate this point. In all of them the participant undergoing motion, the theme, is not the undergoer and is obligatorily marked with *with*; in (3.3a) the theme is also an effector.

Fillmore (1977:78) also noted that in some unexplained cases non-undergoer themes were marked by *of*. However, there does seem to be a principle involved here as well. Consider the sentences in (2.52b) and (2.53b), repeated here as (3.7).

(3.7) a. John drained the pool of water.
     b. Max emptied the box of its contents.

In (3.7) the non-undergoer NPs are themes, the participants undergoing motion. However, they are marked by *of* and not *with*. Themes are marked by *of* with verbs which denote motion from a specified location to a normally unspecified location, whereas *with* occurs with verbs which denote motion to a specified location from an unspecified location. Note the following contrasts.

(3.8) a. John drained the pool of water.
     b. *John drained the pool of water onto the ground.
     c. John drained the water from the pool onto the ground.
(3.9) a. John sprayed the wall with paint.
     b. John sprayed the wall with paint from the can.
     c. *John sprayed paint on the wall from the can.

The difference in semantic orientation between *drain*-type and *spray*-type verbs can be seen clearly in these examples. *Spray* does not allow the locative-source to occur as an argument of the verb; *paint from the can* is a complex NP, as seen in the following cleft sentences.

(3.10) a. It was with paint from the can that John sprayed the wall.
      b. *It was with paint that John sprayed the wall from the can.
      c. *It was from the can that John sprayed the wall with paint.

Contrast these sentences with those in (3.11) in which *from* occurs with an argument of the verb.

(3.11) a. John sent the book to Mary from London.
      b. It was the book that John sent to Mary from London.
      c. It was to Mary that John sent the book from London.
      d. It was from London that John sent the book to Mary.

Verbs like *spray*, then, do not allow the specification of the source location as a verbal argument. *Drain*, on the other hand, allows the locative–goal to occur only if the theme is the undergoer, as in (3.8c); if the locative–source is the undergoer, then the locative–goal may not be present, as (3.8b) shows.[5] This illustrates the 'source' orientation of this class of verbs, and it is just this class of verbs which takes *of* rather than *with* on non-undergoer themes. Because these verbs involve two entities which were previously in contact but which are now no longer, due to the action of the verb, we will label them *removal* verbs, in contrast to *impact* verbs such as *hit* and *load*. These two types are subclasses of achievement verbs in English. They are distinguished in their logical structures as in (3.12).

(3.12) a. $[DO(x,[\ldots])] CAUSE [BECOME \textbf{be-at}' (y, z)]$

$$(=2.51)$$

b. $[DO(x,[\ldots])] CAUSE [BECOME NOT$
$\textbf{be-at}' (y, z)]$ $(=2.54)$

The difference between impact and removal verbs is captured in their logical structures in the contrast between the BECOME **be-at**′ of impact verbs and the BECOME NOT **be-at**′ of removal verbs. Thus we may summarize this discussion of *with* versus *of* by saying that with impact verbs non-undergoer themes are marked by *with*, while with removal verbs they are marked by *of*. Other removal verbs include *empty*, *rob*, and *relieve*.

There are still other uses of *with* which do not conform to the above rule.

(3.13) a. John and Mary went to the party.
b. John went to the party with Mary.
c. Mary went to the party with John.

In the (b) and (c) sentences *with* is used to indicate a participant in what is generally referred to as a comitative relationship, a participant which is a coperformer of the action. Sentences (3.13b–c) express that the action of going to the party was done by the actor accompanied by the participant marked by *with*. This is essentially the same meaning as expressed by the actor with the conjoined NPs in (a). The relationship between (a), on the one hand, and (b) and (c), on the other, has often been described in terms of 'conjunct splitting', in which the conjoined actor has been broken up, and one of the conjoined constituents appears in an oblique *with*-phrase. In the system being developed here, this 'conjunct splitting' is a feature of the semantic representation of the verb. With *go*, for example, which has the logical structure ... **go'** (x), *x* can be either simple or complex, and consequently the logical structure of the sentences in (3.13) would be as in (3.14).

(3.14)   [DO(John/Mary,[**go'** (John/Mary)])] CAUSE
       [BECOME **be-at'** (John/Mary, party)][6]

In this form *John* and *Mary* are coagents, and the differences among the sentences in (3.13) accrue from different actor choices: in (3.13a) both are actor, in (3.13b) only *John* is the actor, and in (3.13c) only *Mary* is the actor. As can be clearly seen from (3.13b-c), agents which are not actors must be oblique phrases marked by the preposition *with*. Agents should, by the hierarchy of accessibility to actorhood, always be actors. However, when an agent does not function as actor, as in these 'split conjunct' examples, then it must occur in an oblique *with*-phrase.

The alternations found in (3.13) are more problematic with effectors and locatives. Example (3.15) presents sentences with more than one effector and (3.16) sentences with more than one actor–locative.

(3.15)   a.   ?The hammer and the crowbar opened the door.
      b.   *The hammer opened the door with the crowbar.
      c.   *The crowbar opened the door with the hammer.

(3.16)   a.   John and Mary saw the accident.
      b.   ?John saw the accident with Mary.
      c.   ?Mary saw the accident with John.

Example (3.15a) is very strange, and (3.15b-c) are clearly unacceptable. Sentence (3.16a) is fine, but the (b–c) sentences are somewhat odd. These sentences show that semantic 'conjunct splitting' is not possible with effectors, difficult with locatives, but fine with agents as in (3.13). Thus *with* may be used to mark a non-actor agent in a situation in which the first argument of DO is complex and only one of its participants occurs as the actor.

This type of conjunct splitting also goes on with undergoers.

(3.17) a. Phoebe served the wine and the cheese.
        b. Phoebe served the wine with the cheese.
        c. Phoebe served the cheese with the wine.

The logical structure underlying these sentences is given in (3.18).

(3.18) [DO (Phoebe, [**do**′ (Phoebe)])] CAUSE [BECOME **have**′ (∅, wine/cheese)]⁷

When both themes occur as undergoer, then the result is the conjoined NP 'direct object' of (3.17a). If, on the other hand, only one of the themes appears as undergoer, then the other one is marked by *with*, as in the (b)–(c) examples. Note that this conjunct splitting does not seem to work with either patients or locatives.

(3.19) a. Fred killed the dog and the cat.
        b. ?*Fred killed the dog with the cat.
        c. ?*Fred killed the cat with the dog.

(3.20) a. Milt hit the desk and the chair.
        b. Milt hit the desk with the chair.   (≠3.20a)
        c. Milt hit the chair with the desk.   (≠3.20a)

Thus it appears that this phenomenon is restricted to themes with respect to undergoer, and to agents with respect to actor.

Another occurrence of *with* is to mark an effector which is outranked for actorhood by an agent and must, therefore, occur in an oblique phrase. These effectors were labeled 'instruments' in Fillmore (1968).

(3.21) a. Bill loaded hay on the truck with a pitchfork.

   b. Harry sprayed paint on the wall with an airgun.

   c. Frank drained the water from the pool with a hose.

(3.21a) has the logical structure given in (3.22).

(3.22) [[DO(Bill,[**do**′ (Bill)])] CAUSE [**do**′ (pitchfork)]]
        CAUSE [BECOME **be-at**′ (hay, truck)]

In (3.22) *Bill* is an agent and *pitchfork*, an effector. An agent outranks an effector as actor, and *pitchfork* must appear in an oblique *with*-phrase as in (3.21a). The same principle also applies to *airgun* in (3.21b) and *hose* in (3.21c). These examples illustrate the same principle as the 'conjunct splitting' examples above: a potential actor which does not occur as actor must be marked with *with*.

With may be said to have two general functions: it marks potential actors, agents or effectors, which do not occur as actor, and it marks (effector–) themes (which are potential undergoers), which do not occur as undergoer. It follows from this analysis that it should be in principle possible to have three *with*-phrases in a single sentence, and it is in fact possible, as (3.23) shows.

(3.23) a. Bill loaded the truck with cartons with a forklift with
        John.

      b. [[DO (Bill/John,[**do**′(Bill/John)])] CAUSE [**do**′
        (forklift)]] CAUSE [BECOME **be-at**′ (cartons,
        truck)]

In (3.23) *with* marks a theme, a (co)agent, and an effector. Because the locative *truck* occurs as undergoer, the theme *cartons* must take *with*. Since only one of the two coagents occurs as actor, the other one is assigned *with*; and because there is an agent, the effector *forklift* cannot be actor and likewise occurs with *with*. We may summarize these two functions of *with* by saying that *with* marks an argument which would be expected to occur as actor or undergoer in terms of the hierarchy in Figure 1 but does not.

   There is an important group of verbs with which a non-undergoer theme is not marked by *with*; it includes *give*, *send*, *hand*, *throw*, and *pass*, which may be termed *transfer* accomplishment verbs.

(3.24) a. John gave the book to Bill.   (= 2.45a)

b.   John gave Bill the book.   (= 2.45b)

(3.25) a.   Mary sent a new pair of footy shorts to Phil.

b.   Mary sent Phil a new pair of footy shorts.

(3.26) a.   Nigel threw the shoes to Bronwyn.

b.   Nigel threw Bronwyn the shoes.

(3.27) a.   *John gave Bill with the book.

b.   ?Mary sent Phil with a new pair of footy shorts.

($\neq$ 3.25b)

c.   ?Nigel threw Bronwyn with the shoes   ($\neq$ 3.26b)

The ungrammaticality of (3.27a) and the non-synonymity of the (b) and (c) sentences to their counterparts in (3.25) and (3.26) illustrate the necessary lack of *with* on the non-undergoer themes. These verbs constitute an apparent exception to the generalization about *with* proposed above.

Given our characterization of core arguments in English as non-oblique as opposed to oblique peripheral arguments, a question must be raised regarding the status of the two non-oblique post-nuclear NPs in the (b) sentences in (3.24)–(3.26), i.e. are they both core arguments? Their non-oblique morphosyntactic status is prima facie evidence that they are core constituents. Further evidence derives from the behavior of adverbs. Normally, an adverb may not occur between the verb and the 'direct object'.

(3.28) a.   John quickly gave the book to Bill.

b.   *John gave quickly the book to Bill.

c.   John gave the book quickly to Bill.

d.   John gave the book to Bill quickly.

Adverbs likewise may not occur between the two post-nuclear non-oblique NPs.

(3.29) a.   John quickly gave Bill the book.

b.   *John gave quickly Bill the book.

c.   *John gave Bill quickly the book.

d.   John gave Bill the book quickly.

The contrast in grammaticality between (3.28c) and (3.29c) is telling evidence that *the book* is a core argument in (3.29). Nonetheless, it is not an undergoer; in sentences like (3.29), *Bill* not *the book* is the undergoer. There is at most one actor and at most one undergoer in a clause (even though they may be complex, as in (3.13a) and (3.17a)), and consequently *book* is a simple theme, even though it is a core argument.

That transfer verbs such as *give* can have three core arguments under certain circumstances has important implications for two of the claims made earlier in this section. It was asserted above that transfer verbs are an exception to the generalization about *with* to the effect that it marks an argument which would be expected to be actor *or* undergoer in terms of the accessibility hierarchy in Figure 1 but is not. Transfer verbs cease to be a serious exception when it is realized that *with* can only mark a peripheral argument, and with transfer verbs the non-undergoer remains a core argument. *With* is therefore excluded by the very definition of 'core argument' in English. What is exceptional about transfer verbs is that they allow three core arguments, not that the non-undergoer core argument is not marked by *with*. The fact that these verbs may have three core arguments calls into question the claim made at the outset of this section that English verbs have no more than two core arguments. However, all of the examples with three core arguments involve undergoer choices which contravene the undergoer accessibility hierarchy in Figure 1; i.e. they all have locative undergoers, and locative is outranked by theme on the hierarchy. This can be seen clearly when we eliminate the third argument from (3.24)–(3.26).

(3.30) a. John gave the book.
       b. John gave Bill.
(3.31) a. Mary sent a new pair of footy shorts.
       b. Mary sent Phil.
(3.32) a. Nigel threw the shoes.
       b. Nigel threw Bronwyn.

In each of these sentences the undergoer must be interpreted as a theme and cannot be understood as a locative. Thus theme is the unmarked undergoer choice with these verbs, locative the marked choice, and it is only when the marked choice is made that these verbs allow three core arguments. Consequently, the claim that English verbs have no more than two core arguments must be reformulated as follows: no verb in English allows more than two core arguments with their unmarked choice for undergoer, but transfer accomplishment verbs require three with the marked undergoer choice.

The fact that these verbs *require* the third core argument with the marked choice of undergoer is significant and shows the close relationship between certain core and peripheral arguments. This is also true with respect to verbs which never take more than two core arguments.

(3.33) a. The man hit the wall.
      b. The man hit the cane.
      c. The man hit the cane against/on the wall.
(3.34) a. The team loaded the trucks.
      b. The team loaded the trucks with books.
      c. The team loaded the trucks onto the ship.

In (3.33a–b) the undergoer can only have a locative interpretation, and the only way *cane* can be understood as an effector–theme is if the unmarked undergoer choice, the locative *wall*, is present as a peripheral argument in a locative prepositional phrase. *Load* differs from *hit* in that it is basically ambiguous as to whether its undergoer is a theme or locative; (3.34a) could have either interpretation (3.34b) or (3.34c). Thus the semantics of the undergoer may in some instances depend on the presence of another argument, a core argument in the case of transfer verbs and a peripheral argument for others.

We now turn our attention to two other common English prepositions, *to* and *from*. Unlike *with* which does not correlate directly with any semantic relation(s), these are a function of the logical structure of the verb they occur with. *To* appears with two kinds of verbs, change of possession and change of location. Change of possession verbs have the logical structure [DO (x, [...])] CAUSE [BECOME **have'** (y, z)], and *to* marks the first argument of BECOME **have'** when it is not the undergoer, as in (3.6a) and (3.24a). The first argument of **have'** (x, y) is a locative (see 2.5, Table 4), and when **have'** is embedded under BECOME this locative becomes a subtype of locative which is typically labeled 'goal' or 'recipient'. We will make use of the term 'locative–goal' to name this relation. The other use of *to* is with motion or change of location activity verbs. We argued in 2.5 that the logical structure underlying motion verbs is **be-at'** (x, y) & BECOME NOT **be-at'** (x, y) $(= 2.35)$. However, another logical structure which would capture motion (as defined in (2.34)) equally well is NOT **be-at'** (x, y) & BECOME **be-at'** (x, y). The first logical structure captures the meaning of verbs like *fall* and *roll* as in (3.35) below, while the second represents the basic meaning of a verb like *run* or *walk* as in (3.36).

(3.35) a. The vase fell off of the table. $\qquad$ $(= 2.36a)$
      b. The ball rolled down the nature strip. $\qquad$ $(= 2.36b)$

(3.36) a. Felix ran to the store.
      b. Tab walked to the door.

Each of these logical structures captures one aspect of the motion of these participants, motion away in (3.35) and motion toward in (3.36), and they may be combined to express both aspects.

(3.37) **be-at'** (x, y) & BECOME NOT **be-at'** (x, y) &
      BECOME **be-at'** (x, z)

The logical structure in (3.37) represents an important part of the meaning of the verb in sentences like (3.38).

(3.38) a. Felix ran from the house to the store.
      b. Tab walked from the table to the door.

In terms of arguments *Felix* and *Tab* are x, *the house* and *the table* are y, and *the store* and *the door* are z in (3.37). *To* marks the z argument, the second argument of BECOME **be-at'**, which is a locative. Thus as with BECOME **have'**, the locative argument of **be-at'** embedded under BECOME is a locative–goal. Indeed, this applies to any state verb with a locative argument which does not appear as undergoer.

(3.39) a. Max showed the book to Alice
      b. [DO (Max, [**do'** (Max)])] CAUSE [BECOME **see'** (Alice, book)]
      c. François taught French to Leon.
      d. [DO (François, [**do'** (François)])] CAUSE [BECOME **know'** (Leon, French)]

Both perception and cognition predicates have locative arguments (see 2.5, Table 4), and in logical structures such as (3.39b, d) they become locative–goals as well, as indicated by their co-occurrence with *to* when they are non-undergoers as in (3.39a, c). Thus we may sum up this discussion of *to* by saying that it marks locative arguments of state predicates embedded under BECOME in the overall logical structure of the verb.

It is not the case, however, that all instances of y in BECOME **be-at′** (x, y) occur with *to*. For example, *load* and *spray* have the logical structure [DO (x,[...])] CAUSE [BECOME **be-at′** (y, z)], and when z is not the undergoer it is marked by *on* or *into* instead of *to*.

(3.40) a. Bill loaded the boxes on the truck.
  b. The guard loaded the gold bars into the vault.
(3.41) a. Fred sprayed the plaster on the wall.
  b. The coffee maker sprayed coffee into the cup.

Similarly, the locative argument of *hit*, the logical structure of which also contains BECOME **be-at′**, may occur with *on* or *against*, depending upon the orientation of the contact.

(3.42) a. Lionel hit the cane on the table.
  b. Lionel hit the cane against the table.

Thus within the system of logical structures developed here, the exact locative preposition which occurs in a given clause may not be uniquely specified in the logical structure of the verb, but rather may be a function of the **be-at′** in the logical structure plus information on the nature of the elements in contact and their orientation (see Dowty 1979:210–11, Cresswell 1978).

The logical structure in (3.37) contains the specification for the preposition *from* in addition to that for *to*, as the sentences in (3.38) show. The crucial part of the logical structure with respect to *from* is BECOME NOT **be-at′** (x, y), which differs from that for *to* only in the presence of NOT as an operator over **be-at′**. The y argument of **be-at′**, when embedded under BECOME NOT, is interpreted as a second subtype of locative, usually labeled 'source'. This gives us three types of locative relations: plain or positional locative in **be-at′** (x, y), locative–goal in BECOME **be-at′** (x, y), and locative–source in BECOME NOT **be-at′** (x, y). This 'source' logical structure has been encountered before in our discussion of removal accomplishment verbs, and when the locative argument of a removal verb is not undergoer, it is marked by *from*.

(3.43) a. [DO (x,[...])] CAUSE [BECOME NOT **be-at′** (y, z)]   (= 3.12b)
b. John drained the water from the pool.
c. Peter stole \$75 from Larry.

Thus *from* signals locative–source with activity verbs of motion, and accomplishment verbs which have BECOME NOT **be-at′** as part of their logical structure.

The locatives that we have been discussing are all represented in the logical structure of the verb with which they occur. There are, however, locatives which are not derived from the logical structure of a verb.

(3.44) a. Max showed the book to Alice in the library.
b. [DO (Max, [**do′** (Max)])] CAUSE [BECOME **see′** (Alice, book)]

There is nothing inherent in the logical structure of *show*, presented in (3.44b), which makes *the library* a locative within the event under consideration; *in the library* would be represented as **be-at′** (x, library), where *x* is the entire logical structure in (3.44b). *In the library* specifies the location of the event or action as a whole, whereas locatives like *against the table* in (3.42b) or *on the truck* in (3.40a) indicate the location of one of the participants in the event or action. This distinction has traditionally been expressed as a contrast between 'inner' and 'outer' locations, *in the library* being an outer locative, and *against the table* and *on the truck* being inner locatives. 'Inner' versus 'outer' status corresponds, in this system, to whether the locative is represented in the logical structure of the verb. Accordingly, we must now recognize two types of peripheral arguments, those which are part of the logical structure of the verb and those which are not. Note that all of the arguments marked by *with* in the uses discussed above would be inner peripheral arguments, since they are derived from the logical structure of the verb. The layered structure of the English clause given in (3.1) must now be revised to reflect the distinction between inner and outer peripheral arguments. (OP = outer periphery, I P = inner periphery.)

(3.45) $_{OP}[_{IP}[_C[NP_N[Predicate]_N(NP)]_C(PP)]_{IP}(PP)\ldots(PP)]_{OP}$

We will now illustrate briefly how this conception of English clause structure, the notions of actor and undergoer, the hierarchy in Figure 1, and the rules of preposition assignment discussed in this section combine in the determination of the morpho-syntactic status of the arguments of a verb. Assuming that the lexical entry for a verb contains a representation of its logical structure, the main question is which arguments will be core and which (inner) peripheral. Let us take the sentence and logical structure in (3.39a, b) as our example. The logical structure is repeated in (3.46).

(3.46)   [DO (Max, [**do**′(Max)])] CAUSE [BECOME **see**′ (Alice, book)]

The first step is to specify the semantic relations of the arguments: *Max* is an agent, *Alice* a locative–goal, and *book* a theme. Assignment of actor and undergoer is the next issue to be resolved. *Max* must be the actor by virtue of being an agent, but there is no such necessary choice for undergoer, as either argument may appear as undergoer. The unmarked assignment in terms of Figure 1 would be the theme as undergoer, yielding (3.47).

(3.47)   Max (actor:agent) showed the book (undergoer:theme) to Alice (locative–goal).

Since *Alice* is not a core argument, prepositional marking with *to* is required. If the marked undergoer choice is made, then the locative–goal *Alice* occurs as undergoer. However, *book* does not appear as a peripheral argument, for *show* behaves like a transfer verb in allowing three core arguments with marked undergoer choices. The resulting sentence is (3.48).

(3.48)   Max (actor:agent) showed Alice (undergoer:locative–goal) the book (theme).

If the verb were *present*, for example, then *the book* would be an inner peripheral argument marked by *with*. Verbs which allow three core arguments are limited in English, and presumably the fact that a verb allows three core arguments would be specified in its lexical entry.

This brief discussion has assumed an active verb form; in Chapter 4 we will discuss passive constructions, and in Chapter 6 complex constructions involving passive and 'raising'.

3.3.2 Eastern Pomo: split-S and fluid-S case marking In this section we will be concerned with the case marking of core arguments in Eastern Pomo, a Hokan language spoken in northern California; the data are from McLendon (1978). Eastern Pomo has a very complex case-marking system, which includes both ergative and accusative patterns depending on the inherent lexical content of the nouns and the semantics of the verb. We will focus our discussion on the inflection of the single argument of intransitive verbs, and we will deal only with sentences with pronominal arguments, in order to keep inherent lexical content (Silverstein's variable I; cf. p. 76) constant.

Eastern Pomo exhibits what Dixon (1979a) calls 'split-S' and 'fluid-S' marking of intransitive 'subjects'. In split-S marking, the single arguments of state and some activity verbs receive undergoer inflection (the same as that of undergoers with transitive verbs), while with other activity verbs their arguments take actor inflection (the same as that of the actor with transitive verbs). This is illustrated in (3.49)–(3.51).

(3.49) a. Xá:s-u:là: wí   ko:kʰóya.
         Rattlesnake-ERG 1sgU bite
         'Rattlesnake bit me.'

      b. Há: mí:pal šá:ǩa.
         1sgA 3MsgU kill
         'I killed him.'

(3.50) a. Há: wá-du:kìya.
         1sgA go
         'I'm going.'

      b. Mí:ƀ   káluhuya.
         3MsgA go-home
         'He went home.'

(3.51) a. Wí   ʔéčkiya.
         1sgU sneeze
         'I sneezed.'

b. Mí:pal xá: ba:kú:ma.
   3MsgU water fall
   'He fell into the water.'

The sentences in (3.49) show the actor and undergoer forms of the first-person-singular pronoun in the context of a transitive verb, as well as the undergoer form of the third-person-masculine-singular pronoun. The intransitive verbs in (3.50) have agentive arguments which appear in the appropriate actor form. Those in (3.51), however, do not have agentive arguments; the 'subject' of (3.51a) is a non-controlling effector, and that of (3.51b) a theme. In these sentences the 'subject' receives undergoer inflection, the same as the 'direct objects' in the transitive sentences in (3.49). McLendon argues that the crucial factor differentiating the participants in the sentences in (3.50) from those in (3.51) is 'protagonist control' (1978:4), a notion expressed in logical structures by the predicate DO (cf. 2.5). Since only those participants which control the action or event in which they are involved can be coded as actors, the notion of actor in Eastern Pomo appears to be virtually equivalent to agent, all other semantic relations receiving undergoer marking when they are core arguments. Other verbs which have undergoer 'subjects' include *be burned, be blistered, forget, bleed, split open, feel heat, dream, belch, be stuck, be tired, feel good, think of, get crippled, become crazy, become wrinkled, become sick, become full, be frightened, become frightened, and get cramped* (McLendon 1978:2–3). Note that both state and achievement verbs are in this group.

The other type of intransitive 'subject' inflection, fluid-S marking, is characterized by variation in the coding of the 'subject' with a given verb, depending upon whether the action is controlled or not in the particular instance being reported. This is exemplified in (3.52)–(3.53).

(3.52) a. Wí   če:xélka.
          1sgU slip/slide
          'I'm slipping.'
       b. Há: če:xélka.
          1sgA slip/slide
          'I'm sliding.'

(3.53) a. Wí   ba:téčki.
       1sgU get.bumped
       'I got bumped (accidentally).'
    b. Há: ba:téčki.
       1sgA get.bumped
       'I got bumped (on purpose).'

The verb *če:xélka* describes a type of motion, and if the protagonist intentionally initiates and controls the notion, then the actor form of the pronoun is used to express this situation, as in (3.52b). If, however, the motion is not intentionally initiated by the protagonist and is not under his control, then this situation is described using the undergoer form of the pronoun, as in (3.52a). Similar considerations apply to the sentences in (3.53) with *ba:téčki* 'get bumped'. The feature of control is crucial for fluid-S marking just as for split-S marking. The verbs in the two groups would have different logical structures. Intransitive verbs which always case mark their single argument as an actor will have DO in their logical structure, whereas those which always have undergoer 'subjects' will lack DO in their logical structures. With fluid-S marking verbs, on the other hand, the occurrence or non-occurrence of DO cannot be specified, since both possibilities are found. Accordingly, in the lexical entry for these verbs the neutral logical structure would be given, e.g. ... **slip′** (x), for *če:xélka* or ... BECOME **bumped′** (x) for *ba:téčki*, with '...' meaning that DO may also be included. Thus **slip′** (x) would be the logical structure for *če:xélka* in (3.52a), DO (x, [**slip′** (x)]) in (3.52b).

Split-S marking is more common than fluid-S marking in the world's languages (see Merlan in press). They both illustrate how case marking may directly signal the semantic function of core arguments. Moreover, they drive home the point made in 2.1 that actor and undergoer are not equivalent to syntactic notions of 'subject' and 'direct object', since there are verbs which have explicitly undergoer 'subjects'.

3.3.3 Dyirbal: the layered structure of the clause in a non-configurational language
One aspect of Dyirbal (Dixon 1972) case marking is the topic of this final section. Silverstein (1976b) presents an analysis of Dyirbal case marking within the framework

sketched out in 3.1, and we will not duplicate it here. Rather, our concern is to show how the various layers or levels of clause structure proposed in 3.2 and amended in 3.3.1 can be distinguished and motivated in a language in which all NP arguments receive some kind of inflection, and word order is totally free. Dyirbal is thus a non-configurational language (see 1.2, 3.2). In order to eliminate the influence of inherent lexical content (Silverstein's variable I), we will deal exclusively with sentences with third-person arguments only.

A few preliminaries are in order. Dyirbal has nine cases, seven of which are relevant to this discussion: absolutive, ergative, dative, instrumental, locative, allative, and ablative. The other two cases, the simple and general genitives, express noun–noun rather than noun–verb relations. The layered structure of the clause is repeated in (3.54).

(3.54) $_{OP}[_{IP}[_C[NP_N[Predicate]_N(NP)]_C(NP) \ldots (NP)]_{IP}(NP) \ldots$
         $(NP)]_{OP}$

Unlike the version in Figure 2, we have distinguished between inner and outer peripheral arguments, as in (3.45). It is our contention that the three levels containing NPs, the core, inner periphery, and outer periphery, can all be clearly differentiated from each other on the basis of behavioral criteria.

No Dyirbal verb has more than two core arguments; if a verb has a single argument, then it is in the absolutive case, and if a verb has two arguments, then they are in the absolutive and the ergative cases. These two cases mark core arguments in simple active clauses in Dyirbal. With a transitive verb in active voice, the ergative NP is the actor and the absolutive NP is the undergoer. That the absolutive case codes a core argument is clear from the fact that it is the case of the single core argument of an intransitive verb and that it has the majority of subject properties, e.g. indispensability. (See Keenan 1976b, Foley & Van Valin 1977, Van Valin 1977b, 1981a.) It is also the zero case, and therefore its argument is morphologically unmarked. There are a number of behavioral properties which show that the ergative NP is a core argument. First it expresses the actor, which controls reflexivization,[8] a property associated with core arguments in other languages, e.g. the German nominative NP and the English 'subject'. Second, the actor is the normal addressee of an imperative, again a property of core arguments cross-linguistically. Finally, only the actor may become the absolutive NP in an antipassive construction (see 4.5). These properties are typical of core arguments, and since the ergative case is the normal vehicle for the expression of the actor, we may conclude that the ergative NP is a core argument in Dyirbal.

An NP in the dative, instrumental, or locative case has none of the properties ascribed above to absolutive and ergative NPs and hence cannot be considered a core argument. It is therefore a peripheral argument, but there is strong evidence that it is an inner rather than an outer peripheral argument. First, like ergative and absolutive NPs, dative, instrumental, and locative NPs may be modified by a relative clause; allative and ablative NPs may not be.

(3.55) Relative clause modifying absolutive NP:
Baŋgul yaṛa-ŋgu balan ḍugumbil ɲina-ŋu-∅
man-ERG woman-ABS sit-REL-ABS
buṛa-n.
see-TNS
'The man is watching the woman who is sitting down.'

(3.56) Relative clause modifying ergative NP:
Bayi yaṛa bangun ḍugumbi-ṛu wayɲḍi-ŋu-ru
man-ABS woman-ERG go.uphill-REL-ERG
buṛa-n.
see-TNS
'The woman who went uphill saw the man.'

(3.57) Relative clause modifying instrumental NP:
Balan ḍugumbil baŋgul yaṛa-ŋgu balga-n yugu-ŋgu
woman-ABS man-ERG hit-TNS stick-IN
baŋgul ɲalŋga-ŋgu maŋga-ŋu-ru.
child-ERG pick.up-REL-IN
'The man hit the woman with the stick that the boy picked up.'

(3.58) Relative clause modifying dative NP:
Balam miraɲ baŋgul yaṛa-ŋgu budi-n
bean-ABS man-ERG take-TNS

    bagun ḍugumbil-gu baŋgul ɲalŋga-ngu buṛa-ŋu-gu.
    woman-DAT   child-ERG   see-REL-DAT
    'The man is taking the beans to the woman that the boy saw.'

(3.59) Relative clause modifying locative NP:
    Bayi yaṛa ɲina-ɲu buni-ŋga ɲadu-ŋu-ra
    man-ABS sit-TNS fire-L   light-REL-L
    baŋgun ḍugumbi-ṛu.
    woman-ERG
    'The man is sitting by the fire which the woman lit.'

The ability to be modified by a relative clause provides a criterion for distinguishing peripheral arguments in Dyirbal into two groups: dative, instrumental, and locative NPs into one, ablative and allative NPs into the other. Note that the locative NP in (3.59) is semantically an inner rather than an outer locative.[9]

    There is a second important difference between the two types of peripheral arguments: the arguments coded by the dative, instrumental, or locative case may under certain circumstances appear as a core argument in the absolutive case, whereas this is not possible for the arguments marked by the allative or ablative case. This is a kind of 'dative shift', and it is exemplified in (3.60)–(3.62).

(3.60) a. Balam miraɲ baŋgul yaṛa-ŋgu wuga-n
          bean-ABS   man-ERG   give-TNS
          bagun ḍugumbil-gu.
          woman-DAT
          'The man gave the beans to the woman.'
      b. Balan ḍugumbil baŋgul yaṛa-ŋgu wuga-n
          woman-ABS   man-ERG   give-TNS
          baŋgum miraɲ-ḍu.
          bean-IN
          'The man gave the woman the beans.'
(3.61) a. Balan ḍugumbil baŋgul yaṛa-ŋgu baŋgu yugu-ŋgu
          woman-ABS   man-ERG   stick-IN
          balga-n.
          hit-TNS
          'The man is hitting the woman with the stick.'

    b. Bala yugu baŋgul yaṟa-ŋgu balgal-ma-n
       stick-ABS man-ERG   hit-IN-TNS
       bagun ḍugumbil-gu.
       woman-DAT
       'The man is using the stick to hit the woman.'

(3.62) a. Bayi yaṟa ḍana-ɲu   yugu-ŋga.
       man-ABS stand-TNS wood-L
       'The man is standing on (the) wood.'

    b. Bala yugu baŋgul yaṟa-ŋgu ḍanay-ma-n.
       wood-ABS man-ERG   stand-COM-TNS
       'The man is standing with some wood (i.e. either stand-
       ing on a block of wood, or leaning against a tree, or
       standing under a tree, or standing holding a stick).'

The sentences in (3.60) involve the classic 'dative-shift' alternation with a verb of giving. In (a) the giver (actor) is in the ergative case, the given (the undergoer–theme) in the absolutive, and the recipient (the locative–goal) is in the dative case. Example (3.60b) represents an alternative coding pattern in which the recipient is the undergoer in the absolutive case and the theme is a peripheral argument in the instrumental case.[10] There is no inflectional change in the verb with the change in coding pattern. In (b) the argument marked by the dative case in (a) is a core argument. The alternation in (3.61) is similar to that in (3.60) except that there is an explicit verbal inflection which signals that the erstwhile peripheral argument is now a core argument. Example (3.61a) presents a simple sentence with an instrumental peripheral argument; in (3.61b) the instrumental argument of the (a) example appears as the undergoer in the absolutive case, and the verb bears a suffix-*ma(l)* which indicates that the verb is in what Dixon calls 'instrumentive' form. A similar situation obtains in (3.62): the verb in (3.62a) is an intransitive verb with a peripheral (inner) locative argument; in (3.62b) the locative is the undergoer and a core argument, and the verb has become formally transitive, having the suffix -*ma(l)* which signals a 'comitative verbal complex'.[11] This comitative suffix thus derives transitive from intransitive verbs through the incorporation of an (inner) locative argument into the core. Each of these three alternations differs from the other two in a number of details, but in each there is variation in the expression of an argument between peripheral status in the dative, instrumental or locative case and core status as an absolutive N P. No such alternation is possible with ablative or allative case-marked arguments. Thus the possibility of appearing as a core argument is a second criterion distinguishing dative, instrumental, and locative N Ps from allative and ablative N Ps, and we conclude that this distinction correlates with the contrast between inner and outer peripheral arguments. The layered structure of the Dyirbal clause may therefore be represented as in (3.63).

(3.63) $_{OP}[$ (A B L) (A L L) $_{IP}[$ (L) (I N) (D A T) $_{C}[$ A B S (E R G) $_{N}[$ Predicate$]_{N}]_{C}]_{IP}]_{OP}$

There is one unresolved question. All of the locatives we have dealt with are inner locatives. Presumably Dyirbal has outer locatives as well, as for example in a sentence like *the man speared a wallaby in the forest*. This analysis predicts that an outer locative N P could not be modified by a relative clause, analogous to allative and ablative N Ps, and, more important, that an outer locative argument could not become a core argument in a comitative construction. It is not possible, unfortunately, to verify these predictions on the basis of the published material on Dyirbal (see n. 9).

The fact that the cases coding locative–goal and locative–source, allative and ablative, respectively, mark only outer peripheral arguments suggests that the logical structure of motion verbs in Dyirbal is different from that of motion verbs in English, since in English locative–source and locative–goal are inner peripheral arguments. This can only be determined conclusively by a full-scale analysis of the semantics of Dyirbal verbs within the framework developed in Chapter 2.

3.4 Case marking in causative constructions

The final topic in the area of case marking that we will discuss concerns case marking in causative constructions. Comrie (1976b) surveyed causative constructions in a wide variety of languages and investigated in particular the ways languages morphosyn-tactically handle the extra argument introduced in the construction. He proposed a case hierarchy of Subject > Direct Object >

Indirect Object > Other Oblique to capture the case marking of the causee in such constructions. Comrie argues that in the paradigm case the causee receives the case marking normally given to the NP occupying the highest position on this hierarchy available in the clause. Because the causer will always be treated as the subject of the clause, subject marking is not available for the causee. When the caused verb is intransitive the causee is treated as a direct object. When it is transitive, the causee is marked as an indirect object, and finally when it is ditransitive, the causee receives some other oblique marking, usually that of the actor of a passive. Comrie illustrates this hierarchy with data from French.

(3.64) a. Je ferai courir *Henriette.*
            'I shall make Henriette run.'
        b. Je ferai manger les gâteaux *à Jean.*
            'I shall make Jean eat the cakes.'
        c. Je ferai écrire une lettre au directeur *par Jean.*
            'I shall make Jean write a letter to the director.'

In (3.64a) the caused verb is intransitive, and the causee *Henriette* is treated as the direct object of the verbal complex *faire courir*. The caused verb is transitive in (3.64b), and its direct object functions as the direct object for the whole clause; consequently, the causee occurs as the indirect object marked by *à*. Finally, in (3.64c) the caused verb is ditransitive, and therefore the only option for the causee is to appear in an oblique form other than *à* in French as the object of the preposition *par* which is used to mark passive agents. In setting up this case hierarchy, Comrie employs purely syntactic criteria. A number of exceptions to the hierarchy have been pointed out since the publication of Comrie (1976b), and in Comrie (1981) he proposes primarily semantic explanations for them.

The question which is of interest here is why the causee should be demoted down the case hierarchy the way Comrie showed that it usually is. In Comrie (1976b) it is noted that there are a number of logically possible ways language could deal with the extra argument added by causativization. For example, rather than demote the causee to an oblique and leave the 'direct object' of the non-causative verb unaffected, languages could demote all of the arguments of the non-causative verb, shifting 'subject' to 'direct object', 'direct object' to 'indirect object', and 'indirect object', to 'other oblique'. Yet this possibility apparently does not occur, whereas the causee demotion described by Comrie seems to be the most common pattern among the languages of the world. Why should this be so? The case hierarchy given above provides a concise and elegant description of the facts, but it is in no sense an explanation of them. An independently motivated explanation for this pattern of demotion is available, however, based on the system of verb semantics and semantic relations developed in Chapter 2 with respect to English.

The causative constructions which Comrie deals with are of two types: morphological causatives, as in, e.g. Turkish, Japanese, Hungarian, Sanskrit, Georgian, and Swahili, and analytic causatives, as in, e.g. French, German, and Jacaltec. It is clear that the verb in a morphological causative is a single nucleus, since the indicator of the causative relation is a simple verbal affix. However, in the case of analytic causatives, it is not obvious that we are dealing with a single, albeit complex, nucleus and hence a single clause. There is syntactic evidence that the constructions in (3.64) are in fact monoclausal. In French, an object pronoun occurs proclitic to its verb, as these examples from Aissen (1974) illustrate:

(3.65) a.   Je l'ai lu.
             'I have read it.'
        b.   Je la chanterai.
             'I will sing it.'
(3.66) a.   Je voudrais le lire.
             'I would like to read it.'
        b.   *Je le voudrais lire.
        c.   Je croyais la connaître.
             'I believed I knew her.'
        d.   *Je la croyais connaître.

In the two simple sentences in (3.65) the object clitic pronoun occurs immediately in front of the verb or the auxiliary. In the more complex sentences in (3.66), the pronoun must occur with the verb of which it is an argument, as in (a) and (c); the (b) and (d) examples are ungrammatical because the pronoun occurs proclitic to the first verb in the sentence rather than to the verb of which it is an argument. In causative constructions as in (3.64), object clitic pronoun placement is as in (3.65) and not (3.66).

(3.67) a. Je le ferai lire à Jean.
'I'll have John read it.'
b. *Je ferai le lire à Jean.
c. Je l'ai laissé chanter à Paul.
'I've let Paul sing it.'
d. *J'ai laissé la chanter à Paul.

In these constructions, *faire/laisser* + Verb, the object pronoun must be placed before the entire verbal complex as in (3.67a, c), which is the pattern found in the simple clauses in (3.65) and not in the complex constructions in (3.66), as the ungrammaticality of the (b) and (d) sentences show. This is strong evidence that these constructions constitute a single clause and consequently that *faire* + Verb constitute a single complex nucleus. Harbert (1977) presents a number of arguments to show that German *lassen* causatives are likewise monoclausal, and in 6.4.3 we show that Jacaltec analytic causatives consist of a single complex nucleus and hence are monoclausal (see also Craig 1977).

These causative constructions thus have a single nucleus and single set of arguments which must be mapped on to the morphosyntactic forms available to the language. Let us consider an example involving the verb *break* as the non-causative verb in the construction. The semantic structure of the nucleus of this construction would be as in (3.68); we will represent *break* as **break'** (x, y) instead of the more complex logical structure in (2.39b) for simplicity of presentation.

(3.68) $[DO (x, [...])] CAUSE [$**break'** $(y, z)]$

In (3.68) x is the causer and y the causee; x is also an agent; and y is an agent and z a patient (cf. (2.39b)). In order to see why the causee, y, gets demoted over the 'direct object' of the non-causative verb, we must appeal to the hierarchy of accessibility to actor and undergoer proposed in Figure 1. In terms of the kind of case-marking rules discussed for English in 3.3.1, x, the argument of the superordinate DO, is the agent which is also the actor; this argument appears as the 'subject' in French and Swahili, the nominative NP in German, Turkish, Hungarian, and Sanskrit, and the ergative NP in Jacaltec. We are now left with the choice of the other core argument, the 'direct object', which is semantically the undergoer. The choice is between the two arguments of *break*, the caused verb in (3.68), and these two arguments are the agent and a patient. By Figure 1 the patient will be the undergoer and hence the 'direct object', since it outranks the agent for undergoer status. With the two core arguments filled, the agent of *break*, the causee, is normally assigned peripheral status, and it is here that there is quite a bit of cross-linguistic variation.[12] The reason why the causee is demoted over the 'direct object' to peripheral status is readily apparent: the other argument of the non-causative verb will always outrank it for undergoer status in terms of Figure 1, and it is the undergoer which appears as the 'direct object'. Thus when the caused verb is transitive, its potential actor will always be blocked from undergoer status by a higher-ranking argument, e.g. a locative, theme, or patient; hence it occurs as an oblique inner-peripheral argument. The hierarchy in Figure 1 explains why it is the causee which gets demoted rather than, e.g. the causee bumping the 'direct object' to 'indirect object'. This explanation is independently motivated in the strongest possible sense, because the hierarchy in Figure 1 was developed with respect to English, *a language which does not even have the causative construction in question.*[13]

We conclude, then, that Figure 1 provides the basis for a principled and independently motivated explanation for the pattern of causee demotion in monoclausal causative constructions characterized in the 'paradigm case' of Comrie (1976b). The cross-linguistic explanatory power of Figure 1 provides indirect support for the system of verb semantics and semantic relations of which it is a part.

4 *Intraclausal syntax*

4.0 Introduction

In the previous chapters we developed a system for the representation of the meaning of various predicate types as well as principles which associated these with the attested clause patterns in English. The hierarchy for accessibility to actor and undergoer in Figure 1 plus the rules of preposition assignment discussed in 3.3.1 account for alternations in English such as:

(4.1) a. John and Mary left early.
       b. John left early with Mary.
(4.2) a. The company supplied the team with uniforms.
       b. The company supplied uniforms to the team.

In this chapter we will examine alternations in clause patterns of a rather different type, those between active and passive clauses, as in (4.3).

(4.3) a. John hit the ball.
       b. The ball was hit by John.

The English active and passive clauses contrast in the assignment of participants to 'subject' position. In the active sentence the actor is 'subject' and the undergoer 'direct object', but in the passive sentence, the undergoer is 'subject' and the actor appears in a prepositional phrase with *by*. Note that these alternations are of a fundamentally different type from those discussed in Chapters 2 and 3. In these examples there is no change in the assignment of NPs to actor or undergoer; rather the difference concerns a change in the grammatical status of the actor and undergoer. The actor remains actor regardless of whether it is 'subject' or an oblique phrase, and the undergoer remains undergoer whether it is 'direct object' or 'subject'.

In this chapter we will analyze in detail alternations of this type, in which the semantic representation of a clause remains constant through a number of differing grammatical forms. Elsewhere (Foley & Van Valin in press) we have referred to these alternations as 'packaging variants', variant clause patterns expressing the same basic semantic information. We will develop a typology of the various possible grammatical constructions employed in natural languages to express packaging variants, such as passive, anti-passive, and topicalization constructions. We will discuss the semantic and pragmatic constraints on these constructions which determine their use and propose some universal statements of passive and antipassive rules in functional terms.

4.1. The notion of pivot

In comparing a pair of active and passive sentences like (4.4),

(4.4) a. The boy hit the ball.
       b. The ball was hit by the boy.

one of the most notable differences concerns the 'subject'. In this active clause the actor is functioning as 'subject', while in the passive clause the undergoer is 'subject'. The English alternation of active and passive clause patterns is a device for presenting either the actor or undergoer as 'subject'. This alternation is a typologically very significant fact about English in that the 'subject' plays the central role in much of the syntax of English. In fact, the most notable feature of the 'subject' notion in English and many other languages is the number of grammatical constructions to which it is central. For example, it is always the target of deletion in complements.

(4.5) a.   Fred wants to see Marsha.
       b. * Fred wants Marsha to see [him].
       c.   Fred wants to be seen by Marsha.

In (4.5a) *Fred* is the 'subject' of both the complement and the matrix verb and is omitted in the complement. In (4.5b) *Fred* is the 'direct object' of the complement and may not be deleted.

Rather the complement must be in the passive form, in which the undergoer *Fred* is the potential but nonoccurring 'subject' of the complement.

'Subject' is also the central NP of many other grammatical constructions in English

Participal relativization

(4.6) a.   The woman scolding the policeman is my mother.

  b.   *The policeman the woman scolding is my father.

  c.   The policeman being scolded by the woman is my father.

'Raising to subject'

(4.7) a.   It seems that Paul caught the wombat.

  b.   Paul seems to have caught the wombat.

  c.   * The wombat seems Paul to have caught.

  d.   The wombat seems to have been caught by Paul.

'Raising to object'

(4.8) a.   John expects that Paul will catch the wombat.

  b.   John expects Paul to catch the wombat.

  c.   * John expects the wombat Paul to catch.

  d.   John expects the wombat to be caught by Paul.

Ellipsis in coordinate structures

(4.9) a.   Oscar went to the store and spoke to Bill.

  b.   *Oscar went to the store and Bill spoke to [him].

  c.   Oscar went to the store and was spoken to by Bill.

In all these constructions the relevant NP in the embedded or second clause which is affected is the 'subject'. In participal relative clauses, only the 'subject' may be relativized. Hence (4.6a,c) are grammatical, while (4.6b) is not. Similarly, in (4.7) only the 'subject' of the embedded clause may occur as the 'subject' of the matrix verb *seem*. Hence (4.7c) is ungrammatical because *wombat* is the 'direct object'. The passivized version (4.7d) is necessary to present *the wombat* as the 'subject' of *seem*. In (4.8) only the 'subject' of the complement clause may occur as the 'direct object' of the verb *expect*. Sentence (4.8c) in which *wombat*, the 'direct object' of the complement, occurs as the 'direct object' of *expect* is ungrammatical. The complement must be passivized, as in (4.8d) so that *wombat* is the 'subject' of the complement and may therefore function as the 'direct object' of *expect*. Finally, in (4.9) only 'subjects' may be deleted in non-initial coordinated clauses. Sentence (4.9b) is ungrammatical if *Oscar* is deleted; a pronoun must occur. However, if the clause is passivized, with *Oscar* as the 'subject', then the NP may be deleted.

From these examples it is clear that the 'subject' is the central NP for much of the cross-clause syntax of English, and further, that the function of the English passive is to allow the undergoer to occur as 'subject', thus meeting this 'subject' constraint in many grammatical constructions. Following Heath (1975) and Dixon (1979a), we now introduce the term *pivot* to cover such an NP type. The pivot of a syntactic construction is the NP which is crucially involved in it; i.e., it is the NP around which the construction is built. In the participial relative clauses in (4.6) the pivot is the NP which must be (i) coreferential with the head noun and (ii) omitted in the embedded clause. In the 'raising' constructions in (4.7) and (4.8) the pivot NP is the one which is apparently 'raised' from the embedded to the main clause (see 6.5). Finally, in the complex sentences involving deletion in (4.5) and (4.9), the pivot NP is the NP in the embedded or non-initial clause which is omitted. Two general types of interclausal syntactic constructions are illustrated in (4.5)–(4.9), namely, those involving the deletion of an NP under coreference with one in a higher or previous clause, i.e. (4.5), (4.6), and (4.9), and those involving the occurrence of an NP in a clause not containing the verb of which it is an argument, i.e. (4.7) and (4.8). The central NP in the first type of construction is the non-occurring NP, and in the second it is the 'raised' NP. These NPs are therefore the pivots of these constructions. These interclausal syntactic facts are complemented by the intraclausal passive construction, which is concerned with presenting a non-actor in a particular syntactic status, and this syntactic status is precisely the one which is crucially involved in these interclausal syntactic constructions. Thus both inter- and intraclausal syntactic facts point unambiguously to one particular NP type as being central to the syntax of the language, and this NP type is the pivot. In these English constructions the pivot is in every case the 'subject' of the clause, and accordingly for English we may equate 'surface syntactic subject' with pivot.[1]

English is like many other languages in having a basic construction, the active, in which the actor is pivot, in contrast to a marked secondary construction, the passive, in which the undergoer is pivot. The marked status of the passive in comparison to the active is indicated in English by the periphrastic passive verb form consisting of the auxiliary *be* plus the past participle. It is important to note that, for English and many other languages, it is the actor which is the unmarked choice for pivot, while the undergoer is the marked choice. Other choices for pivot systems are attested. For example, Dyirbal of north Queensland (Dixon 1972) is the classic case of a language in which the unmarked choice for the pivot is the undergoer, and the marked one, the actor.

(4.10) a. Balan ḍugumbil baŋgul yaṛa-ŋgu buṛa-n.
 woman-ABS(U)man-ERG(A)　　see-TNS
 'The man saw the woman.'

 b. Bayi yaṛa　　bagun ḍugumbil-gu buṛal-ŋa-ɲu.
 man-ABS(A) woman-DAT(U)　　see-ANTI-TNS
 'The man saw the woman.'

As discussed in 3.3.3, Dyirbal is a language with ergative case marking, as in (4.10a), in which the undergoer 'woman' is in the absolutive case and the actor 'man' in the ergative. The absolutive is the case of the pivot, and the undergoer is the unmarked choice for pivot in Dyirbal (Dixon 1979a). Consequently, a special construction, the *antipassive*, exists to allow the actor to function as pivot. Example (4.10b) is an antipassivized clause in which the verb is suffixed with the antipassive suffix -*ŋay* and the case marking of the core arguments is altered. The actor 'man' now occurs in the absolutive, the case of the pivot, and the undergoer in the dative. The antipassive of an ergative language is thus parallel to the passive of an accusative language, in that in both cases a marked choice for pivot is indicated in order to meet the syntactic constraints of the language (see also Kuryłowicz 1946, Silverstein 1976b).

These syntactic constraints vary in strength from language to language to the extent that there are alternative ways of forming a given construction. In English there are two relativization strategies, the participial strategy illustrated in (4.6) and the relative pronoun strategy. Consequently, if a speaker wishes to express the meaning of (4.6b), there are two options: (i) passivization of the relative clause with deletion of the pivot, as in (4.6c), or (ii) the relative-pronoun form *the policeman whom the woman is scolding*. In Dyirbal, on the other hand, there is only one way to form a relative clause, and it necessarily involves the deletion of the pivot in the relative clause, which must be coreferential with the head noun. Consequently, antipassivization is obligatory in certain contexts in Dyirbal, where passivization would not be in English. Accordingly antipassivization plays a larger role in Dyirbal than passivization in English.

Participial relativization

(4.11) a. ŋaḏa bayi yaṛa   bani-ŋu   buṛa-n.
            I(A) man-ABS(U) come-REL see-TNS
            'I see the man who came.'

  b. *Bayi yaṛa   balan ḏugumbil buṛa-ŋu bani-ŋu.
      man-ABS(A) woman-ABS(U) see-REL come-TNS
      'The man who saw the woman came.'

  c. Bayi yaṛa   buṛal-ŋa-ŋu   bagun ḏugumbil-gu
      man-ABS(A) see-ANTI-REL woman-DAT(U)
      bani-ŋu.
      come-TNS
      'The man who saw the woman came.'

In a Dyirbal relative clause the tense suffix of the verb is replaced by the relativizing suffix -*ŋu*, and the verb is inflected for the case of the head noun which in the above examples is ∅, the absolutive case. Example (4.11b) is ungrammatical because the pivot of the relative clause, the absolutively case-marked undergoer *balan ḏugumbil* 'woman', is not coreferential with the head, and it is the ergative NP 'man' which is coreferential and is deleted. In order to form this relative clause correctly, the antipassive must be used as in (4.11c), making 'man' the pivot of the relative clause, so that it may be omitted under coreference with the head noun.

Equi-NP-deletion in purposive construction

(4.12) a. Balan ḏugumbil   baŋgul yaṛa-ŋgu balga-n baḏi-gu.
            woman-ABS(U) man-ERG(A) hit-TNS fall-PURP

'The man hits the woman, causing her to fall.'

* Balan ḍugumbil baŋgul yaṛa-ŋgu wawu-n
woman-ABS(U) man-ERG(A)   fetch-TNS
balan nayinba walmbil-i.
girl-ABS(U) get.up-PURP
'The man fetched the woman to get the girls up.'

c.   Balan ḍugumbil baŋgul yaṛa-ŋgu   wawu-n
woman-ABS(U) man-ERG(A)   fetch-TNS
bagun nayinba-gu walmbil-ŋay-gu.
girl-DAT(U)   get.up-ANTI-PURP
'The man fetched the woman to get the girls up.'

The controller and target of equi-NP-deletion in Dyirbal is the pivot or absolutive NP. In (4.12a) the pivots of the main clause and the purposive clause are both 'woman', resulting in simple ellipsis in the purposive clause. Example (4.12b) is ungrammatical because the pivot of the main clause is 'woman', but the pivot of the purposive clause is 'girls'. The ergative NP of the purposive clause, 'woman', cannot be deleted under coreference with the pivot of the main clause. Rather, the antipassive construction is necessary in the purposive clause, as in (4.12c), to meet the conditions of coreference and omissibility on the pivot.

Ellipsis in coordinate structures

(4.13) a.   Balan ḍugumbil bani-ɲu   baŋgul yaṛa-ŋgu
woman-ABS(A) come-TNS man-ERG(A)
buṛa-n
see-TNS
'The woman came and the man saw [her].'

b. * Bayi yaṛa   bani-ɲu   balan ḍugumbil buṛa-n
man-ABS(A) come-TNS woman-ABS(U) see-TNS
'The man came and saw the woman.'

c.   Bayi yaṛa   bani-ɲu   bagun ḍugumbil-gu
man-ABS(A) come-TNS woman-DAT(U)
buṛal-ŋa-ɲu
see-ANTI-TNS
'The man came and saw the woman.'

Ellipsis in coordinate structures is likewise restricted to pivots. In (4.13a) 'man' is the pivot of the second clause and is elided under coreference with the absolute pivot of the first clause. Sentence (4.13b) is ungrammatical because the non-pivot ergative NP of the second clause is deleted under coreference with the pivot NP of the first clause. The antipassive must again be used, making the actor 'man' the pivot of the second clause instead of the undergoer 'woman'; the pivots of the two clauses are coreferential in (4.13c), and the second may be omitted.

In spite of the fundamental differences in case marking and pivot choice between English and Dyirbal, there is a great deal of functional similarity in their grammatical systems. Both languages use the pivot notion extensively in their interclausal linkages. Both languages have an unmarked choice for pivot, actor for English and undergoer for Dyirbal, and furthermore, both have marked secondary constructions, the passive in English and the antipassive in Dyirbal, for permitting other NP types to function as pivot. Both English and Dyirbal are languages in which the pivot system is largely governed by discourse pragmatic or topicality notions. In both languages the choice of pivot is strongly influenced by the demands of clause linkage under coreference; coreference constraints across clauses can, in fact, be stated in terms of shared pivots. In addition to coreference considerations, factors such as definiteness and givenness may play a central role in the selection of pivots. Given a verb and its arguments (only actor and undergoer are relevant here), the choice of the argument to function as pivot is not determined on semantic grounds; with most transitive verbs in English and Dyirbal either actor or undergoer may be the pivot. Rather, the choice may be determined or at least strongly influenced by discourse factors, e.g. cross-clause coreference, as in (4.9), (4.12), and (4.13), and topicality, as in (4.7) and (4.8). In certain interclausal constructions zero anaphora, which signals that a given argument is coreferential with another argument in the immediate context, is limited to pivots, and this is indicative of the discourse salience of the pivots in them. In sum, in both English and Dyirbal these factors of discourse cohesion affect the choice of pivots, hence the use of passive and antipassive constructions to permit alternative choices of pivots when demanded by context. In both English and Dyirbal pivot choice cannot be stated in purely semantic terms: it is the pragmatic considerations of cross-clause coreference and discourse topicality which are the primary determining factors. Pivots such as these we will term *pragmatic pivots* [PrP].[2]

By labeling the pivots in English and Dyirbal 'pragmatic pivots', we do not mean to downplay their fundamental syntactic nature. As we showed above, pivots are defined in terms of the function of an NP with a particular syntactic status in a clause, in a variety of syntactic constructions. These pivots in English and Dyirbal are 'pragmatic' because pragmatic factors play a major role in the selection of the verbal argument which will assume this syntactic status in a clause. Thus because discourse pragmatic factors such as coreference, definiteness, and givenness are involved in the determination of the syntactic status of the arguments of a verb within a clause, pragmatic pivots represent the *syntacticization* of these discourse factors in clause-internal grammar.

There are other languages in which pragmatic or discourse considerations do not play a crucial role in the selection of pivots. In such languages pivot selection is determined strictly on semantic grounds. Given a verb and its associated arguments, the pivot selection is fixed in such languages; no pragmatically determined alternations like the Dyirbal antipassive are attested in such languages. Choctaw (Heath 1977) is a good example of a language of this type.

(4.14) a. Hattak at   Ø-iya-h.
    man   PVT 3A-go-PRES
    'The maṇ goes.'
   b. Hattak at   Ø-abi:ka-h.
    man   PVT 3U-sick-PRES
    'The man is sick.'
   c. Hattak at   oho:yoh (ã:)   Ø-Ø-pi:sa-h.
    man   PVT woman OBL 3A-3U-see-PRES
    'The man sees the woman.'
   d. Hattak at   oho:yoh (ã:)
    man   PVT woman OBL
    i:-Ø-nokšo:pa-h.
    3DAT-3U-afraid-PRES
    'The man is afraid of the woman.'

Choctaw is a language with both nominal case marking and verbal cross-reference. The affixes on the verb indicate the semantic functions of its arguments (actor, undergoer, locative), while the nominal case marking signals only a binary pivot versus non-pivot distinction. The oblique non-pivot marker *ã:* (< *a-n* 'the-OBLIQUE') is optional, but the pivot marker *a-t* 'the-PIVOT' is obligatory. The choice of which NP is marked by *at* is fixed by the semantics of the predicate and associated arguments, and is not affected by pragmatic considerations like discourse topicality. A semantic hierarchy determines the choice: the highest ranking NP on the hierarchy actor > undergoer > dative is case marked with *at*.[3] In (4.14a-b) there is only one NP in the clause and it receives *at* marking. In (4.14a) it is an actor, and in (4.14b), an undergoer. In (4.14c) *hattak* 'man' is the actor and hence by the hierarchy takes the *at* postposition, while *oho:yoh* 'woman' is the undergoer and occurs with the optional oblique suffix *ã:*. With the verb *nokšo:pa* 'fear', the experiencer functions as undergoer, while the cause is indicated by the dative prefix. As the undergoer outranks the dative NP, the undergoer occurs with *at* and the dative with optional *ã:*, as in (4.14d). These NP case markings are completely determined by the semantic function of the arguments, and not by pragmatic or topicality considerations. There is no passive construction analogous to English which would allow the undergoer of *pi:sa* 'see' (see example (4.14c)) to occur as the pivot with *at*.[4]

The *at* NP clearly functions as a pivot in Choctaw because it is crucial in the linkage of clauses. Because of its extensive verbal cross-referencing, ellipsis of NP arguments is a common feature of Choctaw discourse and is not restricted to pivots. However, the privileged status of the pivot NP is still apparent in that it is the NP monitored by the switch-reference system. Clauses are linked in this language with one of a set of morphemes occurring on the verb of a clause indicating whether the pivot of the clause is the same or different as that of the next clause (see 7.3).

(4.15)   a. $\emptyset$-$\emptyset$-pi:sa-ča: $\emptyset$-iya-h.
             3A-3U-see-SAME.PVT   3A-go-PRES
             'He$_i$ sees him$_j$ and he$_i$ goes.'

         b. $\emptyset$-$\emptyset$-pi:sa-na: $\emptyset$-iya-h.
             3A-3U-see-DIFF.PVT   3A-go-PRES
             'He$_i$ sees him$_j$ and he$_{j|k}$ goes.'

Pi:sa 'see' is a verb with actor and undergoer arguments, so the actor must be pivot, while *iya* 'go' only has one core argument, an actor, which must be pivot. In (4.15a) the two pivots are co-referential, and the verb takes the 'same pivot' suffix *-ča:*. In (4.15b), the two pivots are not coreferential, and so the verb occurs with *-na:*, indicating 'different pivot'.[5]

Although the Choctaw *at* NP is a pivot by our definition above, it is different from the pivots encountered in English and Dyirbal, in that in a Choctaw clause with a given predicate and its associated arguments, the pivot selection is completely predetermined. Most English clauses with two-argument verbs may be in either active or passive form, the choice determined by discourse and clause-linkage constraints. This is not the case in Choctaw. Discourse and topicality considerations do not interfere with pivot selection, which is accomplished on entirely semantic and lexical grounds. Thus the syntactic status of a verbal argument is predictable from either its semantic relations to the verb or the output of a lexical derivational rule, e.g. the Choctaw lexical (medio)passive in (4.77). Pivots like those of Choctaw which are determined in strictly semantic and lexical terms we will term *semantic pivots* [SmP], in contrast to the pragmatic pivots of English and Dyirbal.[6]

The most common type of SmP cross-linguistically is one which conflates the actor argument of transitive verbs with the single argument of intransitive verbs, or in Dixon's (1979a) terms, a pivot grouping A and S together. Most switch-reference systems monitor exactly this notion of semantic pivot, as in the following Kewa examples (Papua New Guinea; Franklin 1971).

(4.16) a. Ní réka-*no*   ágaa lá-lo.
            1sg stand-SAME.SmP talk say-1sgPRES
            'I stood up and am speaking.'

        b. Rúdu yo-*a*   madá na-ria-a.
            short be-SAME.SmP enough NEG-carry-3sgPST
            'It was short and didn't reach.'

        c. Ní réka-*no*   ágaa lá-a
            1sg stand-DIFF.SmP talk say-3sgPST
            'I stood up and he talked.'

In (4.16a) the actors of the intransitive verb of the first clause and the transitive verb of the second are coreferential. By the

definition of SmP above as a conflation of S and A, these would
be the SmPs of their respective clauses, and so the verb occurs
with the switch-reference morpheme -*a*, indicating same SmP.
In (4.16b) there are two intransitive verbs: the first a stative verb
and the second an active one. The stative verb occurs with an
undergoer argument, and the active, with an actor. This distinction is neutralized in Kewa for the purposes of pivot status, as
it operates on a grouping of S and A, with the semantic distinction
between types of S ignored. Again the SmPs of these clauses are
coreferential, so the verb takes the suffix -*a*, indicating same SmP.
Finally, in (4.16c) the S of the first clause and the A of the second
clause are not coreferential, and the verb occurs with the suffix -*no*
for different SmP. Thus the Kewa switch-reference system
operates on an S/A semantic pivot, which is the general pivot in
the language, there being no evidence for any pragmatic pivots.
The S monitored by switch reference in Kewa is always the actor
or undergoer (depending on verb class) as specified in the lexical
entry of the verb. There is no passive rule which changes this basic
lexically determined choice in order to meet discourse constraints.
Pragmatic considerations do not play a role in pivot selection; it
is strictly semantically determined, hence an SmP.

Another language with an S/A SmP is Walmatjari (Australia;
Hudson 1976). As in Kewa, the coreferentiality or non-coreferen-
tiality of SmPs across clauses is crucial in the system of clause
linkage. Walmatjari has a series of suffixes which link a subordinate or coordinate clause to a following clause. What is
common to their use is that they indicate coreferentiality of SmPs.

(4.17) Ṭikiryan-uḷa   ma-ṇa-∅-nja-lu
        return-SAME.SmP INDIC-1EXCL-AUX-3pl-PL
        maṇa-waṇṭi-∅ patjani.
        tree-PL-ABS chopped
        'Having returned we chopped trees.'

The suffix -*uḷa* indicates that the S of the first clause is coreferential to the A of the second. It is clear that -*uḷa* subordination is
controlled by an S/A SmP. Again, like Kewa, Walmatjari presents
no evidence for PrPs, there being no passive or other similar constructions re-arranging basic clause structures for discourse im-
plementation. Kewa and Walmatjari are also parallel in that while

both have ergative case marking for their NP constituents, the SmP pivot system follows an accusative (S/A) grouping, as do the verbal cross-referencing affixes.

An important question here is, why do we find this widespread cross-linguistic propensity for S/A SmPs? The actor notion is basic in the grammar of all languages due to its expressing the controlling and initiating participant in an event. It is semantically the most natural choice for the central participant in an event. Hence, it is the most likely choice for the general pivot of a language. The conflation of S with the A to constitute an S/A semantic pivot is another example of the pervasive tendency in languages to neutralize distinctions in restricted environments. The S function is itself a neutralization of the more basic notions of actor and undergoer. Some S NPs are actors and others are undergoers, depending on the verb class. A good percentage of S NPs are actors, which would qualify as pivots in any case. The remaining S NPs, which are semantically undergoers, are then assimilated to the class of actors to produce a general SmP of S/A. The SmP type, then, is clearly a generalization from the notion of actor, in which the contrast between the two types of arguments of intransitive verbs is neutralized (see also Dixon 1979a).

Many stative–active languages which systematically express in their verbal morphology the contrast between actor and undergoer arguments of intransitive verbs also neutralize this distinction for the purposes of a general S/A SmP. Choctaw (Heath 1977) behaves like this, as does Lakhota. However, there are other stative–active languages which do not collapse actors and undergoers with intransitive verbs to produce a S/A SmP. The Eastern Pomo (McLendon 1978) switch-reference system seems to monitor semantic roles of actor and undergoer directly, not the more abstract S/A SmP. (see 3.3.2 for a discussion of actor and undergoer case marking in Eastern Pomo.)

(4.18) a. Há: káluhu-y   si:má:mérqaki:hi.
        1sgA go.home-SAME went to bed
        'I went home and then went to bed.'
    b. Há: káluhu-qan   mí:ṗ mérqaki:hi.
        1sgA go.home-DIFF 3sgA went to bed
        'I went home and he went to bed.'

c. Há: xá: qákki-qan   wi   ḍa:lál ṭá:la.
   1sgA water bathe-DIFF 1sgU sick   become
   'I took a bath and got sick.'

Examples (4.18a-b) are sequences of two clauses with active intransitive verbs cooccurring with actor NPs. In (4.18a) the actors
are coreferential, and so the verb takes the suffix indicating same
referent, and the actor of the second clause is omitted. In (4.18b)
the actors are non-coreferential, and the verb occurs with the
different-referent suffix. Sentence (4.18c) is the most interesting
example in which an active intransitive verb is followed by an
intransitive achievement verb. The argument of the active verb
is an actor, while that of the achievement verb is an undergoer.
Note that while the actor and undergoer arguments are coreferential, the verb occurs with the different-referent suffix and the
coreferent NP of the second clause is not deleted. This suggests
that Eastern Pomo does not behave like Choctaw and Lakhota
in neutralizing the distinction between actor and undergoer for
a general S/A SmP. Rather the evidence indicates that Eastern
Pomo has no separate syntactic notion of pivot at all, and that
the syntax is directly sensitive to semantic roles like actor or undergoer. There is no intermediary abstract notion of pivot, semantic
or pragmatic, with an important function in the syntax. Other
stative–active languages which group with Eastern Pomo in being
pivotless are Acehnese (Sumatra; Durie 1981) and Arikara (Cad-
doan; Merlan in press).

Stative–active languages are not the only type which seem to
be pivotless from a syntactic point of view. The Daghestani languages of the Caucasus as well as the Lolo-Burmese languages
of the Tibeto-Burman family are also good candidates for this
class. Archi (Daghestan; Kibrik 1979a,b) is an ergative language
lacking any kind of voice opposition. In clause linkage it does
exhibit the normal ellipsis of coreferential NPs but 'the syntactic
or semantic role of NPs imposes no constraints on [it]' (Kibrik
1979a:71).

(4.19) a. Adamli   [k'arāši xit'-boli]   čele
           man-[ERG] down   push-GER stone-[ABS]
           goɪroɪ-abῑi.
           roll-AOR
           'The man rolled the stone, having pushed it down.'

b. [man-ERG [*man-ERG stone-ABS* push down] stone-ABS roll]

c. Os ḣelekulin lo [jab
one hen-[GEN] child-[IVsg-ABS] this-[IIIsg]
liqɪ'ili oẍali]
eagle-[IIIsg-ERG] carry.away-[IVsg-GER]
oqɪali.
disappear-[IVsg-AOR]
'One of the chicks disappeared, carried away by an eagle.'

d. [chick-ABS [eagle- ERG *chick-ABS* carry away] disappear]

e. Bošor [k'oaḣan soli]
man-[Isg-ABS] stick-[IVsg-ABS] hold-[IVsg-GER]
weɪršu.
run-[Isg-AOR]
'The man ran, holding the stick.'

f. [man-ABS [*man-ERG* stick-ABS hold] run]

In each of these sentences one or more NPs in the subordinate clause has been omitted under coreference with NPs in the main clause. The 'full' forms are given in the bracketed English forms with the elements omitted from the Archi sentences in italics. In morphological terms these sentences exhibit ERG=ERG, ABS=ABS, and ABS=ERG coreference; in syntactic terms, they present A=A, S=O, and S=A coreference.

The Archi verbs *bej-eẍas* 'begin' and *k'an* 'want', govern equi-NP-deletion. However, like the sentences in (4.19), and unlike the English sentence in (4.5) and the Dyirbal examples in (4.12), deletion is not restricted to a single NP type in the subordinate clause. The following examples are from Kibrik (1979b).

(4.20) a. Moḣammad-φ nǒk' a-s
Mohammad(I)-ABS house(IV)-ABS build-IVsg
bej-e-w-ẍu.
begin-Isg-TNS
'Mohammad began to build the house.'

b. [Mohammad-ABS [*Mohammad-ERG* house-ABS build] begin]

c. Tor-∅ dija-mu d-irk̄us
3sg(II)-ABS father(I)-ERG IIsg-look.for

bej-e-r-x̌u.
begin-I Isg-TNS
'She began to be looked for by her father.'

d. [she-ABS [father-ERG *she-ABS* look for] begin]

(4.21) a. W-ez   w-irx$_0$mus   ǩ'an-ši   w-i.
I-IsgDAT Isg-work   want-PROG Isg-AUX
'I want to work.'

b. [I-DAT [*I-ABS* work] want]

c. W̌-ez   buwa-mu   w-irǩus
I-IsgDAT mother(II)-ERG Isg-look.for
ǩ'an-ši   w-i.
want-PROG Isg-AUX
'I want my mother to look for me.'

d. [I-DAT [mother-ERG *I-ABS* look for] want]

In (4.20a) the A (ergative NP) in the subordinate clause is omitted under coreference with the S (absolutive NP) of the matrix clause. In (4.20c) however, it is the O (absolutive NP) of the lower clause which has been deleted under coreference with the S (absolutive NP). Similar patterns are found in (4.21) in which the main clause S is in the dative case. This can be seen clearly in the fact that both main and subordinate clause predicates in the (c)-sentences agree with the S of the main clause. Thus in (4.19) there is S = A and S = O coreference, and the latter is particularly significant. Here again there is no definable general pivot for NP ellipsis. Indeed, Kibrik (personal communication) has pointed out that the constraints on the controllers and pivots in coreferential deletion are not a function of the syntactic system of the language but rather follow from the semantics of the matrix predicate.

The lack of syntactic constraints in Archi precludes the existence of definable pivots for them, either semantic or pragmatic. As NP ellipsis does not apply to one particular class of NPs to the exclusion of another, we must conclude that the language does not employ the notion of pivot. Rather, the constraints on morphological and syntactic constructions can be stated directly in terms of semantic roles. Similar findings have been reported for the related language Chechen, by Nichols (1980). The available descriptions of certain languages of the Lolo-Burmese family, such as Lahu (Matisoff 1972) and Lisu (Hope 1974), also indicate a lack of syntactic constraints on NP ellipsis and clause linkage, suggesting that they too are pivotless. This type may in fact be more common in southeast Asia. A careful study of Thai, Khmer, and others from this point of view is needed.

In Van Valin (1980b) and Van Valin & Foley (1980) a typology with respect to the type of pivots languages possess is proposed. Languages in which discourse factors are syntacticized in clause-internal grammar, i.e. languages with a PrP, are termed *reference-dominated* languages, and languages which do not have this syntacticization, i.e. languages with an SmP only or no pivots at all, are labeled *role-dominated* languages. This typology is meant to provide a schema for capturing the differences in clause-internal syntax that we have seen in this section, centered on the notion of pivot. However, the dichotomy between role- and reference-dominated languages is not a simple, binary opposition, for two reasons. First, languages are not strictly divided into those with PrPs and those with SmPs. Some languages have both types; some grammatical processes are sensitive to the PrP and others to the SmP. The classic case of such languages are those of the Philippines. In Schachter (1976, 1977) it was demonstrated that a number of syntactic rules in Tagalog are sensitive to an SmP consisting of S and A, while others involved a PrP, to which a large number of semantic roles are accessible (see 4.3). Second, the distinction between PrP and SmP is itself something of a continuum, as we will see in 4.4 (see p. 167). This typological cline of role-versus reference-dominated languages captures the degree to which the grammatical relations in a language are distinct from the semantic predicate-argument relations indicated in the logical structure of the predicate. Pivots necessarily involve the neutralization of semantic role distinctions for syntactic purposes. An S/A SmP, for example, entails the neutralization of the distinctions between the S of a stative verb and the S of an agentive activity verb in some syntactic construction(s), and consequently this grammatical relation is abstracted from the semantic relations borne by the NPs which occur in it. A PrP is even more distant from semantic relations, since its function is related to the pragmatic, not the semantic, status of a verbal argument. In a language like Archi or Eastern Pomo, on the other hand, where the distinctions among the semantic relations of intransitive 'subjects' to the verb are not neutralized, grammatical relations are not significantly distinct from these semantic relations. Thus we may set up a cline of the distinctness of grammatical relations from semantic relations, with reference-dominated (PrP) languages occupying the end with the greatest distinctiveness, and role-dominated languages (SmP or no pivot) at the other (see Figure 3).[7]

Reference-dominated languages   Role-dominated languages
Dyirbal English Tagalog Choctaw Kewa Archi

Greatest   Least

Figure 3 Distinctiveness of grammatical relations from semantic roles

It should be apparent by now that grammatical relations like 'subject' or 'object' do not play a role as primitives in this theoretical framework. 'Subject' as we have claimed elsewhere (Foley & Van Valin 1977; Van Valin 1977b, 1981a), is not a universal category and may not, therefore, be taken as a primitive. Its properties are divided between the notions of actor and pivot in this theory.[8] 'Object' is also rejected as a primitive. It is largely equivalent to undergoer; but, in some constructions, we make use of the notion 'non-pivot core argument' which is a language-specific concept equivalent to the English notion of 'direct object' (see 3.3.1, 6.5).

4.2 Pivot versus topic

There is a close similarity between the notion of pragmatic pivot and the traditional notion of topic in the sense of 'what the utterance is about'. This similarity is in fact desirable because as we will show in the next section PrPs in at least some languages developed out of earlier topics. But, however close the similarity between these two notions, it is clear that they must be distinguished, for they are structurally quite distinct. Pivots are clause-internal, whereas topics occur external to the clause. Accordingly, many languages can have both in the same sentence, as in these English examples.

(4.22) a. With the sword, the prisoner was quickly dispatched
by the executioner.
b. In Port Moresby I found many diversions.
c. Max I get along with very well.
d. That paper, it was quite interesting.

In all four examples in (4.22) the topic NP is the left-most NP,
then followed by the PrP, the subject NP. In (a) – (c) the topic
and the PrP have different referents, while in (d) the two have
the same referent and the PrP is simply the pronoun *it*. The constructions in (a) – (c) are usually called 'topicalizations', that in
(d) a 'left-dislocation'. In contrasting these forms with pivots
structurally, this distinction is not relevant, and consequently we
will refer to all of the constructions in (4.22) as 'preposed topic
constructions' [PTC].

Before attempting a functional characterization of the notion
of topic and contrasting it with the notion of PrP, it will be useful
to present a summary of the structural differences between them.
There is a large number of fundamental differences in their grammatical behavior across languages, as pointed out by Li &
Thompson (1976), among others.

The first concerns a widespread phonological difference between them. Topics are normally set off from the rest of the
sentence by a pause, while PrPs are not followed by such a pause.

(4.23) a. The sword quickly dispatched the prisoner.
b. With the sword, the prisoner was quickly dispatched.
c. This car gets good mileage.
d. This car, it gets good mileage.

The pause in the (b) and (d) topicalizations is indicated by the
comma after the topic NP.[9] No such pause follows the 'subject'
in the (a) and (c) sentences. Furthermore, if we investigate a variety
of topic NPs in English we discover an interesting pattern: the
more peripheral an NP is, the more natural a topic it is. This
naturalness is indicated primarily by either the omission or
shortening of the pause. Setting NPs such as temporals or outer
locatives are outer peripheral NPs and are the most natural topics
in this sense.

(4.24) a. Yesterday I bought a new car.
       b. In the Sepik I discovered a new language.

Note that the pause following this topic is either very short or non-existent. With inner peripheral NPs such as instruments or goals the pause is more noticeable.

(4.25) a. With the sword, the prisoner was quickly dispatched.
       b. To John, the announcer presented the award.

With core NPs as topics, the pause is most pronounced:

(4.26) a. Silver, I buy all the time.
       b. The plane, the guards loaded with cocaine.
       c. John, the announcer presented with the award.

These data suggest a hierarchy of setting NPs > other oblique NPs (inner peripheral) > core NPs, with the NPs to the left being more natural as topics. The NPs most central to the clause are the most marked as topics, while the most peripheral NPs are the least marked.

    A similar distribution can be found in other languages. In Tagalog, obliquely case-marked setting NPs are the least marked topics. They occur immediately preceding the verb with no intervening particle and no marked pause.

(4.27) Sa palengke b-um-ili aku   ng isda.
       L market   AF-buy 1sgPrP TH fish
       'In the market I bought some fish.'

However, core arguments can only be topics if they are the focused NP and, further, if the particle *ay* is transposed between the topic and the verb.

(4.28) a. Ang isda 'y b-in-ili-$\emptyset$ ng lalake sa palengke
       PrP fish *ay* PERF-buy-THF A man   L market
       'The fish, the man bought in the market.'
       b. *Ng lalake 'y b-in-ili-$\emptyset$ ang isda sa palengke.
          A man *ay* PERF-buy-THF PrP fish L market

Sentence (4.28b) is ungrammatical because the core theme argument has been topicalized without being the focused NP. The Tagalog ranking of peripheral NP over core NPs as potential topics nicely parallels the English facts above, and in both languages core NP topics are explicitly marked, in Tagalog by *ay* and in English by intonation.

A second difference between PrPs and topics concerns voice oppositions: passives or antipassives. Passives and antipassives are by far the most common devices cross-linguistically for altering the unmarked choice for PrPs in a given language. Passives undo the normal choice of actor for PrP and present non-actor arguments as PrP, while antipassives undo the normal choice of undergoer as PrP and allow non-undergoers to be PrP. The important point is that the usual alternative for PrP (and in many languages the only alternative) is the other core argument, the undergoer in the passive and the actor in the antipassive. In many languages, such as German or Italian, only the undergoer can be the PrP in a passive clause, and in other languages, like English, the undergoer is certainly the usual choice for the PrP of a passive. Only a few languages, such as those of the Philippines, allow peripheral NPs to be PrPs. We will discuss and account for this in the next section. Passives (and antipassives) and topicalizations thus have inverse hierarchies for their unmarked choices. Passives and antipassives prefer core > peripheral, while topicalizations prefer peripheral > core.

Parallel to this distinction between voice oppositions and topicalizations is the further point that a PrP is a core argument of the verb, and thus bears a semantic relation to the predicate. A topic need not bear any semantic relation to the verb, but it bears a relation to the sentence as a whole.

(4.29) a. Harry gave the book to Fred at home.
b. Fred was given the book by Harry at home.
c. *Home was given the book to Fred at by Harry.
d. *At home was given the book to Fred by Harry.

Harry and *Fred* are both acceptable as PrPs because as agent and goal, respectively, they are in the logical structure of *give* and thus bear a semantic relation to it. *Home* is an outer peripheral NP and bears no such semantic relation; it therefore may not occur as PrP. However, it is perfectly fine as topic.

(4.30)   a. At home Harry gave the book to Fred.
         b. At home Fred was given the book by Harry.

Correlated with this distinction between PrPs and topics is their difference in morphological coding. Topics are commonly coded by position, either sentence initial or final. PrPs may be coded by position, but in keeping with verbal arguments generally, are more often coded morphologically. In English pre-verbal position is the means of case marking PrPs, just as immediately post-verbal position is the means of coding undergoer. Tagalog codes only topics by position; PrPs are focused NPs and are case marked by *ang*. They may occur in any position following the verb, the order of post-verbal NP arguments being by and large free. However, the topic NP must always occur in the preverbal position.

(4.31)   Sa palengke b-um-ili ng   isda ang lalake.
         L market AF-buy TH fish PrP man

         'In the market the man bought some fish.'

   PrPs, as core arguments, often exhibit other widespread coding properties of core arguments such as verb agreement.

(4.32)   a. The boy is hitting the balls.
         b. The balls are being hit by the boy.
         c. The balls, the boy is /*are hitting them.

Topics *per se* never control verb agreement. Apparent cases of such agreement when core arguments are topicalized are due to the core status of the NP, not its status as topic. Note, e.g. in English, that PrPs cannot be topicalized; rather, a left-dislocated construction must be used.

(4.33)   a.   That paper, it was very interesting.
         b. *That paper, _____ was very interesting.

A trace pronoun is left in the PrP position and it is this pronoun which controls verb agreement, not the topic NP.

   A final difference between PrPs and topics concerns their role in various syntactic constructions. As discussed in 4.1, PrPs are crucial in a large number of constructions in a variety of languages. Their most notable function is in cross-clausal syntax, where they are important as the controllers and targets of NP ellipsis. Topics play no such central role in the syntax of any language (see Li & Thompson 1976: 465–6); they seem instead to be an adjunct to a sentence rather than an integral part of it and are thereby unlikely to play a significant role in its syntax.

This list of differences clearly points out the fact that there is a systematic structural contrast in English and other languages between PrPs and topics. There are likewise systematic functional differences between PrPs and topics. Pivots, insofar as they overlap with 'subjects', would be described in traditional terms as referring to the entity which the clause is about (see Chafe 1976). More important for this discussion is the discourse function of pivots. Givón (1979) has argued on the basis of text counts that PrPs in English are overwhelmingly definite, and it has been widely pointed out in the literature that 'subjects' (PrPs) normally represent given information and the following elements new information, e.g. Halliday (1967), Firbas (1966), Chafe (1972). This suggests that PrPs have an important 'linking' function in discourse, tying a clause to the preceding discourse. This can be seen most clearly in constructions like (4.9), (4.12), and (4.13) in which zero anaphora, which is restricted to the PrP, signals that the PrP of the clause is coreferential with the PrP of the previous clause. This is in effect a syntacticization of this discourse linkage. The pivot is also involved in expression of the speaker's 'empathy' with the participants in the events described (see Kuno 1976, Zubin 1979).

Topics, on the other hand, have a variety of functions depending upon the type of preposed topic construction which one occurs in. We will discuss three of these constructions. The first typically involves a preposed locative or temporal element, as in the English sentences in (4.24) and the Tagalog example in (4.27). Such a topic 'sets a spatial, temporal, or individual domain within which the main predication holds' (Chafe 1976: 50). Further examples of this type of topic are presented in (4.34); they are from the so-called 'topic-prominent' languages of East Asia (Li & Thompson 1976), and involve both individual and locative topics.

(4.34) a. Nèi-xie shù shù shēn   dà.   (Mandarin)
            those   tree tree-trunk big

'As for those trees, [their] trunks are big.'

b. Hɔ   ɔ̄   na-qhɔ̂ yɨ   ve yò.   (Lahu)
   elephant TOP nose   long DECL
   'As for elephants, [their] noses are long.'

c. Nihon wa   Tokyo ga sumi-yoi.   (Japanese,
   Japan TOP Tokyo   easy-live   Kuno 1973)
   'As for Japan, Tokyo is easy to live in.'

d. Sɨgə nya   bə̀   le-ɥ.   (Lisu,
   box TOP burst become-DECL   Hope 1974)
   'As for the box, [it] burst.'

All of these topics set the framework for the following sentence.
The important point about these constructions is that in these
languages they are basic, having none of the marked and stylistic
features of many English topicalizations. Note, again, that the
least-marked topics in English are the setting NPs, those NPs
which most transparently set the domain for the following
sentences. The English sentences in (4.24) are closest in feeling
to the Asian examples above.

The second PTC is topicalization, as illustrated in (4.35).

(4.35) a. John I can't stand.
        b. That car you'll never get to Cleveland in.

In this construction the topic is normally the non-pivot core argument, as in (4.35a), or the object of a preposition, as in (4.35b);
it cannot be the pivot in English (see (4.33)). According to Prince
(1981a, 1982), topicalization has two simultaneous functions:
(i) the sentence-initial NP is marked 'as being either *already evoked*
in the discourse or else in a salient *set relation* to something already evoked in or inferrable from the discourse' (1982:4); and
(ii) the constructions mark an 'open proposition' as already known
and salient, with the open proposition being derived 'by replacing
the ... tonically stressed constituent with a variable' (*ibid.*).[10] She
gives the following examples (# marks discourse infelicity).

(4.36) a. A: You want to see *ET*?
           B: I saw *ET* yesterday.
           B': *ET* I saw yesterday
        b. A: You see every Spielberg movie as soon as it comes
               out.

B: No – I saw *E T* (only) yesterday.

B′: No – *E T* I saw (only) yesterday.

c. A: Why are you laughing?

B: I saw *E T* yesterday. I was just thinking about it.

B′:#*E T* I saw yesterday. I was just thinking about it.

d. A: Sue told me that you were away.

B: Yes, I was. Oh, by the way, I saw *E T* yesterday.

B′:#Yes, I was. Oh, by the way, *E T* I saw yesterday.

The response of B′ in (c) and (d) is infelicitous because the topic *E T* is neither evoked nor inferrable in the context, and the open proposition 'I saw X yesterday' is not known and salient. The following examples cited by Prince are from naturally occurring speech, taken from Terkel (1974). (The antecedent of the topic is in boldface, the topic in italics.)

(4.37) a. 'Then I make a schedule of what's to be done during the day. I try to assign as many tasks as possible to **my staff**, so I can reduce my work. I need two or three additional people. *A couple who are not pulling their weight* I'm in the process of replacing. It's very painful.'

b. 'I have **a recurring dream** in which ... I can't remember what I say. I usually wake up crying. *This dream* I've had maybe three, four times.'

The striking thing about (4.37a) is that the topic NP is *indefinite*; it has been claimed by a number of researchers, e.g. Li & Thompson (1976), that topics must be definite. Example (4.37a) however shows that this is not the case. Rather, as Prince (1981a, 1982) argues, the crucial feature is referentiality. She presents the examples in (4.38)–(4.41) to illustrate this.

(4.38) a. I didn't think you would leave.

b. I told Mary that I wasn't chosen.

c. I brought some books with me.

(4.39) a. You I didn't think would leave.

b. Mary I told that I wasn't chosen.

c. Some books I brought with me.

(4.40) a. I didn't think there would be a fight.

b. I resented it that I wasn't chosen.

c. I brought few books with me.

(4.41) a. *There I didn't think would be a fight.
        b. *It I resented that I wasn't chosen.
        c. *Few books I brought with me.

The topic NPs in (4.39) are all referential, those in (4.41) are not, and only the sentences in (4.39) are grammatical.

The third type of PTC is left dislocation, which differs from topicalization structurally in that instead of a gap in the clause following the topic there is a resumptive pronoun, as in (4.33a); additional examples are given below.

(4.42) a. Those cookies, Max ate them.
        b. *ET*, I saw it yesterday.
        c. Alan, he ought to have his head examined.

Prince (1982) argues that in functional terms there are two distinct left-dislocation constructions in English. The first, LD-1, has the same function as topicalization with respect to the topic NP, namely it is presented as invoked or inferrable in the discourse. However, it differs from topicalization in that it does not mark the open proposition of the adjacent clause as known and salient.

(4.43) a. 'As for making out with **tenants**, it's not like they say. *Good-looking broads*, if they're playing, they ain't going to monkey around with a janitor.'
        b. 'Everybody has their **little bundle**, believe me. I'll bet she had a nervous breakdown. That's not a good thing. *Gall stones*, you have them out and they're out. But *a nervous breakdown*, it's very bad.'

Since the clause in an LD-1 can be new information but the clause in a topicalization cannot, it follows that it should be possible to have sequences of LD-1 – topicalization but not vice versa. Prince (1982) says that only examples of the predicted sequence are found in her corpus.

(4.44) a. 'She had an idea for a project. She's going to use **three groups of mice**. *One*, she'll feed them on mouse chow, just the regular stuff they make for mice. *Another*, she'll feed them veggies. And *the third* she'll feed [Ø] junk food.'

b. 'There were **two things I promised to talk about**. *The first thing*, I looked at it with great care. *The second thing* I didn't look at [∅].'

The second type of left dislocation, L D-2, has a rather different function. According to Prince, 'L D-2 creates a separate information unit for an entity not currently in focus and not represented by an NP in a favored position, e.g. sentence-final, for introducing out-of-focus entities' (1982: 10). A similar analysis of these constructions is proposed in Keenan & Schieffelin (1976). Prince gives the following examples.

(4.45)   a.   'Once when we went to Big Bear and we caught a lot of fish and Suzie Kathy and Betty went to a park and me my mom and dad went fishing. And *this guy* his fishing pole fell down in the water and he had to go down and get it.'

b.   '[Delivering newspapers]'s supposed to be such a great deal. *The guy*, when he came over and asked me if I wanted a route, he made it sound so great. Seven dollars a week for hardly any work. And then you find out the guy told you a bunch of lies.'

In contrast to the topic NPs in topicalization and L D-1, those in (4.45) are being introduced into the discourse for the first time. Thus the discourse function of L D-2 is quite different from that of L D-1 and topicalization.[11]

It should be noted that we have not mentioned contrastiveness as a major function of any of these constructions. Chafe (1976), for example, claims that contrast is the major function of both topicalization and left dislocation. However, it should be clear from the above examples that contrast is not a necessary feature of either construction, since there are examples of both which are not contrastive, e.g. (4.37a,b), (4.43a), and (4.45b). Where the topics are contrastive, e.g. (4.44a,b), it is a function of the particular context. Prince (1981a) argues that topics are contrastive 'just in case (i) a list understanding is induced, and (ii) a salient opposition is inferred in the new information represented in the clause associated with each element' (p. 256). These conditions hold in (4.44a,b), and the topics in the two examples are interpreted contrastively.

We may now summarize this discussion. Pivots are what the sentence is about. As sentences are generally framed about their predicates, which express the event described in the utterance and hence are the *raison d'être* for the utterance, it is logical that the pivot must be an argument of the verb. It would be nonsensical to select an NP as the entity which the sentence is about and combine it with a verb which does not include it as an argument. That would obviate the whole point in selecting that specific verb. Pivots are syntactic in nature, as we argued in 4.1, and a pragmatic pivot is a *syntacticization* of certain discourse relations, one of which is topicality, in the internal structure of the clause. This can be seen in the English and Dyirbal examples in (4.5)–(4.13) in 4.1, in which the choice of the verbal argument to function as PrP is determined by discourse coreference relations. Pivots are always core arguments. Consequently, they exhibit the grammatical properties of core arguments such as verb agreement, and important functions in the syntax of complex sentences. Pivots as core arguments of the verb are internal constituents of the clause and exhibit the case-marking patterns of normal NP clause constituents. Topics are structurally quite distinct from pivots and have different grammatical properties. In particular, they are external to the clause and are not involved, as controller or target, in any intraclausal or interclausal syntactic constructions. The topic NP is very often not a core argument of the verb, and in some cases it may not be an argument of the verb at all, e.g. (4.30), (4.31), (4.34a,b,c). Topics have a variety of discourse functions, depending upon the type of PTC they occur with, but in every case their function is distinct from that of pivots.

4.3 The development of pragmatic pivots from topics: The Philippine case

In the previous section we mentioned the anomaly of Philippine languages in their selection of NP types as PrPs. While the vast majority of languages with PrPs allow only core arguments to the PrPs, Philippine languages are divergent in that they allow certain otherwise peripheral NPs to be PrPs. Given that, as we saw in

4.2, arguments which normally occur as peripheral NPs are more natural as topics than as PrPs, it seems possible that in these languages PrPs might have at least some of the characteristics of topics. In this section we will explore this anomaly and attempt to account for it.

The Philippine system of voice oppositions is called the focus system, as pointed out in 2.7. It presents a number of striking differences from the more usual voice oppositions of active–passive or active–antipassive. Note the following examples from Tagalog (focus affixes on the verb are in italics).

(4.46) a. B-*um*-ili ang lalake ng isda ng pera sa tindahan.
    AF-buy PrP man TH fish IN money L store
    'The man bought fish in the store with money.'

   b. B-in-ili-∅ ng lalake ang isda ng pera sa
    PERF-buy-THF A man PrP fish IN money L
    tindahan.
    store
    'The man bought the fish in the store with money.'

   c. *Ip*-in-*an*-bili ng lalake ng isda ang pera sa
    INF-PERF-buy A man TH fish PrP money L
    tindahan.
    store
    'The man bought fish in the store with the money.'

   d. B-in-ilh-*an* ng lalake ng isda ng pera ang
    PERF-buy-LF A man TH fish IN money PrP
    tindahan.
    store
    'The man bought fish in the store with money.'

Ang marks the focused NP and it corresponds to the PrP in languages like English or Dyirbal. In (4.46a-b) are examples in which a core argument is PrP, actor, and theme respectively, while (4.46c,d) present peripheral arguments, an instrument and an outer locative, as PrP.[12] Further examples of otherwise peripheral NPs as PrP are given in (4.47); in (4.47a) the PrP is a benefactive, and in (4.47b) it is a locative.

(4.47) a. *I*-b-in-ili ng lalake ng isda ang bata.
    BF-PERF-buy A man TH fish PrP child
    'The man bought fish for the child.'

    b. *P*-in-*ang*-isda-*an*   ng lalake ang anau.
    PERF-LF-fish-LF A man PrP lake
    'The man went fishing in the lake.'

The typological classification of Philippine languages in terms of case marking as ergative or accusative, or neither, has been a matter of controversy for some time. Relational grammarians, e.g. Bell (1976), Keenan (1976b), Perlmutter & Postal (1977), and Johnson (1977), have analyzed sentences like (4.46a) as active and (4.46b) as passive, and this implies an accusative analysis. On the other hand, Schachter (1976, 1977) sidesteps this issue by labeling each of the forms in terms of which argument is in focus; accordingly, (4.46a) is actor focus, (b) is goal focus [his term], (c) is instrumental focus, and (d) is locative focus. Recently, it has been suggested that Philippine languages are in fact ergative, e.g. Cena (1979), T. Payne (1982), De Guzman (1983), Gerdts (1983), and Walton (1983). Prima facie evidence for such an interpretation can be found in the following examples from Tagalog and Sama of Pangutaran (Walton 1983).

(4.48)   a.   B-in-asag-∅   ng lalake ang baso.   (Tagalog)
            PERF-break-PF A man   PrP glass
            'The man broke the glass.'   (= 2.81a)
     b.   Nag-basag   ang lalake ng baso.
            PERF/AF-break PrP man   P   glass
            'The man broke a glass.'

(4.49)   a.   ∅-bis   ku   tukul.   (Sama)
            UF-borrow 1sgA hammer (PrP)
            'I borrowed the hammer.'
     b.   N-bis   aku   tukul.
            AF-borrow 1sgPrP hammer
            'I borrowed a hammer.'

In both languages the 'object'-focus forms (patient in Tagalog, undergoer in Sama) take a ∅-focus affix, while the actor-focus forms are morphologically marked. These examples suggest that patient–undergoer is the morphologically unmarked focus choice with transitive verbs. Intransitive verbs are either morphologically unmarked, as in Sama, or have derivational affixes, as in Tagalog (see 2.7).

(4.50) a. Tuwi aku.   (Sama)
            sleep 1sgPrP
            'I sleep.'
        b. *P-um*-ula ang dahon.   (Tagalog)
            um-red   PrP leaf
            'The leaf turned red.'   (= 2.73a)

The affix *-um-* is derivational in (4.50b); it changes *pula* 'red' into an achievement predicate, 'redden' (see 2.7). These examples illustrate a basic ergative case-marking pattern in these two Philippine languages

Cena (1979) presents a number of cogent arguments in support of the view that 'object' focus is the unmarked (in the Praguean sense) focus type in Tagalog. Symmetrical predicates such as *kamukha* 'resemble' (literally 'same face as'), *kasingtaas* 'be as tall as', and *kasama* 'be with' are all obligatorily 'object' focus. Cena notes that just as there are no passive symmetrical predicates in English, there are no actor-focus symmetrical predicates in Tagalog. Verbs taking sentential complements such as *hayaan* 'let', *pilit* 'force', and *palagay* 'consider' must have the (object) complement in focus. Pseudo-verbs such as *gusto* 'want, like to', *dapat* 'must', and *ayaw* 'not want' also take sentential complements but no focus affixation of any kind, and they are always 'object' focus. A number of transitive verbs in Tagalog may occur without any focus affixation, e.g. *kuha* 'get', *dala* 'carry', and *hawak* 'hold', and they must be interpreted as 'object' focus. Finally, there are verbs which can never be actor focus in main clauses, e.g. *takot* 'frighten', *gulat* 'surprise', and *gutom* 'starve', but which can be actor focus only in relative clauses in order to meet the syntactic constraints on relativization to be discussed below. Thus actor-focus verbs form the distributionally restricted class in contrast to 'object'-focus verbs which have a wider distribution, and consequently one may conclude that 'object'-focus verbs in Tagalog are the unmarked focus type.

Cena's arguments concern the opposition between actor focus and patient or undergoer focus. When the oblique focus forms are taken into account, a different picture emerges. The various oblique focus types, e.g. locative, benefactive, and instrument, pattern in certain respects like patient focus, not actor focus. For example, the non-actor-focus types have perfective aspect forms containing the infix *-in-*, as in (4.46b-d) and (4.47a-b), whereas actor-focus verbs never take *-in-*. If patient focus were the unmarked focus type and actor focus the derived type, then it would be expected that the oblique focus types, which are definitely derived, would pattern with actor focus; but this is not the case. Since patient, locative, benefactive, and instrument-focus types pattern together, as opposed to actor focus, this suggests that actor focus should be considered the unmarked type. Further morphological evidence against an ergative analysis for Tagalog can be found in a comparison of (4.46a) with (4.51a-b).

(4.51)   a.   D-um-ating ang lalake.
          um-arrive   PrP man
          'The man arrived.'
      b.   P-um-unta ang lalake (sa tindahan).
          um-go   PrP man   L   store
          'The man went (to the store).'
      c.   P-in-unta-han ng lalake ang tindahan.
          PERF-go-LFA   man   PrP store
          'The man went to the store.'

The infix *-um-* occurs as the actor-focus marker with *bili* 'buy' in (4.46a) and on the intransitive verbs in (4.51a–b); it is missing in the non-actor-focus form in (4.46) and (4.47) with transitive verbs and in the locative-focus form with *punta* 'go' in (4.51c). The distribution of *-um-* follows a clear accusative pattern, and it cannot be claimed that *-um-* is a derivational affix in (4.51a–b) as it is in (4.50b). Thus there is a definite clash between markedness and morphological marking in Tagalog. The situation becomes even more complex when we consider syntax, because, as we will see in 4.5, there is evidence for syntactic ergativity in Tagalog (see p. 178–9). Tagalog defies simple classification as either accusative or ergative, and accordingly we will refrain from forcing it into either category.

Sama, on the other hand, is a much clearer case. The verbal morphology consistently follows an ergative pattern. A strong argument against interpreting undergoer focus as passive and actor-focus forms as active in Sama comes from the fact that Sama has a true passive which is distinct from 'object'-focus forms such as (4.49a).

(4.52) a. Ø-soho'   na   so   N-k'llo ma   kita.
UF-command 3sgA snake(PrP) AF-get OBL us
'He commanded the snake to get us.'

b. Ø-s-*i*-oho'   uk na   so   N-k'llo
UF-PASS-command by 3sgA snake(PrP) AF-get
ma   kita.
OBL us
'The snake was commanded by him to get us.'

c. Ø-b'lla   d'nda kiyakan   kami.
UF-cook girl   food(PrP) ours
'The girl cooked our food.'

d. Ø-b-*i*-'lla   uk d'nda kiyakan   kami.
UF-PASS-cook by girl   food(PrP) ours
'Our food was cooked by the girl.'

So 'snake' is in focus (the PrP) in both (4.52a–b), and in (b) the verb is in a passive form marked by *-i-* and the actor is an oblique marked by *uk*. Similarly in (c)–(d), *kiyakan kami* 'our food' is in focus in both sentences, and in (d) the verb carries the passive infix *-i-* and the actor *d'nda* 'girl' is an oblique marked by *uk*. A major difference between the plain undergoer focus and the passive construction is that the actor may be freely omitted in the passive constructions in (b) and (d) but not in the plain undergoer-focus constructions in (a) and (c). This omissibility correlates with the peripheral status of the actor in (b) and (d). Given the contrast between each pair of sentences, it must be concluded that the Sama constructions in (4.52b,d) are passives and therefore that the plain undergoer-focus constructions in (4.52a,b) are not. It appears, then, that Philippine languages, in so far as they parallel Sama on these points, are ergative languages.

The factors which determine focus selection are primarily discourse-based. Focused NPs in all Philippine languages must be referential and are normally definite. This is in contrast to English and German, which allow indefinite PrPs, although the majority are definite (see Givón 1979, Zubin 1979). If a patient or undergoer is definite, then it must be in focus. Non-patient/undergoers which are not in focus may be interpreted as definite or indefinite, depending upon context, but a non-focused patient/undergoer cannot be interpreted as definite. Thus focus-status in Philippine languages correlates with a particular type of discourse salience, definiteness.

The syntactic role of pivots in Tagalog parallels that in English and Dyirbal to a certain extent. There is some controversy concerning their role in complex sentences. Schachter (1976, 1977) presents the following examples in support of the claim that it is the actor and not the focused NP which can be omitted in certain types of complex constructions.

(4.53) a. Nag-atubili   siya-ng   h-um-iram ng
            PERF/AF-hesitate 3sgPrP-LIG AF-borrow TH
            pera   sa bangko.
            money L bank
            'He hesitated to borrow money from the bank.'
        b. Nag-atubili   siya-ng   hiram-in   ang
            PERF/AF-hesitate 3sgPrP-LIG borrow-THF PrP
            pera   sa bangko.
            money L bank
            'He hesitated to borrow the money from the bank.'
        c. Nag-atubili   siya-ng   hiram-an   ng
            PERF/AF-hesitate 3sgPrP-LIG borrow-LF TH
            pera   ang bangko.
            money PrP bank
            'He hesitated to borrow money from the bank.'

In all three of these sentences the coreferential actor is omitted in the embedded clause, regardless of whether it is in focus or not. Cena (1979), however, argues that non-actor-focused NPs can in fact be deleted in such constructions, presenting the following example and claiming it is a productive sentence type.

(4.54) Gusto ni   John na   ma-suri   (siya) ng doktor.[13]
        want PN/A   LIG OF-examine 3sgPrP A doctor
        'John wants to be examined by the doctor.'

Siya, the focused NP with the 'object'-focus verb *masuri*, can be omitted in the embedded clause under coreference with *John*, *contra* Schachter. Note that in the Sama examples in (4.52a–b) the focused actor in the embedded clause is deleted, but deletion under coreference in Sama does not appear to be restricted to focused NPs. There does appear to be deletion of pivots in co-ordinate structures; the following example is taken from Bloomfield (1917:64), cited in Hopper & Thompson (1980).

(4.55) Si   Andres ay   na-galit,
        PN/PrP Andres TOP PERF/ACHIEV-angry
        nag-tindig   at h-in-anap   niya sa mga
        PERF/INTR-stand.up and PERF-seek 3sgA L PL
        sulok-sulok ng   bahay ang unggo'.
        corners   GEN house PrP monkey
        'Andres got angry, stood up, and searched in all corners
        of the house for the monkey.'

Si Andres is the pivot of *nagalit* 'got angry' and *nagtindig* 'stood up', and occurs only once in a topicalized position before both verbs. In the third clause it is no longer in focus and is not deleted but rather is coded by *niya* '3sg non-focused actor'; the new focused NP is the definite 'object' *unggo'* 'monkey'. Thus there is some evidence that focused NPs are the targets for deletion in complex and compound sentences, albeit weaker than that for English and Dyirbal.

The one construction in which Tagalog focused NPs function exactly like PrPs is the relative clause. Tagalog relative clauses are somewhat like English or Dyirbal participial relative clauses. The head noun must be coreferential with the focused NP of the relative clause. The focused NP is obligatorily deleted under coreference, exactly as with PrPs in English or Dyirbal.

(4.56) a. isda-ng   *i*-b-in-igay   ng lalake sa bata
            fish-LIG THF-PERF-give A man   L child
            'the fish which was given to the child by the man'
        b. bata-ng   b-in-igy-*an*   ng lalake ng   isda
            child-LIG PERF-give-LF A man   TH fish
            'the child which was given fish by the man'
        c. *isda-ng   *nag*-bigay ang lalake sa bata
            fish-LIG AF-give PrP man   L child

> d. *isda-ng   b-in-igy-*an*   ng lalake ang bata
>   fish-L I G P E R F-give-L F A   man   PrP child

Examples (4.56a–b) are grammatical because the head nouns are coreferential with the focused N Ps of the relative clause which are omitted. Examples (4.56c–d) are ungrammatical because the head is coreferential with the theme of the relative clauses, but the focused N Ps are actor and locative respectively. These constructions are exactly parallel to the English and Dyirbal relative clauses in (4.6) and (4.11), and the relativization data suggest that Tagalog focused N Ps should be identified as PrPs.

The focused N P in a Tagalog clause appears to have many of the same properties as the PrP in English and Dyirbal. It is syntactically a core argument, as it is the argument which is coded on the verb. Its clause-internal status is confirmed by the fact, discussed above, that certain verbs require that a particular argument be in focus. It is structurally distinct from a topic, since the latter must occur preverbally, as in (4.27) and (4.28). Syntactically, the focused N P is not as important in cross-clause syntax as the PrP in English and Dyirbal. In these two languages deletion under coreference in complex sentences and coordinate structures is restricted to PrPs, but in Tagalog such deletion is not restricted to focused N Ps. Nevertheless, in syntactic terms the focused N P is clearly a pivot, not a topic. When the discourse function of the focused N P is considered, however, the distinction between PrP and topic becomes blurred, and the Tagalog *ang* phrase seems quite distinct from its English and Dyirbal counterparts. Outer peripheral, i.e. setting, arguments cannot have pivot status in English and Dyirbal, and in English special prominence is accorded them through occurrence in sentence-initial topic position, as in (4.24) and (4.30). In Tagalog, however, outer peripheral arguments may either be topicalized, as in (4.31), or occur as the focused N P, as in (4.46d) and (4.47b). Thus in these latter cases it appears that the focused N P in Tagalog is functioning rather like an English topic, according special discourse status to an outer peripheral argument. Furthermore, the overall discourse function of the focused N P seems to be somewhat different from that of the PrP in English and Dyirbal. We argued in 4.2 that the primary function of PrPs concerns 'discourse linking', and in fact in English and Dyirbal this linking function has been syntacticized in the form of restricted zero anaphora. This cannot be said to be the primary function of the focused NP in Tagalog, for two reasons. First, we saw in (4.53) that zero anaphora is not restricted to the focused NP. Secondly, and more importantly, the constraint that a definite patient/undergoer must be in focus overrides all other discourse considerations. This can be seen clearly in (4.55) in which *Andres* is the primary topical participant in the situation and yet is not in focus in all three clauses; note that in the English translation it is the PrP all the way through. This suggests that discourse linking is not the primary function of the focused NP. Rather, it appears that the primary role of the *ang* phrase is to present NPs as having a particular discourse status, i.e. definiteness, with special emphasis on the 'object' (patient/ undergoer). This function of expressing a particular discourse status rather than discourse linkage *per se* is reminiscent of the functions ascribed to topics in English by Prince (1981a, 1982) in 4.2. Here again we find a functional similarity between the Tagalog focused NP and English topics. Thus it appears that the focused NP in Tagalog is a pivot, and a pragmatic pivot, since discourse factors affect the choice of the NP in focus. However, the discourse function of this PrP is more like that of a topic than of the PrP in English and Dyirbal. We may tentatively characterize the Tagalog focused NP as a *clause-internal topic*, with 'clause-internal' referring to its syntactic status and 'topic' to its function.

This type of hybrid internal topic–PrP is a rare phenomenon, and some explanation of its origin is in order. The relative-clause construction is the crucial nexus in this whole complex system. A relative clause is defined as follows (Keenan & Comrie 1977):

a relative clause ... specifies a set of objects in two steps: a larger set is specified, called the domain of relativization, and then restricted to some subset of which a certain sentence, the restricting sentence, is true. The domain of relativization is expressed by the head NP and the restricting sentence by the restricting clause (pp. 63–4).

The domain of the relative clause is the head NP. Therefore, by this definition, the topic of the relative clause must be the head noun. This point has not been missed by others. Kuno (1973) argued that the head noun must be coreferential to an obligatory deleted topic in Japanese relative clauses. The idea that the head noun is the topic of the relative clause is also behind Schachter's (1973) analysis of relativization. Topicalization of an NP, then, is a likely condition for relativization. However, since the restricting clause is embedded, any topic NP will necessarily be internal to the sentence. This type of topicalization is further constrained by the exigencies of clause linkage and not by any overall considerations of discourse pragmatics, in contrast to the external topics.

In western Austronesian languages an overt form of clause-level topicalization of an NP is required in order to form a relative clause with this NP coreferential to the head. This is most apparent in Palauan, a western Austronesian language of Micronesia. Palauan has a passive-like construction which is very similar in form to a left-dislocation. Compare the following sentences.

(4.57) a. A   ?ad   a mos-terir   a   ngalek.
            ART man   see-3plHUM(U) ART child
            'The man saw the children.'
        b. A   ngalek a le-bos-terir
            ART child   PASS/3sg-see-3plHUM(U)
            a   ?ad.
            ART man
            'The children were seen by the man.'
        c. A   ngalek-ek a s-m-e?er   er a   tereter.
            ART child-my   INTR-sick L ART cold
            'My child is sick with a cold.'
        d. A   tereter a le-se?er   er ngiy a   ngelek-ek.
            ART cold   PASS/3sg-sick L 3sg ART child-my
            'A cold is being sick with it by my child.'

In Palauan only one preverbal NP is allowed, and this is normally the actor, as in (4.57a–b). Other NP types can be placed before the verb, and when this is the case, a special 'passive' construction must be used, as in (4.57b,d). But this so-called passive is radically different from the usual paradigm cases of passive in other languages. Note that while the non-actor occupies topic position, it still agrees as an undergoer in (4.57b) or leaves a pronominal trace associated with its locative preposition in (4.57d). While the actor is removed from the topic position, it is not case marked as oblique, and, further, now controls a type of passive verb agreement which it does not normally control in the active. In no sense could the actor of the passive be viewed as a peripheral constituent. The structure of these 'passives' strongly resembles topicalizations rather than passives, especially in view of the obligatory pronoun traces for the topic NP in its normal position in the clause. These topicalizations are critical in the formation of relative clauses.

(4.58) A   le-bos-terir   a   ?ad
       ARTPASS/3sg-see-3plHUM(U) ART man
       el   ngalek.
       LIG child
       'the children which were seen by the man.'

Palauan exhibits the same relativization constraint as Tagalog, but there are significant differences in the constructions used to meet this constraint. The Palauan construction which permits non-actor arguments is much more transparent in its form as a topicalization than the Tagalog focus system. The trace pronominal elements in the normal clause-internal position of the topicalized NP are clear evidence for this. Further, this is the only type of topicalization in Palauan, whereas Tagalog sentences can have both external and internal topics. The Tagalog focus system is much more extensively used and a more central part of the syntactic system of the language than is the Palauan topicalization construction. Tagalog focused NPs are required in most embedded clauses, including complements, whereas Palauan topicalizations are restricted to relative clauses. The Palauan topic is much closer to the usual notion of external topic in form than is the Tagalog focused NP. This is also true of its function. The Palauan topic is much more restricted in usage. No Palauan verbs idiosyncratically require a particular NP type as topic; the selection is totally contextually determined. But in Tagalog specific verbs may require particular NP types as their focused NPs, as we pointed out above. This indicates that the focus system is more tightly integrated into Tagalog clause structure than Palauan topicalization.

The weight of evidence in western Austronesian languages strongly indicates that the notion of topic, normally external to the clause, has become internal in order to meet relativization constraints. In Palauan there is no motivation for distinguishing external topic from internal topic or PrP, as there is no contrast. However, Tagalog has both notions. A given sentence can contain both an internal topic and an external one. How do we proceed from Palauan with no distinction between internal and external topic to Tagalog, with such a distinction?

An external topic is simply an NP juxtaposed to a sentence as a whole. Given this definition, it is obvious that the likelihood of a specific construction occurring with an external topic is directly related to the sentential status of the construction. The more similarity a clause bears to a normal independent sentence the more eligible it is to occur with an external topic. The more a clause is reduced in its sentential features, i.e. the more it sheds the inflectional and grammatical features of an independent sentence, the less eligible it is for an external topic. This implies that highly sentential embedded clauses would allow external topics in some languages. Note that *that*-clauses in English allow independent external topics.

(4.59) a. It seems to me that, concerning this case, we should apply for reimbursement.
        b. John seems to think that, considering Mary's illness, she shouldn't go to New York.
        c. I don't question that, given their bad record, we should shop elsewhere.

This pattern is more pronounced in Lisu, a topic-prominent language (Li & Thompson 1976) of Thailand. Fully sentential complements generally present an NP as topic, as in these examples in which *Asa* is the topic of the embedded sentence (Hope 1974).

(4.60) a. Ása nya ami khwa-a̱   da-a̱.
            Asa TOP fields hoe-DECL acceptable-DECL
            'It is acceptable for Asa to hoe fields.'

b. Alĕ nya   Ása nya   ami   khwa-ą   tsí
   Ale TOP Asa TOP fields hoe-DECL remember
   mą-ą.
   get-DECL
   'Ale remembers that Asa is hoeing fields.'
c. Alĕ nya   Ása nya   ami   khwa-ą   mu-ą.
   Ale TOP Asa TOP fields hoe-DECL see-DECL
   'Ale saw that Asa was hoeing fields.'

Relative clauses in Tagalog and Palauan differ from the reduced participial forms of English and Dyirbal in that, allowing for the deleted coreferential focused NP, they are fully sentential. The verb in a relative clause in Tagalog is identical to that of a main clause, with all the inflectional possibilities of a main clause. Relative clauses in such languages, then, are potential environments for topicalization, and given the semantic compatibility between topics and the heads of relative clauses noted earlier, it is logical for these languages to utilize topicalization constructions to form relative clauses. This results in a language like Palauan with no distinction between internal and external topic, and topicalization transparently used in the formation of relative clauses.

But the development need not stop here. It is possible for the topic to spread to other less sentential constructions, not necessarily to meet ellipsis constraints, but to express the pragmatic communicative function of topics in embedded clauses. In the process it becomes integrated into the clause and associated with the verb, so that idiosyncratic selections by specific verbs of particular NP types as topic is now possible. In other words, lexical as well as pragmatic factors may play a role in topic selection. Further, now that the topic is integrated within the clause, the way is prepared for a new notion of external topic to be innovated. This is the synchronic situation in Tagalog. We now have in effect a PrP: clause-internal NP which the sentence is about, but as yet does not play a full role in cross-clausal syntax.

Paradigm cases of languages with PrPs like English represent the greatest elaboration of this language type. Here the pivot is employed extensively in the cross-clausal syntax of this language, and there is a sharp distinction between it and the external topic, as discussed in the previous section. The language has a strong preference for one NP type as the unmarked PrP, and special constructions like passives and antipassives which allow other NP types to be PrPs. Further, not only are there pragmatic and lexical considerations involved in the selection of PrP, but structural constraints may be involved as well, as in the obligatory use of passive in some English complements (see (4.5), (4.6), and (4.8)).

The clear preference for the actor as PrP and the marked status of the passive construction presenting the undergoer as PrP suggests a somewhat different scenario for the origin of PrPs for languages like English than for Tagalog. It seems likely that the PrP system in these languages developed from an earlier SmP by gradually generalizing the conditions under which the passive construction was used. The earlier passive construction was simply an intransitive mediopassive or adjectival construction, presenting the undergoer as SmP and expressing a stative condition expressing a state or condition. Gradually, the conditions of its usage extended to meet various syntactic and discourse functions in English. Thus, the pivot in English made a transition from a semantic one to a pragmatic one (see Traugott 1972 for detailed discussion).

The fundamental point to be understood concerns the derivative, secondary status of PrPs. They are topics which have been grammaticalized into the internal structure of the clause. In 4.1 we showed how the most common kind of semantic pivot is basically a generalization of the notion of actor. In this section we have attempted to show that pragmatic pivots are really a special case of the notion 'topic' which has been innovated in certain languages to meet particular grammatical needs. In some languages they are much more prominent than in others. The Philippine languages represent a transitional case in which they still exhibit some of the features of topics. The basic grammatical categories in all languages in this domain are the semantic macroroles, actor and undergoer, and the independent notion of topic. Many of the world's languages, such as Archi or Lisu, operate with just these. Pivots, whether pragmatic or semantic, are derived from these more basic categories.

4.4 Passive constructions

If we inspect an active and passive pair in English we will notice
that two differences in the syntactic status of the N Ps are apparent.

(4.61) a. The boy hit the ball.
        b. The ball was hit by the boy.

The passive construction differs from the active in having the
undergoer as the pivot NP and also in having the actor as an
oblique constituent marked by the preposition *by*. To put it
another way, the actor in a passive is a peripheral NP (inner
peripheral, to be exact). A passive construction, then, differs from
the active construction in two separate, but related, ways: the
occurrence of a non-actor argument, normally the undergoer, as
the pivot of the clause, and the peripheral status of the actor. We
claim that these are separate phenomena because, as we shall see,
there are languages, such as Lango (Nilo-Saharan: Noonan &
Bavin-Woock 1978) which allow non-actor arguments to be pivot
without the actor losing its status as a core argument, as well as
languages like Ulcha (Manchu–Tungus; Nichols 1979b) in which
the actor is eliminated from the clause and is not replaced as pivot
by a non-actor argument. We thus have two separate phenomena,
which commonly (but not necessarily) cooccur. We claim that
universally there are two passive constructions. The first permits
non-actor arguments to occur as the pivot of a clause. We will
refer to this type as the *foregrounding passive*. It is normally found
in languages with a PrP, in which it functions to present non-actor
arguments as the PrP to meet the constraints involved in the linking of clauses in discourse. Examples of the function of this passive
were illustrated with the English data in 4.1. In the other passive
construction the actor may be a peripheral constituent, or it may
be removed entirely from the clause. This type we will term the
backgrounding passive. It is the usual concomitant of the foregrounding passive, as for example in English and German, but,
as we shall see, there are many languages which have backgrounding passives but no foregrounding ones. In this section we develop
a detailed typology of passive constructions along the lines of this
basic division.

Foregrounding passives are associated with the accessibility to

PrP of non-actor arguments. With the exception of the western Austronesian languages discussed in the previous sections, all languages with a PrP restrict the PrPs in passive clauses to core arguments, and commonly to undergoer only. German is one of the languages in which only undergoers may be PrPs in passives.

(4.62) a. Der   Junge hat   das   Butterbrot
            the-NOM boy   have-3sg the-ACC sandwich
            gegessen.
            eat-PASTPART
            'The boy ate the sandwich.'

        b. Das   Butterbrot wurde   von dem
            the-NOM sandwich became-3sg by   the-DAT
            Jungen gegessen.
            boy   eat-PASTPART
            'The sandwich was eaten by the boy.'

The PrP in German is signaled by the nominative case. In the active sentence (4.62a), the actor is the PrP and case marked nominatively, while in (4.62b) the undergoer is the nominative-case PrP. Zubin (1979) has shown the importance of the PrP in the maintenance of discourse cohesion. Like English PrPs, it is the target for ellipsis under coreference in conjoined clauses.

(4.63) a. Der   Junge hat   das   Butterbrot
            the-NOM boy   have-3sg the-ACC sandwich
            gegessen   und dann ____ ist   ins
            eat-PASTPART and then   be-3sg into
            Kino   gegangen.
            movie go-PASTPART
            'The boy ate the sandwich and then went to the movie.'

        b. Die   Frau   sah   den   Mann und ____
            the-NOM woman saw-3sg the-ACC man   and
            schlug ihn.
            hit-3sg 3sgM-ACC
            'The woman saw the man and hit him.'

        c. Er   wurde   zusammengeschlagen und
            3sgM-NOM became-3sg beat.up-PASTPART and
            ____ dann ging   ins Krankenhaus.
                then went-3sg into hospital
            'He was beaten up and then went to the hospital.'

d. Die   Frau   sah   den   Mann und _____
the-NOM woman saw-3sg the-ACC man   and
wurde   gekidnappt.
became-3sg kidnap-PASTPART
'The woman saw the man and was kidnapped.'

In all of these sentences the PrP in the first clause is controlling the ellipsis of the PrP of the second. Whether the PrP is actor or undergoer is irrelevant to the NP ellipsis in these constructions. In (4.63a–b) the PrPs in both clauses are actors, while in (4.63c–d) one is an actor and the other an undergoer in each clause.

Only undergoers, which appear in the accusative case in active clauses, may be PrP in a passive: in particular erstwhile dative arguments do not become PrPs in a passive construction.

(4.64) a. Das   Mädchen hat   mir   ein
the-NOM girl   have-3sg 1sg-DAT a-ACC
Buch geschenkt.
book give (as gift)-PASTPART
'The girl gave me a book.'

b. Mir   wurde   ein   Buch
1sg-DAT became-3sg a-NOM book
geschenkt.
give(as gift)-PASTPART
'I was given a book.'

c. *Ich   wurde   ein   Buch
1sg-NOM became-3sg a-ACC book
geschenkt.
give (as gift)-PASTPART

The NP in the pre-auxiliary position is in the dative case rather than the nominative in (4.64b). Since it is not in the nominative case, we might expect that it is not a PrP, an expectation borne out by its inability to be the controller or target of NP ellipsis.

(4.65) a. *Mir   wurde   ein   Buch von dem
1sg-DAT became-3sg a-NOM book by   the-DAT
Mädchen geschenkt   und
girl   give(as gift)-PASTPART and
sofort   habe   _____ es
immediately have-1sg   3sgN-ACC

verloren.
lost-PASTPART
'I was given a book by the girl and immediately lost it.'
b. *Ich   bin   zu der   Bank gegangen
    1sg-NOM be-1sg to the-DAT bank go-PASTPART
    und ___ wurde   viel   Geld
    and   became-3sg much money
    gegeben.
    give-PASTPART
    'I went to the bank and was given a lot of money.'

These sentences are ungrammatical because in each of them a dative NP is either a controller or target of NP ellipsis. This shows that they are not PrPs. Thus, in German only undergoers, the accusatively case marked NPs in active clauses, may occur as the PrP in a passive.

Other languages are not so restrictive in what arguments are allowed as the PrP in passive clauses. Some languages like those of western Indonesia allow non-actor core arguments in addition to the undergoer to occur as PrP. In Indonesian, goals or benefactives may be core arguments and may be PrPs in passive sentences. A verbal suffix marks the core status of these arguments.

(4.66) a. Ali meng-(k)irim surat itu kepada Hasan.[14]
            Ali ACT-send   letter the to   Hasan
            'Ali sent the letter to Hasan.'
        b. Ali meng-kirim-*kan*   Hasan surat itu.
            Ali ACT-send-SUFF Hasan letter the
            'Ali sent Hasan the letter.'

(4.67) a. Ali mem-beli ayam   itu untuk Hasan.
            Ali ACT-buy chicken the for   Hasan
            'Ali bought the chicken for Hasan.'
        b. Ali mem-beli-*kan*   Hasan ayam   itu.
            Ali ACT-buy-SUFF Hasan chicken the
            'Ali bought Hasan the chicken.'

In the (a) examples, the goal and benefactive NPs are peripheral, and this status is reflected by their being preceded by the preposition *kepada* 'to' and *untuk* 'for'. In the (b) examples these arguments have become core. This is indicated by their immediate postverbal position and the suffix -*kan* on the verb. As peripheral NPs, goals and benefactives are not permissible PrPs, but, as core, they are.

(4.68) a. *Hasan di-bawa   ayam   itu (kepada) oleh Ali.
            Hasan PASS-bring chicken the to   by   Ali
            'Hasan was brought the chicken (to) by Ali.'
        b. Hasan di-bawa-*kan*   ayam   itu oleh Ali.
            Hasan PASS-bring-SUFF chicken the by   Ali
            'Hasan was brought the chicken by Ali.'

(4.69) a. *Hasan di-beli   ayam   itu (untuk) oleh Ali.
            Hasan PASS-buy chicken the for   by   Ali
            'Hasan was bought the chicken (for) by Ali.'
        b. Hasan di-beli-*kan*   ayam   itu oleh Ali.
            Hasan PASS-buy-SUFF chicken the by   Ali
            'Hasan was bought the chicken by Ali.'

The (a) sentences are ungrammatical because regardless of whether the prepositions are present or not, there is no -*kan* suffix on their verb, and, consequently, the goal and benefactive NPs must be peripheral. As peripheral constituents, they are not potential PrPs, and so their passive sentences are ungrammatical.[15] However, in the (b) sentences with the -*kan* suffix indicating their core status, they are possible PrPs, and these passives are grammatical. Indonesian, then, has a less restricted range of options for possible PrPs than German.

Passives are not restricted to morphologically accusative languages, but are also found in ergative languages. Tzotzil, a Mayan language of Mexico, is a language with verbal inflection on a completely ergative pattern (Haviland 1982).

(4.70) a. Bat-em-∅
            go-PERF-3sgABS
            'He's gone.'
        b. S-max-ox-∅.
            3sgERG-hit-PST-3sgABS
            'He hit him.'

The S in (a) and the U in (b) are both indicated by a zero suffix, the suffix for third-singular absolutive, while the A in (b) is the prefix *s-*, the morpheme for third singular ergative. However, whereas Tzotzil is ergative morphologically, its selection for PrP is like German, an accusative language. The actor is the PrP for an active verb, and therefore, unlike German, there is no consistent morphological marking for the PrP. It is absolutive for an intransitive verb, but ergative for a transitive verb. The PrP is always clause final in Tzotzil. But regardless of the morphology the notion of PrP in Tzotzil is like that in German. So when an undergoer is needed as PrP in order to meet a coreferentiality constraint as the target for ellipsis in a subsequent clause, Tzotzil, like German, uses a passive to meet this constraint (Haviland 1982).

(4.71) a. S-mil-ox-∅   Xan li   Petal e.
            3sgERG-kill-PERF-3sgABS John ART Peter
            'Peter killed John.'

     b. mil-bil-∅   yu'un Petal li   Xan e.
         kill-PASS-3sgABS by   Peter ART John
         'John was killed by Peter.'

     c. A   li Petal e bat-em-∅   ta xobel
         ART   Peter go-PERF-3sg-ABS to town
         s-max-ox-∅   li   Anton e.
         3sgERG-hit-PERF-3sgABS ART Anton
         'Peter went to town and hit Anton.'

     d. A   li Petal bat-em-∅   ta xobel max-bil-∅
         ART   Peter go-PERF-3sgABS to town   hit-PASS
         yu'un li   Anton.
         by   ART Anton
         'Peter went to town and got hit by Anton.'

Examples (4.71a–b) correspond as active and passive pair. The passive is formed by marking the actor as an oblique NP with the preposition *yu'un* 'by', dropping the ergative prefix from the verb and suffixing the verb with the passive suffix *-bil*. In (4.71c), 'Peter' is the actor for both the first verb and the second verb and, as the PrP, can be the target for ellipsis in the second clause with no further restructuring. But in (4.71d), 'Peter' is the undergoer of the second verb, and, in order to be the target for ellipsis, it must be the PrP. Consequently, a passive construction must be used to present the undergoer as PrP, exactly as in German.[16] Thus, German and Tzotzil, although contrasting types morphologically, both make use of the same notion of PrP.

The western Austronesian languages such as Tagalog and Palauan are the only cases we have found of languages which allow otherwise peripheral arguments to be PrPs directly without first acquiring core status as in Indonesian. They are the least restricted languages with regard to PrP selection. These languages were discussed in sufficient detail in section 4.3, and we mention them here merely to point out that they represent an extreme development in their lack of constraints on the selection of NP types as PrPs.

Having presented a basic typology of foregrounding passives, we now turn to the backgrounding types. Backgrounding passives are those constructions which function to demote the actor; it may appear as a peripheral argument or, most commonly, it may be eliminated from the clause altogether. The most transparent cases of these constructions are in those languages which suppress the actor but otherwise make no other alteration in the structure of the transitive clause, as in Ulcha (Manchu–Tangus; Nichols 1979b).

(4.72) Ti   dūse-we   hōn-da ta-wuri.
DEM tiger-ACC how-Q do-PASS
'What's to be done about that tiger?'

Note that while no actor appears in the clause in the Ulcha passive, the undergoer remains in the accusative case. Ulcha is a language with semantic pivots rather than pragmatic ones, as pivot selection is strictly determined by verbal semantics. If the actor is present, it must be pivot; no other option is possible. The SmP consists of the usual S/A grouping of NPs which are case marked nominatively. Nominative NPs are those which control and are the target for ellipsis in a simplified switch-reference system.

(4.73) Ti   dūse-∅   ilžu-mi   erke herelu-mi
DEM tiger-NOM stand-SG/SIM slowly turn-SG/SIM
nāntiti ičehneni.
at.them (he).looked
'Standing up, slowly turning around, the tiger looked at them.'

Here the nominative *dūse* 'tiger' is the SmP controlling NP ellipsis in the conjoined clauses. The ellipsis is indicated by the suffixes *-mi* on the verbs. Nichols (1979b) shows that an accusative NP as in the passive of (4.72) does not have this syntactic property, and therefore cannot be a pivot.

Ulcha passives remove the actor SmP from the core of the clause and obligatorily suppress it. No other NP may assume pivot status. Similar backgrounding passives are found in Nanai (Nichols 1979b), Finnish (Comrie 1977), and Ute (Givón 1981).

(4.74) a. Ej   daŋsa-wa   tej   erinčie xola-o-xan
        DEM book-ACC DEM time   read-PASS-PST
        bičin.   (Nanai)
        AUX(PST)
        'The book had already been read by that time.'
    b. Hän-et   jätettiin kotiin.   (Finnish)
        3sg-ACC was.left at.home
        'He was left at home.'
    c. Siváątu-ci 'u-wáy   paxá-ta-xa.   (Ute)
        goat-ACCthe-ACC kȋll-PASS-ANT
        'Someone killed the goat,' or 'The goat was killed.'

In Dutch (Kirsner 1976), on the other hand, the dummy pivot filler *er* occurs in the pivot position occupied by the actor in active sentences. This type of impersonal passive occurs only with intransitive verbs.

(4.75) a. Er   wordt   door de jongens
        there become-3sg by   the boys
        gefloten.
        whistled-PASTPART
        'There is whistling by the boys.'
    b. Er   wordt   door de studenten
        there become-3sg by   the students
        gestaakt.
        strike-PASTPART
        'There is a strike by students.'

These sentences are PrP-less. The *er* is just a dummy pivot holder; it is non-referential and not a PrP. The actor is also not a PrP, but occurs as a peripheral argument. This is indicated by its oblique status, as well as the fact that it no longer controls nor is the target for typical PrP functions like NP ellipsis across clauses.

(4.76) a. De vrouwen lachten   en huilden.
         the women laugh-PST and cry-PST
         'The women laughed and cried.'
     b. *Er   werd   door de vrouwen
         there became-3sg by   the women
         gelachen   en ____ huilden.
         laugh-PASTPART and   cry-PASTPART

        *'There was laughing by the women and cried.'

The function of this construction is clearly to remove the actor from the core and, hence, the pivot position, rather than any promotion of a non-actor argument to PrP. The *er* merely holds the pivot position, but does not function as a PrP.

The Sama passive in (4.52) represents a unique kind of back-grounding passive. Because Sama is ergative, the undergoer is the PrP in an active clause, and consequently any backgrounding of the actor in (4.52b,d) has no effect on the syntactic status of the undergoer, which is already the PrP. In this construction the backgrounding of the actor is independent of pivot considerations.

The most common type of backgrounding passive is a construction in which the transitive verb is detransitivized and often stativized, and only the undergoer is present. The clause is intransitive and so the undergoer is in S function and case marked accordingly, unlike the examples in (4.74), for example. Stativization is a very common effect of backgrounding passives cross-linguistically. Such constructions are often called *mediopassives* or *middle voice* rather than passives. The following examples are from Choctaw (Nicklas 1974) and Chichewa (Bantu; Watkins 1937).

(4.77) a. Bill at okhisa an   tiwwih.   (Choctaw)
           SmP door OBL 3sg-opens-3sg
           'Bill is opening the door.'
       b. Okhisa at   tinwah.
           door SmP open-MEDIOPASS
           'The door is open.'

(4.78) a. Chifuβa chamunthi chirumi-ka.   (Chichewa)
            chest   of-person bite-MEDIOPASS
            'The man's chest is (being) bitten.'
        b. Mwana waŋga wapandi:-ka.
            child   my   beat-MEDIOPASS
            'My child has been beaten.'

Like the backgrounding passives of Ulcha, Nanai, Finnish, and
Ute in (4.72) and (4.74), these constructions require the complete
removal of the actor from the clauses. They differ from them in
that they require detransitivization of the clause and the assumption by the undergoer of S function. Fijian offers an interesting
intermediate case. The backgrounding passive in this language
totally suppresses the actor with the result that the undergoer now
assumes the verbal agreement of S function, but the clause is not
detransitivized or stativized, the verb still occurring with the
transitive suffix.

(4.79) a. E   ∅   a   kau-ti   ira   na   gone na
            CM 3sgA PST carry-TR 3plU ART child ART
            turaga.
            chief
            'The chief carried the children.'
        b. E   ra   a   kau-ti   na   gone (*e na turaga).
            CM 3plS PST carry-TR ART child
            'The children were carried.'

In Fijian a verb occurs with a proclitic indicating person and
number of the S/A SmP, and an enclitic indicating the person
and number of the undergoer. In addition, any transitive verb
must occur with a suffix which indicates its transitivity. In (4.79a),
an active transitive clause, the actor proclitic is ∅ for '3sg' and
the undergoer enclitic is *ira* for '3pl'. Sentence (4.79b) is the corresponding passive and the undergoer now agrees as an S NP,
with the proclitic *ra* '3pl' for A or S. The verb still retains the
transitive suffix and is semantically dynamic not stative (see Foley
1976). Thus, Fijian is like Ulcha, on the one hand, in that the
clause is not detransitivized, while, on the other hand, it is like
Chichewa in that the undergoer is case marked like an S.

Mediopassive constructions are also found in the familiar languages of Europe. These are languages with PrPs, and the undergoer assumes PrP status. Examples from German and Spanish:

(4.80) a. Mein   Wagen wird   (von dem
          my-NOM car   become-3sg by the-DAT
          Mechaniker) repariert.
          mechanic   repair-PASTPART
          'My car is (being) fixed (by the mechanic).'

        b. Mein   Wagen ist   (*von dem
          my-NOM car   be-3sg by the-DAT
          Mechaniker) repariert.
          mechanic   repair-PASTPART
          'My car is fixed (*by the mechanic).'

        c. Das   macht   sich   leicht.
          that-NOM make-3sg REFL easily
          'That is easily done.'

(4.81) a. Se   abre   la   puerta.
          REFL open-3sg the door
          'The door is open.'

        b. Se   quemaron   las   casas.
          REFL burn-PST/3pl the-PL house-PL
          'The houses burned down.'

German has two different constructions for the total suppression of the actor. The regular German foregrounding passive uses *werden* 'become' as its auxiliary, and it can take an overt peripheral actor phrase, as in (4.80a). German also has backgrounding passives and these are formed with *sein* 'be' as the auxiliary; in such constructions, e.g. (4.80b), no actor can be expressed, and the sentence has a stative meaning. Furthermore, German has a construction involving the reflexive pronoun *sich* which serves to allow the undergoer as PrP and permits no expression of an actor; it is illustrated in (c). Spanish has similar reflexive–mediopassive forms as in (4.81).

We have established the existence of two separate passive constructions: backgrounding passives, which remove the actor from the core, either presenting it as an oblique NP or suppressing it entirely, and foregrounding passives, which present non-actor arguments as pivots. Although commonly associated, these functions are logically independent of each other. There are four possible types of languages which result from their interaction. A language can have a backgrounding passive demoting the actor, but resulting in the assumption of pivot status by a non-actor argument, hence a foregrounding passive as well. Choctaw, Chichewa, and Fijian are languages of this type. It is also possible to have a backgrounding passive without this side effect, in which the undergoer does not assume pivot status. Ulcha, Nanai, Finnish, and Ute, as well as the Dutch impersonal passives, exhibit this type. Foregrounding passives permit a non-actor to be PrP. Normally, these require a backgrounding passive side effect in which the actor is removed from the core. The foregrounding passives of German, English, Indonesian, and Tzotzil are all examples of this type.[17] The fourth logical possibility is a language in which there is a foregrounding passive in which non-actors occur as PrP, but in which the actor remains a core argument. This type of language is exemplified by Lango, a Nilo-Saharan language of East Africa (Noonan & Bavin-Woock 1978).[18]

In Lango, the PrP is always the left-most NP in the clause. The actor normally occupies this PrP position. Lango has a foregrounding passive which places the non-actor core argument before the actor argument but no other change is effected in the clause.

(4.82) a. Dákó   ò-jwát-ò   lócà.
            woman 3sgA-hit-3sgU man
            'The woman hit the man.'
        b. Lócà dákó   ò-jwát-ò.
            man woman 3sgA-hit-3sgU
            'The man was hit by the woman.'
        c. Lócà ò-mí-ɔ̀   mɔ̀tbɔ̀t àtín.
            man 3sgA-gave-3sgU gift to child
            'The man gave the gift to the child.'
        d. Àtín lócà ò-mí-ɔ̀   mɔ̀tbɔ̀t-ɛ̀.
            child man 3sgA-gave-3sgU gift to-3sg
            'The child was given the gift by the man.'

The passive is restricted to verbal arguments, as in the examples in (4.82); an outer peripheral NP which is not an argument of the verb cannot be preposed in this construction. The passive PrP occurs first and the remainder of the clause follows it. There is no verbal morphology or case-marking changes associated with the passive. This NP-fronting construction is not topicalization; it is clause-bounded. It can occur in a relative clause, as in (4.83b), and it cannot be used to present an argument of a subordinate clause in main clause-initial position, as (4.83d) shows.

(4.83) a. Búk á'mɛ́ dákó   ò-mí-ɔ̀   lócà dwóŋ
           book REL woman 3sgA-give-3sgU manbig
           'The book that the woman gave the man is big.'

       b. Búk á'mɛ́ lócà dákó   ò-mí-ɔ̀   dwóŋ.
           book REL manwoman 3sgA-give-3sgU big
           'The book that the man was given by the woman is big.'

       c. Dákó ò-dí-ɔ̀   lócà 'ní   'kwál gwènò.
           woman 3sgA-force-3sgU manCOMP steal chicken
           'The woman forced the man to steal the chicken.'

       d. *Gwènò dákó ò-dí-ɔ̀   lócà 'ní   'kwál.
           chicken woman 3sgA-force-3sgU manCOMP steal

True preposed topic constructions of the type discussed in 4.2 are not restricted to verbal arguments, do not occur in relative clauses (Palauan in 4.3 is an exception), and some arguments in subordinate clauses may be the topic of the whole sentence, as in *Those cookies Mary promised not to eat*. The Lango passive lacks all of these features but does have the attributes which are normally associated with clause-internal voice constructions (see Noonan & Bavin-Woock 1978:136–7).

The Lango passive is a foregrounding passive in that the fronted NP controls the typical cross-clausal properties of PrPs.

(4.84) a. Dákó ò-nén-ò   lócà tè   jwâtt-ò.
           woman 3sgA-see-3sgU manand.then hit-3sgU
           'The woman saw the man and then *she* hit *him*.'

       b. Lócà dákó   ò-nén-ò   tè   jwâtt-ò.
           man woman 3sgA-see-3sgU and.then hit-3sgU
           'The man was seen by the woman and then *he* hit *her*.'

In (4.84) the actor and PrP of the second clause with *jwâtt-ò* 'hit-3sg' is determined by coreferentiality with the PrP of the first clause. In (4.84a) in which the first clause is active and the PrP is the actor *dákó* 'woman', then the PrP and actor of the second clause must also be *dákó* 'woman'. However, in (4.84b) the first clause is passive and the PrP is *lócà* 'man', and, therefore, the PrP and actor of the second clause must be *lócà* 'man'. Thus, as is typical with PrPs, the first NP both controls and is the target for NP ellipsis under coreference.

The PrP also is the controller of a cross-clausal switch-reference-like system:

(4.85)   a.   Dákó   ò-kób-ò   ní   ò-cám-ò   rìŋó.
             woman 3sgA-say-3sgU that 3sgA-eat-3sgU meat
             'The woman₍ᵢ₎ said that he/she₍ⱼ₎ would eat meat.'

       b.   Dákó   ò-kób-ò   ní   ɛ̀-cám-ò   rìŋó.
             woman 3sgA-say-3sgU that 3sgA-eat-3sgU meat
             'The woman₍ᵢ₎ said that she₍ᵢ₎ ate meat.'

The verbal prefix for actor in an embedded clause can be either of two forms: ε – which indicates that the actor is coreferential with the PrP of the main clause and *ò-*, which indicates that it is not. That it is the PrP and not the actor which controls this coreference prefix is clear in passive constructions.

(4.86)   a.   Dákó   ò-kóbbì   lócà   ní   ɛ́-'bínó dòk.
             woman₍ᵢ₎ 3sgA-tell man₍ⱼ₎ that 3sg₍ᵢ₎-go back
             'The woman told the man that she will go back.'
       b.   Lócà dákó   ò-kóbbɛ́ ní   ɛ́-'bínó dòk.
             man₍ⱼ₎ woman₍ᵢ₎ 3sg-tell that 3sg₍ⱼ₎-go back
             'The man₍ⱼ₎ was told by the woman₍ᵢ₎ that he₍ⱼ₎ will go back.'

The goal PrP in (4.86b) is coreferential with the *ɛ́-* prefix in the embedding clause indicating same PrP.

In contrast to languages like English or German, however, all evidence seems to indicate that the actor in a passive construction is not a peripheral but a core argument. First, the actor continues to control verb agreement in passives (see examples above), a feature of core arguments. Actors in English passive clauses no longer control verb agreement.

(4.87)   a.   The woman is kissing me.
       b.   I am/*is being kissed by the woman.

But there is stronger evidence as well. Actors, whether in active or passive clauses, are the controllers of reflexivization.

(4.88) a. Lócà ò-kwá-ò   dákó   pìr-έ   kὲnὲ.
           man 3sgA-ask-3sgU woman about-3sg self
           'The man asked the woman about *herself/*himself*.'

       b. dákó   lócà ò-kwá-ò   pìr-έ   kὲnὲ.
           woman man 3sgA-ask-3sgU about-3sg self
           'The woman was asked by the man about *herself/
           himself.'

Whether the actor *lócà* 'man' is PrP or not, the reflexive is always coreferential with it. In English the actor in a passive clause may never be coreferential with a reflexive.

(4.89) a. John talked to Mary about himself.
       b. *Mary was talked to by John about himself.

The fact that actors in passive clauses can control reflexivization in Lango but not in English is due to the fact that in Lango they are core arguments, while in English they are peripheral. Actors are also typically the addressee of an imperative.

(4.90) a. Jwât-á (án).
           hit-1sgU me
           'Hit me!'
       b. án jwât-á.
           me hit-1sgU
           'Hit me!', or 'Let me be hit!'

Here the second person addressee is actor in both the active and passive clauses. But in English, actors in passives are not possible addressees in imperatives.

(4.91) a. Close the door!
       b. *The door be closed (by you)!

This difference in behavior between passive actors in Lango and English reflects their core status in Lango, but peripheral status in English.

     Lango is thus a clear case in which a foregrounding passive does not have backgrounding passive side effects; the actor remains a core argument. The Lango passive parallels Philippine focus systems in a very important respect: in both cases the clause-internal voice system is related to topicalization. We have already discussed the Philippine case in 4.3, and the origins of the Lango passive in a topicalization construction is, if anything, even more apparent. Note that the NP is shifted to the extreme left but no other change is effected. The actor remains in its normal position and there is no passive affixation on the verb. Further evidence is that passives in Lango always leave a trace in the original position of the PrP, either as a verbal affix (4.82) or an object of a preposition (4.83). There can be no doubt of the relatedness of the Lango passive to topicalization, even though synchronically it can no longer be considered a preposed topic construction of the type discussed in 4.2. The reason why passives closely related to topicalization allow the actor to remain a core argument is that a topicalization, being a clause-external function, does not significantly affect the internal structure of the clause; the internal constituents of the clause continue to hold their syntactic and semantic properties. If the topicalization is not fully integrated into the internal structure of the clause, then it may well have syntactic consequences only for the (internally) topicalized argument, the others being unaffected. Hence it seems reasonable that the actor in a passive closely and transparently related to a topicalization would continue to exercise its normal grammatical functions. These Lango facts, then, reinforce the point made in 4.2 and 4.3 that (pragmatic) pivots are grammaticalized topics, representing a syntacticization of certain discourse factors into the internal structure of the clause.

Bantu languages present a passive construction different in certain crucial respects from any discussed thus far. Bantu languages have passive constructions with expressed actors, which are superficially similar to the corresponding English or German sentences. Note these Chichewa examples (Trithart 1979).

(4.92) a. Joni a-na-menya-a   m-ai   w-aŋga.
            John 3sg-PST-hit-INDIC mother my
            'John hit my mother.'
        b. M-ai w-aŋga a-na-meny-*edw*-a   ndi
            mother my   3sg-PST-hit-PASS-INDIC by
            Joni.
            John
            'My mother was hit by John.'

In Chichewa, as in other Bantu languages, verbs always show agreement in class and number with the pivot, e.g. *a-* in (4.92). In an active construction such as (4.92a) the actor controls verb agreement and appears as the preverbal NP. In a passive like (4.92b) the undergoer appears before the verb and controls verb agreement, while the actor appears in an oblique phrase after the verb. The verb is inflected with the passive suffix *-edw* as well. This construction shows a striking similarity to the English passive, and has often been analyzed in a similar way. This would suggest that the Bantu passive, represented here by Chichewa, is a foregrounding passive. But there are several problems with this analysis which suggest that it may not be correct. Unlike foregrounding passives, in which the choice of which NP is PrP is determined by discourse factors, Bantu passives are basically sensitive to inherent semantic factors of the NP arguments of the verbs such as person and animacy (see 3.1; Silverstein 1976b). Trithart (1979) argues that passive is favored when the NP to become subject is higher on the following inherent salience hierarchy: 1st person > 2nd person > proper human > common human > animate > inanimate, or on the following role hierarchy: recipient/benefactive > patient > instrument.

The role hierarchy is simply another version of the inherent salience hierarchy because benefactives and recipients are generally human, patients may be animate or inanimate, and instrumentals are normally inanimate. The Bantu passive simply operates to put higher-ranking NPs on this hierarchy in pivot position. As pivot selection is determined by semantic considerations and not discourse pragmatic ones, it is an SmP.

Other evidence as well suggests that the pivots of Bantu are SmPs and not PrPs. Coreference of NPs in Bantu discourse is monitored by a nominal class concord system with verbal cross-reference. Typologically, such systems are characteristic of PrP-less languages, as discussed in greater depth in 7.2. These examples are from Chichewa (Watkins 1937).

(4.93) a. Mwara   ma-ŋga u-ku:phi   chifukwa
        I Ia-stone I Ia-my I Ia-become. hot reason
        mɔtɔ   wa-ukuru
        I Ia-fire I Ia-big

u-wu-tɛːnth-a.
IIaA-IIaU-burn-INDIC
'My stone is becoming hot because the big fire is burn-
ing it.'
b. Cha-mkɔlɛ cha-nu   chachi-kuːru chi-thaːβ   -a
VI-hostage VI-your VI-valuable VI. A-run. away-
            a-chi-gwir-a   ni
INDIC I.A-VI.U-catch-INDIC is
m-uːnthu.
I-person
'Your valuable hostage is running away and the man
is catching him.'

In these examples the coreference of actor and undergoer across
the clauses is indicated by the verbal concord prefixes. There is
no passive used as is likely to be the case in languages with foregrounding passives. Note that the verb agreement in the second
clause of (4.93b) clearly identifies the person *muːnthu* (class 1)
as the actor with the class 1 prefix in the subject slot and the
hostage *chamkɔlɛ* (class 6) as the undergoer, as the class 6 prefix
is in the undergoer slot. The undergoer of the second clause is
coreferential with the subject of the first clause, as indicated by the
class 6 subject agreement in the first clause, but a passive is not
used. In a language with PrPs and foregrounding passives like
Tzotzil or Indonesian, a passive construction with zero pronominalization of the PrP would be used in the second clause of
an example like (4.93b).

   Although verbal cross-referencing of SmPs for class and number is the normal means of NP coreference monitoring, it is
conceivable that the passive plays a minor role when both actor and
undergoer are of the same class and animacy rank and the undergoer is coreferential with the pivot of the following clause, as in
Swahili (example (4.94) from Hopper & Thompson (1982)).

(4.94) Spekta   Seif a-li-ingia   ndani
        Inspector Seif 3sg-PST-get.in inside
        a-ka-fuat-w-a   na Sajin   Paola na
        3sg-SEQ-follow-PASS-INDIC by Sergeant Paola and

Bwana Musa Hapo.
Mr   Hapo.
'Inspector Seif went inside followed by Sergeant Paolo and Mr Hapo.'

Here the actor and pivot of the first clause is coreferential with the undergoer of the second clause. Consequently, a passive is used in the second clause to make the undergoer pivot. But the actor and undergoer of the second clause are of equal rank in the salience hierarchy so that the semantic factors determining pivot selection are neutralized. The pragmatic factor may then select the pivot. The evidence still seems to suggest that the Bantu pivot is an SmP. Pragmatic factors may play a role only when semantic considerations fail to be decisive. This situation indicates that the dichotomy between SmP and PrP proposed in 4.1 is rather more of a continuum, as the weighting of pragmatic or semantic factors in pivot selection varies across languages. Bantu languages have pivots that are close to the transition point between SmP and PrP. English pivots are more on the pragmatic side, and Dyirbal pivots appear to be the strongest PrPs. We may place some languages discussed along this continuum as in Figure 4.

PrP $\longleftarrow$ $\longrightarrow$ SmP

    Dyirbal   English   Tagalog   Bantu   Choctaw   Kewa

Figure 4 Continuum of pivot types

The Bantu passive is best analyzed as a foregrounding passive but one that operates on semantic pivots rather than pragmatic ones. It is somewhat of an anomaly, in that all other cases of foregrounding passives are in languages with pragmatic pivots,[19] but this may not be unexpected in view of the transitional status of Bantu pivots. These Bantu passives have the usual backgrounding passive side effects, resulting in the removal of the actor from the core.

Our discussion of passive may be summarized as follows. Passives may be divided into two general types according to their function. Passives which serve to remove the actor from the core of the clause are *backgrounding passives*, whereas those which function to permit a non-actor to occur as PrP are *foregrounding passives*. Foregrounding passives are normally found in languages which have PrPs, i.e. in languages in which the choice of pivot is governed by discourse facts of the type discussed in 4.1 and 4.2. Backgrounding passives, on the other hand, are not so constrained and occur in both reference-dominated and role-dominated languages.[20] Table 6 presents the various backgrounding and foregrounding passives we have discussed.

All of the types of passives in Table 6 are exemplified except the foregrounding passive in role-dominated languages in which a non-actor becomes the SmP and the actor retains a core argument. We have been unable to find any examples of such a construction. This is not surprising; SmPs are basically generalizations of the notion of actor, as we argued in 4.2, and therefore it is contradictory for a construction to allow a non-actor to function as SmP but retain the actor as a core argument where it is still a potential pivot. All passives in role-dominated languages involve the elimination of the actor from the core of the clause for this reason.

4.5 Antipassive constructions

In 4.1 we discussed some features of the syntax of Dyirbal (Dixon 1972). Dyirbal is a language in which the undergoer is the unmarked choice for PrP in a transitive clause. In order to have the actor occur as PrP an antipassive construction must be used; the actor occurs in the absolutive case and the undergoer in the dative, and the verb is suffixed with -*ŋay*.

(4.95)   a. Balan ḍugumbil   baŋgul yaṛa-ŋgu buṛa-n.
             woman-ABS(U) man-ERG(A)   see-TNS
             'The man saw the woman.'
         b. Bayi yaṛa   bagun ḍugumbil-gu buṛal-ŋa-ɲu.
             man-ABS(A) woman-DAT(U)   see-ANTI-TNS
             'The man saw the woman.'
         c. Bayi yaṛa   bani-ɲu   bagun ḍugumbil-gu
             man-ABS(A) come-TNS woman-DAT(U)
             buṛal-ŋa-ɲu.
             see-ANTI-TNS
             'The man came and saw the woman.'

Table 6 *Summary of passive constructions*

Role-dominated languages				Reference-dominated languages			
Backgrounding passives		Foregrounding passives		Backgrounding passives		Foregrounding passives	
1. A = X (−A ≠ SmP)	Nanai Ulcha Finnish Ute	1. −A = SmP (A ≠ X)	No known example	1. A = X (−A ≠ PrP)	Dutch (Impersonal)	1. −A = PrP (A ≠ X)	Lango
2. A = X (−A = SmP)	Choctaw Chichewa (-ka mediopass.)	2. −A = SmP (A = X)	Chichewa (-edw pass.) Swahili	2. A = X (−A = PrP)	Spanish (se mediopass.) German (sich mediopass., sein passive)	2. −A = PrP (A = X)	German (werden passive) English Tzotzil Indonesian

A = Actor; −A = Non-actor; X = Non-core (i.e. peripheral or omitted)

    d. Bayi yaṛa   bagun ḍugumbil-gu buṛal-ŋa-ɲu
       man-ABS(A) woman-DAT(U)   see-ANTI-TNS
       wayɲḍi-n.
       go.uphill-TNS
       'The man saw the woman and went uphill.'
       (*'The man saw the woman and [she] went uphill.')

The antipassive version of (4.95a) is presented in (4.95b), and in (4.95c) and (4.95d) the actor PrP is the target and controller of NP ellipsis. Thus the antipassive construction in Dyirbal performs the same basic function as the foregrounding passives in German and English of allowing alternative choices for PrP status. In German and English the actor in the PrP is a simple transitive clause, while in Dyirbal it is the undergoer. Foregrounding passives allow non-actors to occur as PrP, and the Dyirbal antipassive permits non-undergoers to be the PrP. Hence they are functionally parallel constructions. This is illustrated in Table 7.

Table 7 *Foregrounding passive and antipassive*

		I	II
1. Basic pattern	intransitive	S	S
	transitive	A = Prp	U = PrP
2. Altered pattern		Passive	Antipassive
		-A = PrP	-U = Prp

In a system of type I the choices for the PrP in the basic pattern follow the morphological case-marking pattern of a language like German: the A and S are treated alike as the PrP to the exclusion of the undergoer. This morphological pattern is usually termed *accusative*, and we will extend this term to refer to syntactic systems of type I in which the actor is the PrP in the basic pattern. Similarly, the choice of the PrP in the basic pattern in systems of type II parallels ergative case-marking patterns: the undergoer S is a PrP to the exclusion of the A. Accordingly, type II syntactic systems will be called *ergative*. Thus in a language which is syntactically accusative, the foregrounding passive functions to allow non-actors to occur as PrP, whereas in syntactically ergative languages the *foregrounding antipassive* serves to permit non-undergoers to occur as PrP. It must be noted that the syntactic and morphological patterns of a PrP language need not coincide. It is possible for a language to be morphologically ergative and syntactically accusative. Tzotzil, as we saw in 4.4, is an example of this. (See also Van Valin 1981a; 7.4.)

Universally, there is a distinction between two types of antipassives parallel to the difference between foregrounding and backgrounding passives. The foregrounding antipassive illustrated by the Dyirbal construction in (4.95) presents non-undergoer arguments as PrP to meet the constraints involved in the linking of clauses in discourse. The backgrounding antipassive demotes the undergoer to peripheral status, normally suppressing it entirely from the clause.

All languages with PrP selection following an ergative pattern possess foregrounding antipassives which allow the actor to occur as the PrP in order to meet the general coreference constraints associated with PrPs. In Dyirbal (examples (4.95) above), the antipassive marks the actor as the PrP and the undergoer is demoted to peripheral status, marked by the dative (or ergative) case. Foregrounding antipassives of this kind also occur in Yidiɲ (Australia; Dixon 1977) and Greenlandic Eskimo (Woodbury 1977).

(4.96) a. Waguḍa-ŋgu buɲa-∅   giba:l.   (Yidiɲ)
            man-ERG(A) woman-ABS(U) scratch-PST
            'The man scratched the woman.'

       b. Wagu:ḍa-∅   giba-:ḍi-ɲu
            man-ABS(A) scratch-ANTIPAST
            buɲa:-nda.
            woman-DAT(U)
            'The man scratched the woman.'

(4.97) a. Arna-p   niqi-∅   niri-vaa.   (Eskimo)
            woman-ERG(A) meat-ABS(U) eat-INDIC/3sg
            'The woman ate the meat.'

       b. Arnaq-∅   niqi-mik   niri-NNig-puq.
            woman-ABS(A) meat-I(U) eat-ANTI-INDIC/3sg
            'The woman ate some of the meat.'

In these examples the (a) sentences are simple ergatively marked basic clauses. The actor is in the ergative case and the undergoer in the absolutive. The (b) examples are antipassive constructions. The actor is now case marked as absolutive, and the undergoer

is marked as a peripheral argument in the dative case in Yidiɲ
(parallel to Dyirbal), and in the instrumental case in Eskimo. In
both Yidiɲ and Eskimo the antipassive allows the actor to occur
as PrP, in contrast to the basic choice of undergoer, and the undergoer occurs as an optional peripheral constituent.

In addition to foregrounding antipassives, many languages also
possess *backgrounding antipassives*. Backgrounding antipassives
function to demote the undergoer to peripheral status, and in this
way they parallel backgrounding passives in which the actor is
made peripheral. The verb in an antipassive construction is intransitive so the A is case marked as an S, in the absolutive case.
As with backgrounding passives, languages have a range of backgrounding antipassive constructions. The most typical construction is that in which the undergoer is suppressed entirely and
removed from the clause. This again parallels the widespread
actorless backgrounding passive construction. The examples
below are from Yidiɲ and Bandjalang (Australia; Crowley 1978).

(4.98) a. Yiɲḍu:-ŋ   buɲa:-ŋ   mayi-∅
            this-ERG woman-ERG(A) vegetables-ABS(U)
            buga-ŋ.   (Yidiɲ)
            eat-PRES
            'This woman is eating vegetables.'

        b. Yiŋu-∅   buɲa-∅   buga-:ḍi-ŋ
            this-ABS woman-ABS(A) eat-ANTI-PRES
            'This woman is eating.'

(4.99) a. Mali-yu   ḍa:ḍam-bu   mala-∅   bulan-∅
            that-ERG child-ERG(A) that-ABS meat-ABS(U)
            ḍa-ila.   (Bandjalang)
            eat-PRES
            'The child is eating that meat.'

        b. Mala-∅   ḍa:ḍam-∅   ḍa-le-ila.
            that-ABS child-ABS(A) eat-ANTI-PRES
            'The child is eating.'

These examples illustrate the basic backgrounding antipassive
function of undergoer suppression. In the basic transitive clauses
of (a), we have the normal transitive pattern with the verb having
the actor argument in the ergative and the undergoer in the absolu-

tive. The (b) sentences exemplify the backgrounding antipassive. The undergoer does not appear in the clause, and the actor is PrP, case marked as absolutive.

This type of undergoer-suppression antipassive has an interesting specialization in many languages. It often serves as the means of reflexivization. The undergoer is removed from the clause under coreference with the actor, and this is indicated by the antipassive affix in the verb.

(4.100) Wagu:ḍa-∅   bambi-:ḍi-nu.   (Yidiɲ)
         man-ABS(A) cover-ANTI-PST
         'The man has covered himself.'

(4.101) Bayi yaɽa   buyba-yiri-ɲu.   (Dyirbal)
         man-ABS(A) hide-ANTI-TNS
         'The man hid himself.'

In these reflexive examples the undergoer has been suppressed under coreferentiality with the actor, and this is signaled by the antipassive suffix on the verb. This is a backgrounding antipassive function. In Yidiɲ all antipassives whether backgrounding or foregrounding are marked with the suffix *-:ḍi*, but in Dyirbal foregrounding antipassives are generally marked with *-ŋay* (see (4.95) above) and backgrounding antipassives with *-riy* (Heath 1979, Dixon 1979b).

While the languages discussed so far have all exhibited PrP selection of the type characteristic of ergative languages, backgrounding antipassives, unlike foregrounding ones, are not restricted to this type of language. This is because they primarily affect the status of the undergoer independent of pivot considerations. Languages with PrP selection on an accusative pattern, as well as role-dominated languages, also have backgrounding antipassives. Languages with foregrounding passives and backgrounding antipassives are possible, and examples are found in the Mayan language family. We have already seen in our discussion of Tzotzil above that while it is morphologically ergative, it is syntactically accusative, with a basic selection of actor as PrP and a foregrounding passive which places the undergoer as PrP. But Mayan languages also have backgrounding antipassives, i.e. ones which put the undergoer outside the core. The Tzotzil examples are from

John Haviland (personal communication) and the Jacaltec examples from Datz (1980).

(4.102) a. S-mil-ox-Ø   li   Anton e.   (Tzotzil)
            3ERG-kill-PST-3ABS ART Anton
            'Someone killed Anton,' or 'Anton killed someone.'
        b. Mil-Ø-wan   li   Anton e.
            kill-3ABS-ANTI ART Anton
            'Anton killed [someone].'

(4.103) a. X-Ø-s-mak   naj   ix.   (Jacaltec)
            TNS-3ABS-3ERG-hit CL/he CL/she

            'He hit her.'
        b. X-Ø-mak-wa   naj   y-in
            ASP-3ABS-hit-ANTI CL/he 3ERG-on
            ix.
            CL/she
            'He hit on her.'

The Tzotzil sentence in (4.102a) is ambiguous as to whether the postverbal NP *li Anton e* 'Anton' is the actor or undergoer, as the verb is inflected for both third-person-singular actor and undergoer. In (4.102b), however, the occurrence of the suffix -*wan* indicates that the undergoer has been eliminated, and consequently *li Anton e* can only be interpreted as the actor. Thus the -*wan* construction in Tzotzil is a backgrounding antipassive which removes the undergoer from the clause. A similar situation can be found in Jacaltec. The addition of the -*wa* suffix to a transitive verb signals the removal of the undergoer from the core of the clause. It may still occur as a peripheral oblique NP as in (4.103b), and its peripheral status is confirmed by the fact that it may not be questioned, clefted, or relativized upon as it could be in (4.103a). The undergoer may also be deleted altogether as in Jacaltec, yielding *x-Ø-mak-wa* 'he hit [something]'. There is also a construction in Jacaltec in which the undergoer is incorporated into the predicate, losing its status as an independent argument; it is illustrated in (4.104), from Datz (1980).

(4.104) ẍ-∅-mak-wi   ix   naj.
TNS-3ABS-hit-ANTI woman CL/he
'He hits women (women-hits).'

The incorporated undergoer *ix* 'woman' must be generic, and it cannot be modified by noun classifiers, adjectives, or demonstratives. Other examples of ergative languages with incorporating antipassives are Chukchee (Comrie 1978) and Greenlandic Eskimo (Sadock 1980).

There is yet another type of backgrounding antipassive in which the undergoer is still present but is a peripheral argument marked as oblique. These backgrounding antipassive constructions contrast with the normal ergative construction in expressing the incompleteness of the action as it effects the undergoer. Note these backgrounding antipassive examples from Kabardian (Northwest Caucasian, USSR; Catford 1975) and west Circassian (Northwest Caucasian, USSR; Comrie 1978).

(4.105) a. ħe-m   q̇ʷ$ı$pŝħe-r   je-dzaq'e. (Kabardian)
dog-ERG(A) bone-ABS(U) bite
'The dog bites the bone (through to the marrow).'
b. ħe-r   q̇ʷ$ı$pŝħe-m je-w-dzaq'e.
dog-ABS(A) bone-ERG ANTI-bite
'The dog is gnawing the bone.'

(4.106) a. Piśaśa-m   chəy-ər   (West Circassian)
girl-ERG(A) cherkesska-ABS(U)
yadə.
3sg-sews-3sg-TRANS
'The girl is sewing the cherkesska.'
b. Piśaśa-r   chəy-əm   yada.
girl-ABS(A) cherkesska-L 3sg-sews-INTR
'The girl is sewing away at the cherkesska.'

In both of these examples the ergative construction in (a) means that the undergoer is completely affected; and in the case of (4.106) it signals the bringing into being of the undergoer. In the antipassive constructions in (b), the undergoer is only partially or superficially affected by the action. The change effected by the backgrounding antipassive is from a normal transitive clause with ergative case marking to the antipassive intransitive clause in which the actor is case marked as absolutive and the undergoer as locative, reflecting its status as a peripheral argument. There is a change in verbal inflection in (4.106) from transitive in (a) to intransitive in (b).

In all of the antipassive examples examined thus far, each type of antipassive has the other type as a side effect; foregrounding the actor involves backgrounding the undergoer, and vice versa. In the discussion of passives in 4.4, we saw that these two phenomena are logically independent of each other, at least with respect to passivization. Given the strong functional parallelism between passive and antipassive constructions, it is reasonable to assume that these phenomena should be independent in anti-passivization as well. A very important kind of backgrounding passive was the type found in Nanai, Finnish, and Ute, illustrated in (4.74), in which the actor is removed from the clause and no other argument assumes pivot status. This is an example of back-grounding without concomitant foregrounding. The antipassive equivalent of this would have the form in (4.107b), in which the undergoer is eliminated from the clause and the actor remains in the ergative case.

(4.107)   a.   NP-ERG(A) NP-ABS(U) Verb[active]
          b.   NP-ERG(A)   ∅   Verb[antipassive]

We have been unable to find any examples of constructions of this type. The fourth logical possibility would be one in which the actor appears as the pivot and the undergoer remains a core argument; this is the antipassive analog of the Lango passive construction in (4.82)–(4.86). This type of antipassive is attested in the Philippine focus system discussed in 4.3. We argued there that some Philippine languages are basically ergative, and consequently the various non-undergoer-focus forms are antipassives. Examples from Sama are repeated below.

(4.108)   a.   ∅-bis   ku   tukul.   (=4.49)
               U F-borrow 1sgA hammer (PrP)
               'I borrowed the hammer.'
          b.   N-bis   aku   tukul.
               A F-borrow 1sgPrP hammer
               'I borrowed a hammer.'

The actor-focus form in (4.108b) is an antipassive because it allows a non-undergoer to be the PrP. The significant thing about this construction is that the undergoer remains a core argument. The morphological marking of the undergoer *tukul* 'hammer' is the same in both constructions. It is difficult to find syntactic evidence that it is a core argument, because there are no constructions which differentiate between a non-pivot core undergoer and a peripheral undergoer. Nevertheless, it receives the morphological coding of a core argument, unlike the undergoers in the Dyirbal, Yidiɲ and Eskimo antipassives. This is a foregrounding antipassive, because it is used to allow non-undergoers to meet the syntactic constraints on relativization discussed in 4.3, i.e. only the focused NP can be relativized. There is an analogous constraint on WH-question formation to the effect that only a focused core argument may be preposed in a question, and accordingly the antipassive allows non-undergoer core arguments to be questioned. Peripheral arguments need not be focused in order to be questioned, and there is a separate set of question words for them. (Data from Walton 1983.)

(4.109) a. daing Ø-b'lli   d'nda ma   onde'.
            fish UF-buy woman OBL child
            'the fish that the woman bought for the child'

         b. d'nda Ø-b'lli   daing ma   onde'.
            woman UF-buy fish   OBL child
            *'the woman who bought the fish for the child'
            (OK: 'the woman which the fish bought for the child')

         c. d'nda N-b'lli daing ma   onde'.
            woman AF-buy fish   OBL child
            'the woman who bought fish for the child'

         d. onde' Ø-b'lli-an d'nda daing.
            child UF-buy-L woman fish
            'the child for whom the woman bought fish'

(4.110) a. Say Ø-nda' d'nda?
            who UF-see woman
            'Who did the woman see?' (*'Who saw the woman?')

         b. Say N-nda' d'nda?
            who AF-see woman
            'Who saw the woman?' (*'Who did the woman see?')

The single argument of an intransitive verb can always be involved in these constructions, and consequently their pivot is S/U, an ergative pivot like that of Dyirbal. There is thus strong evidence for syntactic ergativity in Sama, and this reinforces the claim made in 4.3 that some Philippine languages are ergative.

In 4.3 we discussed whether Tagalog should be classified as ergative and concluded that it cannot be classified as either ergative or accusative on purely morphological grounds. A number of examples are repeated below.

(4.111) a. B-in-ili-∅   ng lalake ang isda sa tindahan.
          PERF-buy-THF A man PrP fish L store
          'The man bought the fish at the store.'
    b. B-um-ili ang lalake ng isda sa tindahan.
          AF-buy PrP man TH fish L store
          'The man bought some fish at the store.'
    c. B-in-il-han   ng lalake ng isda ang tindahan.
          PERF-buy-LF A man TH fish PrP store
          'The man bought some fish at the store.'

There is some syntactic evidence which seems to point to syntactic ergativity similar to that in Sama. With respect to topicalization and WH-question formation, there are distinct strategies for core and peripheral arguments, and only the constructions involving core arguments are relevant to the question of ergativity. We noted in 4.2 that a core argument may occur in the preverbal topic position only if it is the focused NP, i.e. the PrP. This was illustrated in (4.28), repeated here in (4.112).

(4.112) a. Ang isda 'y b-in-ili-∅   ng lalake sa
          PrP fish *ay* PERF-buy-THF A man L
          palengke.
          market
    b. *Ng lalake 'y   b-in-ili-∅   ang isda sa
          A man *ay* PERF-buy-THF PrP fish L
          palengke.
          market

The same constraint holds with regard to the formation of WH-questions; the preverbal question word must be the focused NP of the clause.

(4.113) a.   Ano ang b-in-ili-∅   mo?
             WH PrP PERF-buy-THF 2sgA
             'What did you buy?'
         b. *Ano ng b-um-ili ka?
             WH TH AF-buy 2sgPrP
             'What did you buy?'

Since these two constructions involve only core arguments, the arguments presented in Cena (1979) for patient focus as the unmarked focus type with a transitive verb (see p. 137) have more force than when both core and oblique focus types are considered. If patient focus is the unmarked focus choice with a transitive verb, it means that topicalization and WH-question formation have an S/P pivot, since the single arguments of intransitive verbs can always be topicalized and questioned. This is an ergative pivot like that in Sama and Dyirbal, and thus these two constructions provide evidence of syntactic ergativity in Tagalog. This is particularly striking in light of the clear accusative patterns found in verbal morphology (see p. 138). Tagalog appears to be a language which combines accusative morphology with at least a limited degree of ergative syntax. In the survey on ergative systems reported in Dixon (1979a), no combination such as this is found. If these are in fact ergative constructions, then the actor-focus forms would have to be considered foregrounding antipassives, since they are used to meet syntactic constraints on unambiguously pragmatically motivated constructions.

Another example of a foregrounding antipassive construction is found in certain Mayan languages. According to Larsen & Norman (1979), in the Kanjobalan, Mamean, and Quichean subgroups of the Mayan family there is a syntactic constraint like the one discussed above which prevents ergative arguments from being questioned, clefted, or relativized. This is illustrated in the following Jacaltec examples from Craig (1977).

(4.114) a. X-∅-w-il   naj
             PST-3ABS-1sgERG-see CL/man
             x-∅-s-mak   ix.
             PST-3ABS-3ERG-hit CL/she
             'I saw the man whom she hit.'
             (*'I saw the man who hit her.')

b. Ha'   ix   x-∅-(y)-il   naj.
   CLEFT CL/she PST-3ABS-3ERG-see CL/he
   'It is she whom he saw.' (*'It is she who saw him.')
c. Mac x-∅-(y)-il   .   naj.
   WH PST-3ABS-3ERG-see CL/he
   'Whom did he see?' (*'Who saw him?')

In order for an ergative NP to be clefted, questioned, or relativized upon, a special construction must be used, as in (4.115).

(4.115) a. X-∅-w-il   naj
            PST-3ABS-3ERG-see CL/man
            x-∅-__-mak-ni   ix.
            PST-3ABS-__-hit-SUFF CL/she
            'I saw the man who hit her.'
            (*'I saw the man whom she hit.')
         b. Ha'   ix   x-∅-__-'il-ni   naj.
            CLEFT CL/she PST-3ABS-__-see-SUFF CL/he
            'It is she who saw him.' (*'It is she whom he saw.')
         c. Mac x-∅-__-'il-ni   naj.
            WH PST-3ABS-__-see-SUFF CL/he
            'Who saw him?' (*'Whom did he see?')

Note that the undergoers in these sentences are not oblique, as in (4.103b), and are still cross-referenced on the verb, as in (4.103a). This shows that they are still core arguments.

There is some controversy as to whether these constructions should be called antipassives. Larsen & Norman (1979) argue that they are analogous to the Dyirbal -*ŋay* construction and hence are antipassives. Craig (1979a), on the other hand, disputes their status as a true antipassive construction. She assumes that a voice construction necessarily involves changes in the grammatical status of both 'subject' and 'object' as compared to the active construction, and since there is no change in the syntactic status of the 'object', she concludes that this is not a voice construction and therefore not an antipassive. However, we have seen a great deal of evidence in these last two sections that this assumption about the nature of voice oppositions is invalid; by this criterion the constructions in Nanai, Ulcha, Finnish, Ute, Dutch, and Philippine languages would not count as voice constructions. We will, therefore, follow Larsen & Norman (1979) in analyzing these forms as antipassives marked by *-ni*, and they are clearly foregrounding antipassives in that they are used to present actors as pivots to meet syntactic restrictions on these three constructions. Jacaltec and certain other Mayan languages present a second example of a foregrounding antipassive without concomitant backgrounding of the undergoer.

The typology of antipassive constructions may be summarized as in Table 8. Only backgrounding antipassives are found in role-dominated languages, demoting the undergoer to the periphery with varying effects. Reference-dominated languages may have both backgrounding and foregrounding antipassives.[21] The backgrounding antipassives in languages with PrPs have functions parallel to those in role-dominated languages, while the foregrounding antipassives present the actor as PrP in order to meet the constraints of NP ellipsis for clause linkage in ongoing discourse, relativization, question formation, or clefting, depending upon the language.

Table 8 *Typology of antipassive constructions*

Backgrounding antipassives		Foregrounding antipassives	
1. U = X (A ≠ Pvt)	No known examples	1. A = PrP (U ≠ X)	Sama Jacaltec (*-ni*)
2. U = X (A = Pvt)	Bandjalang Dyirbal (*-riy-*) Yidiɲ Tzotzil Jacaltec (*-wa, -wi*) Kabardian West Circassian	2. A = PrP (U = X)	Dyirbal (*-ŋay-*) Yidiɲ Eskimo

A = Actor; U = Undergoer; Pvt = Pivot; X = Non-core

4.6 Universal constructions and individual grammars

In the previous sections we developed a typology of passive and antipassive constructions. This allows us to provide universal characterizations of these constructions as in Table 9.

Table 9 *Universal passive and antipassive constructions*

	Passive	Antipassive
Foregrounding	-A = PrP	-U = PrP
Backgrounding	A = X	U = X

We pointed out the further generalization that with few exceptions the foregrounding constructions have the effects of the backgrounding constructions as a by-product. In addition, it is generally the case that the verb or verb complex has some indication that the clause is (anti)passive, either by a verbal affix or auxiliary. The only exceptions to this generalization in the languages discussed above are Lango and Fijian.

The universal statements of passive and antipassive in Table 9 provide the basis for the description of these constructions in individual languages (see 1.2). For example, the English foregrounding passives may be characterized as in (4.116); parenthesized parts of the universal statement indicate common but non-definitive aspects of the construction.

$$(4.116)\ \text{Universal} \qquad \text{English}$$
$$-A = PrP \qquad U = PrP$$
$$(A = X) \qquad A = X\!: by\ NP,\ \emptyset$$
$$(V = V_{passive}) \qquad V = V_{passive}\!: be + PASTPART$$

In English the undergoer is the PrP in the core-initial slot; the non-core actor may either appear as the object of *by* or be omitted altogether. The positioning of these elements in a clause need not be specified in this statement, because it falls out automatically in terms of the layered structure of the English clause given in (3.45). That this construction is defined primarily by $U = PrP$ indicates that discourse factors influence its occurrence. If the top line were $A = X$, then, we would be dealing with a construction whose main motivation is the demotion or, more likely, the suppression of the actor.

As an example of a language-specific antipassive statement, the Dyirbal -*ŋay* construction is characterized in (4.117).

(4.117) Universal   Dyirbal
    -U = PrP   A = PrP
    (U = X)   U = X: DAT/ERG, $\emptyset$
    (V = $V_{antipassive}$)   V = $V_{antipassive}$: V + *ŋay*

The actor in a Dyirbal antipassive is thê PrP, signaled by the absolutive case (for full NPs), and the undergoer may either be omitted or appear in either the dative or ergative-instrumental case, depending upon whether there is already a dative-case-marked NP in the clause.

At the end of 3.3.1, we briefly discussed how the morphosyntactic status of the arguments of a verb may be determined from its logical structure by means of the notion of actor and undergoer, the hierarchy of accessibility/interpretation in Figure 1, and rules of preposition assignment developed in that section. We dealt only with active sentences there, and we will now illustrate the relationship between sentence forms and verbal logical structures in both voice types. Voice deals only with the morphosyntactic status of actor and undergoer and not with the determining of which arguments in the logical structure of the verb are linked to them; moreover, it has no effect on preposition assignment (see Chapter 3, n.4).

There is a very important constraint which governs the mapping from logical to syntactic structure and likewise the interpretation of logical structures from syntactic structures. This is the *completeness constraint*, stated below.

All of the arguments explicitly specified in the logical structure of a verb must be realized syntactically in any sentence containing that verb, and vice versa.[22]

In simple sentences this constraint specifies that the number of syntactic-argument positions in a clause must match up with the number of filled semantic-argument positions in the logical structure of the verb in the clause.

The logical structure we will analyze is that of *load*, given in (4.118).

(4.118) [DO (Bill, [**do′** (Bill)])] CAUSE [BECOME **be-at′** (hay, truck)]   (=2.51)

This logical structure may be realized in four ways in English,

depending upon undergoer choice and voice. It is mapped onto
the basic English clause structure given in (4.119).

(4.119) $_{OP}[_{IP}[_C[NP \quad _N[VERB]_N \quad (NP)]_C \quad (PP) \quad \ldots \quad (PP)]_{IP}$
$(PP) \ldots (PP)]_{OP}$

The semantic relations of the arguments of *load* are *Bill* = agent,
hay = theme, and *truck* = locative. *Bill* must be the actor by virtue
of being an agent, according to Figure 1. Either *hay* or *truck* may
be the undergoer, with the other being a prepositionally marked
inner peripheral argument. These two possibilities are displayed
in (4.120).

(4.120) a. *Bill*   = agent   = actor
       hay   = theme   = undergoer
       truck = locative = *on*____

     b *Bill*   = agent   = actor
       truck = locative = undergoer
       hay   = theme   = *with*____

Having established the core arguments and the prepositional
marking of the non-core argument, we may now look at the role
of voice, which, as noted above, relates solely to the morphosyntactic status of the two core arguments. Both of the possibilities
in (4.120) have active and passive versions. The active forms with
the actor as PrP are given in (4.121), the passive forms with the
undergoer as PrP in (4.122).

(4.121) a. Bill loaded the hay on the truck.   (= 4.120a)
     b. Bill loaded the truck with the hay.   (= 4.120b)
(4.122) a. The hay was loaded on the truck by Bill. (= 4.120a)
     b. The truck was loaded with the hay by Bill.
       (= 4.120b)

If we were to reverse this process, i.e. to attempt to link the
NPs in (4.121)–(4.122) with the logical structure $[DO(x,[\ldots])]$
CAUSE [BECOME **be-at**$'$ (y, z)], all we would need to know
would be the voice of the verb, which would tell us whether the
PrP is actor or undergoer, and the preposition of the inner
peripheral argument, which would tell us indirectly the semantic
relation of the undergoer. The voice of *load* in these sentences

signals that *Bill* is the actor, and in terms of Figure 1 we would expect him to be an agent. This logical structure does have an agent argument, x, and therefore $Bill = x$. Undergoer is more complex. *Hay* is the undergoer in (4.121a) and (4.122a), and it cooccurs with a locative NP, *truck*. The logical structure of *load* has only two non-agent arguments, a locative and a theme, and since *truck* must be the locative by virtue of its preposition, *hay* must be y, the theme. Filling in NPs for the variables we arrive at the logical structure in (4.118). In the other pair of sentences, *truck* is the undergoer, and *hay* is the peripheral argument marked by *with*. *With*, unlike *on*, does not uniquely identify its NP as having a particular semantic relation. Given that the two non-agent arguments of *load* are theme and locative, we can deduce that the NP marked by *with* is the theme, since non-core (i.e. non-undergoer) themes, but not locatives, occur with *with*. Hence the undergoer must be the locative argument, and we again arrive at $hay = y$ and $truck = z$, as in the logical structure in (4.118). These two possibilities may be summarized as in (4.123).

(4.123) a. *Bill* = actor = agent
             hay = undergoer = theme
             truck = *on*____ = locative
         b. *Bill* = actor = agent
             truck = undergoer = locative
             hay = *with*____ = theme

All of these possible mappings and interpretations meet the completeness constraint (p. 183). Examples (4.123) and (4.120) differ according to the perspective of the analysis. If we start from something like (4.118), we must first determine the semantic relations of the arguments, the actor and undergoer choices, and then the preposition assignment. If, on the other hand, we start from actual sentences as in (4.121)–(4.122), determining which NPs are actor and undergoer is primary, and their semantic relations are deduced from them plus the prepositions marking the inner peripheral arguments. This is summarized in Figure 5. Thus the system developed in Chapters 2 and 3 allows both mapping from logical structures to sentences and interpretation from sentences to logical structures.

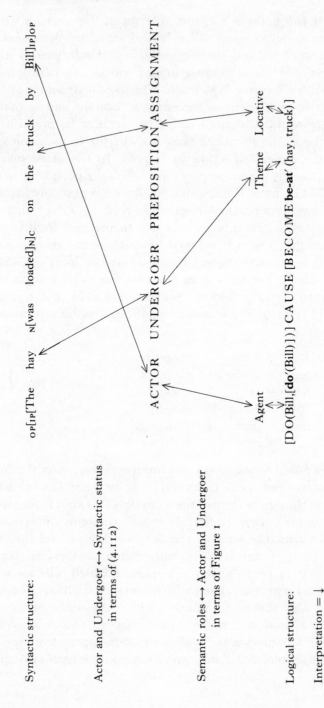

Syntactic structure:

Actor and Undergoer ↔ Syntactic status
    in terms of (4.112)

Semantic roles ↔ Actor and Undergoer
    in terms of Figure 1

Logical structure:

Interpretation = ↓
Mapping   = ↑

Figure 5 Mapping between logical structure and syntactic structure

5 *Juncture and operators*

5.0 Introduction

In this chapter we begin the presentation of the theory of clause-linkage systems. Specifically we will develop the theory of juncture – the level at which clauses are joined. In 3.2 we presented a theory of clause structure in terms of a layered structure of grammatical units, smaller units within larger. We will employ these layered units of the clause as fundamental analytic categories in RRG. Universally, it is appropriate to propose a tripartite division of clausal units. These units are the nucleus, the core, and the periphery. The innermost layer of the clause is the nucleus. It corresponds to the predicate, generally a verb. The next layer is the core. It consists of the core arguments of the verb, normally the pivot plus additional arguments, depending on the valence of the verb. The outermost layer is the periphery. The peripheral layer consists of all other constituents of the clause, typically setting NPs and secondary participants, which are arguments represented in the logical structures of the verb. See 3.2, 3.3.1, and 3.3.3 for detailed discussion.

We may represent the layered structure of the clause diagrammatically as Figure 6; see also Figure 2.

$$_P[\text{(Oblique NPs) } _C[\text{NP (NP)}_N[\text{Predicate}]_N]_C]_P$$

PERIPHERY   CORE   NUCLEUS

Figure 6 The layered structure of the clause

5.1 Juncture

The application of this system to the analysis of interclausal
relations is very straightforward. As a working hypothesis we propose that a token of any layer – nuclear, core, or peripheral – may
be joined to any other token of its same type. Constructions built
up by this means we will refer to as a *juncture* of the corresponding
type, and any individual member unit of this juncture we will
refer to by the technical term *junct*. Peripheral junctures will be
represented by a single line (–), core by a double line (=),
and nuclear by three parallel lines (≡). The resulting junctures
may be represented as in Figure 7. A nuclear juncture is a construction with a complex nucleus. It is a single unit, and all core
and peripheral arguments are arguments of this complex nuclear
element. In core-level junctures two cores, each with its own
nucleus and core arguments, are joined together to form a larger
complex core. The peripheral arguments must be shared by both
cores, as they form a single complex unit within the peripheral
layer. Peripheral junctures involve the joining of two clauses with
independent peripheries. Differences within the juncts are permitted at the level of juncture and below, but everything above
it must be shared by both juncts (see 6.2 for more detailed discussion).

$$_P[\,(NP)\ldots(NP\ _C[NP\,(NP)\ _N[\text{Predicate}]_N]_C]_P\ -$$
$$_P[\,(NP)\ldots(NP)\ _C[NP\,(NP)\ _N[\text{Predicate}]_N]_C]_P$$

Peripheral Juncture

$$_P[\,(NP\ldots(NP)\ _C[NP\,(NP)\ _N[\text{Predicate}]_N]_C\ =$$
$$_C[NP\,(NP)\ _N[\text{Predicate}]_N]_C]_P$$

Core Juncture

$$_P[\,(NP)\ldots(NP)\ _C[NP\,(NP)\ _N[\text{Predicate}]_{NN}\ \equiv\ _N[\text{Predicate}]_N]_C]_P$$

Nuclear Juncture

Figure 7 Juncture types

The simplest kind of constructions which illustrate junctures at the nuclear and core layers are serial-verb constructions. They are constructions in which verbs sharing a common core argument are merely juxtaposed with no complementizers or intervening conjunctions. They are common in many languages, especially those of West Africa, Southeast and East Asia and Papua New Guinea.

(5.1) a. Igede (Nigeria) (Pike 1967:3)
        àhì hû   óló   chū.
        we take load put.on.head
        'We carried the load.'

     b. Yoruba (Nigeria) (Bamgbose 1974:17)
        ó   mú   ìwé   wá.
        3sg took book came
        'He brought the book.'

     c. Yessan–Mayo (Papua New Guinea) (Foreman 1974:100)
        An rini peti wur-tí.
        1sg him send go. inside-FUT
        'I will send him inside.'

     d. Vagala (Ghana) (Pike 1967:4)
        ù   kpá kíyzèé mòng ówl.
        3sg take knife cut   meat
        'He cut the meat with a knife.'

     e. Thai (A. Diller, personal communication)
        Dèk khɨɨn nansɨ̌ hây khruu.
        boy return book give teacher
        'The boy returned the book to the teacher.'

     f. Mandarin (Thompson 1973)
        Tā lā-kāi   le   mén.
        3sg pull-open PERF door
        'He pulled the door open'

Serial verb constructions always contain two or more predicates, sharing a common core argument. It is not necessary for the verbs to share all core arguments, as (5.1d) and (5.1e) indicate. In these two examples, the verbs have the same actor, but different undergoers.

In an analysis in terms of the layered structure of the clause, these constructions are composed of junctures of nuclei or cores.[1]

Serial-verb constructions are thus of two basic types, those formed by nuclear junctures and those from core junctures. The contrast between nuclear-layer and core-layer junctures is discussed in Olson (1981). His discussion concerns Barai, a Papuan language of Papua New Guinea. He supplies the following examples.

(5.2) a. Fu fi fase isoe.
            3sg sit letter write
            'He sat down and wrote a letter.'
        b. Fu fase fi isoe.
            3sg letter sit wrote
            'He sat writing a letter.'

(5.2a) and (5.2b) correspond to core layer and nuclear layer junctures respectively, as represented by the structures in (5.3).

(5.3) a.

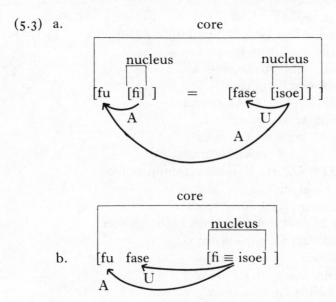

In the core-layer juncture of (5.2a) and (5.3a) the core arguments of each nucleus are selected independently and are core arguments only of their specific nuclei, although the type of core-layer serial construction in (5.2a) requires the actors of the two nuclei to be coreferential. The nuclear juncture in (5.2b) and (5.3b) requires a single core for the composite nucleus. Thus, the complex nucleus [fi ≡ isoe] takes a single set of actor and undergoer arguments.

Olson (1981) presents several arguments to support this analysis. The first concerns the intonation patterns over (5.2a and b). Barai intonation is characterized by an early sharp rise in pitch, coming to an early peak over the first high-pitched stressed syllable. Then, there is a gradual fall over the remainder of the contour with the final syllable dropping sharply in pitch. The core-layer juncture shows two of these contours, with the second contour beginning at the seam of the juncture:

(5.4) -Fu fi fase isoe.
     3sg sit letter write

However, the nuclear-layer juncture only has one such contour:

(5.5) Fu fase fi isoe.
     3sg letter sit write

Two intonation contours in (5.4) as opposed to one in (5.5) argues that (5.4) is a more complex structure than (5.5). In the analysis presented here, this is in fact the case. Sentence (5.4) consists of two separate nuclei and their individually associated cores joined together to form a complex core unit, whereas (5.5) consists only of two nuclei joined together to form a single complex nucleus associated with a single common core.

Another argument concerns the scope of certain adverbs. Barai has a class of adverbials which modify the nucleus like *isema* 'wrongly'. As nuclear-level modifiers, they take a whole nucleus, whether simple or complex, as their scope. Thus, in a core-layer juncture they may modify either verb, but in a nuclear-level juncture, they must modify both simultaneously.

(5.6) a. Fu isema fi fase isoe.
       3sg wrongly sit letter write
       'He sat wrongly and wrote a letter.'
   b. Fu fi fase isema isoe.
       3sg sit letter wrongly write
       'He sat down and wrote the letter wrongly.'
   c. Fu fase isema fi isoe.
       3sg letter wrongly sit write
       'He wrongly sat writing a letter.'

    d. *Fu fase fi isema   isoe
       3sg letter sit wrongly write

In (5.6a–b) the adverb is independently modifying either one of the nuclei. This is grammatical because these are core-layer junctures. However (5.6c–d) are nuclear-layer junctures and, as *isema* is a nuclear modifier, it must modify both verbs simultaneously as in (5.6c). Example (5.6d), in which it occurs between the two verbs and can only modify the following verb is ungrammatical.

A parallel constraint operates with negation. Barai has two negatives. One of them, *ba*, is a peripheral-layer negative which negates the entire clause and roughly means 'it is not the case that'. Interestingly, it is the only element which ever follows the verb in heavily verb-final Barai. This is in keeping with its peripheral status, as the verb is the last core-layer constituent in Barai. The other negative, *naebe*, is, like *isema* above, a nuclear-layer negative and exactly parallels it in behavior.

(5.7) a. Fu naebe fi fase   isoe.
         3sg NEG sit letter write
         'He did not sit down, but did write a letter.'
      b. Fu fi fase   naebe isoe.
         3sg sit letter NEG write
         'He sat down, but did not write a letter.'
      c. Fu fase   naebe fi isoe.
         3sg letter NEG sit write
         'He did not sit and write a letter.'
      d.*Fu fase fi naebe isoe.
         3sg letter sit NEG write

Naebe, as a nuclear-layer negative, can modify either nucleus in core-layer junctures, as in (5.7a–b), but must modify both verbs in a nuclear-level juncture, as in (5.7c). Example (5.7d), in which it occurs between the verbs in a nuclear juncture and, thus, could modify only the second, is ungrammatical. These arguments present a convincing case for a distinction between core-layer and nuclear-layer junctures in Barai. A distinction in serial-verb constructions between nuclear and core junctures can also be found in other languages. In the examples in (5.1) above, (5.1c) is an example of a nuclear juncture, while the others are all core junctures. Scrutinizing the examples further, it is noteworthy that only Yessan–Mayo, the language of (5.1c), is verb final, while the others are all verb medial. This brings up the important typological generalization that extensive nuclear junctures are a widespread feature of verb-final serializing languages (see Foley & Olson in press).

Having established the existence of nuclear and core junctures and explored some of the differences between them, we now wish to contrast these with peripheral junctures. Peripheral-layer junctures are those in which two grammatical units with independent peripheries, cores, and nuclei are joined. It is the loosest type of juncture but exhibits the richest inventory of grammatical and semantic distinctions. Core junctures differ from peripheral junctures in generally having strong coreferentiality constraints on the core arguments of the individual cores constituting the juncture. With nuclear junctures, of course, the question does not ever arise, because by definition all members of the junct must have the same core arguments. The most common restriction for core junctures is for A–A or S–A coreference between the cores. The Akan sentence (5.8) from Schachter (1974) exhibits this constraint.

(5.8) Kofi yɛɛ adwuma maa Amma.
       Kofi did work   gave Amma
       'Kofi worked for Amma.'

It is ungrammatical if the actors are different:

(5.9) *Kofi yɛɛ adwuma Kwaku maa Amma.
       Kofi did work   Kwaku gave Amma

This A–A/S–A constraint is widespread among languages with serial–verb constructions, as the following show.

(5.10) a. Thai (A. Diller, personal communication)
            Sùk ʔaw máy maa.
            Sook take wood come
            'Sook brought the wood.'
        b. Yoruba (Stahlke 1970)
            Mo mú ìwé wá   ilé.
            1sg took book come home
            'I brought a book home.'

    c. Igbo (Lord 1975)

    ọ́   gà-fè-rè   ụ́lọ̀ ákwụ́kwọ́.

    3sg go-pass-FACT school

    'He passed the school.'

Other languages are less restrictive and allow core junctures to be formed on the basis of U–A or U–S coreference, as in this Barai example (Olson 1981).

(5.11) Na ki-ia   bu va-e.

       1sg say-3pl 3pl go-PST

       'I spoke to them; (causing) they went' or 'I made them go.'

In this example the undergoer of 'say' is coreferential with the S of 'go'. A causative meaning is usual in core junctures of this type. Examples in other languages with this coreference constraint are:

(5.12) a. Yoruba (Bamgbose 1974)

        Olú lo   aṣọ náà gbó.

        Olu used dress the wore. out

        'Olu used the dress and it wore out' or 'Olu wore the dress out.'

    b. Igbo (Lord 1975)

        ọ́   tụ̀-fù-rù   ákwụ́kwọ́.

        3sg throw-lost-FACT paper

        'He threw the paper and it got lost' or 'He threw away the paper.'

In some cases core-layer junctures can be ambiguous, the interpretation depending on how the coreference constraint is interpreted, as in this example from Thai, supplied by A. Diller (personal communication).

(5.13) John khàp rót chon khwaay taay.

       John drive car collide buffalo die

    1. 'John drove the car, collided with a buffalo, and it (the buffalo) died.'

    2. 'John drove the car, collided with a buffalo, and it (the car) stalled.'

    3. 'John drove the car, collided with a buffalo, and he (John) died.'

Example (5.13) is three ways ambiguous. This ambiguity is determined by whether the S of *taay* 'die' is coreferential with the U of *chon* 'collide' which is *khwaay* 'buffalo' (reading 1), or coreferential with the U of *khàp* 'drive' which is *rót* 'car' (reading 2), or finally, coreferential with the A of *khàp* 'drive' and *chon* 'collide', which is John (reading 3). Thus, readings 1 and 2 arise from differing interpretations of the U–S constraint, whereas reading 3 is by the A–S constraint.

Because peripheral junctures are formed by combining peripheries each with their own nucleus and core we would not expect coreference constraints between core arguments to be built into the formation of the junct. Rather, peripheries can be freely joined to form a variety of different types of peripheral junctures. In such a situation it is clear that determination of coreferentiality of constituents across peripheral junctures can be problematic, and languages have developed a number of devices to accomplish just this end. They will be the subject of Chapter 7; we will illustrate one such device, switch-reference. Switch-reference indicates whether the A or S of one junct in a peripheral juncture is coreferential with that in the following junct, as in these Kewa examples (Franklin 1971).

(5.14) a. Ní réko-a   ágaa lá-lo.   (=4.16)
         1sg stand-SAME.SmP talk say-1sgPRES
         'I stood up and am speaking.'

       b. Ní réka-no   ágaa lá-a.
         1sg stand-DIFF.SmP talk say-3sgPST
         'I stood up and he talked.'

(5.15) a. N'í'. ma-adaalu   yaa-wa   keda
         1sg CAUSE-long be-SAME.SmP heavy
         ma-paa-ru.
         CAUSE-make-1sgPST
         'I made it long and heavy.'

       b. Nipú ma-rúdu   yaa-nia   ní
         3sg   CAUSE-short be-DIFF.SmP 1sg
         ma-adaalu   paa-ru.
         CAUSE-long make-1sgPST
         'He made it short and I made it long.'

Junctures marked by switch reference such as these in Kewa, are clearly peripheral because peripheral constituents are freely permitted in each of the juncts. In (5.14b), for example, it is possible to specify different locations for the two juncts in the juncture. In these examples we have suffixes monitoring the co-referentiality of the actor in the two clauses, -*a*/-*wa* for coreferential actors and -*no*/-*nia* for non-coreferential actors. Peripheral junctures allow such systems because coreferentiality restrictions are not built into the juncture itself, as they are with core-layer junctures.

A second significant difference between core and nuclear junctures, on the one hand, and peripheral, on the other, concerns the elaboration of the morphological marking of the juncture. Nuclear and core junctures are often marked by juxtaposition and the range of possible semantic relations between the two juncts in the juncture is rather restricted. The range of semantic relations in nuclear and core junctures is generally a feature of the nature of the juncture itself. So, for example, core junctures with A–A/S coreference often express a relation of simultaneity between the two juncts and those with U–A/S coreference generally express a causative relation in which an action affecting the undergoer of the first juncture brings about a change of state or action in the second. Because of their relatively restricted range of semantic relations, languages generally have not developed an elaborate morphology for indicating them in nuclear or core junctures. Most commonly, no marking, i.e. simple juxtaposition, is used, but, in any case, the degree of morphological marking is always less for nuclear and core juncture than for peripheral ones. Peripheral junctures are not constrained in their formation in the same way and allow a wide range of semantic relations to exist between the juncts. As a result, languages generally have a large inventory of morphemes to express these relations. English subordinating and coordinating conjunctions are an example of such morphemes. Other languages such as Kewa (Franklin 1971) may use a series of verb affixes to perform this function, often simultaneously functioning as a switch-reference device. We will investigate this in greater detail in Chapter 7.

Core and nuclear junctures also differ from peripheral junctures in that the individual juncts may not be separately specified for tense or mood. Tense and mood, as we shall argue in 5.3, are sentential modifiers, and, since core and nuclear junctures are surrounded by a common outer-peripheral layer, this same tense and mood constraint is understandable. There is no reason to expect this constraint to apply in peripheral junctures, because they allow independent peripheries for the two juncts. Thus, in Akan (Schachter 1974) serial-verb constructions which are junctures at the core layer there is no possible independent tense choice for the verbs of the two juncts.

(5.16) a. Mekɔɔe mebaae.
             1sg went 1sg came
             'I went and came back.'
      b.*Mekɔɔe maba.
             1sg went 1sg have.come

Example (5.16a) is an acceptable serial construction in that both verbs are inflected for past tense. Sentence (5.16b) is ungrammatical because the first verb is inflected for past, but the second for perfect. This kind of sequence of tenses can only be expressed grammatically with a conjoined structure, corresponding to a peripheral juncture.

(5.17) Mekɔɔe na maba.
         1sg went and 1sg have.come
         'I went and have come back.'

Akan serial-verb constructions also require the same mood inflection in each junct.

(5.18) Frɛ Kofi bra.
        call Kofi come
        'Call Kofi and come!'

In (5.18) the imperative mood obligatorily applies to both verbs.

5.2 Serialization and the lexicon

The most widespread function of complex-verb constructions in both nuclear and core junctures is as a valence increaser. A familiar example of the use of junctures to perform this function is found in the well-known periphrastic causative constructions. To form a causative of a verb, i.e. to introduce the new argument of causer for the verb, a special causative auxiliary must be used in a nuclear juncture. (French examples from Aissen 1974.)

(5.19) a. Je le ferai   lire à Jean.
            1sg it will. have read by John
            'I'll have John read it.'
        b.*Je ferai   le lire à Jean.
            1sg will. have it read by John
        c. Je l'ai   laissé chanter à Paul.
            1sg it have let   sing   by Paul
            'I let Paul sing it.'
        d.*J'ai   laissé la chanter à Paul
            1sg have let   it sing   by Paul

Faire (future form: *ferai*) 'make' and *laisser* 'let' are the causative auxiliaries in French. In these examples they are used with the two argument verbs *lire* 'read' and *chanter* 'sing' to allow a third core argument, the causer, to be introduced. There are clearly nuclear junctures because, as we argued in 3.4, the object pronouns governed by the causativized verbs must occur proclitic to the causative verb, i.e. before the complex nucleus, as in (5.19a, c). Examples like (5.19b, d) in which the object pronoun occurs immediately before the causativized verb which governs it, i.e. inside the complex nucleus, are ungrammatical. This parallels the behavior of the Barai nuclear adverbs in (5.6) and (5.7) and demonstrates that the juncture is nuclear.

Many languages have a very productive use of verb serialization to introduce core arguments parallel to the French use of causative auxiliaries. Certain verbs are specialized in use to indicate the addition of specific kinds of core arguments. So given a basic transitive verb, a juncture between that verb and *give* would be formed to introduce a benefactive argument. This juncture could be either at the nuclear or core layer. Cross-linguistically, the most common verbs in this usage are *give*, which adds benefactives or goals, and *take*, which adds instruments, manner NPs, and comitatives. The junctures involved can be either nuclear or core, depending on the language.

Yimas, a language of Papua New Guinea, uses *give* in a nuclear juncture to express a benefactive or goal core argument.

(5.20)   Awt ŋa-kra-yawra-mpi-warasa-ŋa-n.
fire   I M P-2sg-1pl-get-*mpi*-return-give-PRES
'You get and come back with fire for us.'

The goal benefactive 'us' is introduced by *ŋa* 'give' and appears as a core argument with the verbal prefix *kra*- '1pl'. In such constructions Yimas does not distinguish the goal from the benefactive reading.

Many languages use *give* in core junctures to introduce arguments, either as goals or benefactives.

(5.21)   Goals added:
a.   Yoruba (Stahlke 1970)
Mo mú ìwé wá fún ê.
1sg took book came gave 2sg
'I brought you a book.'
b.   Thai (A. Diller, personal communication)
Dèk khỉin nansỉi hây khruu.
boy return book give teacher
'The boy returned the book to the teacher.'

(5.22)   Benefactive added:
a.   Anyi (Van Leynseele 1975)
ǎjó tɔ̌   àlɛ̀ɛ̀ mɑ̃̀ Kaši.
Ajo cook-HAB food give Kasi
'Ajo cooked food for Kasi.'
b.   Kasem (Hewer 1976)
ò sàŋe wùdíu ō pā bá.
3sg cooked food 3sg give 3pl
'She cooked food for them.'

The benefactive reading seems to be favored with activity verbs and the goal, as expected, with motion verbs, but the range of serial constructions with 'give' varies widely from language to language. Furthermore, in some languages, such as Yoruba and Anyi, different constructions are employed for the two meanings (although in Anyi both contain the verb *mã* 'give'). In other languages, such as Yatye, a construction with serial 'give' is ambiguous as to the two possible roles.

'Take' seems associated with the introduction of adverbial-like arguments such as instruments, comitatives, or manner NPs.

Barai uses 'take' in a nuclear juncture to add an instrumental core argument.

(5.23) Fu burede ije   sime abe ufu.
3sg bread   DEF knife take cut
'He cut the bread with a knife.'

Ufu 'cut' is a transitive verb with the core arguments actor and undergoer. In a nuclear juncture with *abe* a further core argument, an instrument semantically, is present in the clause.

In the serializing languages of West Africa the use of 'take' in core junctures to add a range of adverbial-like arguments is extremely widespread, as these examples from Anyi (Van Leynseele 1975), and Yoruba (Stahlke 1970) show.

(5.24) Instrument:
    a. Kòfí fà   dàdìé kpè   nyǎmá   (Anyi)
        Kofi take-HAB knife cut-HAB string
        'Kofi cut the string with a knife.'
    b. Mo fi   àdá   gé igi nâ.   (Yoruba)
        1sg take machete cut tree the
        'I cut the tree with a machete.'

(5.25) Manner:
    a. Kòfí fà   ŋglě   dì jùmâ   (Anyi)
        Kofi take- HAB intelligence eat work
        'Kofi works intelligently.'
    b. Mo fi   ǫgbǫ̀n   gé igi.   (Yoruba)
        1sg take cleverness cut tree
        'I cut the tree cleverly.'

(5.26) Comitative:
    Kòfí fà   mwǎ-!mɔ́ kɔ̀   sùá   !nṹ. (Anyi)
    Kofi take-HAB sheep-PL go-HAB house inside
    'Kofi goes into the stable with the sheep.'

The use of serialization in nuclear junctures brings up an important issue in the theory of lexical entries. The core layer relates to the nucleus as a whole, so when a nucleus is complex, the core arguments are a function of the whole nucleus, not any particular verb within it. How then are the core arguments determined with complex nuclei consisting of two or more verbs differing in their logical structures? For this we would need a set of correspondence principles for associating the arguments in the logical structures of the verb in the juncture. To illustrate this consider the Yimas example:

(5.27) Uraŋ   ki-mpu-kra-yawra-ŋa-t.
       coconut (V) Vsg-3pl-1pl-get-give-PERF
       'They got the coconut for us.'

Here we have a nuclear juncture of the verbs 'get' and 'give' resulting in three core arguments, an actor, undergoer and goal/ benefactive. 'Get' has the logical structure:

(5.28)   a. $[DO(x,[\ldots])]$ CAUSE [BECOME **have**$'$ $(y,z)]$,
          where $x = y$
      b. $[DO(they,[$**do**$'$ $(they)])]$ CAUSE [BECOME **have**$'$
         (they, coconut)]

'Give' has the logical structure in (5.29). (Cf. (2.45c).)

(5.29)   a. $[DO(x,[\ldots])]$ CAUSE [BECOME **have**$'$ $(y,z)]$
      b. $[DO(they,[$**do**$'$ $(they)])]$ CAUSE [BECOME **have**$'$
         (we, coconut)]

This kind of serial construction is one with A = A/S coreference. Yimas has both this type and serialization with U = A/S coreference, but with these two verbs the latter type is not available. Therefore x in (5.28a) is the same as x in (5.29a), which because it is an agent (first argument of DO), it must be the actor. The theme, 'coconut', is again coreferential for both verbs and will constitute the second core argument. The two verbs have different locative–goals, 'they' for 'get', and 'us' for 'give'. 'They', the locative goal of 'get', is already the actor and, hence, a core argument. This, then, leaves the third core-argument position open for 'us', which is realized by the verbal prefix form *kra-* '1pl'. As it is the goal of the verb 'give', its semantics as the goal/ benefactive of the overall clause is straightforward.

     Now let us turn to the Barai nuclear juncture in (5.23). In Barai 'cut' is a transitive verb with core arguments actor and undergoer. A tentative logical structure for 'cut' is given in (5.30).

(5.30) a. [DO(x,[...])] CAUSE [BECOME **cut′** (y)]
       b. [DO(he,[**do′** (he)])] CAUSE [BECOME **cut′**
           (bread)]

Take has the same logical structure as 'get'.

(5.31) a. [DO(x,[...])] CAUSE [BECOME **have′** (y,z)]
       b. [DO(he,[**do′** (he)])] CAUSE [BECOME **have′** (he,
           knife)]

Just as in the Yimas example, actor–actor coreference is required
in the juncture in (5.23). The two logical structures must combine
in such a way that *sime* 'knife' becomes part of the logical structure
of *ufu* 'cut'. This is achieved if the logical structure of *abe* 'take'
becomes the first argument of CAUSE in the logical structure
of *ufu* in (5.30a); this would yield (5.32).

(5.32) [[DO(he,[**do′** (he)])] CAUSE [BECOME **have′** (he,
        knife)]] CAUSE [BECOME **cut′** (bread)]

In terms of the actor–undergoer hierarchy in Figure 1, 'he' will
be the actor and 'bread' the undergoer. *Sime* 'knife' is a theme
by virtue of being the second argument of **have′**, but because
it is part of the first argument of CAUSE, i.e. part of the causing
event, it receives an effector–theme, or instrument, interpretation.

   In some cases it seems simpler to view the use of the verb 'take'
in a lexical construction as simply adding atomic predicates to
the logical structure of the base verb, instead of adding the complete logical structure of 'take' which then combines with the
logical structure of the main verb. In such languages, 'take'
behaves much like the valence-increasing morphemes discussed
for Tagalog in 2.7 by adding atomic predicates to a simpler basic
logical structure. This is probably the result of diachronic re-
analysis of the function of 'take' from an earlier Barai-like use.
In these languages the nucleus is actually related to a single logical
structure, albeit derived, rather than two logical structures linked
together by juncture.

   This type of serialization is very common in Yatye, a Kwa
language of southeastern Nigeria (Stahlke 1970). In this language,
verbs like 'close', 'open', 'break', 'split', or 'fall' are entered in
the lexicon as basic stative verbs with the logical structure **verb′**
(x). Any adjustment to this requires a serial construction with *abà*,

which, although it does not occur independently, looks suspiciously like, and in some constructions can occur interchangeably with, *awa* 'take'. *Abà* is undoubtedly a verb, however, in that it is inflected for tense and mood and can undergo agentive nominalization. Note the following Yatye paradigm for *iku* 'close' (Stahlke 1970):

(5.33) a. Utsì ikù   **closed**′ (x)
      door close
      'The door is closed.'   (stative)

     b. Utsì abà ikù   BECOME **closed**′ (x)
      door   close
      'The door closed.'   (achievement)

     c. ìwyi abà utsì ikù.   [DO(x,[...])] CAUSE
      child   door close   [BECOME **closed**′ (y)]
      'The child closed the door.'   (accomplishment)

     d. òtsi abà utsì ikù   [**do**′(x)] CAUSE
      stick   door close   [BECOME **closed**′ (y)]
      'The stick closed the door.'

     e. ìwyi abà òtsi ikù   utsì
      child   stick close door
      'The child closed the door with a stick.'
      [DO(x,[...])] CAUSE [**do**′ (y)]] CAUSE
      [BECOME **closed**′ (z)]

In (5.33a) we see the basic use of the verb *ikù* 'close' as a stative verb with the logical structure **closed**′ (x). With the addition of *abà*, an achievement verb can be formed with the derived logical structure BECOME **closed**′ (x). In (5.33c–e) we see further uses as a valence increaser adding agents and effectors (DO and **do**′ predicates and the connective CAUSE). This pattern follows the theory of verb aspect proposed by Dowty (1979) and discussed in 2.3. It is possible to have a variant of (5.33e) with two occurrences of *abà*, one for the agent (DO argument), and one for the effector (**do**′ argument).

(5.34) ìwyi abà òtsi abà ikù   utsì.
      child   stick   close door
      'The child closed the door with a stick.'

A further variant in the use of serial verbs in valence increasing is found in certain languages of New Guinea in which this function is combined with the building up of verbal units of complex meaning. Not only does serialization increase the number of core arguments, but each verb in the juncture contributes its meaning to that of the composite unit. Dani, a Papuan language of New Guinea (Bromley 1981), requires periphrastic conjugation with serial verbs to express transitivity. Verbs involving a change of state are regarded as intransitive with the logical structure BECOME **verb**′ (x). With the single exception of *wat* 'hit, kill' all such change-of-state verbs must be transitivized by means of a nuclear juncture, with one of the following set of verbs: *hei* 'put', *ha* 'see', *et* 'give' (*et* does not occur as an independent verb, but its semantics in junctures indicate 'give'). It is these verbs to which are added the affixes indicating the person and number of the actor and undergoer.

(5.35) a. Hakki   pa ≡ m-et-h-e.
            bananas cut ≡ 1sgU-give-FACT-3sgA
            'He cut bananas and gave them to me.'
        b. N-esi   pa ≡ n-eeik-h-e.
            1sg-hair cut ≡ 1sgU-see-FACT-3sgA
            'He cut my hair.'
        c. Hakki   pa ≡ n-akeik-h-e.
            bananas cut ≡ 1sgU-put-FACT-3sgA
            'He cut bananas and put them aside for me.'

The conjugations of these verbs are very complex. *Eeik* and *akeik* are suppletive variants of *ha* and *hei*, respectively. *Pal* 'cut' can never be inflected transitively by itself. It must occur in a serial construction with one of these verbs. Note that these verbs are not simply meaningless auxiliaries added to introduce a second core argument. Rather they contribute their own meaning to that of the whole nucleus. Thus, the meaning of 'give' and 'put' is transparent in (5.35a, c). *Ha* 'see' in one of these nuclear junctures adds a locational or directional meaning, perhaps not so obvious in (5.35b) (although a close approximate translation might be 'he cut *at* my hair'), but quite transparent in (5.36).

(5.36) a. Seke tumu⁷ ≡ n-eeik-h-e.
            spear thrust ≡ 1sgU-see-FACT-3sgA
            'He thrust a spear at me.'
        b. I   kesa ≡ n-eeik-h-e.
            water pour ≡ 1sgU-see-FACT-3sgA
            'He poured water on me.'

The meaning of 'see' in nuclear junctures is rather different from its meaning as an independent verb and this will need to be stated in its lexical entry (as with the Barai verb *abe* 'take').

In Dani we see the transition point between the productive use of serialization to build up complex nuclei and cores in expressing composite semantic notions, and the more restricted specialized use in introducing core arguments. The Dani nuclear junctures perform both functions simultaneously. Most Barai and Yimas serializations perform the prior function and only constructions with Yimas *na-* 'give' and Barai *abe* 'take' are specialized for the latter. The Barai and Yimas pattern seems to be the general one for most serializing languages. Serialization is used primarily to build up complex verbal units and, only secondarily, to allow for the core arguments to be present in a clause. The extensive use of serialization to build up complex verbal units is illustrated below from a variety of languages.

(5.37) Yimas
        a. Kaykut na-n-ma-mpi-yawra-mpi-wambaki-k.
            hornbill 3sgU-3sgA-other-*mpi*-get-*mpi*-throw-
                                                        REMPAST
            'He got a hornbill again and threw it down.'
        b. Mamparŋkat   ya-na-park-mpi-kapik-mpi-
            coconut branches 3sgU-3sgA-split-*mpi*-break-*mpi*-
                                warkɨ-k.
                                tie-REMPAST
            'He split, broke into small pieces, and tied together the coconut branches.'
(5.38) Barai (Olson 1981)
        a. Fu do   ij-ia   barone na.
            3sg water DEF-L die   lay
            'He lay dead in the water.'

b. E   ije   fu a-nafa-fu-o   kan-ia buvua i.
   man DEF 3sg child-PL-3sg-POSS kill-3pl cut.up eat
   'The man killed, cut up, and ate his children.'

c. A   na ine   tua   kore-j-ie.
   2sg 1sg stick break. off throw-TRANS-2sg
   'You broke off and threw a stick at me.'

(5.39) Alamblak (Papua New Guinea; Bruce 1979)
   a. Wifërt fir-gënNgi-me-t-a.
      wind   blow-cold-REMPAST-3sgA-1sgU
      'The wind blew on me and I got cold.'
   b. Yimar këmbrur muh-hambre-më-r-r
      man   possum climb-search-REMPAST-3sgA-
      mis-n.
      3sgU
      tree-L
      'The man climbed a tree, searching for a possum.'

(5.40) Igbo (Lord 1975)
   a. ọ́ tụ̀-fù-rù   ákwúkwọ́.
      1sg throw-lost-FACT paper
      'He threw the paper and it got lost.' or
      'He threw away the paper.'
   b. ó bú-lá-rá   íté.
      1sg carry-go home-FACT pot
      'He carried the pot home.'

It is abundantly clear from these examples that serialization is
a highly productive process which results in complex nuclei or
cores with composite meanings derived from those of the constituent juncts. These composite meanings result from the logical
structures of the individual juncts, as we discussed earlier with
the valence-increasing function of 'give' and 'take'. This usage
is only a specialization of the general pattern illustrated in the
four languages above. The meaning of the composite is derived
by associating the logical structures in the manner outlined above.

   It is very important to contrast clearly the valence-increasing
function of serial verbs with the functions of the prepositions
discussed in 3.3.1. Prepositions are not valence-increasing morphemes. They function basically as oblique case markers indicating that an NP is a peripheral constituent, as well as indicating
the semantic function of the NP. The NP may function as an

argument present in the logical structure (inner periphery) or not (outer periphery), but in any case the NP involved is a peripheral constituent. These claims apply equally to oblique cases in a nominal case-marking language (see 3.3.3). On the other hand, any argument introduced by a serial verb is a core argument of that verb and a core argument of the juncture as a whole. In one sense the functions of serial verbs and prepositions/oblique case markers are similar in that they mark NPs which are *not normally* core arguments of the main verb of the clause. Prepositions/ oblique case markers indicate peripheral or non-core constituents explicitly, while serial verbs introduce arguments into the core which are not present in the logical structure and hence not basic core arguments. From this point of view we can see a relatedness of function. Both their similarity and their contrast are brought out clearly in this Thai example (A. Diller, personal communication):

(5.41) a. Kháw tàt yâa   dûay mîit.
            1sg   cut grass with knife
            'He cuts grass with a knife.'
        b. Kháw ʔaw mîit pay tàt yâa.
            1sg   take knife go cut grass
            'He cuts grass with a knife.' or
            'He uses a knife to cut grass.'

Tàt 'cut' is a verb with two core arguments in Thai and would have a logical structure similar to the Barai verb 'cut' in (5.30). Both (5.41a) and (5.41b) have three NP constituents associated with the verb. An instrumental NP can be expressed as a peripheral constituent with a preposition *dûay* 'with, along with, too' or as a core constituent with the serial verb *ʔaw* 'take'. There is an important difference in meaning. Diller reports that an instrument marked with *dûay* is out of focus, of secondary or peripheral importance, whereas when an instrument is expressed in a serial construction with *ʔaw*, it is highlighted and of central importance. This correlates with a difference in peripheral versus core status. Note, though, the parallelism of behavior between the preposition and the serial verb: They both indicate an NP which is not normally core for the two-argument verb *tàt* 'cut'.

It is also a well-known fact about language change that serialized verbs like 'give' and 'take' are often gradually re-analyzed into adpositions or case markers (Lord 1973, Clark 1978). This is readily accountable in terms of this analysis. As the serialized verb loses its verbal status, the core juncture ceases to be a juncture (there are no longer two equivalent juncts), and becomes a simple non-composite core. Because the constituent introduced by the serial verb is not a basic core argument, present in the logical structure of the verb, it must be the case in a simple non-composite core that it is a peripheral constituent. Consequently, the serialized verb is re-analyzed as an adposition marking a peripheral constituent related to a simplex core. Thus, the change in form class from verb to adposition also accounts for the concomitant partial change in function.

5.3 Operators

Corresponding to each of the three layers is a set of operators which have as their scope the corresponding layer. They have scope in the same way that negatives and quantifiers have scope. They are not constituents of the layer, but are operators over the entire layer. These operators are usually marked morphologically as affixes or clitics to the nucleus, the central constituent of the clause. The most common operators are the usual categories of verb inflection, tense, aspect, and mood, etc., but, as we will see, these inflectional possibilities correspond to operators of different layers. This is reflected in the ordering constraints in different languages for these inflectional categories.

We will start with the most basic contrast in verbal inflection categories, tense and aspect. The distinction between these two was drawn clearly in Jakobson's 1957 classic paper 'Shifters, verbal categories, and the Russian verb.' Distinguishing the speech act and its participants from the reported event and associated participants, Jakobson defines aspect as characterizing 'the narrative event itself without involving its participants and without reference to the speech act' (Jakobson 1971:134), while tense 'characterizes the narrated event with reference to the speech event' (Jakobson 1971:135). There is a clear distinction. Tense locates the time of the reported event with respect to the time of the speech event. The reported event can be before (past), simultaneous with (present), or after (future) the speech event. Further distinctions are possible: the reported event can be a long time before (remote past), not so long before, such as a week to a few days (near past), or just yesterday (immediate past), as well as a long time ahead (remote future), or tomorrow (immediate future). Yimas is a language of this type; it distinguishes three past tenses, a present tense and two future tenses. Tense is crucially concerned with grounding the reported event in the real world, expressing its temporal orientation with regard to the present act of speaking. Its function is much like the peripheral setting NPs like temporals or locatives, and tense is, in fact, a peripheral-layer operator.

Aspect is fundamentally different. As Jakobson points out, it is not at all concerned with the present speech act or its participants. Nor is it directly concerned with the participants of the reported event itself. Aspect simply expresses the temporal structure of the reported event without reference to anything else. All events, no matter how brief, take place over a period of time, but for practical purposes we can distinguish events of very short duration, punctual or non-durative, from those of longer duration which we term durative events. Among durative events we may distinguish those of homogeneous unchanging internal structure, states, from those having an internal structure of distinct changing phrases, which we call actions. The various inflectional categories languages present are directly related to these notions. When reporting an event the speaker chooses a particular point from which to view the internal temporal phrases of the event. If the event is viewed as complete and of no continuing relevance, then the perfective or non-durative aspect may be used. The imperfective indicates the event is not complete and may highlight the internal development of the event. Subtypes of the imperfective include the habitual and progressive. Finally, the event may be viewed as complete, but its consequent result may be of continuing relevance. This is the perfect aspect. In all cases aspect is concerned with the structure of the narrated event itself. The speech event and its participants are of no importance.

Aspect is an operator over the nucleus. This is entailed by defining it as the category expressing the temporal structure of the event itself without regard to its participants. It is not concerned with core arguments referring to the participants in the event, nor with peripheral constituents like setting NPs which place the event in time and space with respect to the speech act. Only the predicate is within its scope, and accordingly it is a nuclear operator.

We have claimed that aspect is a nuclear operator, while tense is a peripheral one. In languages which have both of these as separate inflectional categories, this scope difference is reflected in ordering constraints for the corresponding morphemes. Aspect occurs closer to the verb stem, the nucleus, than does tense. In Kewa (Franklin 1971) both aspect and tense are verbal suffixes, but aspect comes immediately after the verb stem followed by tense.

(5.42) a. íra-paa-ru.
        cook-PERF-1sgPST
        'I finished cooking it.'
    b. íra-waa-ru.
        cook-IMPF-1sgPST
        'I cooked part of it.'

Such ordering constraints are widespread in the languages of the world. To illustrate with another unrelated language, consider the heavily prefixing language Tiwi of Australia (Osborne 1974).

(5.43) ŋə-ru-untiŋ-apa.
       1sg-PST-DUR-eat
       'I was eating it.'

Again, the aspect morpheme is closer to the nucleus than the tense morpheme. We know of no cases of the inverse order of the two inflectional categories, in which tense is closer to the stem than aspect.[2]

One of the ways for aspect to be indicated is by a serial verb construction with a stance verb like 'sit', 'stand', or 'live' for progressive aspect and 'finish', 'throw away', or a similar verb for perfective aspect. These are not verbs in a nuclear juncture, but rather an aspectual operator realized by a verb stem and a predicate within its scope. Note the contrast between a nuclear juncture, and an operator plus nucleus construction with *tū* 'stand' in these Fijian examples (Parke 1981).

(5.44) a. E   viri-tū-ra   na   duru na   tūraga.
           CM put-stand-TR ART post ART chief
           'The chief erected the post.'
    b. E   viri-a   tū   na   duru na   tūraga.
           CM put-TR PROG ART post ART chief
           'The chief is placing the post.'
    c. E   viri-tū-ra   tū   na   duru na   tūraga.
           CM put-stand-TR PROG ART post ART chief
           'The chief is erecting the post.'

In (5.44a) we have a nuclear juncture with the two verbs *viri* 'put' and *tū* 'stand'. This is demonstrated by the transitive suffix occurring after *tū* 'stand', but clearly applying to both. Note that *viri* 'put' and not *tū* 'stand' is the transitive predicate semantically. In (5.44b) we find an operator plus nucleus construction. The nucleus is the simple transitive verb *viri* 'put', to which is added the transitive suffix. The operator *tū* occurs after the transitive suffix, and indicates progressive aspect. Finally, in (5.44c) we have two occurrences of *tū*; one as a member of a nuclear juncture, the other as the progressive aspect operator. Fijian has a parallel construction with *oti* 'finish' to indicate perfective aspect.

(5.45) E   viri-tū-ra   oti   na   duru na   tūraga.
        CM put-erect-TR PERF ART post ART chief
        'The chief has already erected the post.'

The use of intransitive verbs as operators to the nucleus to indicate aspect is not limited to stance verbs and 'finish'. For example, Yoruba uses 'come' and 'go' to indicate inceptive aspect (Bamgbose 1974). 'Go' is the general inceptive, while 'come' indicates abrupt inception.

(5.46) a. ó   ńsùn   lọ.
          3sg sleeping go
          'He is falling asleep.'
    b. ọmọ náà ké wá
          child the cry come
          'The child cried suddenly.'

Lisu (Tibeto-Burman; Hope 1974) also uses serials as nuclear operators to express aspect. The operator follows the nucleus and the tense morpheme is a suffix to the operator.

(5.47) a. Ása dza dzà γə-ų.
   Asa rise eat PERF-PST
   'Asa had eaten his rice.'

   b. Ásanya   gwa   lwé ye tyă-ą
      a   TOP there roll go PROG-NPST
      'Asa is rolling away over there.'

Sentence (5.47b) is an example of a composite nucleus formed by a nuclear juncture modified by the operator aspect morpheme. Tense, as an outer-layer operator, occurs joined to the aspectual operator, not to the verbs of the juncture. Again, we find an ordering constraint such that aspect is closer to the nucleus than tense, as the theory predicts it should be.

The other common nuclear operators are directionals. These express a directional orientation of the nucleus, whether the action is up, down, toward, or away from some point of reference (see Fillmore 1971). They are common in many languages of Melanesia and elsewhere. Here are some examples from Yimas of Papua New Guinea.

(5.48) a. I-na-l-cay-pra-n.
   3sgU-3sgA-down-see-come-PRES
   'She saw (the canoe) while coming down.'

   b. Na-wi-aykrasa-pu-k.
   3sgA-up-shout-go-IRR
   'She shouted up.'

The prefix (*i*)*l*- 'down' and *wi*- 'up' indicate the directed orientation of the action. In (5.48b) no literal movement is intended, merely the direction in which the actor shouted.

Kewa also has directional suffixes and provides evidence that, of the two nuclear operators aspect and directionals, aspect is the more inner. For when a verb is inflected for both aspect and directionals, aspect occurs immediately following the verb stem, followed by the directional, followed in turn by tense.

(5.49) a. íra-pa-niaa-ru.
   cook-PERF-down-1sgPST
   'I burned it downward (as a hill).'

   b. íra-pa-saa-ru.
   cook-PERF-up-1sgPST
   'I burned it upward (as a hill).'

The other general category of verb inflection in addition to aspect and tense is mood or modality. These terms have been used in confusing and overlapping ways in the Western grammatical tradition to cover *three* grammatical categories (see e.g. Lyons 1968), which must be clearly distinguished. Mood, first of all has been used to describe illocutionary force (J. Austin 1962, Searle 1969). Imperative mood, the mood of commands or exhortations, is the most transparent example of this usage, but some of the uses of the Latin subjunctive, e.g. in expressing wishes or en-treaties, are also examples of mood expressing illocutionary force.

Other uses of the Latin subjunctive indicate a different gram-matical category, sometimes referred to under the separate name of modality. This is the variable of actuality of the event, whether it has been realized or not. We will borrow the term *status* from Whorf (1956) for this notion. Status is often viewed as a binary distinction between realis–irrealis, and some languages use just such a binary distinction. However, within the irrealis dimension many languages recognize further distinctions, whether the action is necessary, or likely, or merely possible. So within the realis–irrealis poles we may have a continuum such as (5.50):

(5.50)   real ← necessary – probable – possible → unreal

The middle points in this scale are expressed in English by the modals *must, will, can* and *may*. In Latin the real is expressed by the indicative, and the unreal by the subjunctive. In Lisu (Hope 1974), the status category is expressed by a set of intransitive verb stems which immediately follow the main verb and which take the tense suffix.

(5.51)   a. Ása nya   ami khwa wa̧-a̧.
            Asa TOP field hoe   obligatory-NPST
            'It is obligatory for Asa to hoe the field.'
         b. Ása nya   ami khwa da-a̧.
            Asa TOP field hoe   acceptable-NPST
            'It is acceptable for Asa to hoe the field.'
         c. Ása nya   ami khwa khù-a̧.
            Asa TOP field hoe   normal-NPST
            'It is normal for Asa to hoe fields.'

In these examples we find the proposition that Asa hoes fields followed by an intransitive verb stating the reality status of the proposition, whether it is obligatory, normal or just acceptable. A similar effect is obtained in English by using modal adjectives as the predicates in complement structures as in the translations above. In addition to modal auxiliaries, such modal adjectives are ways of expressing the category of status in English.

There is yet a third category subsumed under the terms mood/modality. This can be seen in the following Lisu sentences by comparing them with (5.51) above.

(5.52)   a. Ása nya   ami khwa kwá̠-a̠.
         Asa TOP field hoe   mentally. able-NPST
         'Asa is able (knows how) to hoe the field.'
      b. Ása nya   ami khwa da-a̠.
         Asa TOP field hoe   able-NPST
         'Asa is (physically) able to hoe the fields.'
      c. Ása nya   ami khwa bala-a̠.
         Asa TOP field hoe   able-NPST
         'Asa is free to hoe the field.'

Note the difference in meaning between (5.51) and (5.52), especially the (b) examples. The (b) examples are identical utterances but have quite different meanings. Example (5.51b) expresses that in the scheme of things it is acceptable for Asa to hoe the fields, but this does not entail that he is able to do so. Example (5.52b) expresses that Asa has the ability to hoe the fields, but, of course, this need not entail that it is acceptable in the scheme of things for him to do so. Two different grammatical categories are involved here. The sentences in (5.51) are examples of the category status, while (5.52) involves a distinct grammatical category, which we will term *modality*. Jakobson (1971:135) expressed well the semantics of modality when he defined mood as characterizing 'the relation between the narrated event and its participants with reference to the participants of the speech event'. More particularly, modality characterizes the speaker's estimate of the relationship of the actor of the event to its accomplishment, whether he has the obligation, the intention, or the ability to perform it. In a sense, modality is connected to status, although it is a distinct category, in that when an actor is obliged to carry out an action, one might infer a high likelihood that the event will become a reality, but when he is merely able to perform it, one would infer no such probability. Thus, within the general domain of mood/ modality, we must distinguish three different grammatical categories: illocutionary force, status, and modality.

All of these categories are operators, but they are not all operators at the same layer. Modality is an operator of the core layer, having both the nucleus and its core arguments in its scope. This follows from the semantics of modality in that it expresses the relationship between the actor and his accomplishment of the action. This is apparent from the Lisu examples and their translation in (5.52). Status is a peripheral operator; it expresses the reality status of the entire proposition and bears no direct relation to the nucleus or to any of its core arguments. The entire proposition is within its scope, and hence it is a peripheral argument. This can be seen in the Lisu examples of (5.51) and their English translations. The contrast between modality and status as operators at different layers is clearly brought out in the following Lisu sentences.

(5.53) a. Ása nya   ami khwa xạ-ạ.
           Asa TOP field hoe   good-NPST
           'Asa is good at hoeing the field.'
       b. Ása nya   ami khwa-ạ   xạ-ạ.
           Asa TOP field hoe-NPST good-NPST
           'It is good that Asa hoes the field.'

The verb *xạ-* 'good' can function as either a modality operator or a status operator. Sentence (5.53a) is an example of its use as a modality operator. Tense occurs suffixed to the modal because it is a peripheral operator and the ordering reflects their relative scope. In (5.53b) the verb functions as a status operator, an operator at the periphery. Tense occurs on both the main verb and the operator because both operators are peripheral. There seems to be no clear difference in their relative ordering in Lisu, so tense occurs before and after the status operator.

More evidence for the distinction between modality and status and their assignment as operators at different layers will be provided in the next section. We may summarize the structure of the nuclear and core layers and their associated participants as Figure 8.[3,4]

$$(\text{MOD } \underbrace{[\text{NP} \,(\text{NP})} \,(\text{DIR } (\text{ASPECT } \underbrace{[\text{Predicate}])))]}$$
$$\text{CORE} \qquad\qquad\qquad \text{NUCLEUS}$$

Figure 8 Core and nuclear operators

We have proposed two operators over the periphery so far, tense and status, and we may inquire as to the relative ordering between them. This, however, is rather difficult to establish, as the two categories are very closely related. Obviously, the temporal orientation of an event with regard to the time of the speech act is crucially important to the reality status of the event. Much more research is needed to establish conclusively the ordering of tense and status, and it is possible that their relative ordering varies from language to language, but present evidence indicates that status is inside of tense, i.e. status has scope over the periphery, and tense has scope over status and the periphery. In other words, the likelihood of the proposition along the realis-irrealis dimension is first established, and then the temporal orientation of this modified proposition is established with respect to the time of the speech act. Evidence to support this comes from several sources. In Latin and Ancient Greek the inflectional possibilities for tense are determined on the basis of the mood inflection. In Latin, the indicative is inflected for three tense possibilities – present, past, and future – while the subjunctive is only inflected for two – present and past. In Ancient Greek, the indicative is inflected for two tenses – the present and past – while the subjunctive and optative are not inflected for tense at all, only for aspect. These facts suggest that status is a more basic category than tense, and is, therefore, a more inner operator.

Still more evidence is suggested by diachronic trends in this area. It seems that the basic tendency in diachronic developments for clause operators is for more-inner operators to be re-analyzed as operators over outer layers. Aspectual categories are often re-analyzed as tense oppositions (Kuryłowicz 1964). For example, in colloquial French and German, the former perfect aspect now signals past tense. The more-inner operator, aspect, has become re-analyzed as the more-outer, tense. This diachronic trend of inner to outer bears on the question of the relative order of tense and status in several ways. First of all it is a common diachronic development for a future tense to come from an earlier subjunctive mood. In other words, the specification of irrealis in the status category is realized as the most indefinite and unreal tense category. The Latin future tense in the indicative comes from an earlier subjunctive mood (Buck 1933). Such a development is likely to be the ultimate fate of the English modal *will*, which in Old English indicated modality: intend, want (modality) > likely (status) > future tense (Traugott 1972). It is very likely that such a drift is the source of the future tense in most languages. For example, in Yimas of Papua New Guinea, the verbal desiderative suffix *-k* also marks irrealis and is the base suffix in both the immediate future *-kiak* and the remote future *-kit*. However, for English this argument can be viewed to cut both ways, because the past-tense forms of the modal auxiliaries indicating status are often used to express a greater degree of unreality.

(5.54) a. John may go.
        b. John might go.
(5.55) a. John can do it.
        b. John could do it.

The (b) sentences express a lesser degree of likelihood for the event. These seem to indicate a drift from tense to status, as opposed to the developments of the future tense, which indicates a shift from status to tense. This again shows the very close relationship between the two categories, but the sum total of the evidence, we feel, favors an order of tense outside of status. One final bit of evidence for this view comes from the ordering of peripheral auxiliary elements for a number of creoles of independent origins (Bickerton 1974, 1981).

(5.56)

		Tense	Status	Aspect
a.	*Sranan* (South	ben	sa	e
	America)	anterior	irrealis	durative
b.	*Haitian Creole*	te	ava	apres
		anterior	irrealis	durative
c.	*Hawaiian Creole*	been	go	stay
		anterior	irrealis	durative

This rigid invariant order from two independent English-based creoles (a and c) and one French-based creole (b) motivates well the position of status inside of tense.

In addition to status and tense, there are two other peripheral operators. The next peripheral operator in relative ordering is the category of evidentials. It follows tense, and it takes within its scope the entire periphery as well as the more-inner peripheral operators. Evidentials mark the truthfulness of the proposition in terms of the way the speaker has ascertained this. Did he see with his eyes? Is it hearsay? and so on. Kewa (Franklin 1971) has verbal suffixes indicating evidential status. It possesses a simple binary distinction: was the action seen or not? They occur exactly in the expected position as outer-peripheral operators—after the tense morpheme.

(5.57) a. íra-a-na.
            cook-3sgP S T-seen
            'He cooked it (I saw it).'
        b. íra-a-ya.
            cook-3sgP S T-unseen
            'He cooked it (hearsay, I didn't see it).'

The evidentials occur after the tense suffixes because they take tense within their scope. They comment on the truthfulness of a specific event located in a particular time, not the truthfulness in general of such events.

Evidentials are a common category of verb inflection in American Indian languages. In Imbarura Quechua (Cole & Hermon 1981), evidentials are a set of clitics whose placement in main clauses is free, subject to discourse factors. Tense morphemes always occur suffixed to the verb. When the evidentials are suffixed to the verb, they must follow the tense morpheme, again demonstrating the more outer status of the evidential operator.

(5.58) Juan cri-n-mi   Maria Juzi-ta
        Juan believe-3sg-firsthand Maria Jose-A C C
        ricu-shca-ta.
        see-P S T/N M Z-A C C
        'Juan believes that Maria saw Jose (I know this by first-hand knowledge).'

Further evidence for the wider scope of evidentials can be found in the fact that evidential morphemes such as *-mi* cannot occur in the complement clause in a sentence like (5.58), while the tense of the complement can be independent of that in the main clause. The evidential operator thus has scope over the entire sentence, whereas each tense operator has scope over its respective clause.

English does not have a set of evidential verbal suffixes or verbal auxiliaries, but possesses this operator type nonetheless. The function of evidentials is performed by certain sentential adverbs like *obviously, evidently, seemingly*, etc. Consider the following examples.

(5.59) a. Evidently, it is possible for little green men to live on the moon.
   b. *It is possible for little green men to live evidently on the moon.
(5.60) a. Obviously, it is likely that John will be late again.
   b. *It is likely that John will obviously be late again.

As we pointed out above, modal adjectives like *possible* and *likely* are status operators, as we have claimed, and are more-inner peripheral operators than the evidential operators like *evidently* and *obviously*. Therefore, the required ordering of the operator is as in the (a) examples in which the status operator occurs after and is within the scope of the evidential. The opposite order in which the evidential is within the scope of status operator is ungrammatical.

Bellert (1977) points out an important distinction between modal adjectives and modal adverbs along these lines. She points out that while modal adjectives modify a proposition by expressing its reality status, modal adverbs modify the *truth* of the proposition, not the proposition. By this view modal adverbs would be evidentials and not status morphemes. She points out that sentences like

(5.61) a. Probably, John will come.
   b. Certainly, John can do it.

are paraphrasable as:

(5.62) a. It is probably true that John will come.
   b. It is certainly true that John can do it.

Such paraphrases are impossible for the modal adjectives.

(5.63) a.   It is probable that John will come.
        b.   *The truth that John will come is probable.
        c.   It is certain that John can do it.
        d.   *The truth that John can do it is certain.

Further, it is possible to have both a modal adjective and a modal adverb in the same sentence.

(5.64) a.   Certainly, it is possible that John will come.
        b.   Probably, it is necessary for John to cut down the tree.

In (5.64) the modal adjectives express the reality state of the event and the modal adverbs express the speaker's assessment of the truth status of the potential or necessary event. This suggests that the modal adverbs are the outer-peripheral operators, evidentials. This is corroborated by the fact that the adverbs cannot be under the scope of the adjectives.

(5.65) a.   *It is possible that John will certainly come.
        b.   *It is necessary for John probably to cut down the tree.

Finally, while the constructions with modal adjectives can be questioned, those with modal adverbs cannot.

(5.66) a.   It is possible that John will come?
        b.   Is it certain that John can do it?
        c.   *Will John probably come?
        d.   *Can John certainly do it?

It is certainly acceptable to question the truth of the reality status of an event by a yes–no question as in (5.66a–b), but to question the truth of an event and at the same time evaluate it by a modal adverb is nonsensical. Consequently, questions with modal adverbs are unacceptable. The sum of the evidence clearly supports the contention that while modal adjectives are indicators of status, modal adverbs are evidentials.

The outermost operator is illocutionary force, taking the entire periphery as well as the other peripheral operators, status, tense, and evidentials, within its scope. An earlier analysis which also argued in essence that illocutionary force is the outermost operator can be found in Ross (1970). This view is amply supported by the sentence patterns of the Papuan languages of the Highlands of New Guinea. These languages are characterized by sentences of enormous length, in which chains of verbs with reduced inflectional possibilities are followed by a single final verb which marks the end of the sentence. The inflection diagnostic of final verbs is suffixation for illocutionary force. The reduced medial verbs may *never* be inflected for illocutionary force, although in some languages they may be for tense, albeit restrictedly. Note this example from Fore (Papua New Guinea; Scott 1978):

(5.67) Mae-ʔte kana-ma-ki-na
        get-SIM come-SEQ-LINK-3sgA
        na-mu-y-e.
        1sgU-give-3sgA-DECL
        'He got (it) and came and gave (it) to me.'

Here the illocutionary force marker -*e* 'declarative' only occurs on the last verb, but its scope is over the two previous verbs as well. Similar sentences but of enormous length are quite common in Fore. Scott (1978) presents a text in which 37 medial verbs occur with no marking for illocutionary force before a single final verb with the -*e* suffix indicating declarative.

   Lisu (Hope 1974) marks illocutionary force primarily by a tone on the tense morpheme: mid tone for declarative (-a̠), falling tone for interrogative (-â), and low tone for imperative (-a̠). Imperative may also be expressed by the absence of a tense morpheme altogether. Illocutionary force, the outermost peripheral operator, is thus expressed through a suprasegmental over the next outermost operator, tense. Lisu also has an additional way of expressing more specific types of speech acts. It possesses a set of sentence-final speech-act particles such as *na* 'surprise', *lê* 'warning', *há* 'wonder', *xù* 'complaint', *læ* 'confirmation', *mâ* 'expectation', etc. These always occur in absolute final position in the sentence, reflecting their status as the outermost illocutionary-force operators:

(5.68) a. ŋwa áthà   nya lì-a̠   na.
            1sg machete TOP heavy-NPST SURPRISE
            '(I'm surprised that) my machete is heavy.'

    b.　ŋwa áthà　　nya　lì-ạ　　　　　lê.
　　　　1sg　machete TOP heavy-NPST WARNING
　　　　'(I warn you that) my machete is heavy.'

    c.　ŋwa áthà　　nya　lì-ạ　　　　　xù
　　　　1sg　machete TOP heavy-NPST COMPLAIN
　　　　'(I complain to you that) my machete is heavy.'

English has a set of illocutionary-force adverbs which are discussed in some detail in Schreiber (1972). The illocutionary-force adverbs include *frankly, candidly, confidentially, briefly,* and others. These adverbs modify the illocutionary force of the sentence, expressing the speaker's view of the nature of the message he is transmitting or the form preferred by the speaker of the anticipated addressee's response. Sentences with these adverbs are paraphrasable by sentences with explicit performative verbs modified by these adverbs.

(5.69)　a.　Honestly, you are wrong.
　　　　b.　I am telling you honestly that you are wrong.
(5.70)　a.　Truthfully, did you lie to me?
　　　　b.　I request that you tell me truthfully whether you lied to me.

Both examples in (5.69) express the speaker's assertion that he is speaking in an honest fashion. The adverb is part of the illocutionary force of the sentence. In (5.70) the adverb expresses the speaker's request that the addressee speak truthfully in his response. It is the general pattern for these adverbs to be speaker oriented in statements, but addressee oriented in requests.

(5.71)　a.　Frankly, John is a fool.
　　　　b.　I am telling you frankly that John is a fool.
(5.72)　a.　Confidentially, John lost the case.
　　　　b.　I am telling you confidentially that John lost the case.
(5.73)　a.　Seriously, did you like the book?
　　　　b.　I request that you tell me seriously whether you liked the book.
(5.74)　a.　Confidentially, did John lose the case?
　　　　b.　I request that you tell me confidentially whether John lost the case.

As modifiers of illocutionary-force operators, these adverbs must

include evidentials like modal adverbs within their scope, and this
is certainly the case.

(5.75) a. Confidentially, John is probably going to be late.
      b. *Probably, John is confidentially going to be late.
      c. I am telling you confidentially that it is probably true
         that John is going to be late.

(5.76) a. Frankly, it is certainly possible that John won't meet
         his sales target.
      b. *Certainly, it is frankly possible that John won't meet
         his sales target.
      c. I am telling you frankly that it is certainly true that
         it is possible that John won't meet his sales target.

The order of the (a) examples in which the illocutionary-force
adverb precedes the evidential adverb reflects the relative scope
of the two operators and is the only grammatical possibility. The
(b) examples in which the order is switched are ungrammatical.
The (c) examples are paraphrases of the (a) examples, explicitly
indicating the relative scope of the operators. Example (5.76)
is especially interesting in that it contains three peripheral
operators, status (*possible*), evidential (*certainly*), and illocutionary
force (*frankly*), and their relative scopes are clearly delineated in
the paraphrase in (5.76c).

We may summarize the discussion in this section of the
operators and their associated layers in Figure 9. The ordering
of the operators reflects their scope relations, illocutionary force
having scope over all other operators and all constituents of every
layer, and aspect having scope only over the nucleus. We have seen
that the order of verbal affixes with reference to the verb reflects
the scope relations of the operators they express. Bybee (1983)
presents a survey of 50 languages from all areas of the world with
respect to the question of the order of verbal affixes, and in every
case where an order can be established (see n. 2), it follows the
ordering predicted in Figure 9. It is interesting to note that
Tesnière (1939) proposed the following very similar universal
order of verbal affixes: voice, aspect, tense (of aspect), mode, tense
(of mode).[5]

(ILLOC FORCE (EVID (TENSE (STATUS [L ... In (MOD[NP (NP) (DIR (ASPECT [Predicate])])])))

NUCLEUS

CORE

PERIPHERY

(...) = OPERATORS

[...] = Constituents

Figure 9 The layered structure of the clause with operators

5.4 English auxiliary order

In the previous section we discussed the English system for the outer operators, evidential and illocutionary, but we have not yet investigated how English codes the more-inner operators of aspect, modality, status, and tense. These are expressed by the various verbal elements. In this section we will develop an analysis of the English auxiliary and demonstrate how the ordering of the auxiliary elements directly reflects the relative ordering of the operators. Comparing the ordering of the inner operators with the ordering of the auxiliary elements in (5.77) and (5.78), we see at first glance a perfect match-up of the English order of (5.78) and the universal template in (5.77).

(5.77)   tense   status   modality   aspect

(5.78)   T N S   modal   PERF   PROG   PASS

We now wish to justify in detail the mapping of (5.77) – (5.78). The innermost auxiliary element, passive *be*, does not express an operator of the type discussed in the previous section. Consequently, its position with respect to the verb is governed by totally different principles and lies outside the scope of this discussion. Voice is a nuclear modification, since it deals with the syntactic expression of the arguments of the nucleus, and therefore its position immediately adjacent to the nucleus is not surprising. Moreover, as Comrie (1976a) notes, in many languages there is a complex interaction between voice and aspect, the innermost operator.

Aspect has a very complex realization in English. A great deal of effort has been expanded by other scholars to account for the fact that while English verbs can be inflected for both progressive and perfect aspect, the morphemes can only occur in the sequence perfect–progressive, the sequences progressive–perfect, progressive–progressive, and perfect–perfect being blocked. Semantic arguments accounting for these constraints have been presented in Schachter (1980). We accept his arguments, and will not concern ourselves with these ordering constraints for the aspectual morphemes themselves. Here we are only concerned with demonstrating how English aspectual inflection with *have* and *be* conforms to the universal template of (5.77).

English has an aspectual system composed of three distinctions, two of them (perfect and progressive) morphologically marked, and the third, unmarked. Consider the following paradigm in the past tense:

(5.79) a. John wrote. $\emptyset$
          b. John was writing.   progressive
          c. John had written.   perfect
          d. John had been writing.   perfect–progressive

Analyzing this system in terms of two binary features we have:

		PERF	PROG
(5.80) a.	John wrote.	−	−
b.	John was writing.	−	+
c.	John had written.	+	−
d.	John had been writing.	+	+

This analysis requires us to recognize three aspectual categories with the following feature definitions:

(5.81)   a. $\emptyset$ b. perfect   c. progressive
                 −PERF   +PERF   −PERF
                 −PROG   −PROG   +PROG

with the proviso that the perfect and progressive can cooccur with the same verb.

The perfect and progressive aspects are well known. The zero aspect corresponds to the simple tense form of the verb and is found in two tenses.

(5.82) a. John writes.
          b. John wrote.

Following Bull (1960), we claim that English presents a simple two-way tense distinction expressed by its bound morphemes: a zero form (*-s* in third singular) versus a dental suffix form. The form with the dental suffix is correlated with a definite past-time reference,

(5.83) a. John killed the bear.
          b. Harry slept in the barn.

while the zero form is not closely associated with a single signification but shows a range of meanings:

(5.84) a. Universal statements not associated with a particular time
  1. Lions are carnivores.
  2. Spinach is good for you.
  b. Habitual actions extending into present
  1. John works from 9 to 5.
  2. I travel overseas every year.
  c. Present time
  1. Harry throws the ball to Sam.
  2. I now leave you to find your own devices.
  d. Definite future time
  1. The train leaves at 5.
  2. Harry leaves for France tomorrow.

We cannot claim that the zero form in English signifies present tense if we want to account for its future use in (5.84). Rather, the zero form must be defined negatively with regard to the dental suffix past-tense form. The zero form signifies non-past tense and nothing more. Any more precise meaning is supplied by other elements in the sentence such as the temporal adverbs in (5.84d), which force a future interpretation. We must always be careful to distinguish the sense of morphemes from their pragmatic entailments in context. English has a simple two-way tense distinction: dental suffix (past) versus zero (non-past). Any further meanings that have been ascribed to zero are due to inference. This principle of distinguishing the meaning of grammatical morphemes from their implications is very important, and we will see further examples.

Returning now to the zero aspect in English, it is the unmarked aspect, both morphologically and semantically. Its specific meaning is determined to some extent by its interaction with tense specification. With past tense, it marks a completed past action, without any of the implications of a resulting state with continuing relevance, expressed by the perfect. It expresses an act, pure and simple, located in past time. In the non-past tense, it expresses a rather wider range of meanings, outlined in (5.84) above. Fundamental to them all seems to be the idea of the irrelevance of the internal temporal structure of the event. Again, it expresses an act, pure and simple, in non-past time. The vagueness of the meaning of the zero aspect is to be expected in view of its unmarked status.

The English zero aspect corresponds in a very striking way to what is called the aorist in comparative Indo-European studies (see Kuryłowicz 1964). Friedrich (1974) argues that the aorist aspect is the unmarked aspect in Ancient Greek. It is the 'normal aspect for expressing an activity simply as an act or event, as action pure and otherwise undefined .... There is a tendency for the aorist to be used as the residual [i.e. unmarked W A F/R V V] aspect, whenever there is no need or desire to express the relevance of another aspect' (McKay 1977:138–9). This semantic unmarkedness of the aorist is also matched by its morphological form. As Friedrich (1974) points out, of the three aspectual contrasts in Greek, aorist, perfect, and imperfect, the aorist is morphologically of the simplest composition. The aorist is unrestricted as to the form of the stem, being consonantal, thematic, or athematic, whereas the other two aspects are restricted, and, further, the bare root of the stem is most often shown in the aorist aspect. The specific uses of the Ancient Greek aorist also correspond to the English zero aspect. Both are most commonly used in the past, being semantically most compatible with the past, but can be used in the non-past to express timeless universal statements, as well as for vivid descriptions of actions (see McKay 1977:144–5). A three way aspectual contrast seems just as well motivated for English as for Ancient Greek.

The analysis of *be* as a progressive morpheme seems non-controversial, but the claim that *have* is a morpheme signaling perfect aspect is in need of some justification, in view of McCawley's (1971, 1981) analysis of it as a past-tense morpheme. A cursory view suggests this cannot be true because there are many sentences containing *have* which are not past tense.

(5.85)   a.   John has lived in Paris for five years.
  b.   John has known Mary a long time.
  c.   Peter has been overweight for too long.

All these sentences are in the non-past tense and express a condition which began in the past but is still applicable in the present.

If these are only to hold in the past, the past tense with zero aspect must be used.

(5.86) a. John lived in Paris for five years.
 b. John knew Mary a long time.
 c. John was overweight too long.

These sentences all mean that the condition existed in the past, but has now ended. The only case where it is plausible to claim that *have* is a tense marker is in infinitives, in which the contrast between past tense and perfect aspect is neutralized.

(5.87) a. John arrived/*has arrived at 2:00 yesterday.
 b. John has drunk a gallon of beer by now.
 c. John had already met Sue when he married Cynthia.

(5.88) a. John is believed to have arrived at 2:00 yesterday.
 b. John is believed to have drunk a gallon of beer now.
 c. John is believed to have already met Sue when he married Cynthia.

Example (5.88a) is the infinitive version of the past-tense form in (5.87a), and here have plus past participle seems to signal past tense (note the ungrammaticality of *have* plus past participle with a past adverb in (5.87a)). However, this is no argument that *have* is a past-tense marker in all of its uses, because the past meaning in (5.88) is easily inferred from the basic perfect meaning in this context of neutralization. We conclude, then, that the auxiliary *have* must be analyzed as a perfect morpheme, and not a past-tense morpheme.

Turning now to modals, we note that both status and modality are matched to the English modal auxiliaries in the correspondence in (5.77) and (5.78). The English modals are ambiguous in that they express both categories. This can be seen by considering the following English sentences.

(5.89) a. John must leave now.
 b. John may climb that tree.

These sentences are both ambiguous. Example (5.89a) can mean either that it is a logical necessity that John leave now, or that John is obliged to leave now. Example (5.89b) can mean that it is possible that John will climb that tree or that John has permission to climb that tree. This is the well-known difference between the epistemic and deontic meanings of English modals (Hofmann 1976; Lyons 1977). The first meaning of each sentence is the epistemic one, expressing the values of the event along the realis–irrealis dimension. Epistemic modals express status. The second meaning of each modal is the deontic one and this corresponds to the category of modality. The fact that modality is a core operator and status a peripheral one explains the differences in syntactic behavior between the two readings of the modal auxiliaries. Consider the following sentences:

(5.90) a. John must leave.
       b. John has the obligation to leave.   (deontic)
       c. It is necessary for John to leave.   (epistemic)

(5.91) a. John can climb that tree.
       b. John has the ability to climb that tree.   (deontic)
       c. It is possible that John will climb that tree.
                                  (epistemic)

(5.92) a. John may write that letter.
       b. John has permission to write that letter.   (deontic)
       c. It is possible that John will write that letter. (epistemic)

The (a) sentences are ambiguous between the deontic and epistemic meaning of the modal. The (b) examples paraphrase explicitly the deontic meaning of the modals. They predicate a relation between the action *John* and the performance of the various acts. The (c) examples are paraphrases of the epistemic meaning. In these examples, a predication along the realis–irrealis dimension is made of the entire reported event – the act itself and its participants. The paraphrases with the epistemic adjectives *necessary* and *possible* are not acceptable if the actor is subject:

(5.93) a. *John is necessary to leave.
       b. *John is possible to write that letter.

Another bit of evidence for the assignment of the deontic and epistemic interpretations of the modals to two different layers of the clause concerns the ordering constraints when two modal elements are present in a single clause.

(5.94) a. John may have to leave.
       b. John could be able to write that letter.
       c. John has to be able to do it.

Note that in these examples the first modal must have the epistemic reading and the second the deontic, i.e. (5.94 a–c) are paraphrasable as (5.95 a–c) respectively.

(5.95) a. It is possible that John has the obligation to leave.
       b. It is possible that John has the ability to write that letter.
       c. It is necessary that John has the ability to do it.

In all cases the first modal corresponds to the epistemic meaning, *possible* or *necessary*, and the second to the deontic, *obligation* or *ability*. Note the obligatory ordering is epistemic before deontic. The sentences are ungrammatical if the order is switched.

(5.96) a. *John has to may leave.
       b. *John was able to can write that letter.
       c. *John was able to have to do it.[6]

This ordering constraint also accounts for the meanings of the double modal constructions found in dialects of the southern United States.

(5.97) a. John might could do it.
       b. Don't get so far ahead – I may not could make it.[7]

These sentences can only mean

(5.98) a. It is possible that John is able to do it.
       b. It is possible that I will not be able to make it.

in which the first modal is epistemic and the second, deontic, corresponding to the ordering constraint proposed.

    Such double-modal dialects, rather than being some sort of peculiar aberration, are in fact a logical and predictable variant in terms of the theory presented here. Deontic modals express modality, an operator at the core layer, while epistemic modals express status, a peripheral operator. A sentence containing a modal of both types is perfectly reasonable, provided the deontic modal is within the scope of the epistemic, and this is precisely what we find in examples like (5.97).

A final argument for the assignment of deontic and epistemic to different layers concerns diachronic developments for the English modals. Recall that above we proposed the generalization that more-inner modals tend to be re-analyzed as more-outer. For the modals, the general tendency is for deontic modals to take on the meaning of epistemic modals, and not vice versa. For example, in Old English, the ancestors of the present-day modal auxiliaries were main verbs and only had meanings associated with the deontic uses, such as 'know', 'intend', 'be able to', and 'be obliged' (Traugott 1972). This is true, as well, of their cognate forms in Modern German *können* 'be able', *müssen* 'be obliged to', *sollen* 'to be required to', and *wollen* 'want, desire, intend'. Diachronically, the deontic meanings, corresponding to the core operator of modality, are more basic in the history of English; the modals have expanded from the core operator of modality to take on as well the function of the peripheral operator, status.

Tense in English is a very straightforward category, a simple binary opposition between past and non-past as we argued above. What is commonly called the future tense in English is not a tense at all, but rather a specification of the status of an event by the epistemic use of the modals *will* or *shall*. Tense attaches to the first auxiliary element. This is to be expected from its status as an outer operator. Some examples follow in Table 10.

Table 10 *The English auxiliary*

Tense	Status-modality	Aspect	Verb	Form
a. non-past	can	PERF	go	can have gone
b. past	$\emptyset$	PROG	go	was going
c. past	$\emptyset$	PERF	go	had gone
d. past	$\emptyset$	$\emptyset$	go	went

In (a) the non-past is a zero morpheme, so no change is effected. In (b–c) the past-tense morpheme affects the first overt auxiliary element, the aspect morphemes *be* PROG and *have* PERF, converting them into their corresponding past forms *was* and *had*. In (d), the only overt element is the main verb so past attaches to it, converting *go* into the past-tense form *went*.

It has long been known, e.g. Jespersen (1924), Chomsky (1957), that *do*-support occurs in English whenever the attachment of tense is blocked. To take one example, negation in English is permissible at all three levels – nuclear, core, and peripheral. As an outer-peripheral operator, tense is always more peripheral than the negative morpheme because peripheral negation falls into the status category which is inside of tense. The attachment of tense is blocked by the negative morpheme, because it is not allowed to cross the more-inner negative. Thus tense cannot occur on a main verb preceded by a negative. Rather, this orphan tense morpheme is realized by the auxiliary *do*.

(5.99) a. non-past – negative – $\emptyset$ – $\emptyset$ – write = does not write
        b. past – negative – $\emptyset$ – $\emptyset$ – write   = did not write

Finally, we wish to consider briefly the interaction of illocutionary force with the auxiliary elements in English. We will be concerned with the three basic distinctions of illocutionary force: imperative, interrogative, and declarative. Declarative sentences in English are the unmarked case. No change is effected in the sentence or auxiliary element. Imperative sentences are distinguished by the obligatory absence of the tense morphemes, as well as of the modals. However, aspect inflection is still possible in imperatives, as these examples (Gazdar, Pullum & Sag 1982) demonstrate.

(5.100) a. Be studying your Spanish when I get home!
        b. Don't dawdle! For Pete's sake have left the room by the time she gets back.

The most interesting formation is that for interrogative illocutionary force in yes–no questions. This is indicated by having tense occur as the first element in the clause. This is accomplished syntactically by placing the tense-bearing auxiliary element before the subject.

(5.101) a. Is John going?
        b. Has John left?
        c. Has John been going to work regularly?
        d. Can John go?
        e. Could John kill it?
        f. Could John have gone there?

If the sentence occurs with zero status, modality, and aspect morphemes, then there is no auxiliary element to be placed before the subject. In such cases, tense still occurs before the subject to signal yes–no questions, and *do* must occur so that the bound tense morpheme will have a constituent to attach to.

(5.102) a. Does John know that?
    b. Did John go?

It should be noted that in related languages such as German, *do*-support is unnecessary because the language allows a tensed main verb to occur before the subject in yes–no questions.

In this section we have presented an analysis of the English auxiliary and demonstrated how the ordering of the elements reflects the universal template of the operators. That the English auxiliary system can be analyzed in such a straightforward way in terms of the theory of operators is very strong support for this theory, which was developed on entirely independent grounds.

5.5 The layered structure of the clause in configurational and non-configurational languages

In 1.2 and 3.2 we briefly discussed the notion of 'non-configurational language', i.e. a language which lacks English-style syntactic constituent structure, e.g. Dyirbal (see 3.3.3), Warlpiri (Hale 1979), Lakhota (Van Valin in press). In languages with little or no constituent structure the layered structure exclusively determines the occurrence of specific NP constructions, in particular, the occurrence and position of peripheral arguments. This is illustrated in the following Fore examples (Scott 1978).

(5.103) a. Naninta: mae-ma-ki-na   ʔma:-ʔta
             food   get-SEQ-LINK-3sgA here-L
             ʔyaga:-ne nka-mu-y-e.
             pig-my   3sgU-give-3sgA-DECL
             'He gets food and he gives it to my pig here.'
      b. Ma:-ʔta ʔnaninta: mae-ma   yaga:-ne
             here-L food   get-SEQ pig-my
             nka-mu-y-e.
             3sgU-give-3sgA-DECL
             'He gets and gives food to my pig here.'

Example (5.103a) is a peripheral juncture in which each clause has its own independent periphery. Consequently, the peripheral locative argument *ma:ʔta* 'here' may occur in the second junct. The peripheral juncture is marked by the suffix *-ki* to the medial verb. This is always diagnostic of peripheral junctures in Fore.

Example (5.103b) is a core juncture, and this is indicated by the lone suffix -*ma* on the verb, neither -*ki* nor an actor-concord market being present. In a core juncture the two cores share a common periphery. Consequently, the peripheral constituent must occur before the core juncture and is a constituent of the juncture as a whole in (5.103b). A sentence in which it occurs in the second junct of the core juncture is ungrammatical because it is not possible in a core juncture for there to be a peripheral constituent which modifies the second core independent of the first.

(5.104) *Naninta: mae-ma   ma:ʔta ʔyaga:-ne
          food   get-SEQ here-L pig-my
          nka-mu-y-e.
          3sgU-give-3sgA-DECL
          'He gets food here and gives it to my pig.'

A similar situation is found in Barai (Olson 1981).

(5.105) a. Fu fi-na   mufuo   fase isoe-ke.
             3sg sit-SAME late.afternoon letter write-FUT
             'He will sit and in the late afternoon will write a
             letter.'
         b. Mufuo   fu fi fase isoe-ke.
            late.afternoon 3sg sit letter write-FUT
            'In the late afternoon he will sit and write a letter.'

Example (5.105a) is a peripheral juncture, indicated by the switch-reference monitoring suffix -*na* 'same actor' (see 7.3). The peripheral constituent *mufuo* 'late afternoon' may freely occur in the second junct. However, (5.105b) is a core juncture, as the verbs are simply juxtaposed with no connector. The peripheral constituent must occur before the core juncture and function as a constituent of it as a whole. A sentence in which it occurs in the second junct of a core juncture is ungrammatical, for the same reason that (5.104) is ungrammatical.

(5.106) *Fu fi mufuo   fase isoe.
           3sg sit late.afternoon letter write

Both Fore and Barai are non-configurational languages, and in both the layer structure is the primary determinant of constituent assignment. Consequently a peripheral constituent with a core juncture must modify the juncture as a whole. If it is to modify only one verb, as in (5.103a) and (5.105a), then a peripheral juncture must be used.

If we look at a language in which constituent structure plays a central role, such as English, we find a different situation.

(5.107) a. John is thought to have murdered Mary in the church yesterday.
        b. In Russia Andropov is believed to be working for peace in southern Africa.
        c. Yesterday Fred persuaded John to wash his car in the river tomorrow.

These constructions in English are core junctures, as we will motivate in detail in the next chapter. What is important about those core junctures in English is the fact that the two juncts in the juncture may independently select peripheral arguments. In (5.107a) *yesterday* and *in the church* are peripheral constituents related to the verb *murder* and bear no relation to the verb *think*. They function as constituents of the second junct in the juncture, not of it as a whole. In (5.107b), *in Russia* is a peripheral locative of the first junct, while *in southern Africa* is a peripheral locative to the second junct. Neither locative relates to the core junct as a whole, but only to one of the juncts. Similarly, in (5.107c), *yesterday* belongs to the first junct, both *in the river* and *tomorrow* to the second.

English thus allows juncts in core junctures to select their peripheral constituents independently, in contrast to Fore and Barai. The reason for this lies in the importance of constituent structure in the syntactic organization of English sentences. Constituent structure supplies a hierarchical organization of phrasal or clausal constituents in English sentences. It identifies the relations between predicates and constituents, especially syntactically inert NPs like peripheral ones. Thus in English the domain of setting locatives and temporal outer-peripheral arguments is delimited by the constituent relations within each junct in the sentence, and consequently it is possible for each junct to have independent peripheral constituents (but not peripheral operators). However, in languages which lack constituent structure as a sentential syntactic organization device, the layered structure is the only means for circumscribing the relations between the predicate and its arguments, and the domain of setting peripheral arguments. Because core junctures have a single periphery, and there is nothing to delimit the domain of a peripheral setting NP in a non-configurational language, it is not possible for such an element to modify only one junct, as the ungrammaticality of (5.104) and (5.106) shows.

6 *Nexus*

6.0 Introduction

In Chapter 5 we further developed the notion of the layered structure of the clause with reference to the problems of clause linkage. Having established the levels at which juncture may be effected, we now turn our attention to the nature of the syntactic linkage between two clauses. This is the problem of *nexus*. It must be emphasized from the outset that nexus and levels of juncture are independent parameters in clause linkage. A given type of nexus, e.g. coordination, may occur at all three levels (nuclear, core, and peripheral), and, conversely, at a given level of juncture, e.g. peripheral, all of the nexus possibilities to be discussed below are found. Thus the level and type of linkage must be carefully distinguished.

As noted at the beginning of Chapter 5, a theory of clause linkage is crucial for analysis of both clause-internal morphosyntax and cross-clause coreference maintenance systems. Silverstein (1980b, 1981) argues that case marking in a clause is sensitive to the linkage relationship of that clause to adjacent clauses (see 3.1). Moreover, the choice of discourse coreference maintenance device is very often governed by the nexus–juncture combination obtaining between two clauses (see 6.4.4, 7.5). A theory of clause linkage thus unites the internal morphosyntax of the clause with the complex structures of the sentence and ultimately of discourse.

In 6.1 a typology of nexus types will be proposed and its interaction with the layered structure of the clause examined in 6.2. A hierarchy of clause–linkage relationships will be presented in 6.3 and 6.4, and illustrated with data from English, Quechua, and Jacaltec. In 6.5, certain problems of English complex sentences will be addressed within this framework.

6.1 A typology of nexus types

The two varieties of nexus which have been recognized traditionally are coordination and subordination. In coordinate nexus neither conjunct is embedded in the other, and the two are in a whole–whole equivalence relation. The lack of embedding in a sentence like (6.1a) is obvious, whereas the whole–whole equivalence relation of the juncts is revealed only when certain tests are applied, as in (6.1b).

(6.1) a. The man bought some soap, and the woman will look for a new dryer.

     b. The man bought some soap, and the woman will look for a new dryer, won't she?

We argued in 5.3 that illocutionary force is the outermost peripheral operator, and the fact that the conjuncts may have different illocutionary force indicates that they are independent at the outermost level of the clause, hence are complete clauses in themselves. Neither clause is dependent on the other in any way, and therefore the relation between them is one of whole–whole equivalence. Subordination differs from coordination in two ways. First, one of the two juncts is embedded in the other. Secondly, they are in a part–whole relationship, with the subordinate junct dependent upon the superordinate junct. This is illustrated in (6.2).

(6.2) a. Bertrand believes that Bronwyn ate the last biscuit.

     b. Because Johann kicked the vase over, it broke into pieces.

In (6.2a) *that Bronwyn ate the last biscuit* is the subordinate junct which functions as an argument of *believe* and hence as a part of the superordinate junct *Bertrand believes* ( ); the two juncts together constitute a single unit. (But cf. 6.2.2.) In (6.2b) the subordinate junct is adverbial in nature, and again the two juncts form a composite unit. The illocutionary force test shows that no independent specification is possible in subordinate juncts; the subordinate junct must have the neutral, unmarked form of a statement.

(6.3) a. *Bertrand believes that Bronwyn ate the last biscuit, didn't she?

    b. *Because did Johann kick the vase over, it broke into pieces.

    c. Does Bertrand believe that Bronwyn ate the last biscuit?

    d. Because Johann kicked the vase over, did it break into pieces?

The examples in (6.3a–b) are ungrammatical because the subordinate juncts are questions, but the superordinate ones are assertions. The opposite situation in which the superordinate junct is a question and the subordinate junct is in the unmarked form is perfectly acceptable, as in (6.3c–d). The difference in behavior with regard to illocutionary force of the superordinate and subordinate juncts is due to the nature of the nexus. Because the subordinate junct is embedded in the superordinate one in a part–whole relationship, an outer peripheral operator like illocutionary force only applies to the superordinate junct, the subordinate clause always being presupposed, backgrounded, although stated, information. The position of the subordinate clause with regard to illocutionary force is much the same as that of a core NP with regard to the tense of its governing verb. Tense sets the time of the action of the governing verb and the core NP arguments are not in essence modified by it, their referential value being determined in themselves. In these cases of subordinate nexus, the illocutionary force is a feature of the superordinate junct, and the subordinate junct is unaffected by it, but remains semantically backgrounded, but stated, information. The subordinate junct is dependent on the superordinate junct in that because illocutionary force may never be specified, it may never function as a complete utterance but must always occur in combination with a superordinate junct.

In contrasting these two kinds of nexus, we have been employing two different oppositions: embedded versus non-embedded juncts, on the one hand, and dependence versus independence relations between the juncts on the other. In most discussions of nexus, embedded is considered to be equivalent to a part–whole or dependence relation, and non-embedded to a whole–whole or independence relation. Yet these correlations are not the only possible ones. Consider a construction in which there are two clauses such that neither is embedded in the other, but one is dependent upon the other for some feature, e.g. tense inflection. Such a construction would be neither coordinate nor subordinate. These three possibilities may be represented in terms of features as in (6.4).[1]

(6.4) a. − embedded − dependent = coordination
       b. + embedded + dependent = subordination
       c. − embedded + dependent = ?

We have already seen examples of the first two types of nexus. Examples of the third possibility can be found in nuclear and core-level verb serialization of the type discussed in 5.1; a number of examples are repeated below.

(6.5) Na-bu-wul-cay-pra-kiak.   (Yimas)
       3sgU-3plA-afraid-try-come-REMPAST
       'They tried to make him afraid as he came.'

(6.6) a. Fu fi fase isoe.   (Barai)
           3sg sit letter write
           'He sat (down) and wrote a letter.'
       b. Fu fase fi isoe.
           3sg letter sit write
           'He sat writing a letter.'

(6.7) a. Fémí fa   ilèkùn náà ṣí.   (Yoruba)
              pull door the open
           'Femi pulled the door open.'
       b. Ebí   pa   ọmọ náà kú.
           hunger strike child the die
           'The child starved to death.'

Examples (6.5) and (6.6b) are nuclear serializations, and (6.6a) and (6.7) are core-level. None of the predicates in these serial constructions is embedded in any other. In the Barai (Olson 1981) sentences, for example, *fi* 'sit' is not an argument of *isoe* 'write' (and vice versa); the two form a complex nucleus in (6.6b) sharing the core arguments *fu* 'he' and *fase* 'letter', as well as all other core and peripheral level operators and constituents, while in (6.6a) the two nuclei share an actor argument and constitute a complex core which would take a single set of peripheral-level

a. Coordination: −embedded, −dependent

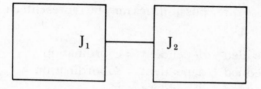

b. Subordination: +embedded, +dependent

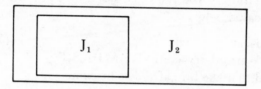

c. Cosubordination: −embedded, +dependent

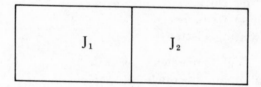

Figure 10 Three nexus types

constituents and operators. There is thus no embedding and each verb is dependent upon the other in terms of shared arguments and operators. The same is true of the Yimas and Yoruba (Lord 1974) examples. This third type of nexus in which two non-embedded juncts join together in a dependence relationship we will label *cosubordination*, following Olson (1981) in which this concept was originally developed.

These three nexus types may be represented as in Figure 10,

taken from Olson (1981). In our analysis of clause linkage, then, we will employ three kinds of nexus rather than the traditional two: coordination, subordination, and cosubordination. In [– embedded] nexus types, i.e. coordination and cosubordination, whether a juncture is dependent upon another is determined solely with reference to the operators over the level of the juncture; e.g. in a non-embedded peripheral juncture, dependence is with respect to the peripheral operators of illocutionary force, evidentials, status, and tense. Thus the operators discussed in 5.3 play a crucial role as a diagnostic of nexus type. The essential point with respect to this three-way distinction among nexus types is that dependence is *not* equivalent to embeddedness. That is, whether a clause is dependent in some way upon another clause is independent of whether it is embedded as an argument of another clause. As we will see, many languages possess construc-tions in which one unit is dependent upon another and yet is clearly not embedded in it.

It is very important to note that our uses of the terms subordina-tion and coordination do not correspond to the traditional ones. Subordination is strictly defined in terms of the part–whole embedding relation. When syntactic patterns indicate that one of the juncts in a construction should not be considered as an embedded constituent of the other, then such a construction will not be analyzed as subordinate nexus, regardless of traditional usage. Further tests will then determine whether the nexus is coordinate or cosubordinate. Our use of the term coordinate is even further removed from the traditional one and must be sharply distinguished from the notion of conjunction, which is not often done in discussions of clause linkage. Coordinate nexus applies to any construction in which the juncts are not in a part–whole relationship, i.e. one junct is not embedded in the other, and both juncts may be independently specified for the operators at the given level of juncture. Cosubordinate nexus differs from co-ordinate in that the juncts may not be independently specified for such operators, but are under the scope of a single operator. Coordinate nexus may be viewed as being overall the least-marked nexus type, and this is in fact indicated by its being negatively defined, i.e. it is the nexus type in which there is no part–whole embedded relationship and in which there is no shared scope of operators. In what follows, the reader may be startled to find familiar constructions labeled in an unfamiliar way as coordinate nexus. Confusion will be minimized if it is remembered that coordinate nexus simply means that the criteria for either of the other two nexi, subordinate or cosubordinate, are not met by the construction in question.

6.2 Interaction of nexus and juncture

In this section we discuss the interaction of nexus and juncture. Since there are three types of nexus and three levels of juncture, there are nine logically possible juncture–nexus combinations. The unmarked pattern of clause linkage is to have units of the same type linked: periphery with periphery, core with core, nucleus with nucleus. Hence the three nexus types provide three distinct ways to join periphery and periphery, core and core, and nucleus and nucleus. We begin with coordinate nexus.

6.2.1 Coordinate nexus   Coordinate nexus is most commonly found in peripheral junctures. Because the two juncts do not yield a composite unit at the peripheral level, each must select independently for peripheral constituents, i.e. locative and temporal adverbials, and peripheral operators such as tense, status and illocutionary force. This was illustrated for English in (6.1) and further examples are given below.

(6.8)   a. The man discussed the news with a stranger in the bar, and his girlfriend will arrive at a restaurant in half an hour.
   b. We thought Fred might bring a few friends to the party, but why did he bring the entire rugby team?
   c. Make yourself at home, and I'll fix us a snack.

(6.9)   a. Fu iviama va-ko   ro   na   (Barai)
      3sg now   go-IMMFUT CONJ 1sg
      nituage   va-ke.
      day.after.tomorrow go-FUT
      'He is about to go now, but I will go the day after tomorrow.'

    b. A keke-i   ro   fu be va-e.
       2sg arrive-PST CONJ 3sg Q go-PST
       'You arrived, but did he go?'

(6.10) a. Lócà ò-yìt-ò   gɔ̀t   (Lango)
       man 3sgA-climbed-3sgU mountain
       ò-lùb-ɔ̀   dákó.
       3sgA-followed-3sgU woman
       'The man climbed the mountain toward the
       woman.'
       (Literally: 'The man climbed the mountain;
       he followed the woman.')
    b. Téd   ríŋô á-bín-ó
       cook-IMP meat 1sgA-go-3sgU
       cɔ̀mmò.
       eat-INF
       'Cook the meat [and] I'll eat it.'

The two clauses in (6.8a) have different tenses and peripheral constituents, while those in (6.8b–c) differ in illocutionary force. The same differences are found in the Barai sentences in (6.9); the two juncts in (a) have distinct tenses, while in (b) they contrast in illocutionary force. The examples in (6.10) are from Lango; Noonan & Bavin-Woock (1981) label them 'paratactic' constructions because of the lack of an overt conjunction. Each junct can stand by itself as a separate speech act, and both need not have the same illocutionary force, as in (6.10b) (E. Bavin, personal communication). Because these constructions allow each junct independent selection of the outermost peripheral operator, illocutionary force, they involve coordinate nexus at the peripheral level.

Coordination in core junctures is not as common as that in peripheral junctures. Such a construction would involve two independent cores, each with its own set of core constituents and operators; the two juncts would share higher-level operators such as tense and illocutionary force. A clear example of core-level coordinate nexus is from Barai (Olson 1981). The main core-level operators in Barai are the pragmatic pivot and certain mode particles (-*me* 'casual', -*ka* 'intensive', -*te* 'dubitative') which occur bound to pronominal PrPs. In core coordination, each junct has its own PrP, either of which may occur with a mode particle as in (6.11).

(6.11) a. Na e   ije   k-ia   bu-me   va-e.
            1sg person DEF say-3plU 3pl-CAS go-PST
            'I spoke to the people, [and] they just went.'

      b. Na-ka   e   ije   k-ia   bu
            1sg-INTENS person DEF say-3plU 3pl
            va-e.
            go-PST
            'I really spoke to the people, [and] they went.'

Olson notes that there is a significant pause between the two juncts in sentences such as these; there is no such pause with core-level cosubordinate nexus. Both juncts are under the scope of the peripheral operators of tense and illocutionary force; no such differences between them are allowed.

(6.12) a *Na e   ije   k-ia-e,   bu-me
            1sg person DEF say-3plU-PST 3pl-CAS
            va-ke.
            go-FUT
            'I spoke to the people, [and] they will just go.'

      b. *Na-ka   e   ije   k-ia,   bu be
            1sg-INTENS person DEF say-3plU 3pl Q
            va-e.
            *go-PST.
            'I really spoke to the people, [and] did they go?'

      c. A be   e   ije   k-ia,   bu-me   va-e.
            2sg Q   person DEF say-3plU 3pl-CAS go-PST
            'Did you speak to the people [and] did they just go?'

The two juncts in (6.12a) are marked for different tenses, and the result is ungrammatical; note that in (6.11) tense is marked only on the second verb and has scope over the whole sentence. The occurrence of the question marker *be* in the second conjunct of (6.12b) likewise yields an ungrammatical sentence; the only possibility is for it to occur in the first conjunct, as in (6.12c), in which case it has scope over the whole sentence just like the tense suffix on the final verb. Thus the Barai sentences in (6.11) illustrate the combination of core juncture with coordinate nexus.

Core coordination is also found in English in the so-called accusative plus infinitive construction, as in (6.13).

(6.13) a. Philip believes Doreen to have tickled the poodle.
      b. Fred got John to wash his car.

Two syntactic tests show that the infinitival complements are not embedded as core arguments of the finite predicate, passivization (which is inapplicable to *get*) and clefting.

(6.14) a. *Doreen to have tickled the poodle is believed by Philip.
      b. Doreen is believed by Philip to have tickled the poodle.

(6.15) a. It is Doreen who Philip believes to have tickled the poodle.
      b. *It is Doreen to have tickled the poodle that Philip believes.
      c. *It is to have tickled the poodle that Philip believes Doreen.

(6.16) a. It is John who Fred got to wash his car.
      b. *It is John to wash his car that Fred got.
      c. *It is to wash his car that Fred got John.

Passivization in (6.14) shows that only *Doreen* and not *Doreen to have tickled the poodle* is a syntactic argument of *believe* and the latter is not a single constituent. This is borne out by the clefting test in (6.15); the same clefting facts hold in (6.16) for (6.13b). (See also Postal 1974, Bach 1977, Cole & Hermon 1981). These facts point to *Doreen to have tickled the poodle* and *John to wash his car* not being embedded under *believe* and *get*, respectively, and hence the nexus in these examples cannot be subordinate. Because the two juncts share a core argument, *Doreen* in (6.13a) and *John* in (6.13b), the level of juncture must be the core. In order to ascertain whether coordination or cosubordination is involved, we have to look at the core-level operator in English, modals (See 5.3).

(6.17) Philip must believe Doreen to have tickled the poodle.
(6.18) Fred can get John to wash his car.

We are concerned here with the deontic meanings of modals, 'obligation' for *must* and 'ability' for *can*. It is quite clear in these examples that the modal has scope only over the verb in the first junct; the obligation in (a) holds only between *Philip* and *believe*, and only Fred's ability, not John's, is at issue in (b). Consequently, (6.17) cannot mean 'Philip is obligated to believe Doreen to be (have been) obligated to tickle the poodle', and (6.18) cannot be interpreted as 'Fred is able to get John to be able to wash his car'. Thus the core operators of English do not have scope over the whole construction, and consequently there is no dependency relation between these non-embedded core junctures. The constructions in (6.13) are, therefore, examples of coordinate nexus at the core level. Note that they have single peripheral operators of tense and illocutionary force. Tense is impossible in an English infinitive, and independent specification of illocutionary force in the second junct is ungrammatical.

(6.19) a. *Philip believes Doreen to have tickled the poodle, hasn't she?

   b. *Fred got Mary to wash his car, doesn't/didn't she?

The dependency relation in this construction is only at the peripheral and not the core level.

   Coordinate nexus at the nuclear level involves two nuclei with independent aspectual or directional marking. Nuclear coordinate nexus is very rare, but we have found examples in two unrelated languages of Papua New Guinea, Alamblak (Bruce 1979) and Barai (Olson 1981).

(6.20) a. Fu vazai ufu furi   numu akoe.   (Barai)
           3sg grass cut finish pile   throw.away
           'He finished cutting, piled, and threw
           away the grass.'

   b. Wa-yarim-ak-ni-n-m-ko.   (Alamblak)
           IMP-DIR-get-go-2sgA-3plU-DIR
           'Get them toward me and go up [there].'

In both of these examples we are dealing with nuclear junctures in which individual nuclei receive individual aspectual inflection, as in the Barai example, or directional modification, as in the Alamblak example. The aspectual operator *furi* modifies only *ufu* 'cut' in (6.20a). There are two directionals in (6.20b), *-yarim-* 'toward speaker' and *-ko* 'up from speaker', and they each modify a different verb in the nuclear juncture. Thus in neither sentence does any verb share a nuclear-level operator with another verb. They do, of course, share all core and peripheral arguments and operators.

6.2.2 Subordinate nexus Subordinate nexus is the type in which one junct is embedded in the other, and, consequently, the juncts function as a composite unit. Subordinate nexi are widespread in languages, but are found at only two of the three levels of juncture.

Subordinate nexus at the peripheral layer is very common in many languages. The best-known examples are adverbial clauses in which a clause is subordinated and functions as an adverbial modifier of the main clause, as in these English examples.

(6.21) a. Because John kissed her, Mary burst into tears.
      b. After Bruce left, the party really hotted up.
      c. If you don't stop that, I'll scream!

The nexus is subordinate, the subordination being indicated by the subordinating conjunctions *because*, *after*, *if*. Note, as mentioned above, that the subordinate clause may not be independently specified for illocutionary force.

(6.22) a. *Mary burst into tears, because/after/if did someone kiss her?
      b. *I'll scream because/after/if kiss me!

Also, since adverbial clauses function as adverbial modifiers or constituents of the main clause, they must be considered peripheral elements of the main clause.

Such subordinate adverbial clauses are widespread in other languages.

(6.23) a. Hel ilotaka-he   k'ũ ičhũhã le   (Lakhota)
         there 2sgA-sit-CONT PST while this
         wa-kage.
         1sgA-make
         'While you were sitting there, I made this.'

b. B-in-i-bili-∅   ng lalake ang isda   (Tagalog)
   IMPF-buy-THF A man   PrP fish
   dahil sa na-gu-gutom   siya
   because AF-IMPF-hungry 3sgPrP
   'The man is buying the fish because he is
   hungry.'

c. Sáá pú-lupa-gá   píra-   (Kewa)
   1dl go-1dlPRES-because sit-
   lepaa-pe.
   2pl/IMP-IMM
   'Because we two are going, you all sit down
   now.'

The adverbial clause in the Lakhota example in (6.23) functions
as a temporal modifier of the main clause, while in the Tagalog
and Kewa examples it is in a causal relation to the main clause.
Subordinate nexus at the peripheral level is thus a common
phenomenon in the languages of the world.

Subordination at the core level involves the embedding of either
a core as a core constituent (i.e. argument) or a full clause with
independent periphery and some freedom of peripheral operators,
usually tense; the second type appears to be much more common
than the first. This example of core embedding comes from Barai.

(6.24) a. Juare ij-ia   a   ni   ije g-a-ne.
          garden DEF-L 2sg IMP 3sg look-3sgU-IMP
          'Look at it (there) in the garden!'
       b. Juare ij-ia   a   ni   [mave n-one
          garden DEF-L 2sg   IMP pig 1sg-POSS
          sak-a-mo]   g-a-ne.
          bite-2sgU-PRES/HAB look-3sgU-IMP
          'In the garden look for [it]: my pig bites!'

The first example has a simple pronominal object *ije* 'it', while
in the second the core *mave n-one sak-a-mo* 'my pig bites' replaces
ije. This is a 'naked' core without any peripheral arguments, as
none are possible in this construction. Moreover, the tense
inflection in the embedded core is constrained by that of the superordinate junct.

English gerunds are a type of core subordination. Gerunds are basically clauses stripped of all of their peripheral operators and usually reduced to just the verb plus core arguments. They function as arguments of the main clause.

(6.25) a. Max's losing the election surprised everyone.
b. Mary was very concerned about Harold's being so despondent.
c. Alex was angry about Larry's sleeping through dinner.
d. Felix regretted Bill's having lost his job.

English differs from Barai in that oblique constituents are permitted in gerunds.

(6.26) a. Fred's whistling at Mary in the library caused him to get kicked out.
b. Walter's sending the bouquet to Louise was an empty gesture.

Despite the possible occurrence of peripheral constituents, gerunds in English exemplify the embedding of a reduced clause (ideally a simple core, as in Barai) as a core argument.

The embedding of an entire clause as a core argument is quite common in languages, and this commonness belies its unique character. In all of the other juncture–nexus combinations dis-cussed in this section, the units linked are of the same type: nucleus with nucleus, core with core, periphery with periphery. Here, however, we have a periphery linked with a core or, more specifically, embedded in it. This is quite striking, because peripheries are more inclusive than cores, and therefore the sub-ordinate junct may contain higher-level constituents and operators than the superordinate junct. This asymmetry relates directly to certain paradoxical features of these constructions.

(6.27) a. Max reported/believed that Louise will arrive in London tomorrow.
b. That Louise will arrive in London tomorrow was reported/believed by Max.

(6.28) a. That Louise will arrive in London tomorrow surprised everyone.
b. That Louise will arrive in London tomorrow is very likely.

The prima-facie evidence for the core status of *that*-clauses in English is (a) that they passivize as in (6.27), and (b) that they can occur in the PrP slot, as in (6.28). They function as core arguments of the main clause predicate, and therefore the linkage type is core subordination. Many verbs, however, do not take *that*-clauses as core arguments. Zwicky (1971) and Emonds (1976) argue that the complements of 'manner of speaking verbs understood communicatively' are not objects akin to those in (6.27a).

(6.29) a. Morris whined that night was falling.
        b. *That night was falling was whined by Morris.
        c. *It was whined by Morris that night was falling.

(6.30) a. One guest growled to the waiter that an hour was long enough.
        b. *That an hour was long enough was growled to the waiter by one guest.
        c. *It was growled to the waiter by one guest that an hour was long enough.

Verbs like *whine*, *shriek*, *growl*, and *mumble* can have *that*-clauses, but they do not undergo passivization. Zwicky and Emonds conclude from this that they are not direct objects; they are therefore peripheral arguments, since peripheral arguments do not normally undergo passivization in English (see 4.2). Other verbs which have peripheral *that*-clauses include *seem*, *appear*, *persuade*, *convince*, *remind*, and *tell*.

(6.31) a. It seems/appears that Fred has been elected treasurer.
        b. Abigail persuaded/convinced Lance that she had not gone out with Rudy.
        c. Felix reminded Nigel that he was supposed to meet Holly at the Uni.
        d. The vet told Lucy that her pet wombat would recover.

Seem and *appear* have only one core argument, which in (6.31a) is the dummy pivot filler *it*; the *that*-clause is an inner peripheral argument. All of the other complement-taking predicates in (6.31) have two core arguments in addition to a *that*-clause, which is again peripheral. Moreover, extraposition is possible with all sentential pivots.

(6.32) a. It was reported/believed by Max that Louise will arrive in London tomorrow.
    b. It surprised everyone that Louise will arrive in London tomorrow.
    c. It is very likely that Louise will arrive in London tomorrow.

Here again the *that*-clause appears as a peripheral argument.

When these constructions are examined with respect to level operators, it is immediately obvious that they are not at all like the core–core embedding in Barai but rather like peripheral subordinate clauses. *That*-clauses have independent peripheries and independent tense selection in many cases, just like adverbial peripheral subordinate clauses. They may not, however, be independently specified for illocutionary force, the outermost peripheral-level operator, which is uniquely a feature of the superordinate clause.

(6.33) a. *Max believed that Louise will arrive in London tomorrow, won't she?
    b. *Tim reported that why did Noel lose his keys?
    c. *It seems that what has Olivia bought this time?
    d. *Alex convinced Bob that when will Elsa leave for Brisbane?

As with adverbial clauses, *that*-clauses cannot have distinct illocutionary force from the main clause (see 6.1). Since core operators like modals do not have scope over the core of the subordinate clause and peripheral operators like status and tense may be independently specified for the two juncts, these clauses have a dependency relation in terms of operators at the peripheral rather than the core level. This is the paradoxical feature of sentences like (6.27) alluded to earlier: by clause-internal criteria there is core-level juncture, but from the interclausal perspective of operators, the juncture is peripheral. Notice that the paradox is solely with respect to constructions like (6.27) and (6.28), and not (6.29), (6.30a), (6.31), and (6.32) in which the *that*-clause is a peripheral argument. These latter constructions follow the overwhelming tendency toward linkage of units of the same type. This leads us to the following proposal: the unmarked syntactic status for a *that*-clause in English is as a peripheral (more specifically, an inner peripheral) argument. Hence (6.29a), (6.30a), (6.31), and (6.32) all represent the unmarked pattern with respect to *that*-clauses. For such a clause to occur as a core argument is marked, and the most highly marked syntactic status for a *that*-clause is occurrence as PrP.

There is syntactic evidence supporting the highly marked status of sentential PrPs. First, they may not be embedded. (Some of the following examples are from Emonds 1976.)

(6.34) a. *For that you pay this tax to be necessary would be an inconvenience.
　　　 b. For it to be necessary that you pay this tax would be an inconvenience.
　　　 c. *I don't believe (that) that you study history hurts you.
　　　 d. *Although that the house is empty may depress you, it pleases me.
　　　 e. *The salesman who that I bought a car seemed most important to was a southerner.
　　　 f. The salesman who it seemed most important to that I bought a car was a southerner.

Note that the extraposition of the *that*-clauses in (b) and (f) remedies the ungrammaticality; replacing the clauses with gerunds renders the others grammatical. Secondly, sentential PrPs inhibit the formation of WH-questions and drastically reduce the acceptability of yes/no questions.

(6.35) a. *Why did that Mary liked old records irritate him?
　　　 b. Why did it irritate him that Mary liked old records?
　　　 c. *Did that Mary liked old records irritate him?
　　　 d. Did it irritate him that Mary liked old records?

Again, extraposition of the *that*-clause to peripheral status results in grammatical sentences. Third, sentential PrPs are islands, and all extraction out of them is blocked, hence the 'Sentential Subject Constraint' of Ross (1967); the same extractions are possible when the clause is extraposed.

(6.36) a. *What did that Mary liked irritate him?
　　　 b. What did it irritate him that Mary liked?

    c.   *The old records which that Mary liked irritated him
        are over in the corner.

    d.   The old records which it irritated him that Mary liked
        are over in the corner.

These facts correlate with the highly marked status of PrP *that*-clauses as opposed to their unmarked status as peripheral arguments. It should be noted that Emonds (1976) takes an even stronger position, contending that such clauses never occur as core arguments but rather are always either extraposed, as in (6.27a), or topicalized into COMP, as in (6.27b) and (6.28) (see 1976:126–135).

Non-PrP *that*-clauses are not as marked as sentential PrPs, and their exact syntactic status is somewhat ambiguous. If we compare (6.27a) with (6.29a) or (6.30a), there is no overt indication that the *that*-clause in (6.27a) is core but those in the others are peripheral. There are in fact no grounds for analyzing them as core arguments in such constructions, and even if the main clause is passive, the *that*-clause may remain a peripheral argument. This captures the difference between (6.27b) and (6.32a). In (6.27b) *that Louise will arrive in London tomorrow* must be regarded a core argument, since it has assumed PrP-hood in the passive construction. In (6.32a), on the other hand, it remains a peripheral argument, so that when the main verb is passivized, there is no argument to fill the PrP slot and accordingly the (in this case cataphoric) pivot filler *it* occurs. (See 6.5 for more details of mapping from semantic to syntactic structure in complex sentences.) Thus non-PrP *that*-complements need not be considered core arguments, even with verbs which allow them to occur as the PrP in a passive construction.

We have argued that the occurrence of a junct with independent periphery and tense as a core argument of another predicate is highly marked syntactically, and that the unmarked syntactic status of such juncts is as a peripheral argument. English thus has two types of peripheral subordinate clauses, adverbial clauses and *that*-clauses. There is, however, an important difference between them. Because a *that*-clause is represented in the semantic structure of the complement-taking predicate it will always be an *inner* peripheral argument (cf. 3.3.1). Adverbial clauses, on the other hand, are not directly related to the semantic structure of the main-clause predicate, and moreover they typically characterize some aspect of the spatio-temporal context in which the state of affairs of the main clause is situated. Consequently adverbial clauses are constituents of the *outer* periphery of the clause.

We have discussed only English in this section, and it is not possible to present detailed analyses of the core versus peripheral status of such subordinate juncts in other languages here (cf. 6.4.3 for a discussion of this construction in Jacaltec). However, because of the principle of linkage of like units, we may assume that the embedding of a nearly fully sentential junct into a core will always yield a syntactically marked construction and that languages will develop means, e.g. extraposition, to alleviate this asymmetry. It may be objected that the widespread occurrence of this construction is counterevidence against attributing a marked syntactic status to it. This objection overlooks the functional basis of the construction: reporting speech. The basic function which all such constructions have is the expression of indirect discourse. In many languages, particularly Papuan languages, this is the only function it may have, and consequently in such languages these complements occur only with verbs of saying. The nearly fully sentential nature of the subordinate junct follows from its function: the clause reports an utterance which specifies a particular state of affairs, and both its spatio-temporal parameters and the relationship between the time of the reported utterance and that of the state of affairs are expressed, resulting in an independent periphery and tense operator in the clause. Languages such as Dyirbal which lack a distinction between direct and indirect discourse do not have constructions of this type. Once languages have grammaticalized these indirect discourse complements, their use may spread to other verbs, especially cognition verbs.

Subordination appears not to exist at the nuclear level. Such a construction would involve the embedding of a naked nucleus in another nucleus, which is in principle impossible. It is possible for a nucleus to function as a core argument of another nucleus, but this would be core subordination, not nuclear. No examples of this type have been found, even in languages with extensive nuclear junctures such as Barai and Yimas.

6.2.3 Cosubordinate nexus   The final nexus type to be considered is cosubordinate nexus. This nexus type is not traditionally recognized and was first proposed in Olson (1981). It is characterized by two juncts which are in a dependency relation, but neither of which is embedded in the other. The lack of embedding contrasts cosubordinate with subordinate nexus, although both result in a composite unit, while the dependence between the juncts distinguishes cosubordinate from coordinate nexus, although both involve the non-embedding of the juncts. Cosubordinate nexus is found at all three levels of juncture.

Cosubordinate nexus at the peripheral level is best illustrated by the clause-chaining and switch-reference phenomena widely found in Papuan and American Indian languages. In this construction, bound morphemes monitor the sameness or difference of the primary participants between two juncts (see 7.3). The juncts are not in a subordinate relationship, as one junct is not embedded in the other. However, a dependency relation exists between the juncts in that they must have the same illocutionary force and share the same absolute tense. Note the following examples from Kewa (Franklin 1971).

(6.37) a. Nipú ípu-la   pare ní paalá
        3sg   come-3sgPRES but 1sg afraid
        na-pía.
        NEG-be: 3sgPRES
        'He is coming but I am not afraid.'

   b. Ní réka-no   ágaa lá-a.
      1sg stand-DIFF.SmP talk say-3sgPST
      'I stood up and he talked.'

   c. Ní réko-a   ágaa lá-lo.
      1sg stand-SAME.SmP talk say-1sgPRES
      'I stood up and am speaking.'

   d. Nipú táá-ma   pámua-la.
      3sg   hit-SAME.SmP walk-3sgPRES
      'He is hitting it while walking.'

   e. Roto-mé   tá-a   pae ake-me   tá-a
      stick-ERG hit-3sgPST or what-ERG hit-3sgPST
      pae.
      or
      'A stick hit him, or what hit him?'

f. Pora póá   míru rú-nane
    door strike-IMP snake inside-DIR
    ípu-la-ga.
    come-3sgPRES-because
    'Close the door, because the snake is coming inside!'

Sentence (6.37a) is a typical example of a peripheral juncture with coordinate nexus. The juncts are connected by a coordinating conjunction *pare* 'but', and each can stand alone as an independent utterance. Note that each verb is inflected for the person and number of the actor as well as tense. Sentences (6.37b–d) contrast with (6.37a) in that they exhibit cosubordinate nexus at the peripheral level. In these examples only the final verb is inflected for the person and number of the actor (SmP) and for tense. The verb of the first junct in all three examples merely takes a suffix indicating whether the SmPs are different (6.37b) or the same (6.37c–d). In same SmP constructions a distinction is made as to whether the events expressed by the two juncts are sequential (6.37c) or simultaneous (6.37d). The juncts in a peripheral layer cosubordinate nexus must share not only the same tense, but also the same illocutionary force. If they differ in illocutionary force, a coordinate nexus must be used, as in (6.37e), or one of the juncts must be embedded in a subordinate nexus, as in (6.37f).

The same contrast between coordinate and cosubordinate nexus in peripheral junctures is found in other languages, e.g. Tonkawa (Hoijer 1949).

(6.38) a. Tekeke?e:k š?a:pa-ta   ke-yaše-w.
            in.that.bush hide-SAME 1sgU-watch-IMP
            'Hide in that bush and watch me.'
        b. Tekeke?e:k š?a:pa-w   ?e:-ta   ke-yaše-w.
            in.that.bush hide-IMP and-SAME 1sgU-watch-IMP
            'Hide in that bush and watch me.'

Sentence (6.38a) is an example of cosubordinate nexus; only the final verb is inflected for imperative illocutionary force although its scope is over both juncts. There is no conjunction, the same SmP morpheme is merely added to the verb of the first junct. Sentence (6.38b) is a coordinate nexus. A coordinating conjunction *?e:-* 'and' is used to which the same SmP morpheme is added.

Note that each verb has imperative inflection. Each of the juncts in (6.39b) can stand as independent utterances, as would be expected of a coordinate nexus. This is not true of (6.38a). The first junct does not have its own inflection for illocutionary force and therefore is dependent upon the second junct; thus it may not be an independent utterance. The second verb may, however, since it carries the sentential features of the whole unit. Constructions parallel to these in Kewa and Tonkawa are widespread and can be found, for example, in Washo (Jacobsen 1967), Chickasaw (D. Payne 1980) and Barai (Olson 1981). Cosubordinate peripheral junctures of this type with switch-reference morphology are a common feature of many language families, especially those with verb-final word order. (See 7.3 for more detailed discussion.)

Languages like English exhibit a different kind of peripheral cosubordination. It is illustrated in (6.39).

(6.39)   a.   Max went to the store and bought some beer.
        b.   Fred has already left Santa Fe and should arrive in New Orleans tomorrow.

These sentences with the PrP of the second junct omitted under coreference with that of the first are similar to the examples of peripheral coordination in English in (6.1) and (6.8a) in certain respects; each conjunct may have distinct peripheral constituents and tense choices. However, there is a significant difference between them: the conjuncts in (6.1) and (6.8) may have different illocutionary forces as in (6.8b–c), whereas sentences such as (6.39) may not. This can be seen in (6.40)–(6.41).

(6.40)   a.   John went to work but forgot his briefcase, didn't he?
        b.   John went to work, but he forgot his briefcase, didn't he?
        c.   John went to work, but did he forget his briefcase?
        d.   John went to work, but did forget his briefcase./*?
        e.   What did Max go to the store and buy?

(6.41)   a.   *Bob has a new car and is going off for the weekend, isn't he?
        b.   Bob has a new car, and he is going off for the weekend, isn't he?

    c. *Zeke has always been a troublemaker, but why did rob
a bank?

    d. *What did Max go to the store and he buy?

When there is an interrogative tag on one of these sentences, the
illocutionary force operator must have the entire sentence under
its scope; this can be seen in (6.40a), in which both juncts must
be considered part of the question, and in (6.41a) in which the
tag explicitly refers to only the second junct, rendering the
sentence ungrammatical. When the second junct has a pronominal
PrP as in (6.41b), then the sentence is grammatical. There is no
zero anaphora in (6.40b), and the scope of the operator is variable;
it may be interpreted as being over only the second junct, with
the first being an independent assertion, or it may be over both
juncts as in (6.40a). Questions with core-initial tense are not
possible when there is zero anaphora as in (6.40d) and (6.41c),
but are possible in the coordinate constructions in (6.8b), (6.40c).
That the scope of the illocutionary force operator is over the whole
sentence is clearest in (6.40e), in which the question word is an
argument of the verb in the second junct.[2] Note further that these
two juncts are also under the scope of the same tense operator;
the verb in the second junct is tenseless. This is the result of the
fact discussed in 5.4 that sentence-initial tense is the marker of
interrogative illocutionary force in English. The two clauses thus
share both tense and illocutionary force peripheral operators.
When there is no zero anaphora in the second junct, as in (6.41d),
the result is ungrammatical. This is further evidence that zero
anaphora in the second junct correlates with the illocutionary force
operator having scope over the whole sentence.

    Similar facts can be adduced for German.

(6.42) a. Jürgen is in die Stadt gegangen und hat Kleider
gekauft, nicht war?
'Jürgen went to town and bought clothes, didn't he?'

        b. Jürgen ist in die Stadt gegangen, und er hat Kleider
gekauft, nicht war?
'Jürgen went to town, and he bought clothes, didn't
he?'

These examples are exactly parallel to (6.40a–b) in their possible interpretations. In (6.42a), with zero pronominalization of the PrP of the second junct, both juncts must be interpreted as being under the scope of the interrogative operator, whereas in (6.42b), in which there is no zero anaphora, two readings are possible, one identical to (6.42a) and the other with only the second junct under the scope of the tag. These constraints on the illocutionary force of juncts which otherwise select tense independently distinguish the zero anaphora constructions in (6.39), (6.40a, e) and (6.42a) from those in (6.1), (6.8), (6.40b–c), (6.41b) and (6.42b). Since there is no embedding relationship between the juncts and they form a single unit with respect to the illocutionary force operator, such constructions must be considered cosubordinate rather than coordinate peripheral junctures.

Cosubordinate nexus at the core level occurs in numerous languages. The core-level verb serialization constructions in (6.5)-(6.7) discussed in Chapter 5 are examples of this nexus type. We repeat a few examples from the discussion of serialization in Chapter 5 here.

(6.43) a. Mo mú ìwé wá ilé.   (Yoruba)
            1sg take book come home
            'I brought a book home.'
        b. Sùk ʔaw máy maa.   (Thai)
            Sook take wood come
            'Sook brought the wood.'
        c. ɔ-de   siká   nó maa me.   (Twi)
            3sg-take money the give 1sg
            'He gave me the money.'
        d. Olú lo aṣọ   náà gbó   (Yoruba)
            Olu use dress the wear. out
            'Olu wore out the dress.'

These are all examples of core-layer serialization in that the verbs share a core argument and core operators and all peripheral constituents and operators. As the arguments in Chapter 5 demonstrated, there is no embedding involved here, and the serialization construction is a composite unit. They are, then, instances of cosubordinate nexus.

English has a variety of core cosubordination which is analogous to the verb serialization in (6.43). It involves stance verbs and a following non-finite verb ending in *-ing*.

(6.44) a. Paul sat playing his guitar for hours.
      b. Zelda lay reading a book in bed.
      c. Matthew stood singing on a street corner.

These involve cosubordinate nexus because unlike (6.13), modals have scope over both predicates.

(6.45) a. Paul can sit playing his guitar for hours.
      b. Matthew must stand singing on a street corner for thirty minutes because he lost his bet with Ernie.

Can in (6.45a) does not express Paul's ability to sit but rather his ability to sit playing the guitar, and therefore it has scope over both verbs. Similarly in (6.45b) *must* signals an obligation not simply to stand but to stand and sing. Because the first verb in each sentence is intransitive, there can be no question of embedding being involved, and because the core-level operator in question (modals) has both juncts within its scope, they form a composite unit with respect to it. Accordingly, sentences like (6.44) are instances of core-level cosubordination.

The most common type of nexus at the nuclear level is cosubordinate. In such a construction the nuclei share aspectual or directional inflection; they all must be under the scope of a single operator. This distinguishes them from the nuclear co-ordinate constructions in (6.20).

(6.46)   Wa-rim-ak-ni-n-m.   (Alamblak)
          IMP-DIR-get-go-2sgA-3plU
          'Get them and go away from me!'

(6.47) a. E   viri-tū-ra   na   duru na   (Fijian)
        CM put-stand-TR ART post ART
        tūraga.
        chief
        'The chief erects the post.'
      b. E   viri-tū-ra   tū   na   duru
        CM put-stand-TR CONT ART post
        na   tūraga.
        ART chief
        'The chief continues to erect the post.'

(6.48) a. Fu kai   fu-one   kume-fie   va.   (Barai)
        3sg friend 3sg-POSS call-listen   continue
        'He continued calling and listening for his friend.'
    b. *Fu   kai   fu-one   kume-va-fie.
        3sg   friend 3sg-POSS call-continue-listen

In the Alamblak example (Bruce 1979) in (6.46), there is a single directional affix, *-rim-* 'away from speaker', which modifies both *-ak-* 'get' and *-ni-* 'go', in contrast to (6.20b) in which each verb was modified by a different directional. The nexus in (6.46) is cosubordinate. The verbs *viri-* 'put' and *tū-* 'stand' are serialized in Fijian (Parke 1981) to yield a transitive verb meaning 'to erect', as in (6.47a). When aspectual modification is added (signaled by *tū-* 'stand'), the operator obligatorily has scope over both nuclei, as (6.47b) shows. Finally in the Barai examples in (6.48) we see that unlike (6.20a), an aspectual operator cannot occur between the nuclei in the juncture but rather must occur after them and modify the whole complex nucleus. Comparing (6.20a) and (6.48) we see a clear contrast between coordinate and cosubordinate nexus at the nuclear level.

6.2.4 Summary The interaction of nexus and juncture discussed in the previous sections may be summarized as in Table 11.

Table 11 *Nexus and juncture possibilities*

Nexus: Juncture	Coordinate	Subordinate	Cosubordinate
Peripheral	*Conjunction* English (6.1), (6.8) Barai (6.9)	*Adverbial clause* English (6.21) Lakhota, Tagalog, Kewa (6.23)	*Switch-reference* Kewa (6.37) Tonkawa (6.38)
	Parataxis Lango (6.10)	*That-Clause* English (6.31)	*CONJ with zero anaphora* English (6.39) German (6.42a)
Core	*Parataxis* Barai (6.11)	*Core embedding* Barai (6.24b) English (6.25)	*Verb serialization* Yoruba, Thai, Twi (6.43)
	ACC plus INF English (6.13)	*Clause embedding* English (6.27b), (6.28b)	English (6.44).
Nuclear	*Verb serialization* Barai (6.20a) Alamblak (6.20b)	Non-existent	*Verb serialization* Alamblak (6.46) Fijian (6.47) Barai (6.48)

6.3. Semantic relations of clause linkage

Having set out a general typology of possible syntactic clause-linkage types, we now turn to the question of the semantic aspects of the syntactic relationships between clauses or, more precisely, between the relevant levels of clauses. The basic proposition to be explored here is: there is a direct correlation between the semantic relationships holding between two clauses (or subparts thereof) and the syntactic linkage between them, such that the closer the semantic relationship, the tighter the syntactic linkage. The consequences of these linkage possibilities for both clause-internal and cross-clause syntax will also be examined.

6.3.1 Syntactic bondedness hierarchy   The nine possible juncture–nexus combinations discussed in 6.2 represent the interaction of two independent sets of variables, the level of the clause involved and the nature of the syntactic relationship. If one analyzes each set in terms of the sententiality of the relevant elements, then these nine combinations may be ordered into a *syntactic bondedness hierarchy* which captures the relative strength of the syntactic bond between two juncts in a complex construction. Looking at the levels of the clause, it is immediately obvious that the peripheral layer is the most sentential and the nuclear level the least. The peripheral layer of the clause surrounds the nucleus and the core, which together contain the predicate and its core arguments, and includes all extra-core constituents. The nucleus contains only the predicate and hence is the least sentential of the three. The core falls in between having verbal arguments as constituents, but lacking peripheral constituents. Thus the levels of the clause may be ranked as follows with respect to their sententiality.

(6.49)   PERIPHERY > CORE > NUCLEUS

The ordering of nexus types is not so straightforward and must be established with respect to the independence and scope of the operators on the three levels. Coordinate nexus allows the greatest independence of the operators; because there is no dependence between the two juncts, each junct has independent operators at the level of the juncture with scope over it alone. A junct which has its own operators is more sentential than one which is dependent upon another clause for some operator. In subordination the embedded junct is less sentential than the juncts in coordinate nexus. At the peripheral level they are always dependent upon the main clause with respect to illocutionary force but may have independent operators up through tense. At the core level the linked junct in both coordinate and subordinate nexus is independent of the other junct with respect to the core operator modality. We saw this in the Barai example in (6.11) and (6.24b), and in the English core coordinate examples in (6.17)–(6.18). The following examples illustrate this for core subordination in English with gerunds.

(6.50) a. Fred can forgive John's leaving the party early.
   b. Laura must overlook Tom's having an affair with her best friend.

As one would expect, the deontic modal in the main clause in these sentences has scope over only the main-clause actor and predicate; the subordinate juncts are unaffected. There are syntactic grounds, however, for considering gerunds less sentential than the infinitives of core coordination in English; see Ross (1973) for detailed discussion. There is no contrast between the two nexus types at the nuclear level. We may conclude that the linked clause is less sentential in subordinate than in coordinate nexus. There is no question that the sententiality of the juncts in coordinate nexus is greater than in cosubordinate nexus, for there is always operator dependence in cosubordination and never any in coordination. When contrasting subordinate and cosubordinate nexus at the peripheral and core levels, we find clear evidence that subordinate juncts are more sentential than cosubordinate juncts. At the peripheral level in English, neither construction may independently select illocutionary force, but in the cosubordinate construction in (6.39) the dependent junct is missing a core argument (the PrP) and is dependent upon the previous clause with respect to the specification of this argument. Such a relation is impossible in the subordinate nexus, as the core arguments of the subordinate clause are always fully specified. Moreover there is no constraint in subordinate nexus types to the effect that the superordinate and subordinate juncts must have any coreferential arguments. In core junctures a similar contrast obtains; a gerund need not share any arguments with the main clause, whereas the participle in a cosubordinate nexus such as (6.44) must. Indeed, in English, cosubordination in peripheral and core junctures always requires both shared operators and arguments. The linked junct in cosubordinate nexus is, then, less sentential than that in subordinate nexus. We thus arrive at the following ranking of nexus types in terms of the potential sententiality of the linked junct.

(6.51)   COORDINATE > SUBORDINATE >
         COSUBORDINATE

The hierarchies in (6.49) and (6.51) generate markedness relations between levels of juncture and nexus types. For every kind of juncture there is an unmarked nexus type; these are presented in (6.52).

(6.52)   Unmarked juncture – nexus combinations
     a. Peripheral junctures – coordinate nexus
     b. Core juncture   – subordinate nexus
     c. Nuclear juncture   – cosubordinate nexus

These markedness relations yield the following claim: if a language has only one nexus type at a particular level of juncture, it will be the unmarked one. We can see an example of this with respect to nuclear junctures. Nuclear coordination is very rare, and all of the languages in which we have found it also have nuclear cosubordination, e.g. Alamblak and Barai (compare (6.20a) with (6.46), (6.20b) with (6.48a)). On the other hand, languages such as French, Fijian and Jacaltec all have cosubordinate nexus at the nuclear level (see (3.64), (6.47) and (6.80), respectively) but lack nuclear coordinate nexus. Thus it appears that in nuclear junctures cosubordination is the unmarked nexus type.

The two hierarchies in (6.49) and (6.51) may be combined into the syntactic bondedness hierarchy presented in Figure 11.[3]

Nuclear cosubordination	↑ Strongest
Nuclear coordination	
Core cosubordination	
Core subordination	
Core coordination	
Peripheral cosubordination	
Peripheral subordination	
Peripheral coordination	Weakest

Figure 11 Syntactic bondedness hierarchy

This hierarchy represents a cline of the variable strength of the syntactic bond or link between two units. The eight juncture–nexus combinations represent the main divisions of the cline, within which several construction types may fall. For example, two different varieties of peripheral cosubordination were discussed in 6.2.3, conjunction with zero anaphora as in English and German and clause chaining with switch-reference as in Kewa and Tonkawa, and there are clear grounds for considering the juncts in clause chains more tightly linked than those in the other construction. While both constructions require common illocutionary force over all juncts, tense is likewise constrained in clause chains but may not be in the conjoined clauses. Accordingly, since the clause chains are more constrained in terms of peripheral operators than the conjoined clauses, they must be considered more tightly bound, even though both constructions are instances of peripheral cosubordination. Since there are four peripheral operators, there are four possible distinct degrees of dependence in peripheral cosubordination: illocutionary force only with all others independent; illocutionary force and evidentials with all others free; illocutionary force, evidentials and tense, with only status independent; and all four shared between the two clauses. Predictably, there is an inverse correlation between the strength of the syntactic bond and the sententiality of the conjuncts, as argued above, with peripheral coordination having the most sentential juncts and nuclear cosubordination the least.

Variation in the closeness of the semantic relationship between units correlates transparently with the strength of the syntactic link. Two nuclei which fall under the scope of the same aspect operator and share all core arguments and peripheral constituents (nuclear cosubordination) are obviously more closely related semantically than two nuclei which have distinct aspect operators, core arguments, and peripheral constituents and operators (peripheral coordination). The operators on the various levels of the clause, which are of crucial importance for determining the level of juncture, all have semantic value, and consequently juncts which share a particular operator, e.g. obligation modality at the core level, have more in common semantically than those which do not. Similarly, juncts which share constituents have closer semantic ties than those that do not. Juncts in core coordination and cosubordination, for example, usually share arguments; verb serialization is built upon shared actor or undergoer arguments, and in the accusative-plus-infinitive construction in a language like English one of the core arguments acts semantically as an argument of the second junct and syntactically as an argument of the first (see 6.5 below). With respect to the comparative semantic weight of operators versus constituents at a particular level, joint constituents are indicative of a closer semantic relationship than common operators above. Thus, as one ascends the hierarchy in Figure 11, one finds no shared constituents or operators in peripheral coordination at the bottom, and more and more shared operators and constituents as one approaches the top. In multiclause constructions, then, the closeness of semantic relationship correlates with the tightness of the syntactic link between clauses.

6.3.2 Interclausal semantic relations hierarchy The various constructions captured in Figure 11 are used to express a variety of semantic relations, e.g. causation or simultaneous action. These relations may likewise be ordered hierarchically, as in Figure 12. Like the predicate–argument semantic relations hierarchy in Figure 1, this hierarchy presents a cline of semantic relations, with the labeled relations being major points along the

Causative   ↑ Strongest
Modality
Psych-action
Jussive
Direct perception complements
Indirect discourse complements
Temporal adverbial clause
Conditionals
Simultaneous actions
Sequential actions: overlapping
Sequential actions: non-overlapping
Action–action: unspecified | Weakest

Figure 12 Interclausal semantic relations hierarchy

continuum. A finer-grained division with more explicitly labeled relations is certainly possible, but Figure 12 is adequate for the purposes of this discussion. The causative relation is much discussed and needs no elaboration here. Modality is expressed in English by verbs like *try, start, manage, stop, cease,* and *continue.* Psych-action includes the semantic range of sentences like *John wanted to go, forgot to go, remembered to go,* and *decided to go.* Jussive is the relation between verbs like *order* and *tell* and their complements, e.g. *Max ordered Fred to leave.* Direct perception complements, e.g. *Leon saw Phil washing his car,* are next, followed by indirect discourse complements which subsumes the complements of cognition and propositional attitude verbs as well. Temporal adverbial clauses and conditionals are well known and require no comment. The next three relations are best illustrated with data from Papuan languages, since they often make these distinctions explicitly. The following examples are from Barai (Olson 1981).

(6.53) a. Bu ire i-ko   no vua kuae.
     3pl food eat-CONJ 1pl talk say
     'They were eating food, and at the same time we were talking.'

   b. Bu ire i-na   vua kuae.
     3pl food eat-CONJ talk say
     'They ate food and then told stories.'

c. Na va-ekiro   isuame   una   rua-ke.
1sg go-CONJ tomorrow do again come-FUT
'I will go and then (after an interval) will return tomorrow.'

Sentence (6.53a) involves two clauses expressing simultaneous actions, indicated by the conjunction -*ko*. The next two sentences have sequential events, overlapping, i.e. in this case the second event begins immediately after the termination of the first, in (6.53b), and non-overlapping, i.e. there is a significant time period between the events in (6.53c). The end point on the cline refers to two clauses which are linked without any specification of any kind of relation between them.

(6.54) John walked slowly down the street, and the next launch of the space shuttle has been delayed three weeks.

No semantic relation of any kind is explicitly coded in (6.54), unlike the examples in (6.53).

This semantic hierarchy complements the syntactic hierarchy in Figure 12, and taken together, the two provide an etic grid for the analysis of interclausal relations (Figure 13).

Nuclear cosubordination ↑	Causative
Nuclear coordination	Modality
Core cosubordination	Psych-action
Core subordination	Jussive
Core coordination	Direct perception complement
Peripheral cosubordination	Indirect discourse complement
Peripheral subordination	Temporal adverbial clause
Peripheral coordination	Conditionals
	Simultaneous action
	Sequential action: overlapping
	Sequential action: non-overlapping
	Action–action: unspecified

Figure 13 Interclausal Relations Hierarchy [IRH]

Just as in other domains, e.g. grammatical relations, there is no one-to-one correlation of syntactic and semantic relations. Accordingly, one of the most important questions to be investigated in the analysis of clause linkage in a language is how particular semantic relations are realized syntactically. For example, as we will see in 6.4.3, in Jacaltec temporal adverbial clauses and indirect discourse complements fall together in peripheral subordination. It is equally possible that a given semantic relation may be realized more than one way syntactically. For example in Barai simultaneous action may be expressed by peripheral cosubordination, as in (6.53a), or by peripheral co-ordination, as in (6.55).

(6.55) Na kofu mubu-koga Vito fu are   Umuate
        1sg coffee pick-CONJ   3sg place
        ij-ia   va.
        DEF-L go
        'I was picking coffee, and at the same time Vito was going to Umuate village.'

The same variation exists cross-linguistically as well, and there-fore not only the inventory of syntactic clause-linkage categories in different languages but also the relationship between the syntactic and semantic parts of the IRH in them are important topics for investigation.

There is one significant claim about the interaction of the two hierarchies inherent in the IRH. Given the inventory of syntactic clause-linkage categories in a language, it will always be the case that the strongest semantic relations will be expressed in the most tightly linked syntactic configurations found in the language, the weaker relations in the less tightly linked constructions. Thus, for example, if a language has only core and peripheral junctures, causative, modality and psych-action relations will be realized in the most tightly linked core junctures the language has. As this example makes clear, we are not claiming that a particular semantic relation, e.g. causative, always has the same syntactic realization, e.g. nuclear cosubordination, across languages. This claim also does not preclude the possibility documented above, that a particular semantic relation may have more than one syntac-tic manifestation; we claim only that one of these realizations must be consistent with this generalization. If, for example, causation can be expressed more than one way in a language, one of those ways must be in the most tightly linked construction found in the language.

We will discuss the interaction of the two parts of the IRH in detail here only with respect to Jacaltec in 6.4.3. Givón (1980) surveys a large number of languages with reference to the syntactic realization of the semantic relations between causative and indirect discourse complement in the IRH, and his findings are in accord with our general claim that the tightness of the syntactic linkage between two clauses correlates with the closeness or strength of the semantic relation between them.

6.3.3 Silverstein's hierarchy of clause–clause logical relations These syntactic and semantic relations between clauses have been explored in another context in Silverstein (1976b, 1980b). Silverstein's primary concern is split case-marking, and he shows that certain splits in ergative languages are a function of the strength of the syntactic link between two clauses. His hierarchy of logical relations between clauses is presented in Figure 14.

Figure 14 Logical relations of clauses

Ergative
languages

probability of antipas-
. sivization
suspension of agent
hierarchy

probability of normal
forms, nominalization
degree of formal distinctness from unlinked clause
markedness of connexion

∧ possessive
habitual actor
habitual agent
relative clause (making definite
   reference)
purposive complement
desire complement
indirect discourse complement
temporal adverbial clause
if – then
disjunction
conjunction
clause sequence (sequitur)
clause sequence (non-sequitur)

The effects of tighter linkage are to the left of the arrow and will be discussed in detail in 6.4. As in the hierarchy in Figure 13, the strength of the link increases the higher one goes up the hierarchy. It may be divided into three sections. The first contains the two steps labeled 'clause sequence' at the bottom. They refer to unlinked pairings of clauses; i.e. pairs of clauses which have no syntactic connection between them. 'Non-sequitur' refers to the fact that the clauses 'just happen to be in the order S_1–S_2 ... with no implicative *sequitur*, no semantic connection ...' (1980b:13). Clause sequence (sequitur) involves some semantic but no syntactic relationship between the clauses.

The second section of the hierarchy in Figure 14 concerns clauses which are explicitly linked syntactically; it subsumes the steps between 'conjunction' and 'purposive complement'. The semantic hierarchy in Figure 12 is in effect an expanded version of this segment of Silverstein's hierarchy. The logical relations of this part of the hierarchy are expressed in terms of particular construction types. Silverstein's claim is that the logical (i.e. semantic) relation in a purposive complement (e.g. *John went to the store to buy some beer*) relates the two clauses more closely than that in conjunction or disjunction, and consequently the syntactic ramifications for the linked clause will be greater in a purposive complement than in conjoined clauses, for example. The final section of the hierarchy includes the top four steps, from 'relative clause' to 'possessive'. Unlike the previous two sections, this one is not concerned with clause sequences, linked or unlinked, but rather with complex noun phrases. Within this NP hierarchy, NP + relative clause is the most loosely linked construction and NP_{POSS} ($\pm$NP) the most tightly linked, with habitual agent/ actor constructions falling in the middle. Since we are primarily concerned with clause–clause linkage in this chapter, we will not discuss complex NP phenomena.[4]

The claim embodied in Silverstein's hierarchy in Figure 14 is the same as that of the IRH. The two hierarchies differ in a number of crucial respects. First, Silverstein's is purely semantic; the syntactic aspects of clause linkage are not expressed in terms of syntactic linkage categories but rather in terms of generalizations about the specific morphosyntactic consequences of increasingly tight logical relations between clauses. A hierarchy of linkage categories such as Figure 11 complements rather than contrasts with Silverstein's morphosyntactic generalizations. Secondly, the hierarchy in Figure 14 is wider in scope than the IRH, since it includes complex NPs and syntactically unlinked clauses in addition to clause–clause linkage. In the next section we will attempt to incorporate Silverstein's generalizations in Figure 14 into the framework developed in this chapter and Chapter 5.

6.4 Morphosyntactic consequences of clause linkage

We have argued that there is a direct correlation between the tightness of the semantic and syntactic links between clauses, and this is expressed in the Interclausal Relations Hierarchy [IRH] in Figure 13. In order for this hierarchy to be something more than just a taxonomy of clause-linkage categories, it must be associated with cross-linguistically valid claims about other phenomena. Silverstein in fact proposes a number of such generalizations, which were found in Figure 14. They cover the syntactic correlates of the strength of the syntactic bond between two clauses, and they are repeated below.

The higher up the IRH the linkage type between two clauses is:

(a) *General*
    1. The greater the probability of nominative–dative case marking ('normal forms').
    2. The greater the probability of nominalization.
    3. The greater degree of formal distinctness from unlinked clause.
    4. The greater markedness of the connection.

(b) *Ergative languages*
    1. The greater the probability of antipassivization.
    2. The more likely the suspension of ergative case marking governed by the agent hierarchy.

All of these phenomena are manifestations of a single general principle, which Silverstein expresses as follows.

As we move up the hierarchy of linkage types, there seems to be greater and greater formal distinctness of the surface structure remnants of what could be constructed as full 'kernal' clauses for the linked (or dependent) members of the pair under consideration. At one extreme are possessive NPs, indicating the possessor of some Noun (or Nominal) in the independent (or relatively more independent clause); at the other end are clauses indistinguishable from their unlinked forms. In between is a whole range of formal de-formations of erstwhile independent clause surface structure (1980b:14).

In other words, the linked or dependent clause will undergo certain alterations from its independent form, and the tighter the link is, the greater these alterations or 'de-formations' will be. In a language with VO word order, the dependent clause normally follows the non-dependent clause, whereas in languages with OV order the reverse is generally true. In the subsequent sections we will investigate the various generalizations proposed by Silverstein in order to elucidate the consequence of the IRH for intra- and interclausal syntactic processes.

6.4.1 Nominalization One of the most significant consequences of a strong syntactic bond between two clauses is the increased likelihood of the dependent clause occurring in a nominalized form. Silverstein's claim is that if a language nominalizes dependent clauses at a certain point on the hierarchy, it will likewise nominalize everything above that point. Languages differ greatly in their use of nominalization in clause linkage, and we will compare English and Quechua in this regard.

English employs nominalization in only a very limited way in clause linkage, the primary example being gerunds in core subordination, as illustrated in (6.25) and (6.26). Imbabura Quechua (Cole & Hermon 1981), on the other hand, makes much more extensive use of nominalization than English. It appears that all clause linkage at the core level involves nominalization of the dependent clause. Object complements and desire complements are formed with one of a set of nominalizing verbal suffixes which also indicate tense, and the nominalized clause receives accusative case marking. (Both S–V–Clause and S–Clause–V orders are possible.)

(6.56) a. Juzi   yacha-n ñuca   Maria-ta
       Jose-NOM know-3sg 1sg-NOM Maria-ACC
       juya-j-ta.
       love-PRES/NMZ-ACC
       'Jose knows that I love Maria.'

    b. Juzi   ñuca-ta   yacha-wa-n   Maria-ta
       Jose-NOM 1sg-ACC know-1sg-3sg Maria-ACC
       juya-j-ta.
       love-PRES/NMZ-ACC
       'Jose knows me to love Maria.'
    c. Wawa-ca   muna-n lichi-ta
       child-TOP want-3sg milk-ACC
       ufya-na-ta.
       drink-FUT/NMZ-ACC
       'The child wants to drink milk.'

These examples (from Cole & Hermon 1981) illustrate an object complement in (a), raising-to-object in (b) and a desire complement in (c).[5] The subordinate junct in (6.56) is nominalized by -*j*-, which also signals present tense; there is no requirement that the tense in the subordinate clause be the same as that in the main clause.

(6.57) Juzi   yacha-n Juan   chaya-shca-ta.
       Jose-NOM know-3sg Juan-NOM arrive-PAST/NMZ-
       ACC
       'Jose knows that Juan has arrived.'

Sentence (6.56b) is a 'raising' construction in which the pivot of the subordinate clause functions as the accusative argument of the verb in the main clause. Cole & Hermon (1981) shows that it has most of the major syntactic properties of the English accusative-plus-infinitive construction in (6.13), e.g. allows reflexivization and reciprocalization and blocks disjoint reference. One significant difference between the English and Quechua constructions lies in the fact that the nominalized clause in Quechua retains its independent tense marking, whereas in English the complement clause loses its tense inflection when it becomes an infinitive. The desire complement in (6.56c) is more tightly bound than the 'raising' construction because the tense of the nominalized clause must be either future or subjunctive and consequently it lacks the independent tense selection of (6.56a–b). In both constructions the interpretation of the pivot of the nominalizing clause derives from a main-clause argument.

    Thus, Imbabura Quechua employs nominalization extensively

in clause–clause linkage, whereas English does not. In particular, core junctures require it. In certain varieties of Quechua there is a different set of clause-linkage devices in peripheral junctures which do not involve the nominalization of the dependent clause, and, further, switch-reference marking is involved in certain nexus types (see Levinsohn 1978, Weber 1980). This contrast between English and Quechua regarding the variable function of nominalization in clause linkage follows the IRH in that it is found in the higher and not lower range of hierarchy.

6.4.2 Case-marking elaboration and reduction The primary focus of Silverstein (1976b, 1980b) is the explanation of split case marking in ergative languages and more generally, an understanding of the various factors which affect case marking in all types of languages. Silverstein makes two interrelated claims which are relevant to this discussion. First, he argues that the fundamental case-marking opposition in human languages is nominative–dative, with elaborations of this basic system following principles akin to those governing the elaboration of color-term vocabularies proposed by Berlin & Kay (1969). This is represented by the schema in Figure 15.

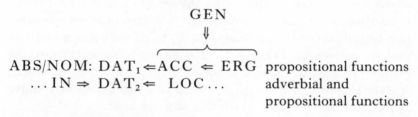

$$\text{GEN}$$
$$\Downarrow$$
$$\overbrace{\text{ABS/NOM: DAT}_1 \Leftarrow \text{ACC} \Leftarrow \text{ERG}} \quad \text{propositional functions}$$
$$\dots \text{IN} \Rightarrow \text{DAT}_2 \Leftarrow \text{LOC} \dots \quad \text{adverbial and}$$
$$\quad\quad\quad\quad\quad\quad\quad\quad \text{propositional functions}$$

Figure 15 Case hierarchies

Thus, just as a distinct term of 'red' in a language implies the existence of terms for 'white' and 'black', the existence of a distinct genitive case in a language implicates a further distinction between nominative (absolutive) and dative. The same is true with respect to the occurrence of separate ergative or accusative cases (see Silverstein 1976b: 162). The dative is in fact elaborated in two directions: one involves the propositional functions mentioned above, and the other adverbial and propositional functions such as instrumental and locative.

This relates to the I R H in the following way. The more tightly linked the dependent clause is to an adjacent clause, the more the case-marking possibilities in it are reduced. 'Case-marking is "telescoped" into a reduced or minimal system, gradually in some languages, more abruptly in others, as we climb the hierarchy of linkage types' (Silverstein 1980b: 15). This is taken to its extreme at the top of the hierarchy where only genitive (or if there is no genitive, then dative) case is possible. This reduction of case-marking possibilities can be seen in English nominalizations; a gerund allows genitive, accusative, and dative case marking, e.g. *the man's giving him to her*, an action nominal only genitive and dative, e.g. *his gift of the book to Mary*, and finally an agent noun only genitive, e.g. *the book's buyer*. Thus one generalization inherent in the I R H is expressed by Silverstein as follows: 'the NP adjuncts of nominalized constructions never have a greater case-elaboration than non-nominalized ones, and generally have far fewer' (1980b: 15). The upshot of this is that what a particular case marking signals in a clause can only be understood with reference to the clause-linkage environment in which the clause occurs. 'The point is, we cannot interpret the reading for a particular case-marking relative to a system of case-marking oppositions, without knowing the placement of the relevant clause in a structure of discourse linkage: the genitive in an independent non-linked 'kernal' clause-sentence is, as an indicator about any underlying propositional role, something different from the genitive in a tightly linked noun of agency construction' (ibid.) A clear example of this will be found in a discussion of Jacaltec syntax and case-marking in the following section.

In 6.3.1 we argued that the strength of the syntactic bond between two clauses correlates with the possibility of independent expression of notions like tense and illocutionary force; the tighter the linkage, the more these are constrained. In the same way the case-marking possibilities in a clause are reduced as the tightness of linkage increases. Just as the actual interpretation of the future-tense nominalizer *-na* in Quechua depends on whether it is in a construction like (6.56a, b or c), so the interpretation of case marking in a clause depends on the syntactico-semantic linkage environment in which it occurs.

6.4.3 Antipassivization and suspension of ergative case marking

Silverstein proposes two effects of tighter linkage specifically with respect to ergative languages: an increasing probability of antipassivization and of a suspension of the agent hierarchy governing ergative case marking. The result of these changes is tightly linked forms with nominative–dative case marking in the dependent junct. We will illustrate this aspect of the IRH through an examination of clause linkage in Jacaltec. The primary source of data is Craig's excellent presentation (1977); additional data are drawn from Day (1973) and Datz (1980).

A few preliminary remarks about Jacaltec clause structure are in order. Word order in simple independent clauses is VAU. The verb is prefixed for tense,[6] carries affixes cross-referencing the person and (in non-third persons) number of the two core arguments, and has an irrealis-future tense suffix.

(6.58)   a.   X-∅-to-pax   heb naj   winaj.
           PST-3ABS-go-back PL CL/the man
           'The men returned.'

       b.   X-∅-aw-il   ix.
           PST-3ABS-2sgERG-see CL/she
           'You saw her.'

       c.   Ch-∅-s-lok-o'   naj   winaj
           NPST-3ABS-3ERG-buy-FUT CL/the man
           no'   txitam.
           CL/the pig
           'The man will buy the pig.'

There is no inflection on core NP arguments to indicate their syntactic function; actor is distinguished from undergoer solely by word order. Noun classifiers, glossed, e.g. 'CL/the' or 'CL/she', function as anaphoric pronouns, as in (6.58b). The ergative morphemes are also used to mark possessors, e.g. *hin-xañab* (1sgERG-sandal) 'my sandals', and objects of prepositions, e.g. *y-ul te' ñah* (3ERG-in CL/the house) 'in the house'.

Jacaltec clause–clause linkage possibilities fall into two groups, the main formal feature distinguishing them being whether both clauses are tensed or only one is. Correlated with the tense feature are the following properties: (1) only tensed clauses may be negated, (2) *an* placement may not operate across the boundary of a tensed clause, and (3) noun-classifier deletion may not operate across the boundary of a tensed clause. The sentence-final particle *an* signals the presence of a first person participant in a clause; only one is permitted per clause.[7]

(6.59) a. Ch-in   to an
        NPST-1sgABS go 1p
        'I go.'

(6.59) b. Ch-in   ha-mak   an.
        NPST-1sgABS 2sgERG-hit 1p
        'You hit me.'

Noun-classifier deletion involves the omission of coreferential noun classifiers; verbal cross-reference morphemes are unaffected in multiclause constructions.[8]

(6.60) a. *X-$\emptyset$-(y)-il   naj$_i$ s-mam
        PST-3ABS-3ERG-see CL/he$_i$ 3ERG-father
        naj$_i$.
        CL/he$_i$
        'He$_i$ saw his$_i$ father.'

      b. X-$\emptyset$-(y)-il   naj$_i$ s-mam $\emptyset$.
        PST-3ABS-3ERG-see CL/he$_i$ 3ERG-father
        'He$_i$ saw his$_i$ father.'

      c. X-$\emptyset$-(y)-il   naj$_i$ s-mam
        PST-3ABS-3ERG-see CL/he$_i$ 3ERG-father
        naj$_j$.
        CL/he$_j$
        'He$_i$ saw his$_j$ father.'

      d. *X-$\emptyset$-(y)-il   naj$_i$ s-mam $\emptyset$.
        PST-3ABS-3ERG-see CL/he$_i$ 3ERG-father
        'He$_i$ saw his$_j$ father.'

The interaction of *an* placement and noun-classifier deletion with the boundaries of tensed and non-tensed clauses will be discussed below.

We begin with the most weakly linked constructions, peripheral coordination. Jacaltec lacks a sentential conjunction analogous to English *and*, and clauses are simply juxtaposed. If the two verbs are intransitive or the second is intransitive, as in (6.61a) then nothing more is required; if the non-initial verb is transitive, as in (6.61b), then the suffix -*n(i)* must be added to it.

(6.61) a. X-∅-to   ix   maxatic'a x-∅-ul
       PST-3ABS-go CL/she never   PST-3ABS-come
       ix.
       CL/she
       'She went, and she never came back.'

     b. X-∅-ul   naj Pel   x-in-(y)-il-ni
       PST-3ABS-come CL Pedro PST-1sgABS-3ERG-
                      naj   an.
       see-SUFF CL/he 1p
       'Pedro came, and he saw me.'

     c. X-∅-(y)-iche-coj   ix
       PST-3ABS-3ERG-start-on CL/she
       x-∅-s-lah-ni   y-unin
       PST-3ABS-3ERG-finish-SUFF 3ERG-child
       ix.
       CL/she
       'She started it, and her child finished it.'

There are explicit conjunctions akin to *or* and *but*.

(6.62) a. Ch-on   to chinabul   mato
       NPST-1plABS go Huehuetenango or
       ch-on   cani.
       NPST-1plABS stay
       'Are we going to Huehuetenango, or are we staying?'

     b. Ch-in   to hecal   an yaj ch-ach
       NPST-1sgABS go tomorrow 1p butNPST-2sgABS
       can beti'.
       stay here
       'I will go tomorrow, but you stay here.'

     c. X-in-(y)-il   naj   an yaj mach
       PST-1sgABS-3ERG-see CL/he 1p but NEG
       x-∅-(y)-al   naj.
       PST-3ABS-3ERG-say CL/he
       'He saw me, but he didn't say it.'

In each of these examples both conjuncts have the same tense and illocutionary force. There is no statement to the effect that same tense is a necessary feature in any of the discussions of these constructions, and we will assume that there is none, since they contrast with constructions which have tense constraints to be discussed below. The following examples illustrate the lack of an illocutionary force constraint, at least in the juxtaposed construction.

(6.63) Way-oj   ab   hon   mach mac ay   yoc
        sleep-SUFF EXH 1pl ABS NEG WH exist interest
        j-in.
        1plERG-in
        'Would that we sleep, nobody cares about us!'

The first junct has exhortative illocutionary force, the second declarative. Note that noun-classifier deletion has not been in effect in these sentences; the omission of the coreferential noun classifiers in the second conjuncts of (6.61a, b, c) and (6.62c) would render these examples ungrammatical. Furthermore, the placement of *an* in (6.62c) is limited to the first conjunct; were it located at the end of the entire sentence, the result would be ungrammatical. In these constructions *an* must occur in the same junct as the element inflected for first person. The islandhood of tensed clauses with respect to these rules is clear in these examples.

There are two forms of peripheral subordination in Jacaltec, adverbial clauses and *that*-clauses. Adverbial clauses are illustrated in (6.64).

(6.64) a. X-∅-'ayc'ay   naj   bay
           PST-3ABS-fall CL/he where
           x-∅-(y)-il   naj   no'   cheh.
           PST-3ABS-3ERG-see CL/he CL/the horse
           'He fell where he saw the horse.'
      b. Ch-in   tzotel t-(y)-et   ix   an
           NPST-1sgABS talk   AUG-3ERG-to CL/she 1p
           yuñe   ch-∅-sta'wi   ix   w-et
           so.that NPST-3ABS-answer CL/she 1sgERG-to
           an.
           1p
           'I will talk to her, so that she will answer me.'

c. Lañan ∅ hin-tx'ah-ni xil kape an
PROG 3ABS 1sgERG-wash-SUFF clothes 1p
yet xc-ach huli.
when PST-2sgABS come
'I was washing clothes, when you came.'

d. X-∅-'ayc'ay naj yet
PST-3ABS-fall CL/he when
x-∅-(y)-il-ni naj ix.
PST-3ABS-3ERG-see-SUFF CL/he CL/she
'He fell when he saw her.'

The adverbial clause in each sentence is fully tensed, and noun-classifier deletion does not take place in (a) and (b). The placement of *an* is constrained again to the junct in which the inflected element occurs; note in (6.64b) that the first person participant in the second clause is the object of a preposition. The verb in first clause in (6.64c) is not inflected for tense but rather for progressive aspect; aspectual inflection will be discussed in detail below. Note that when a temporal adverbial clause has a transitive verb, as in (6.64d), it takes the suffix -*n(i)* just as in (6.61c); an intransitive verb in such an adverbial clause, e.g. (6.64c), does not require -*n(i)*.

The Jacaltec equivalents of English *that*-clauses are exemplified in (6.65).

(6.65) a. X-∅-(y)-al naj chubil xc-ach
PST-3ABS-3ERG-say CL/he that PST-2sgABS
y-il naj.
3ERG-see CL/he
'He said that he saw you.'

b. X-∅-aw-abe tato ch-in
PST-3ABS-2sgERG-hear that NPST-1sgABS
to-j hecal an.
go-FUT tomorrow 1p
'You heard that I will go tomorrow.'

As in English, these clauses appear to be the core arguments of the verb; they are cross-referenced by the 3ABS affix ∅. However, unlike in English, there are facts which show that such clauses are in fact never core constituents. First, all core and peripheral constituents must occur between the verb and the subordinate clause.

(6.66) a. X-∅-(y)-al   naj   t-(y)-et
           PST-3ABS-3ERG-say CL/he AUG-3ERG-to
           anma   chubil x-∅-(y)-il   naj
           people that   PST-3ABS-3ERG-see CL/he
           ix.
           CL/she
           'He said to people that he saw her.'
       b. X-∅-(y)-al   naj   t-(y)-et
           PST-3ABS-3ERG-say CL/he AUG-3ERG-to
           anma   y-ul   parce ewi   chubil
           people 3ERG-in park   yesterday that
           chi-m-hul-uj   naj   presidente
           NPST-may-3ABS come-FUT CL/the president
           coñob.
           village
           'He said to people yesterday in the park that the
           president may come to the village.'

This is readily accounted for if we assume that the clauses are peripheral rather than core constituents in all cases; indeed, in a theory like RRG which lacks syntactic movement transformations, this is the only possible analysis. Secondly, sentential 'subjects' provide no evidence for core status, as peripheral constituents intervene between verb and clause here as well.

(6.67) a. X-∅-'ec'le   y-iñ   hin-c'ul   chubil
           PST-3ABS-cross 3ERG-in 1sgERG-stomach that
           kin   hecal.
           fiesta tomorrow
           'It crossed my mind that it is fiesta tomorrow.'
       b.*X-∅-'ec'le   chubil kin   hecal   y-iñ
           PST-3ABS-cross that   fiesta tomorrow 3ERG-in
           hin-c'ul.
           1sgERG-stomach
           'It crossed my mind that it is fiesta tomorrow.'

Thus, there are no unambiguous cases of core status for the subordinate clause in Jacaltec analogous to those involving sentential pivots in English, and moreover the facts of (6.66)–(6.67) strongly support the peripheral status of such clauses. We conclude, then, that *chubil*-clauses in Jacaltec are realizations of peripheral subordination.

These subordinate clauses have independent tense selection, as (6.65b) illustrates. That noun-classifier deletion is not allowed across the boundary of this kind of tensed subordinate clause is shown in (6.65a) and (6.66a). The possibility of negation in such a clause and the affect on *an* placement are exemplified in (6.68).

(6.68) a. X-∅-(y)-al   hin-mam   an chubil
           PST-3ABS-3ERG-say 1sgERG-father 1p that
           mach ch-∅-ul-uj   naj.
           NEG NPST-3ABS-come-FUT CL/he
           'My father said that he will not come.'
      b. *X-∅-(y)-al   hin-mam   chubil
           PST-3ABS-3ERG-say 1sgERG-father that
           mach ch-∅-ul-uj   naj   an.
           NEG NPST-3ABS-come-FUT CL/he 1p
           'My father said that he will not come.'

The ungrammaticality of (6.68b) shows that *an* must occur before the *chubil*-clause. These clauses are identical to adverbial clauses with respect to independent tense choice, possibility of negation, blocking noun-classifier deletion, and constraining *an* placement.

It was mentioned above that there are constructions in which tense choice is constrained in one of the conjuncts. Contrast (6.62b) with (6.69a).

(6.69) a. Ch-in   to hecal   an cat   ha-can
           NPST-1sgABS go tomorrow 1p SEQ 2sgERG-stay
           beti'.
           here
           'I will go tomorrow, and you will stay here.'
      b. Ch-∅-(y)-oche   ix   ∅
           NPST-3ABS-3ERG-like CL/she 3ABS
           s-tahtze-'   te'   cenya
           3ERG-cook-FUT CL/the banana

```
cat    Ø        s-lo-ni-toj                    ix
SEQ 3ABS 3ERG-eat-SUFF-up  CL/she
te'.
CL/them
```
'She likes to cook the bananas and (then) she eats them.'

Examples (6.62b) and (6.69a) differ only in the device used to link two otherwise semantically identical clauses. In (6.62b) the conjunction *yaj* 'but' is used, and each clause has independent non-past tense marking. However, the future tense interpretation derived from the adverb *hecal* 'tomorrow' is a feature of only the first conjunct in (6.62b), as the second has a present tense reading. In (6.69a), on the other hand, there is no conjunction, and the second conjunct is not inflected for tense but rather for what Day and Craig call the 'sequential aspect'; the internal structure of this conjunct is the same as that of the first clause in (6.64c) and will be discussed below. In this example the scope of the temporal adverb *hecal* is over the whole sentence, and consequently both juncts receive a future-tense interpretation. Illocutionary force is likewise the same for both juncts.

(6.70) Peba te'   pulta cat   Ø   haw-a-ni-coj
        close CL/the door SEQ 3ABS 2sgERG-put-SUFF-on
        s-tel   te'.
        3ERG-bar CL
        'Close the door and put on the bar!'

The second junct is interpreted as a command even though it lacks the formal feature of an imperative clause with a transitive verb. Thus because in this construction the second junct is not embedded but is dependent upon the first junct for illocutionary force and tense, (6.70) involves cosubordinate nexus at the peripheral level. A second example is given in (6.69b).

The other Jacaltec construction which has contrained tense choices serves to express simultaneous actions. Two clauses are juxtaposed (the second taking *-n(i)* if transitive), and the first always has non-past tense, the tense of the second clause being that of the whole sentence; if it is future tense, then both verbs must have the suffix *-oj*.

(6.71) a. ẍ-Ø-tzebi   naj   x-Ø-'el-tij
       NPST-3ABS-laugh CL/he PST-3ABS-come-out
       naj.
       CL/he
       'He came out laughing.'
    b. Ch-in   xubli   an
       NPST-1sgABS whistle 1p
       x-Ø-(h)in-tx'ah-ni   xil kape an
       PST-3ABS-1sgERG-wash-SUFF clothes 1p
       'I washed the laundry whistling.'
    c. Ch-Ø-'ok-oj   naj
       NPST-3ABS-cry-FUT CL/he
       ẍ-Ø-to-j   naj.
       NPST-3ABS-go-FUT CL/he
       'He will go crying.'

Because the scope of the tense operator is obligatorily over both clauses, the nexus is again cosubordinate. Both types of co-subordination block noun-classifier deletion, as (6.69b), (6.70), and (6.71a, c) show, and *an* placement is likewise constrained, as in (6.69a) and (6.71b). There are no examples in either Craig or Day involving negation in these constructions, although it is possible.

We have examined Jacaltec constructions illustrating all three peripheral nexus types, and there are four morphosyntactic features common to all of them: (1) both juncts are formally inflected for tense or aspect; (2) each junct may be negated; (3) noun-classifier deletion may not occur across such a juncture; (4) the particle *an* cannot be separated from its governing element across such a juncture. Thus peripheral junctures form a well-defined group in Jacaltec and can be easily distinguished from core and nuclear junctures, which lack all of these features, as we will see.

The second major type of Jacaltec clause-linkage construction is characterized by the formal inflection of only the initial junct for tense (or aspect), and consequently only the first junct may be negated.[9]

(6.72) a. ẍ-∅-tz'a   hin-c'ul   ha-to
           NPST-3ABS-burn 1sgERG-stomach 2sgERG-go
           an.
           1p
           'I am sad that you are going.'

  b. *ẍ-∅-tz'a   hin-c'ul   mat
      NPST-3ABS-burn 1sgERG-stomach NEG
      ha-to   an.
      2sgERG-go 1p
      'I am sad that you are not going.'

  c. ẍ-∅-tz'a   hin-c'ul   ta   mach
      NPST-3ABS-burn 1sgERG-stomach that NEG
      ch-ach   to-yi   (*an).
      NPST-2sgABS go-AUG   1p
      'I am sad that you are not going.'

(6.73) a. Ch-∅-(y)-oche   naj   hin
           NPST-3ABS-3ERG-like CL/he 1sgABS
           y-il-a'   (*naj).
           3ERG-see-FUT CL/he
           'He likes to see me.'

  b. *Ch-∅-(y)-oche   naj   mat
      NPST-3ABS-3ERG-like CL/he NEG
      hin   y-il-a'.
      1sgABS 3ERG-see-FUT
      'He likes not to see me.'

  c. Ch-∅-(y)-oche   naj   ta   mach
      NPST-3ABS-3ERG-like CL/he that NEG
      ch-in-y-il   naj.
      NPST-1sgABS-3ERG-see CL/he
      'He likes not to see me.'

Comparing the (a) and (c) examples in each group of sentences, we see that the verb in second junct in (a) has no tense or aspect prefixation and is inflected only for an ergative argument; if the verb is transitive, the absolutive argument occurs as a free-standing pronoun, as in (6.73a). The non-finite juncts cannot be negated, as (b) shows, and in order to negate them they must be changed into a finite clause with a complementizer, as in (c). These examples also illustrate the fact that non-finite juncts do not constrain *an* placement or block noun-classifier deletion. In (6.72a) *an* occurs sentence-finally immediately following a verb without a first person argument; the governing first person element is in the first junct. Were *an* to occur between *hin c'ul'* my stomach' and *ha-to* 'you go', the result would be ungrammatical. This contrasts sharply with sentences like (6.72c) and (6.69a) in which *an* cannot occur sentence-finally and must be in the same junct as the first person argument. Thus as far as *an* placement is concerned there is no internal clause boundary in constructions like (6.72a). Similarly, noun-classifier deletion is not only possible but obligatory in such constructions.[10] An occurrence of *naj* in the second junct of (6.73a) would render it ungrammatical; when the second junct takes on a finite form plus a complementizer as in (6.73c), the rule is blocked. With respect to noun-classifier deletion, such constructions have no internal clause boundary. The (a) sentences in (6.72) and (6.73) illustrate *core* junctures in Jacaltec, which are clearly distinguished from peripheral junctures by this cluster of morphosyntactic properties.

There are two types of core-level nexus in Jacaltec, subordinate and non-subordinate. In core subordination the untensed junct is an argument of the tensed one, cross-referenced by the $\emptyset$ third person absolutive affix on it; (6.73a) is an example of this nexus type. Because the subordinate junct carries no peripheral operators, the asymmetry of core subordination with tensed clauses discussed with respect to English in 6.2.2 does not arise. The construction in (6.73a) is very much like the Barai core embedding in (6.24b). Further examples of this juncture–nexus combination are presented in (6.74).

(6.74) a. X-$\emptyset$-(y)-il   ix   hin
             PST-3ABS-3ERG-see CL/she 1sgABS
             ha-mak-ni   (an).
             2sgERG-hit-SUFF 1p
             'She saw you hit me.'
      b. X-$\emptyset$-w-ilwe $\emptyset$
             PST-3ABS-1sgERG-try 3ABS
             hin-watx'e-n   kap   camïxe (an).
             1sgERG-make-SUFF CL/the shirt   1p
             'I tried to make the shirt.'

   c. Ø-w-ohtaj   Ø   hin-watx'e-n
       3ABS-1sgERG-know 3ABS 1sgERG-make-SUFF
       kap   camïẍe (an).
       CL/the shirt   1p
       'I know how to make the shirt.'

   d. Ch-Ø-aw-iche   ha-munlayi.
       NPST-3ABS-2sgERG-begin 2sgERG-work
       'You begin to work.' (literally: 'you begin it – you work')

   e. Ch-Ø-ichi   ha-munlayi.
       NPST-3ABS-begin 2sgERG-work
       'You begin to work.' (literally: 'it begin – you work')

   f. Ø-s-kan   hin-c'ul   Ø
       3ABS-3ERG-want 1sgERG-stomach 3ABS
       w-il-a'   naj   (an).
       1sgERG-see-FUT CL/he 1p
       'I want to see him.'

In all of these sentences the second junct functions as a core argument of the first, filling the third person absolutive slot. The peripheral operators of tense and illocutionary force have scope over the whole sentence.

Aspectual marking is achieved by embedding a core under a higher predicate; the aspect markers are *lañan* 'progressive', *cat* 'post-sequentive', and *lahwi* 'presequentive'. According to Day (1973), *lañan* is a stative predicate meaning 'long and flexible', *lahwi* is an intransitive verb meaning 'finish', and *cat* is derived from *cata* 'come'.

(6.75) a. Lañan ha-wayi.
           PROG 2sgERG-sleep
           'You are sleeping.'

      b. Lañan hach   s-mak-ni   naj.
           PROG 2sgABS 3ERG-hit-SUFF CL/he
           'He is hitting you.'

(6.76) a. Ch-on   wa'i cat   Ø
           NPST-1plABS eat SEQ 3ABS
           cu-tx'ah-ni   cu-munlabal.
           1plERG-wash-SUFF 1plERG-dish
           'We eat and then we wash our dishes.'

b. Lahwi   w-ul   an xc-in
PRESEQ 1sgERG-arrive 1p PST-1sgABS
to wa'-oj   an
go eat-INF 1p
'and after I arrived, I went to eat'

The progressive aspect may occur in simple independent clauses, as in (6.82), but *cat* and *lahwi* are possible only in clause-linkage environments, and, as we argued above, they are found in peripheral cosubordinate nexus (see also (6.69)).

The other nexus type found at the core level was labeled 'non-subordinate' above, because the data necessary for distinguishing coordinate from cosubordinate nexus are not available in any of the sources on Jacaltec we have investigated. Modals are the primary core operator, and it was their different scope possibilities which differentiated coordinate from cosubordinate nexus at the core level in English (cf. (6.17), (6.44)). In the absence of comparable examples in Jacaltec we are unable to specify the nexus type definitively. The main feature separating non-subordinate from subordinate constructions is that the second, non-tensed junct is not an argument of the tensed junct. An example of this is (6.72a). The verb in the first junct is intransitive and has *hin-c'ul* 'my stomach' as its single core argument; the second junct is independent, having no argument in common with the first. Aside from these body-part idiom constructions, the other core non-subordinate junctures involve a coreferential core argument between the juncts.

(6.77) a. Xc-in   to Ø   w-il-a'   naj
PST-1sgABS go 3ABS 1sgERG-see-INF[11] CL/he
(an).
1p
'I went to see him.'
b. Xc-ach   to sajch-oj.
PST-2sgABS go play-INF
'You went to play.'
c. Ch-Ø-(y)-iptze   naj   ix   hach
NPST-3ABS-3ERG-force CL/he CL/she 2sgABS
s-mak-ni.
3ERG-hit-SUFF
'He forces her to hit you.'

    d. Xc-ach   w-iptze   ha-canalwi   an.
       PST-2sgABS 1sgERG-force 2sgERG-dance 1p
       'I forced you to dance.'

    e. Xc-ach   ichi ha-munlayi.
       PST-2sgABS begin 2sgERG-work
       'You began to work.' (literally: 'you began – you work')

The only form in which the coreferential core argument is not coded on the second junct is (6.77b) in which an intransitive verb follows a verb of motion; this equi-NP-deletion also occurs with verbs of desire, but only when the verb in the second junct is intransitive.

(6.78) a.   Ch-$\emptyset$-(y)-oche   naj   canalw-oj.
          NPST-3ABS-3ERG-like CL/he dance-INF
          'He likes to dance.'

      b.   *Ch-$\emptyset$-(y)-oche   naj   col-o'
          NPST-3ABS-3ERG-like CL/he help-INF
          hach.
          2sgABS
          'He likes to help you.'

      c.   *Ch-in   to col-o'   hach.
          NPST-1sgABS go help-INF 2sgABS
          'I go to help you.'

In both types of core-level nexus, the dependent junct occurs in a form quite distinct from that in peripheral junctures. In addition to the lack of tense marking (see n. 11), the case-marking pattern is one in which ergative morphemes cross-reference both transitive and intransitive 'subjects' and independent absolutive pronouns indicate the transitive object, thus yielding an accusative schema. Moreover, transitive verbs are suffixed with -$n(i)$ or, if the tensed verb is one of motion, desire or causation, with the infinitive marker. However, as (6.77c) shows, this is not an absolute constraint, and if sentences like (6.77a) are themselves embedded, then -$n(i)$ is obligatory.

(6.79) a.   X-$\emptyset$-(y)-ilwe   naj   s-to $\emptyset$
          PST-3ABS-3ERG-try CL/he 3ERG-go 3ABS
          y-il-n-oj   ix
          3ERG-see-SUFF-INF CL/she
          'He tried to go to see her.'

    b. C'ul ∅   y-oche-ni   ix   ∅
       good 3ABS 3ERG-like-SUFF CL/she 3ABS
       s-watx′e-n-oj   s-ba.
       3ERG-make-SUFF-INF 3ERG-REFL
       'It is good that she likes to arrange herself.'

We will return to -*n(i)* suffixation and the accusative case-marking pattern below.

The most tightly linked clause–clause constructions are direct causative constructions with *a'a'* 'cause', which are nuclear co-subordination. (These constructions are known as predicate-raising causatives in the generative semantics literature; see Shibatani 1976.) This is the only construction in which a transitive verb appears as a true infinitive stripped of all arguments. The absolute argument of the non-causative verb is coded as the absolutive argument of *a'a'*, and its ergative argument occurs as an oblique (cf. 3.4).

(6.80) a. Ch-∅-(y)-a'   ix   xew-oj
         NPST-3ABS-3ERG-cause CL/she rest-INF
         naj.
         CL/he
         'She makes him rest.'
      b. Ch-∅-(y)-a'   xew-oj ix
         NPST-3ABS-3ERG-cause rest-INF CL/she
         naj.
         CL/he
         'She makes him rest.'

(6.81) a. X-in-y-a'   naj
         PST-1sgABS-3ERG-cause CL/he
         mak-a'/*mak-ni   t-aw-et.
         hit-INF/hit-SUFF AUG-2sgERG-to
         'He made you hit me.'
      b. X-in-y-a'   mak-a' naj
         PST-1sgABS-3ERG-cause hit-INF CL/he
         t-aw-et.
         AUG-2sgERG-to
         'He made you hit me.'

c. X-∅-(y)-a'   mak-a' s-ba
PST-3ABS-3ERG-cause hit-INF 3ERG-REFL
naj   t-aw-et.
CL/he AUG-2sgERG-to
'He made you hit him.'
(Literally: 'he made you hit himself'.)

Each of these sentences has a single periphery and single core which subsumes a complex nucleus in which each individual nucleus contributes one core argument, both of which are cross-referenced on the causative verb. Note that -$n(i)$ is not possible on a transitive verb in this construction, as (6.81a) shows. Reflexivization is clause-bounded in Jacaltec, as Craig (1977) shows, and (6.81c) constitutes syntactic evidence that they are monoclausal. The ability of the non-causative verb to occur adjacent to the causative verb inside the noun classifiers is unique to nuclear-juncture causative construction. Nuclear versus core causatives with intransitive verbs can be distinguished on this basis.

(6.82) a. X-∅-(y)-iptze   ix   naj   canalw-oj.
PST-3ABS-3ERG-force CL/she CL/he dance-INF
'She forced him to dance.'
   b. X-∅-(y)-iptze   canalw-oj ix   naj.
PST-3ABS-3ERG-force dance-INF CL/she CL/he
'She forced him to dance.'

(6.83) a. X-∅-(y)-iptze   ix   naj
PST-3ABS-3ERG-force CL/she CL/he
s-canalwi.
3ERG-dance
'She forced him to dance.'
   b.*X-∅-(y)-iptze   s-canalwi ix
PST-3ABS-3ERG-force 3ERG-dance CL/she
naj.
CL/he
'She forced him to dance.'

Craig (1977) describes equi-NP-deletion as being optional with causative verbs, but it would appear that the lack of subject coding on the second junct is a function of the level of the juncture: no coding in a nuclear juncture, ergative coding in a core juncture. It should be noted that equi-NP-deletion with motion and desire verbs is obligatory but is not part of a nuclear juncture.

(6.84) a.   X-$\emptyset$-to   naj   sajch-oj/ *s-sajchi.
         PST-3ABS-go CL/he play-INF 3ERG/play
         'He went to play.'
    b. *X-$\emptyset$-to   sajch-oj naj.
         PST-3ABS-go play-IN CL/he
         'He went to play.'

Motion and desire verb complements such as this are core junctures.

The final Jacaltec construction to be discussed is not a clause–clause structure but rather a complex NP; namely, relative clauses. Their structure is illustrated in (6.85).

(6.85) a. X-$\emptyset$-w-il   naj   x-$\emptyset$-to
         PST-3ABS-1sgERG-see CL/man PST-3ABS-go
         ewi   (an).
         yesterday 1p
         'I saw the man who went yesterday.'
    b. X-$\emptyset$-w-il   naj
         PST-3ABS-1sgERG-see CL/man
         x-$\emptyset$-s-mak   ix   (an).   (=4.114a)
         PST-3ABS-3ERG-hit CL/she 1p
         'I saw the man whom she hit.'
         (*I saw the man who hit her.')
    c. X-$\emptyset$-w-il   naj
         PST-3ABS-1sgERG-see CL/man
         x-$\emptyset$-__-mak-ni   ix   (an).   (=4.115a)
         PST-3ABS-__-hit-SUFF CL/she 1p
         'I saw the man who hit her.'
         (*I saw the man whom she hit.')

Relative clauses have a number of interesting properties. First, they are tensed and therefore can be negated, as in (6.86a). Nevertheless, *an* placement is not constrained in (6.85) and (6.86a) and noun-classifier deletion is likewise not blocked in (6.86b).

(6.86) a. Ø-w-ohtaj   naj   mach
            3ABS-1sgERG-know CL/man NEG
            x-Ø-munla   tu' (an).
            NPST-3ABS-work that 1p
            'I know that man who is not working.'
        b. Mat   Ø-y-ohtaj   ix   naj
            NEG 3ABS-3ERG-know CL/she CL/man
            x-Ø-__-mak-ni   (*ix)   y-ul
            PST-3ABS-__-hit-SUFF CL/she 3ERG-in
            parce.
            park
            'She does not know the man who hit her in the park.'

Thus despite being tensed like the clauses in peripheral junctures, relative-clause boundaries do not affect *an* placement or noun-classifier deletion. Secondly, transitive verbs take the suffix -$n(i)$ if the head noun functions as the actor of the verb in the relative clause; the ergative cross-referencing affix is also omitted. This deletion of the ergative marker and suffixation of -$n(i)$ may be considered a kind of antipassivization, and Larsen & Norman (1979) have argued that it is analogous to the *ŋay* antipassive construction in Dyirbal (see 4.5). There is, however, a significant difference between Dyirbal and Jacaltec antipassivization: in Dyirbal the *ŋay* construction can occur in a simple, independent clause (although its primary function is as part of a clause-linkage reference maintenance system – see 7.4), whereas in Jacaltec this form of antipassivization is possible only as part of certain syntactic processes, and therefore simple, independent antipassivized clauses are impossible. In addition to relativization, deletion of the ergative marker and suffixation of -$n(i)$ are also involved in the clefting and WH-questioning of the actors of transitive verbs.

(6.87) a. Ha'   ix   (= 4.114b)
            CLEFT CL/she
            x-Ø-(y)-il   naj.
            PST-3ABS-3ERG-see CL/he
            'It is she whom he saw.' (*'It is she who
            saw him.')

b. Ha'   naj   (= 4.115b)
CLEFT CL/he
x-∅-__-'il-ni   ix.
PST-3ABS-__-see-SUFF CL/she
'It is he who saw her.' (*'It is he whom
she saw.')

(6.88) a. Macx-∅-__-'il-ni   naj.   (= 4.114c)
WH PST-3ABS-3ERG-see CL/he
'Whom did he see?' (*'Who saw him?')

b. Macx-∅-__-'il-ni   naj.   (= 4.115c)
WH PST-3ABS-__-see-SUFF CL/he
'Who saw him?' (*'Whom did he see?')

Craig (1977) argues that in relativization, clefting, and WH-question formation antipassivization is a mechanism for disambiguating actors from undergoers, for without it sentences like (6.87a) and (6.88a) would be potentially ambiguous as to the syntactic function of the core arguments, since there is no way to tell whether the single post-verbal NP is located in the actor or undergoer slot. It should be noted that these three syntactic operations all result in precisely the same structure, i.e. an NP followed by a clause which has lost an (NP) argument.

We are now in a position to summarize the clause–clause linkage phenomena of Jacaltec. In Table 12, '+tense' means both juncts are tensed, '−tense' both are not: '+an, +NCD' means neither an placement nor noun-classifier deletion are constrained, '−an, −NCD' means they are restricted; 'IF' stands for illocutionary force.

The most striking feature of this table is the sharp break between peripheral and non-peripheral junctures. Peripheral junctures allow tensed clauses with ergative case marking which block noun-classifier deletion and restrict an placement. Core junctures, on the other hand, have only one tensed clause with ergative case marking, the other being tenseless and having an accusative case-marking schema; these junctures do not block noun-classifier deletion nor constrain an placement. The nuclear juncture causative construction is a single clause with a single set of arguments; the dependent verb is reduced to a bare infinitive, and it is the only construction in which transitive verbs so occur.

Table 12 *Jacaltec clause–clause linkage categories*

Juncture–nexus	Features	Examples
Nuclear cosubordinate	−tense, bare infinitive (causative with *a'a'*)	(6.80)–(6.81)
Core non-subordinate	−tense, +*an*, +NCD	(6.77)–(6.79)
Core subordinate	Accusative case marking Transitive verb + -*n(i)*	(6.79)–(6.83)
Peripheral cosubordinate	+tense, -*an*, −NCD Ergative case marking Same tense, IF required Transitive verb + -*n(i)* (Simultaneous action)	(6.69)–(6.71)
Peripheral subordinate	+tense, -*an*, −NCD Ergative case marking Same IF required Transitive verb + -*n(i)* (Temporal adverbial)	(6.64)–(6.68)
Peripheral coordinate	+tense, -*an*, −NCD Ergative case marking Transitive verb + -*n(i)* (Juxtaposition)	(6.61)–(6.63)

Silverstein (1976b, 1980b) claims (cf. p. 274) that in ergative languages tighter linkage results in increased probabilities of antipassivization of the linked member, and of accusative case marking in it; both of these predictions are realized in Jacaltec. The case-marking pattern in the linked junct shifts from ergative to accusative with the change from peripheral- to core-level junctures; in nuclear junctures the case marking of the dependent unit has been totally integrated into that of the tensed verb. Antipassivization in Jacaltec is tied up with the suffix -*n(i)*, which occurs on at least some transitive verbs in all of the peripheral and core linkage categories. As discussed in 4.5, antipassivization typically entails two changes in a clause with a transitive verb: (1) the verb is detransitivized, and (2) the actor may assume pivot status. Both of these aspects are involved in relativization, clefting, and WH-question formation, as we saw in (6.85)–(6.88).

In order to appreciate the function of -*n(i)* in core and peripheral junctures, it is necessary to recognize the strong bias in favor of intransitive verbs in the grammar of this language. In peripheral coordination, intransitive verbs may be juxtaposed without alteration to form chains of clauses, and they likewise occur in temporal subordinate clauses and in simultaneous action constructions without modification, e.g. (6.61a), (6.64c), and (6.71a).

Passivized transitive verbs have the linkage privileges of intransitive verbs and never take *-n(i)*. In core junctures only the single arguments of intransitive verbs may undergo equi-NP-deletion, e.g. (6.71a), and 'promotion' (Craig 1977) to be the absolutive argument of an intransitive aspectual verb (compare (6.74e) with (6.77e)). In this context the apparently multifunctional *-n(i)* can be seen to have one basic function: to allow transitive verbs the same linkage possibilities as intransitive verbs. Accordingly, the effect *-n(i)* has on a clause will vary according to the demands of the syntactico-semantic linkage environment; the stronger the syntactic bond between the clauses is, the greater the effect of *-n(i)* will be on the dependent clause. In peripheral junctures, *-n(i)* serves to detransitivize transitive verbs only to the extent necessary to allow them to combine with intransitive verbs or to occur in temporal adverbial clauses. The only evidence of detransitivization is the form of the future–irrealis suffix, which expresses a peripheral operator. Because the linkage involves only the outermost level of the clause, the core is unaffected, and consequently the addition of *-n(i)* does not disrupt the case marking of core arguments or alter their syntactic status. In core junctures, however, the core of the clause is the locus of the linkage, and therefore any alteration for clause-linkage purposes could not leave it unscathed. Since it is a core juncture, the dependent junct will have no tense marking, and this affects the coding of core arguments. The absolutive case marker is normally bound to the tense prefix, and with tense gone it must occur as a free-form pronoun, leaving only the ergative marker still bound to the verb. The verb itself is formally detransitivized and takes the intransitive irrealis–future suffix *-oj* (see (6.79)). The syntactic status of the ergative argument has been modified; although it still cannot be omitted by virtue of equi-NP-deletion, it is now freely extractable.

(6.89) a. Mac x-∅-aw-il   ∅
           WH PST-3ABS-2sgERG-see 3ABS
           s-mak-ni   ix.
           3ERG-hit-SUFF CL/she
           'Who did you see her hit?'
           'Who did you see hit her?'

b. Ø-w-ohtaj   naj
   3ABS-1sgERG-know CL/man
   x-Ø-aw-il   Ø   s-mak-ni
   PST-3ABS-2sgERG-see 3ABS 3ERG-hit-SUFF
   ix.
   CL/she
   'I know the man who you saw her hit.'
   'I know the man who you saw hit her.'

Moreover, for some speakers, promotion is applicable to anti-passivized transitive clauses.

(6.90) a.   X-Ø-ichi   hach   hin-mak-ni.
            PST-3ABS-begin 2sgABS 1sgERG-hit-SUFF
            'I began to hit you.'
       b (*)Xc-in   ichi hach   hin-mak-ni.
            PST-1sgABS begin 2sgABS 1sgERG-hit-SUFF
            'I began to hit you.'

In the dialect in which (6.90b) is grammatical, the syntactic consequences of $-n(i)$ antipassivization are unambiguous. Also in this dialect the derived subject of a passive construction may be promoted, thus confirming that the promoted argument in (6.90b) is indeed a derived intransitive subject. Thus because junctures of this type involve the core of the clause and its constituent arguments, $-n(i)$ affects them directly, whereas in peripheral junctures they are insulated from it. In other words, in peripheral junctures $-n(i)$ antipassivization involves only superficial detransitivization, in particular the expression of a peripheral operator, whereas in core junctures both aspects of antipassivization come into play. The non-occurrence of $-n(i)$ in nuclear junctures such as (6.81a) follows directly from this analysis: antipassivization is a core phenomenon in that it involves the nucleus and its core arguments, and consequently it cannot apply to a single nucleus in a nuclear juncture independent of the core arguments of the complex nucleus. The dependent nucleus in sentences like (6.80) and (6.81) no longer has any core arguments of its own which could be affected by antipassivization. Hence the distribution of $-n(i)$ in Jacaltec complex sentences is readily explained in terms of the layered structure of the clause and the theory of nexus types presented here.

Looking at the semantic relations expressed by the Jacaltec linkage categories, we find that the pattern follows that specified in the IRH. Causative relations appear in nuclear cosubordinate nexus, as in (6.80)–(6.81), the most tightly linked category. Modality, psych-action and direct-perception complements are expressed through core subordination, as the examples in (6.80) show. Causatives with *iptze* 'force' appear to fall into the jussive category, occurring in core non-subordinate (almost certainly coordinate) nexus (cf. the English example in (6.18)). Indirect discourse complements and adverbial clauses fall together in peripheral subordination. Simultaneous action is coded in both peripheral cosubordinate (e.g. (6.71)) and subordinate (e.g. (6.64d)) nexus. A variety of relations appear in peripheral coordination. Thus the semantic relations manifested by the syntactic linkage categories of Jacaltec are the ones which are predicted by the IRH.

Jacaltec provides an excellent example of the value of the IRH as an analytical tool and conforms to two effects of tighter linkage posited by Silverstein for ergative languages: an increasing probability of antipassivization and of a shift to accusative case marking. These data also exemplify the point of the previous section concerning the interpretation of case marking. Ergative in a clause in a peripheral juncture is not the same as the ergative in a core juncture, since in the former it cross-references only the actor of a transitive verb but in the latter the actor of a transitive and the single argument of an intransitive verb. The same is true with respect to adpositional case marking; -*et* 'to' signals a different semantic function of its object in a nuclear-juncture causative construction with a transitive verb, as in (6.81), from the one it indicates in simple independent clauses.

(6.91) X-∅-(y)-a'   ix   te'   hum
        PST-3ABS-3ERG-give C L/she C L/the book
        t-aw-et.
        A U G-2sgE R G-to
        'She gave the book to you.'

In (6.81) the object of -*et* is the actor of the infinitival transitive

verb, whereas in (6.91) it is a recipient (indirect object). Thus
the clause-linkage phenomena of Jacaltec illustrate the claims of
the I R H regarding case marking, antipassivization, and the shift
from ergative to accusative case marking in ergative languages.

6.4.4 Reference maintenance in tight linkage   One of the
correlates of the I R H not mentioned in Figure 14 and in Silverstein's generalizations (p. 274) concerns the interaction of clause
linkage with cross-clause coreference maintenance systems. Since
these are the main topic of Chapter 7, the discussion here will
be brief. Silverstein characterizes this interplay as follows. 'If a
language uses a special form for co-reference relations over a
logical connexion at a certain point [of the I R H], it will use at
least that mechanism for everything above, and possibly even more
elaborate formal distinctions' (1976b: 163).

One type of coreference device is restricted zero anaphora as
in English and many other languages, and we can use data from
English to demonstrate this point. English uses zero anaphora for
the junctures between peripheral cosubordination and core cosubordination.

(6.92) a. Max forgot his notebook and had to buy another one.
            (Peripheral cosubordination).
        b. John forced Mary to bake an apple pie. (Core co-
            ordination)
        c. Phil regretted leaving Mary. (Core subordination)
        d. Morris stood glaring at the heretic. (Core cosubordina-
            tion)

Jacaltec relies on noun classifiers for coreference in peripheral
junctures, while in core-level linkage and relative clauses noun-
classifier zero anaphora is found. Omission of verbal cross-
reference morphemes is possible only in the most tightly linked
forms, i.e. core non-subordinate nexus with an intransitive verb
in the dependent junct, nuclear cosubordination, and some
relative clauses. Various systems of discourse coreference
maintenance and their interaction with juncture and nexus will
be discussed in more detail in 7.5.

6.4.5 Markedness relations in clause linkage Two other points in Figure 14 and the summary on p. 274 deserve brief mention. The correlation between tightness of linkage and the degree of formal distinction of the dependent clause from the form of an unlinked clause is amply exemplified in the Jacaltec data. In peripheral junctures, clauses with intransitive verbs occur in unmodified form, while in some constructions transitive verbs must have the suffix -$n(i)$. Linkage at the core level results in major formal deformation of the linked clause, regardless of the transitivity of its verb, and nuclear junctures require the dependent verb to be stripped of all arguments. These deformations are summarized in the 'features' column of Table 12.

The increasing 'markedness of connexion' up the IRH is reflected in Jacaltec, as in other languages, by restrictions on the elements which may be involved in the juncture. These restrictions relate to the non-linked clause or verb. In Jacaltec peripheral junctures, there are virtually no restrictions on what verbs may occur in either clause. In core junctures, on the other hand, the range of verbs which can occur in the non-linked clause is limited to a relatively small number, e.g. motion, cognition, desire, causation, and aspect. The restriction is most severe at the nuclear level, where only *one* type of verb is possible, i.e. causative, and only one verb may occur in this juncture–nexus combination with both transitive and intransitive verbs, i.e. *a'a'* 'make, cause'. This increasing markedness of the linkage goes hand-in-hand with the formal transformations of the morphosyntax of the clause. It is interesting to note that this syntactico-semantic markedness is inversely proportional to the likelihood of morphological marking of the connection. The greatest variety of conjunctions and other morphological means for joining two elements is found invariably in the less tightly linked constructions, while at the top end of the IRH simple juxtaposition is the rule, particularly in nuclear junctures.

6.4.6 Summary In this section we have proposed an interclausal relations hierarchy which orders the nexus–juncture combinations discussed in 6.2 along a cline of increasing strength of the syntactic bond or link between two clausal or subclausal units. The tightness of the syntactic connection between two units is directly related to the closeness of the semantic relationship holding between them. Silverstein has proposed a number of morphosyntactic correlates of the increasing tightness of linkage, and these were discussed and illustrated with data drawn from English, Imbabura Quechua, and Jacaltec.

6.5 Aspects of English core junctures

In this section we will deal with certain aspects of English core junctures, concentrating on infinitival constructions and the much-discussed problem of control (see e.g. Rosenbaum 1967, Jackendoff 1972, Chomsky 1980a). The central examples are presented in (6.93).

(6.93) a. Bill seems to have won the lottery.
       b. Max tried to escape from prison.
       c. Larry forgot to lock the gate.
       d. Fred persuaded Mary to give him title to her estate.
       e. Alice promised Ellen to leave early.

The control problem is that of determining which main clause argument is the 'subject' of the infinitive, and most discussions have centered around sentences like (6.93d) and (6.93e). In addition, we will also discuss the accusative-plus-infinitive construction in (6.94), which is a core juncture but is not a control structure analogous to the constructions in (6.93b–e).

(6.94) a. Jimmy expects Harry to win the race.
       b. Carl considers himself to be splendid on television.

It was pointed out in 5.1 that core junctures typically require that the two cores share a core argument and that the coreference pattern between the two cores is either S/A–S/A or U–S/A. The S/A–S/A pattern was illustrated in (5.8) and (5.10), repeated here as (6.95), and the U–S/A pattern was exemplified in (5.11) and (5.12), repeated here, as (6.96).

(6.95) a. Akan (Schacter 1974)
          Kofi yɛɛ adwuma maa Amma.
             did work ˊ gave
          'Kofi worked for Amma.'

    b. Thai (A. Diller, personal communication)
        Sùk ʔaw máy maa.
         take wood come
        'Sook brought the wood.'
    c. Yoruba (Stahlke 1970)
        Mo mú ìwé wá   ilé.
        1sg took book come home
        'I brought a book home.'
    d. Igbo (Lord 1975)
        ọ́ gá-fè-rè   ụ́lọ̀ ákwụ́kwọ́.
        3sg go-pass-FACT school
        'He passed the school.'

(6.96) a. Barai (Olson 1981)
        Na ki-ia   bu va-e.
        1sg say-3pl 3pl go-PST
        'I spoke to them; (causing) they went' or 'I made them
        go.'
    b. Yoruba (Bamgbose 1974)
        Olú lo aṣọ náà gbó.
          use dress the wore. out
        'Olu used the dress and it wore out' or 'Olu wore the
        dress out.'
    c. Igbo (Lord 1975)
        ọ́ tụ̀-fù-rù   ákwụ́kwọ́
        3sg throw-lost-FACT paper
        'He threw the paper and it got lost' or 'He threw away
        the paper.'

The patterns of coreference found in these examples of verb serialization are also found in the English core junctures in (6.93): S/A–S/A in (6.93b–c, e) and U–S/A in (6.93d). Consequently, any theory of control proposed for the English examples should also apply to analogous core junctures in other languages.

    Two of the most important theories of control advanced within the framework of generative grammar are the 'minimal distance principle' of Rosenbaum (1967) and the networks of coreference based on thematic relations proposed in Jackendoff (1972). The 'minimal distance principle' states that the matrix-clause argument which is coreferential with the 'subject' of the infinitive is the one closest to it, where distance is measured in terms of the number of nodes in the phase-structure tree between the NP nodes under consideration (see Rosenbaum 1967:17–18). This principle accounts for (6.93b–d) but not for (6.93e); verbs such as *promise* and *vow* are exceptions to it, since the closest NP in terms of nodes or tree branches is not the controller. Moreover, because it involves counting nodes and branches in a phrase-structure tree, its application is limited to configurational languages only. Jackendoff's proposal, on the other hand, is semantically rather than syntactically based. He argues that the controller should be specified in the lexical entry of the comple-ment-taking predicate as part of the 'network of coreference' which the verb is involved in. With any given verb the controller is determined on the basis not of structural configurations or grammatical relations, but rather of thematic relations. Thus with *get*, as in (6.97), the theme is always the controller, regardless of its syntactic position, while with *promise*, as in (6.98), the source is always the controller.

(6.97) a. John got leave.
        b. Bill got John to leave.

(6.98) a. John promised to leave.
        b. John promised Bill to leave.

This approach avoids the two major problems noted with respect to the minimal distance principle: there is no glaring class of exceptions, and it applied equally to non-configurational as well as to configurational languages. However, Jackendoff does not attempt to derive the source control of *promise* or the theme control of *get* from the semantics of these verbs in any principled way, and consequently the specification of the controller in the lexical entry is ultimately arbitrary and non-explanatory.

Chomsky (1980a, 1981c) adopts the minimal-distance principle to handle the majority of control phenomena, and to handle *promise* he proposes an arbitrary feature, [+SC], where 'SC' is 'subject control', to be added to the lexical entry of *promise*-class verbs. This is a somewhat redundant formulation, however, because the marking of some verbs as [+SC] entails that all others are [−SC]; consequently, the controller with every complement-taking predicate is specified by an arbitrary feature $[\pm SC]$ in its lexical entry. Invoking the minimal distance principle adds nothing to this and is superfluous.

Radford (1981) raises crucial objections to these last two solutions to the control problem.

Firstly, arbitrary lists of properties associated with predicates have no predictive or explanatory value: ask the question 'How do you know this is a verb of subject control?', and you get the non-answer 'Because it's listed as a verb of subject control in the lexicon.' Secondly, treating *control* ... as a *lexically governed* phenomenon implies that control properties are entirely arbitrary, and hence will vary in random fashion from dialect to dialect, or language to language: this would lead us to expect that the counter-part of [(6.93d)] in some other dialect or language would have subject control rather than nonsubject control ... But as far as we know, this is not the case (p. 381).

Neither Jackendoff's nor Chomsky's approaches have any predictive or explanatory power, and accordingly it is an entirely accidental fact about languages that these control patterns recur cross-linguistically. Radford goes on to suggest a potentially more explanatory solution: 'it seems likely that the question of whether a control predicate takes subject control or nonsubject control will ultimately turn out to follow directly from the meaning of the predicate concerned' (*ibid.*)

We will now develop a semantic theory of control, following Radford's suggestion. It will be noticed immediately that this problem is restricted solely to two-argument complement-taking predicates such as *force, persuade, discourage, convince, promise, vow,* and *ask*. We may divide these verbs into two groups, one with verbs of saying and the other with all other verbs. Looking at the non-verbs-of-saying first, we find that all of them have a basically causative meaning, from strongly implicative verbs like *force* or *make* to non-implicative verbs like *persuade, encourage,* and *convince*, and they all have undergoer control. Note that it is undergoer and not direct object which is the relevant notion.

(6.99) a. Bill persuaded Max to sing.
        b. Max was persuaded by Bill to sing.

(6.100) a. The burglar forced Larry to open the safe.
        b. Larry was forced by the burglar to open the safe.

In these pairs of sentences the undergoer is the controller regardless of its syntactic status. That causative verbs have undergoer control follows from the semantics of causation, since the participant acted upon in the causing event is the actor of the caused event. We predict, then, that causative complement-taking predicates will always have undergoer control.

Turning to verbs of saying, we see that there is a clear semantic distinction which correlates with whether a verb has actor or undergoer control.

(6.101)   a.   Max invited Fred to sit down.
          b.   Max ordered Fred to sit down.
          c.   Max told Fred to sit down.

(6.102)   a.   John promised Mary to leave early.
          b.   John vowed to Mary to leave early.
          c.   John asked Mary what to do.

All of the sentences in (6.101) illustrate undergoer control, those in (6.102) actor control. Again, it is the notion of actor rather than syntactic subject which is relevant, as (6.103) shows.

(6.103)   a.   Mary was promised by John to leave early.
          b.   Mary was asked by John what to do.

The actor is the controller in these examples, just as in (6.102). If we examine the types of illocutionary acts which these verbs may be involved in, we note that all of the verbs in (6.101) are used to make what Searle (1975) calls *directives*, while those in (6.102) are employed to make either *commissive* illocutionary acts, as in (6.102a,b), or *interrogatives*, as in (6.102c). Searle characterizes directives as 'attempts ... by the speaker to get the hearer to do something. They may be very modest "attempts," as when I invite you to do it or suggest that you do it, or they may be very fierce attempts as when I insist that you do it' (1975:255). Given the semantics of directive illocutionary acts, it is not surprising that the verbs which express these acts have undergoer control. Indeed, they are in essence a kind of 'verbal causative' in which the speaker/actor tries to get the addressee/undergoer to perform some action by means of an utterance. These verbs differ primarily from the causative verbs discussed above in that with these the causing event is always verbal whereas with the others it is not. There is thus a strong common semantic thread linking causative and directive verbs, all of which have undergoer control.

Verbs expressing other illocutionary acts have actor rather than undergoer control. In the case of *vow* and *promise* this follows directly from the semantics of commissive speech acts: 'Commissives then are those illocutionary acts whose point is to commit the speaker . . . to some future course of action' (Searle 1975:356). With *promise* and *vow* the speaker is realized grammatically as the actor, and accordingly these verbs have actor control. There are no such clear-cut semantic grounds for interrogatives like *ask* in (6.102c) to have actor control, but there is a strong reason why they do not have undergoer control, namely, their non-causative/ directive meaning. Generalizing over both commissives and interrogatives, we may say that verbs of saying which do not express directive illocutionary acts do not have undergoer control, and this is complemented for commissive verbs by the inherent semantics of commissive speech acts.

The semantic theory of control may be summarized as follows. Undergoer control is a feature of causative verbs and directive speech-act verbs. Verbs not falling into either of these two groups have actor control. This theory of control avoids all of the problems discussed with respect to Rosenbaum's, Jackendoff's, and Chomsky's proposals. It applies equally to configurational and non-configurational languages, unlike a purely structural theory like the minimal-distance principle. It accounts for the control facts not only in the English examples in (6.93) but also in the serial-verb constructions in (6.95) and (6.94). It does not involve any arbitrary features, e.g. [±SC], or any arbitrary specification of the controller in the lexical entry of a verb. Rather, the choice of the controller follows from the meaning of the verb.

This semantic theory of control makes an interesting prediction with respect to verbs of saying. In talking about the 'meaning' of these verbs we have dealt with the illocutionary acts they may express rather than their lexical meaning. It follows, then, that if a given verb can be used in both directive and non-directive speech acts, then its control properties would vary depending upon the type of illocutionary act it denotes, undergoer control in a directive, actor control in a non-directive. Such a case is exemplified in (6.104).

(6.104) a. John asked Bill to sing something.
         b. John asked Bill what to sing.

The speech act in (6.104a) is a directive, and there is undergoer control. In (6.104b), however, the speech act is not a directive but rather a request, and accordingly there is actor control, just as the theory predicts. None of the other three theories of control can account for the switch in control in (6.104). The semantic theory also predicts that there will be no control at all in examples like (6.105).

(6.105) Bill was asked what to do.

Control is stated in terms of actor and undergoer, not syntactic notions like subject and direct object, and in a non-directive use of *ask* there is actor control. Because the actor of *ask* is not expressed in the passive clause in (6.105), the theory predicts that there should be no control (or arbitrary control, following Chomsky 1980a), and this is in fact the case; *Bill* is not the controller in (6.105). Examples similar to (6.104) are pointed out in Radford (1981).

(6.106) a. John pleaded with Bill to leave.
         b. John pleaded with Bill to be allowed to leave.

Plead with in (a) expresses a directive speech act, and consequently *Bill* is the controller. In (b), on the other hand, *plead with* is not a directive; (6.106b) could be paraphrased as 'John asked of Bill that he be allowed to leave', ignoring the begging connotation of *plead*. This is clearly a request and not a directive, and as predicted *John* rather than *Bill* is the controller. Here again the choice of the controller depends upon whether the verb expresses a directive illocutionary act or some other kind. As Radford notes, examples such as these argue strongly against any theories of control which involve specifying the controller in the lexical entry of the verb, since some verbs can have more than one possible controller. In Chomsky's framework, for example, *ask* would have to be specified [+SC] if its complement is an indirect question but [−SC] if it is an infinitive, hardly an enlightening solution.

Even worse, *plead with* would be [+SC] with an infinitival complement composed of '*allow* [+PASS] + infinitive', otherwise
[−SC]. The ability of the semantic theory of control to predict
and account for the facts in (6.104)–(6.106) provides strong support for it.

Having established a theory of control, we now turn to the syntax
of the junctures themselves. The first constructions to be examined
are the infinitival complements of single argument verbs like *try*,
manage, remember, forget, decide, and *want*. By 'single argument'
is meant that in these junctures these verbs have only one core
argument; when they occur as the nuclei of independent clauses,
they normally have two core arguments. This valence shift need
not be specified in the lexical entries for the verbs in this class,
for it appears that the only complement-taking predicates which
may have two core arguments in a core juncture are the causative
and speech-act verbs mentioned in our discussion of control above.
At this point we claim only that this is a general principle of English
clause linkage, but further cross-linguistic research may determine
that this principle is in fact universal. Examples of core junctures
with these verbs are given in (6.107).

(6.107) a. Larry tried to buy some beer without an ID.
         b. Ian tried to be examined by a specialist.
         c. Helen remembered to lock the gate.
         d. The Prime Minister declined to be interviewed.
         e. The candidate wanted to be photographed kissing a
             baby.
         f. Ursula decided to leave early.
         g. Tom forgot to be ready at 7.30.

One fact that emerges from these examples is that the controller
need not function as an actor in the linked core; as (b), (d), (e),
and (g) show, it may be an undergoer, and, in (b), (d), and (e),
the undergoer of a passive construction. Thus the non-occurring
core argument of the linked core cannot be specified as actor or
undergoer but rather is the pivot; or perhaps more accurately,
the non-occurring core argument corresponds to the pivot argument if the core occurred in a simple independent clause. This
is the case in all core junctures in English, irrespective of the
valence of the non-linked clause. This fact, along with the principle

proposed above regarding the number of core arguments of the complement-taking predicate, precludes the need for any 'like-subject constraint' on these verbs of the type proposed in Perlmutter (1971). In a non-subordinate core juncture, the two cores must share a common argument, which in the linked clause is always the potential pivot argument. By virtue of their semantics these verbs will have only one core argument in such a juncture (the actor), and since it is the only core argument in the non-linked clause, it must be the controller. Accordingly, it and the potential-pivot argument of the linked core must always be coreferential. This follows from the principle governing the valence of complement-taking predicates, the necessary involvement of the potential-pivot argument of the linked clause, and the nature of non-subordinate core junctures, and hence no specific coreference constraint is required.

The syntactic structure of these junctures may be represented as in (6.108).[12]

(6.108) a. $_P[_{C1}[NP1]\ _N[PRED]_N]_{C1} = _{C2}[\emptyset\ _N[PRED$
$(\pm PASS)]_N \ldots]_{C2} \ldots]_P$

b. $_P[_{C1}[Helen\ _N[remembered]_N]_{C1} = _{C2}[to\ _N[lock]_N$
the gate$]_{C2}]_P\ (= 6.107c)$

The nexus type in this construction appears to be cosubordinate, because the relevant operator, root modals, has scope over both cores. This is illustrated in (6.109).

(6.109) a. Ian must try to be examined by a specialist.
b. Helen should have remembered to lock the gate.
c. The Prime Minister may decline to be interviewed, if he so wishes.
d. Ursula can try to leave the party early.

In (6.109a), what is it that Ian is obliged to do: 'try' or 'try to be examined'? Similarly in (b), what is it that Helen ought to have done: 'remember' or 'remember to lock the gate'? In both cases the answer seems to be the second one, the one which includes both cores. Thus in these junctures the two clausal units share a core argument and the core operator, and accordingly the nexus is cosubordinate (cf. 6.2.3).

In 3.3.1 and 4.6 we dealt with the mapping relationships between semantic logical structures and simple sentences, and the same basic principles are involved with complex sentences as well. There is, however, the additional problem of specifying 'co-reference' between logical structures, since in these junctures the two cores must share a core argument. This can be achieved by means of the 'completeness constraint' stated earlier (p. 183). In simple sentences this constraint specifies that the number of syntactic-argument positions in a clause must match up with the number of filled semantic-argument positions in the logical structure of the verb in the clause. In a complex sentence it guarantees the correct coreference relations between the arguments in the logical structures of the verbs in the sentence. We will use (6.107c) to illustrate this. The logical structures for *remember* and *lock* are given in (6.110).

(6.110) a. **remember**$'$ (Helen, $\emptyset$)
        b. $[DO(Helen,[\textbf{do}'(Helen)])]$ CAUSE [BECOME **locked**$'$ (gate)]

The semantic relations of the arguments are straightforward: *Helen* is the locative of *remember* and the agent of *lock*, and *gate* is the patient of *lock*, and *Helen* is also the actor of *remember* and *lock*, *gate* the undergoer of *lock*, following the hierarchy in Figure 1. The mapping of these arguments into the structure in (6.108a) is straightforward. *Helen* is the only argument of *remember* and occupies the NP1 slot in Core$_1$. There are two possible mappings of the arguments of *lock* (cf. 4.6). One is for the actor to be the pivot and the undergoer to be the post-verbal object; *gate* would occupy the post-nuclear core slot in Core$_2$, but there is no slot for *Helen*, the actor, in Core$_2$. Since *Helen* already occurs as the pivot of Core$_1$, however, there is no problem in terms of the completeness constraint. Arguments from distinct logical structures can be mapped into the same syntactic position only if they are referentially identical. The actor of *lock* is not realized directly but rather is the shared argument of the core juncture. This yields (6.108b). The other possible mapping would have *gate* chosen as the pivot. *Helen* would then occur as an inner-peripheral argument marked with *by*, but because there is no pivot slot in Core$_2$, there is no possible syntactic realization for *gate*. Consequently, the completeness constraint is violated, and this mapping is ruled out. Thus in this case the completeness constraint guarantees coreference between the appropriate arguments in the two logical structures, because without coreference a complete mapping between logical and syntactic structures is not possible.

The next set of verbs to be discussed are 'subject raising' verbs like *seem*, *appear*, and *certain*. These verbs differ from *try, et al.* in taking a logical structure as their single argument rather than an individual nominal of some kind. As a result, in core junctures the shared argument corresponds to a single argument in the logical structure of the linked verb which occurs syntactically as the pivot of the complement-taking predicate. The sentences in (6.111) exemplify this with *certain*.

(6.111)   a.   That Helen locked the gate is certain.
          b.   It is certain that Helen locked the gate.
          c.   Helen is certain to have locked the gate.

In (a) the single argument of *certain* is a full clause; in (b) it is the (cataphoric) pivot-filler *it* with the clause occurring as an inner-peripheral argument. (See 6.2.2. for some discussion of these constructions.) The construction of interest here is (c), the non-subordinate core juncture. It has the syntactic structure given in (6.108a), i.e. the same as the examples in (6.107). The logical structure underlying (6.111c) is, however, very different from that underlying (6.107), as is the mapping between them. The logical structure of (6.111c) is presented in (6.112).

(6.112)   **certain′** ([DO(Helen,[**do′**(Helen)])] CAUSE
          [BECOME **locked′**(gate)])

Each argument in (6.111c) occurs only once in (6.112), and thus we are not dealing with a coreference problem as we were in (6.110). *Certain* is the predicate in $Core_1$ in (6.108a), and its pivot must come from the logical structure of *lock*. If the actor of *lock* were to be its pivot, then *Helen* would occur as NP1, with *gate* in the post-nuclear slot in $Core_2$. The result would be (6.113).

(6.113) $_P[_{C_1}$[Helen $_N$[is certain]$_N$]$_{C_1}$ =
          $_{C_2}$[to $_N$[have locked]$_N$ the gate]$_{C_2}$]$_P$[13]

If, on the other hand, the undergoer of *lock* were chosen as its pivot, then the result would be (6.114).

(6.114) $_\text{P}[_{\text{C}_1}[\text{The gate }_\text{N}[\text{is certain}]_\text{N}]_{\text{C}_1} =$
$_{\text{IP}_2}[_{\text{C}_2}[\text{to }_\text{N}[\text{have been locked}]_\text{N}]_{\text{C}_2}$ by Helen]$_{\text{IP}_2}]_\text{P}$[14]

In both cases the pivot of *certain* is an argument of *lock*, and the 'raising' which other theories attempt to capture by means of a syntactic rule exists here only in the mapping from logical to syntactic structures. In transformational theory (6.111a) is taken as the basic form with (b) and (c) derived by means of syntactic rules of subject-to-subject raising and extraposition. No such rules need be posited within the framework developed in this chapter, because each of the sentences in (6.111) exhibits a distinct juncture–nexus combination: core subordination in (a), peripheral subordination in (b), and core cosubordination in (c). At this point we will say only that these juncture–nexus possibilities are listed in the lexical entry for each verb. Further research may well reveal that the juncture–nexus combinations that a predicate may be involved in are a function of its semantics.

We now turn our attention to the transitive complement-taking predicates discussed above with respect to the theory of control. The two major types in terms of control are illustrated in (6.115).

(6.115) a. Max reminded Helen to lock the gate.
b. Helen promised Max to lock the gate.

The syntactic structure of these sentences is given in (6.117),

(6.116) a. $_\text{P}[_{\text{C}_1}[\text{NP}_1 \ _\text{N}[\text{PRED}(\pm \text{PASS}]_\text{N} \ \text{NP}_2]_{\text{C}_1} =$
$_{\text{C}_2}[\emptyset \ _\text{N}[\text{PRED}(\pm \text{PASS})]_\text{N} \ ...]_{\text{C}_2} \ ...]_\text{P}$
b. $_\text{P}[_{\text{C}_1}[\text{Max }_\text{N}[\text{reminded}]_\text{N} \ \text{Helen}]_{\text{C}_1} =$
$_{\text{C}_2}[\text{to }_\text{N}[\text{lock}]_\text{N} \text{ the gate}]_{\text{C}_2}]_\text{P}$

The logical structure of *remind* is presented in (6.125), that of *lock* in (6.110b).

(6.117) [DO(Max,[**do**′(Max)])] CAUSE [BECOME **remember**′ (Helen, $\emptyset$)]

The mapping from logical to syntactic structure is no different from that with verbs like *try*, and *remember*. With *remind*, *Max* is an agent and the actor, *Helen* is a locative and the undergoer; *Max* occurs in the NP1 pivot slot, *Helen* in the NP2 slot, and the clause is active voice. With *lock*, *Helen* is an agent and the actor, *gate* is a patient and the undergoer. There is only one possible mapping of the arguments of *lock*; *gate* must occur in the post-nuclear NP2 slot in $Core_2$, for there is no other possible slot for it and the completeness constraint would otherwise be violated. Because the two *Helen*-arguments are referentially identical, they are both mapped onto the same syntactic slot in $Core_1$. In mapping from syntactic to logical structure, the theory of control comes into play, as it determines which argument of $Core_1$ functions as an argument in the logical structure of the predicate of $Core_2$.

Consider now the sentence in (6.118).

(6.118) a. Max reminded Helen to be examined by the doctor.
  b. $_P[_{C1}$[Max $_N$[reminded]$_N$ Helen]$_{C1} =$
      $_{IP2}[_{C2}$[to $_N$[be examined]$_N$ by the doctor]$_{IP2}]_P$

The logical structure of *examine*, an activity verb, is the same as that of *look at* or *watch* (see 2.5): $DO(x, [\mathbf{see}' (x,y)])$. In this case $x = the\ doctor$, an agent and the actor, and $y = Helen$, a theme and the undergoer. The mapping of $Core_1$ in (6.118) would be the same as in (6.116b). In $Core_2$ there is again only one possible mapping which satisfies the completeness constraint. *Helen*, the undergoer, must be treated as the potential pivot and mapped into NP2 of $Core_1$. This necessitates a passive construction in $Core_2$, and accordingly *doctor*, the actor, must occur in a *by*-prepositional phrase. If *doctor* were treated as the potential pivot, then there would be no syntactic slot available for it and the completeness constraint would be violated. In both (6.116b) and (6.118b) there is only one possible mapping in $Core_2$, but this does not hold with respect to $Core_1$, as both sentences in (6.119) are fully grammatical.

(6.119) a. Helen was reminded by Max to lock the gate.
  b. Helen was reminded by Max to be examined by the doctor.

Thus the only complexity which these verbs exhibit over single-argument verbs such as *try* and *remember* is the possibility of passivization in $Core_1$, otherwise the mapping follows exactly the same principles and parameters.

The final group of verbs to be discussed are those which in earlier transformational theory governed a syntactic rule of 'raising to object'. It includes *believe, expect, assume, acknowledge, suppose,* and *consider*, among others. Like *seem*-class verbs, they permit three nexus–juncture combinations, as illustrated in (6.120).

(6.120) a. Max believed that Helen locked the gate.
b. That Helen locked the gate was believed by Max.
c. Max believed Helen to have locked the gate

In (6.120a) the linkage is peripheral subordination and in (b) core subordination (see 6.2.2); in (6.120c) it is core coordination (see 6.2.1). The nexus of interest is (c), the 'raising' construction. The syntactic structure of (c) is presented in (6.121).

(6.121) a. $_P[_{C_1}[NP_1 \ _N[PRED]_N \ NP_2]_{C_1} =$
$_{C_2}[\emptyset \ _N[PRED(\pm PASS)]_N \ldots]_{C_2} \ldots]_P$
b. $_P[_{C_1}[Max \ _N[believed]_N \ Helen]_{C_1} =$
$_{C_2}[to \ _N[have \ locked]_N \ the \ gate]_{C_2}]_P$

The syntactic structure in (6.121a) is the same as that in (6.116a), and thus both *persuade*-type and *believe*-type verbs occur in the same syntactic structure.[15] The difference between these two types of complement-taking predicates is the number of arguments which the verb in $Core_1$ supplies. It was pointed out above that the only verbs which have two core arguments in a core juncture are causative verbs and verbs of saying (see p. 311). All of the verbs of the *persuade*-class fall into this group, and none of the *believe*-class verbs do. Thus by this principle *believe*, etc. may supply only one core argument to $Core_1$ and it will always be the actor. Accordingly, the argument in the NP_2 slot must come from the logical structure of the predicate in $Core_2$. The logical structure for *believe* is **believe′** (x,y) (see 2.5) and that for *lock* is given in (6.110b). The logical structure underlying the sentences in (6.120) is presented in (6.122).

(6.122) **believe′** (Max,([DO(Helen,[**do′** (Helen)])] CAUSE
[BECOME **locked′** (gate)]))

The mapping parallels that for *seem*-class predicates. *Believe* is the verb in $Core_1$, and *Max* is its actor, which appears in the NP_1 pivot position. There is no additional argument of *believe* to fill the NP_2 slot. *Lock* is the verb in $Core_2$, and *Helen* is its actor and *gate* its undergoer. The potential pivot argument of $Core_2$ fills the open position in $Core_1$, just as with *seem*-class predicates.

If the actor is the potential pivot, then *Helen* appears in the un-filled core argument position in $Core_1$, and the result is (6.121b). If, on the other hand, *gate* is the potential pivot of *lock*, then it occurs in $Core_1$, yielding (6.123).

(6.123) a. Max believed the gate to have been locked by Helen.
       b. $_P[_{C_1}[Max \ _N[believed]_N \ the \ gate]_{C_1} =$
           $_{IP_2}[_{C_2}[\ to \ _N[have \ been \ locked]_N]_{C_2} \ by \ Helen]_{IP_2}]_P$

There are two more possible mappings from (6.122): if the actor of *believe* does not function as pivot and the NP_1 pivot slot is left open, then the potential pivot of $Core_2$ will appear as the pivot of $Core_1$.

(6.124) a. Helen was believed by Max to have locked the gate.
       b. $_P[_{IP_1}[_{C_1}[Helen_N[was \ believed]_N]_{C_1} \ by \ Max]_{IP_1} =$
           $_{C_2}[to_N[have \ locked]_N \ the \ gate]_{C_2}]_P$

(6.125) a. The gate was believed by Max to have been locked by Helen.
       b. $_P[_{IP_1}[_{C_1}[the \ gate_N[was \ believed]_N]_{C_1} \ by \ Max]_{IP_1} =$
           $_{IP_2}[_{C_2}[to_N[have \ been \ locked]_N]_{C_2} \ by \ Helen]_{IP_2}]_P$

These last two sentences illustrate the much-discussed interaction between passive and 'raising' in which the actor or undergoer of $Core_2$ appears as the pivot of $Core_1$. As in the case of *seem*-class 'subject raising' predicates, there is no actual syntactic raising of an argument from one clause to another. Rather, the 'raising' is all in the mapping from logical to syntactic structure in which an argument of the predicate of $Core_2$ occurs in a core-argument slot in $Core_1$. The potential pivot of $Core_2$ fills the open-argument position in $Core_1$, which may be either pivot as in (6.124)–(6.125) or post-nuclear 'object' as in (6.121b) and (6.123).

We thus have two broad classes of complement-taking predicates in these English core junctures. One class includes *try*- and *persuade*-class predicates. In junctures with these verbs, two arguments, one from the predicate in each core, are mapped onto a single core argument position in $Core_1$ under conditions of referential identity. With *try*-class verbs the double mapping is into the actor/pivot slot; with *persuade*-class verbs, it is into the undergoer, the exact syntactic position of which is determined by the voice of the verb. These verbs were labeled 'equi-verbs' in the transformational literature, e.g. Rosenbaum (1967). The other class includes predicates like *seem* and *believe* which always have an unfilled core-argument position in their clause in a core juncture. This open slot is filled by an argument (the potential pivot) of the predicate in the linked clause. There is no mapping of two arguments from different verbs into a single argument slot as with the other class of verbs. These predicates were called 'raising verbs' in the transformational literature, e.g. Postal (1974). Both *try-* and *seem*-type verbs occur in the same syntactic structure, i.e. (6.108a), and they differ in that *try*-verbs supply the single-core argument of Core$_1$ whereas *seem*-verbs do not. Similarly, both *persuade-* and *believe*-type verbs occur in the syntactic structure in (6.116a), and they contrast with respect to the number of (potential) core arguments they supply to Core$_1$: *persuade*-verbs provide two, whereas *believe*-verbs provide only one, the actor. Thus these English core junctures reduce to two basic syntactic structures which differ with respect to the number of core arguments in Core$_1$ and two classes of verbs, each of which occurs in both syntactic forms.

6.6 Appendix: a note on creativity

One of the major issues in linguistic theory since the beginning of the generative era has been 'linguistic creativity', i.e. the ability of native speakers to produce and understand an (in principle) infinite number of sentences (see 1.1). Chomsky and his followers have maintained that this aspect of human linguistic ability can only be captured and ultimately explained in terms of a system of generative rules incorporating the property of recursion. How else, it is argued, could a speaker employing finite means be able to produce and understand an infinite number of sentences?

The framework developed in this and the last chapter provides an alternative account of linguistic creativity. In language-acquisition terms, a child needs to learn only two things: (1) the layered structure of the clause, and (2) the nexus types (at most three) in the language. These provide the means for forming the clause-linkage constructions discussed in this chapter, which are recursive in that clauses (and subparts thereof) may be linked iteratively. For example, two nuclei could be joined to form a complex nucleus, and the core containing the complex nucleus could be linked to another core in a core juncture. The resulting complex clause could then be connected to other clauses in a series of peripheral junctures. The languages we have looked at in these two chapters exhibit iterated linkage at all three levels of juncture and in more than one nexus type at each level. The finite means available to the native speaker are the three levels of clause structure with their accompanying operators and the three nexus relationships; with them a speaker can construct an infinite number of utterances of potentially infinite length. If one adopts the generative grammar goal of specifying all and only the grammatical sentences of a language, then of course there must be constraints on clause linkage, and we have discussed a number of such constraints in this chapter, e.g. markedness relations in 6.3.1, the interaction of the syntactic and semantic hierarchies in 6.3.2, and the constraints on core junctures discussed in 6.5. In short, the theory of nexus and juncture in RRG provides an alternative means for capturing the creative aspect of language use.

7 Systems of discourse cohesion: reference–tracking mechanisms

7.0 Introduction

In the previous two chapters, in presenting the theory of interclausal relations, we have been primarily concerned with constructions with nuclear and core junctures. In this chapter we will discuss in some detail constructions formed with peripheral junctures. Peripheral junctures are the loosest type, and they have the weakest constraints on their formation. As we mentioned in Chapter 5, core junctures are often constrained so that the juncts share at least one common core NP, while the members of a nuclear juncture by definition must share all NP arguments. But peripheral junctures are not constrained in this way. The juncts need not, and frequently do not, have any NPs in common. Consequently, a major consideration in peripheral junctures is the monitoring of coreference for the arguments in the juncts. Peripheral junctures, by virtue of the wide range of semantic relations expressed by them, are common in all forms of discourse, so the monitoring of coreference of core arguments across them is a central function of the grammar of any language. The use of full noun phrases to refer to all participants in each junct is a potential solution to this problem, but not an actual one, given the pervasive tendency in language to omit or pronominalize given and topical information. Therefore, the problem of participant identification in an ongoing discourse is a very real one. In this chapter we will investigate the systems languages have evolved to fulfill this function.

7.1 A typology of reference-tracking mechanisms

There appear to be four basic systems for signaling the reference relations of NP arguments in discourse, and a given language may employ one or more of them. Two of these systems were mentioned briefly in Chapter 4: pragmatic pivots [PrPs] in combination with voice oppositions, and switch reference (see 4.1, 4.4). In the first system junctures are formed on the basis of co-referential PrPs, which are normally realized by zero anaphora in the linked units. English is an example of a language which makes use of this system.

(7.1) a.   Fred wants to see Marsha.   (= 4.5)
       b.   *Fred wants Marsha to see [him].
(7.2) a.   Max persuaded Freda to see Marsha.
       b.   *Max persuaded Fred Marsha to see [him].
(7.3) a.   Oscar went to the store and spoke to Bill.   (= 4.9)
       b.   *Oscar went to the store and Bill spoke to [him].

In (7.1a) and (7.3a) there is PrP–PrP coreference, while in (7.2a) there is U–PrP conference; in each case the PrP in the linked clause is zero. The (b) examples are ungrammatical because there is PrP–U and U–U coreference in which the undergoer in the linked clause occurs as zero in the non-pivot core argument ('direct object') position. In order for the co-referential argument in the linked clause to be omitted in zero anaphora, it must be potential PrP (see 6.5), and this is achieved if the linked clause is passive, as in (7.4).

(7.4)   a.   Fred wants to be seen by Marsha.
       b.   Max persuaded Fred to be seen by Marsha.
       c.   Oscar went to the store and was spoken to by Bill.

In every case the zero-pronominalized argument must be the PrP of its clause, and accordingly the active–passive voice opposition plays an important role in this system. We will discuss this type of reference-tracking mechanism in more detail in 7.4, and we will refer to it as a 'switch-function' system, since it tracks a particular referent across clauses with the verbal morphology indicating the semantic role function of the referent in each clause.

The other system mentioned in Chapter 4 is switch reference, which is illustrated by the Kewa examples in (7.5) and the Choctaw examples in (7.6).

(7.5) a. Ní réko-*a*   ágaa lá-lo.   (=(4.16))
           1sg stand-SAME.SmP talk say-1sgPRES
           'I stood up and am speaking.'

       b. Ní réka-*no*   ágaa lá-a.
           1sg stand-DIFF.SmP talk say-3sgPST
           'I stood up and he talked.'

(7.6) a. $\emptyset$-$\emptyset$-pi:sa-ča: $\emptyset$-iya-h.   (=(4.15))
           3A-3U-see-SAME.SmP   3A-go-PRES
           'He$_i$ sees him$_j$ and he$_i$ goes.'

       b. $\emptyset$-$\emptyset$-pi:sa-na: $\emptyset$-iya-h.
           3A-3U-see-DIFF.SmP   3A-go-PRES
           'He$_i$ sees him$_j$ and he$_{j|k}$ goes.'

In this system the verbal morphology indicates whether a particular NP in the first clause is coreferential with a particular NP in the following clause. Most commonly switch-reference morphology signals S/A SmP–S/A SmP coreference or non-coreference, although there are languages in which it works on a different basis. We will examine switch-reference systems in detail in 7.3.

The third type of reference-maintenance system we will call the 'gender system'. Such a system involves the overt morphological coding of a classification of NPs, although it need not be on the basis of sex. These morphological distinctions are carried by anaphoric elements; anaphoric elements of the same class can be interpreted as coreferent, while those of different classes cannot. English provides an illustration of a simple version of this system.

(7.7) a. John decided to talk to Mary about *her* dog because *it* had been causing problems in the neighborhood.

       b. *She* was very surprised, as *she* had no idea that *it* had been getting into other people's garages and garbage cans.

       c. *He* was pleased that *she* did not react defensively to *his* mentioning the situation.

English has a three-way classification of nouns based on animacy

and sex which is manifested only in third-person singular pronouns. When there is only one noun of each class in a discourse,
as in (7.7), then coreference relations are unambiguous. Many
languages which employ the gender system make much more
elaborate distinctions than English does, as we will see in
7.2.

The final type of discourse cohesion system is that exemplified
by the languages of Southeast and East Asia, such as Thai or
Japanese. These languages are characterized primarily by the lack
of any of the previous three systems. Zero anaphora is heavily
used in these languages but assignment of coreference is often
determined by the subtle use of sociolinguistic variables and is
not directly signaled in the linguistic form. In particular,
honorific speech levels such as those found in Japanese and Korean
can be exploited for the purpose of indirectly specifying reference.
Rules of conversational inference based on cultural knowledge
(Gumperz 1982) also play a major role in the assignment of
coreference for the participants in the discourse. Sentences are
often multiply ambiguous and subject to different interpretations
depending on the knowledge the hearer brings to the task. All
languages use inference to a significant degree in their assignment
of coreference among NPs, but in these languages it has been
elevated to the status of a fine art. These features may be correlated
with the high value the cultures in which these languages are
spoken place upon indirectness and ambiguity in speaking. In any
case, these languages must be recognized as presenting a fourth
system of discourse cohesion, one we will call the 'inference
system'. Presumably, there are other means to identify participants in these languages, but inference does play a much more
prominent role in them than in languages with any of the other
three systems. These Asian languages all have classifier systems,
but they do not play a crucial participant-tracking role in discourse, parallel to the gender classes of languages with gender
systems like Yimas. Classifiers may function as pronouns, but they
are by no means obligatory. Zero anaphora is probably more common, in fact. We will have nothing more to say about inference
systems in this chapter; see Hinds (1978) for a discussion of
Japanese anaphora and Li & Thompson (1979) for an analysis
of zero anaphora in Mandarin Chinese discourse.

The typology of reference-tracking systems presented in this section is summarized as follows: (a) Switch function; (b) Switch reference; (c) Gender; (d) Inference.

Each of the first three will be discussed in detail in the following sections, and in 7.5 we will explore the interaction and cooccurrence of the various systems.

7.2 Gender systems

Grammatical gender is a classification of nouns which in most cases is based on perceived properties of the referents of the nouns. The most common basis is according to animacy and sex. Thus, English pronouns in the singular are divided on this basis: *he* (masculine), *she* (feminine), and *it* (inanimate). Animals may be assigned to either the *he/she* human class or the *it* inanimate class depending on semantic factors like status or emotional involvement. The family dog is likely to be *he* or *she*, but a snake or, even more likely, a mosquito will be *it*. Other European languages use a similar sex-based classification for animate beings, but extend this classification in an arbitrary way to inanimate objects with no clear semantic basis. In a number of Papuan languages, on the other hand, the sex-based classification for animate or human beings is also extended to inanimate things, but with a clear semantic basis. In Alamblak (Bruce 1979) for instance, masculine gender with inanimate objects denotes long thin things, while feminine denotes short, fat and round objects. Here we see the sex basis of gender classification in combination with the other most common basis, shape. In languages with a large number of gender distinctions, such as Bantu languages, shape often plays a major role in the assignment of NPs to gender classes. However, the semantic uniformity of the classes is often not perfect, a number of seemingly arbitrary assignments having been made.

A very unusual basis for the assignment of nouns to gender classes is found in two unrelated language groupings in the Sepik basin of New Guinea, the Torricelli languages and the Lower-Sepik Family. In these languages, in addition to assignment of some nouns to classes on the usual basis of sex, animacy, etc., we find most inanimate nouns assigned to classes on the basis of their phonological shape. Thus, in Yimas of the Lower-Sepik Family, nouns ending in *-nk* belong to one class, those in *-mp* to another, those in *-i* to another, those in *-nt*, *-p*, *-k*, and *-r* to another, and so forth. There is no semantic basis to these assignments, simply shared phonological shape. We do not know of such systems being reported outside of the Sepik area of New Guinea.

Languages in which gender functions as the dominant system of discourse cohesion are common. They are found along the north coast of New Guinea, especially in the Sepik area, among the non-Pama-Nyungan languages of northern Australia, throughout central and southern Africa, in the Caucasus, and in Central and South America.[1] Languages of this type are characterized by cross-referencing on the verb for the number and gender class of the core arguments of the verb which are then generally realized by zero anaphora in the junct itself. Discourse in languages of this type is characterized by chains of verbs heavily inflected with cross-referencing affixes and with relatively few nominal adjuncts.

This description of a language using the gender system is an idealized case, but as a good thumbnail sketch of such a language we will examine Yimas of the Lower-Sepik Family, spoken in New Guinea. Yimas is a thoroughgoing gender system language, with ten major gender classes and a half dozen or so minor classes. Four of the major classes have membership determined on semantic grounds: one denotes female humans, another, male humans, a third, higher animals, like dogs, pigs or crocodiles, and the last, plants, which serve a useful function within the culture. Membership in the other major classes, as noted above, is determined by the final one or two phonemes of the stem. Nouns are inflected only for number in Yimas: singular, dual and plural. Case marking is rudimentary; there is a single oblique case marker *-n/-nan*, marking locatives and instruments. The roles of other NP types are indicated by verbal inflection, there being no nominal case marking for them. Word order among NPs is free, but the verb is generally final.

Concord for gender class and number is extensive. Possessives and adjectives must agree with their head nouns in gender class and number and therefore need not stand immediately

juxtaposed to them. Core arguments of the verb, actor, undergoer, and dative, for basic and derived ditransitive verbs, are cross-
referenced on the verb by a series of verbal prefixes. These prefixes
cross-reference the gender class and number of the NP. Table
13 gives the noun marker and the corresponding verb prefix for
singular and plural in each of the major ten classes. From a glance
at the table we see that while there are ten distinct classes from
the point of view of the nominal endings (and adjectival concord
endings not included here), the distinction between certain classes
is neutralized in the verbal prefixes. For example classes I–III
are not distinguished in the verbal prefixes for both singular
and plural (class III, however, is distinguished from I and II
in the dual). Furthermore, V merges with I–III in the singular.
In the plural, the verbal prefixes for IV, V, VII, VIII and
some nouns in X are identical, whereas these are all distinguished
in the singular (and in the dual, which is formed by adding
the dual marker -l to the singular prefix forms). Although we
see extensive neutralization of class distinctions in the verbal
prefixes, we still find a seven-way contrast in the singular and
five-way contrast in the plural, suggesting that the gender system
plays a considerable role in the grammar of Yimas.

The gender class system carries most of the load of referential
tracking in Yimas. An NP whose referent is known or given does
not normally appear overtly: it is simply represented by the
cross-referencing affix on the verb. The given information status
of the NP can be acquired either by previous mention in the
text or by being shared knowledge of the interlocutors, either as
a cultural or an environmental given. Thus, in traditional nar-
ratives, with their culturally well-known stock of characters, it
sometimes occurs that a participant is introduced only by the
verbal prefix, without ever having occurred as a full NP. Need-
less to say, this leads to no end of confusion on the part of the
uninitiated member of the audience, the linguist.

This pervasive tendency to represent given NPs only by the
verbal affixes results in a very distinctive style for Yimas discourse.
Yimas discourse is characterized by a very high ratio of verbs to
nouns, on an average, eight verbs to every noun. Full NPs are
new information. New information NPs are not normally cross-
referenced by the verbal affixes, but once their status as given

Table 13 *Yimas gender class markers*

		I male human	II female human	III higher animals	IV plants	V	VI	VII	VIII	IX	X
sg	N	∅	-maŋ	∅	-um	-p, -k -nt, -r	-ŋk	-mp	-i	-aw	-uk/-uŋk
	V	-na	-na	-na	-mu	-na	-kt	pt	i-	-wa	-ku
pl	N	-um	-put	-wi	-ŋi	-ra, -t -i, -ŋkat	-ŋki	-mpat	-mpit	-ut	-at/uŋki
	V	-pu	-pu	pu-	ya-	ya-	-kia	ya-	ya-	ura-	ya-/kwia-

is established, they are then realized by the verbal affixes. Depending on the salience of the NP its given status may extend over a wide stretch of text even without further mention. In one text, that of the creation myth, a particularly important prop in the story is introduced, talked about for a few lines and then ignored for a reasonably long stretch of the text, running about three pages. It is, then, reintroduced, but only by means of the verbal prefix. It retained its given status through three pages without mention. There were no other nouns of its class and number occurring in the text to that point. Given the reasonably large number of distinctions in the system of verbal prefixes, this is the normal pattern. The only frequent situation in which two members of the same class and number may occur in the same text is with animate participants, especially those of classes I and II. Yimas has a special way to deal with this problem, which we shall discuss below.

The following Yimas text illustrates the points made thus far.

(7.8) a. Tay ŋariɲ   waŋkia   awl-ɨk
        tomorrow beams-IXsg get-PURP
      ipa-na-wa-kiak.
      1pl-FUT-go-FUT
      'Tomorrow we will go get beams.'

(7.8) b. Ipa-wa-ntut   Paŋkaymat
      1pl-go-REMPAST   place name
      wa-kay-awkawku-awl-kiantuk-imp-ɨn
      IXsg-1pl-gather-get-FARPAST-SEQ-OBL
      wa-kay-pampay-wapat-mpi-timpasa-kiantut.
      IXsg-1pl-DUR-climb-SEQ-place.down-
      FARPAST
      'We went to Pankaymat and after we collected
      (beams), we climbed and put (them) down (here).'

    c. Ma-ŋariɲ   tumpuntut ipa-wa-ntut
      other-tomorrow early   1pl-go-REMPAST
      Pakanan   pusiŋki   awkura-k
      place name rafters-VIpl gather-PURP
      'Another morning we went to Pakanan to gather
      rafters.'

d. Kia-kay-awkura-kiantuk-imp-in   timal
    VIpl-ipl-gather-FARPAST-SEQ-OBL sun
    mpa-nan   kia-kay-pampay-arapal-kia ntut   tak.
    one-OBL VIpl-ipl-DUR-come.out-FARPAST here
    'After we gathered (them) in one day, we carried
    (them) out to here.'
e. Kia-kay-timpasa-kiantut.
    VIpl-ipl-put.down-FARPAST
    'We put it down.'
f. Ma-ŋariŋ   ipa-wa-ntut   iraki
    other-tomorrow ipl-go-REMPAST wood-VIIIsg
    al-ik   Irukat.
    cut-PURP place name
    'Another day we went to Irukat to cut wood.'
g. I-kay-wa-ka-al-nsuk-imp-in
    VIIIsg-ipl-go-SEQ-cut-REMPAST-SEQ-OBL
    i-kay-pay-pra-kiantut
    VIIIsg-ipl-carry-come-FARPAST
    i-kay-tal-wapal-mpi-timpassa-kiantut.
    VIIIsg-ipl-hold-climb-SEQ-put.down-
    FARPAST
    'After we went and cut (it), we carried it back and
    climbed up with it and put it down.'
h. Ipa-mampi-warasa-mpi-wa-kiantut   muraŋk-in.
    ipl-again-return-SEQ-so-FARPAST outboard-OBL
    'We went back again with an outboard motor.'
i. Ipa-ya-kiantut
    ipl-come-FARPAST
    i-kay-tal-wapat-mpi-timpasa-kiantut.
    VIIIsg-ipl-hold-climb-SEQ-put.down-FARPAST
    'We came and we carried it and put it down.'

This bit of text nicely illustrates all the typical features of
Yimas discourse: the very high ratio of verbs to nouns, the extensive use of complex serial verb constructions sharing the same

core arguments, and the use of the verbal prefixes as reference-tracking morphemes for given information. In (a) the NP *waŋkia* 'beams', belonging to class IX, is introduced. In (b) it is twice referred to simply by the verbal prefix for this class *wa-*. Similarly, the noun *pusiŋki* 'rafters' in (c) is realized by the prefix *kia-* in (d) and (e), while the noun *iraki* 'wood', introduced in (f), is tracked by the prefix *i-* in (g) and (i).

Yimas also well illustrates the principle presented at the beginning of this chapter that reference-tracking mechanisms are predominantly a feature of peripheral junctures, because in such junctures, determination of coreference of NPs across the juncts is a potential problem, while with core junctures coreference of certain key NP arguments is a necessary constraint on the formation of the juncture. In Yimas verbs in juncts joined at the peripheral level occur with the cross-referencing verbal prefixes, whereas verbs in core junctures may not take verbal prefixes cross-referencing the core NPs, even when they are given information. Coreference of a particular core NP is built into the juncture and other core NPs may not be cross-referenced, but must occur as nouns or free pronouns. Consider these examples:

(7.9) a. Patn   wu-ru-mpwi   na-kasapal.
       betelnut get-NMZ-DEP 3sg-forget
       'He forgot to get betelnut.'

     b. *Na-wu-ru-mpwi   na-kasapal.
       3sg-get-NMZ-DEP 3sg-forget
       'He forgot to get (it).'

(7.10) a. Patn   wu-ru-mpwi   na-kra-i.
       betelnut get-NMZ-DEP 3sg-1pl-say
       'He told us to get betelnut.'

     b. *Na-wu-ru-mpwi   na-kra-i.
       3sg-get-NMZ-DEP 3sg-1pl-say
       'He told us to get (it).'

These are examples of complement constructions, formed by core junctures. These constructions are marked by the nominalizing suffix *-ru* and the dependent verb marker *-mp(w)i* attached to verb of the complement. Sentence (7.9) exemplifies coreference between the actors of the main verb and the complement verb, while (7.10) is formed by coreference between the undergoer of the main verb and the actor of the complement verb, as predicted by the theory of control developed in 6.5. Coreference of this type is critical to the formation of these core junctures in Yimas. Cross-referencing by verbal affixes is impossible in the complement junct, as shown by the ungrammaticality of (7.9b) and (7.10b). This correlation of verbal cross-referencing with peripheral junctures in Yimas is further evidenced by the usual co-occurrence of the cross-referencing affixes with the tense suffixes. If a verb can occur with a tense suffix, it can generally take the cross-referencing affixes. If it cannot occur with tense suffixes, it generally cannot take the cross-referencing affixes. As tense is a peripheral operator, this is strong evidence for the association of the cross-referencing affixes with peripheral junctures. The verbs in the complements above in (7.9) and (7.10) may not occur with tense suffixes as befits their core-juncture status.

One final point in Yimas grammar needs to be considered. The text in (7.8) is rather atypical in that there is only one animate participant 'we' which functions as the actor for all verbs. Rather more common is to have more than one animate participant, each of which alternates as actor as the text progresses. This could present potential problems of ambiguity, as humans and higher animals have the same cross-referencing verbal prefixes: *na-* for singular and *pu-* for plural (see Table 13). Yimas solves this problem by making a distinction between two types of third persons. In a peripheral juncture, if the actor of a junct is the same as that of the previous junct, it is simply realized by the verbal cross-referencing affix. If there is a change in the actor, but the actor is given information, it is normally signaled by an overt pronoun formed by the base of the distal deictic plus the adjective concord endings, which cross-reference the class and number of the actor. The verb will also agree with the actor in the normal way. Compare these examples:

(7.11) a. Na-ma-tampulanta-put-t na-n-tu-t.
            3sg-in-run-go-PERF   3sgU-3sgA-kill-PERF
            'He ran in and he killed him.'

b. Na-ma-tampulanta-put-t mi-n
3sg-in-run-go-PERF   DISTAL.ADJcII-III
na-n-tu-t.
3sgA-kill-PERF
'He ran in and was killed by him.'

Sentence (7.11a) will be interpreted as indicating coreference between the actors of the two clauses. Example (7.11b) is ambiguous. It could be a version of (7.11a) with contrastive emphasis on the actor, but generally it would be interpreted to indicate that the actor of the second junct is a different, but given, animate participant.

This Yimas mechanism is an example of a 'fourth-person' system in which the category of third person is subdivided into different deictic-based categories.[2] We may view this as a type of gender system, but one in which the classification of the noun is not inherent in the noun itself, but is assigned to the noun in a given discourse, according to its salience in relation to the other participants. These fourth-person systems are common in the American-Indian languages of North America.

The classic example of a 'fourth-person' system is found in Algonquian languages, and we will take Plains Cree (Wolfart 1973) as our representative. The term 'fourth person' is somewhat misleading, for what we are dealing with is two types of third-person categories and not a distinct fourth-person category (see Wolfart 1973:16–20). The two types of third person have been traditionally labeled *proximate* and *obviative*. If there is only one third-person argument in a clause, then it must be proximate; if there are two, one must be proximate and the other obviative.

(7.12) a. Pimohtē-w   nāpēw-∅
walk-3PROX man-PROX
'The man is walking along.'
b. Wāpam-ē-w   nāpēw-∅   atim-wa.
see-SUFF-3PROX man-PROX dog-OBV
'The man sees the dog.'

There is only one third-person argument in (7.12a), and it is obligatorily proximate. In (7.12b), however, there are two third-person arguments, and one of them must be marked proximate and the other obviative. The choice of the proximate NP in such a situation is discourse-conditioned. Bloomfield characterizes the proximate NP as follows: 'The proximate third person represents the topic of discourse, the person nearest the speaker's point of view, or the person earlier spoken of and already known' (1962: 38).

The selection of the proximate NP in sentences like (7.12b) is discourse-conditioned and not affected by whether an NP is actor or undergoer; *atim* 'dog' could be proximate in (7.12b). Even though this proximate–obviative contrast is discourse- rather than semantically based, it does interact with the complex system for coding actor and undergoer found in Algonquian languages known commonly as an *inverse-person marking* system. Role coding is based on the interaction of the system of verb affixes, which express only inherent lexical content (in the sense of Silverstein (1976b); see 3.1) and not grammatical function, and the category of direction. First- and second-person arguments are coded by prefixes, third-person by suffixes; the form and position of the person-marking affix is unrelated to whether it expresses the actor or undergoer.

(7.13) a. Ni-wāpam-ā-w.
            1sg-see-SUFF-3sg
            'I see him.'
        b. Ni-wāpam-ik   (< ni-wāpam-ekw-w).
            1sg-see-SUFF-3sg
            'He sees me.'

In both of these examples *ni-* codes a first-person argument and *-w* a third-person argument (it is deleted by a morphophonemic rule in (7.13b).), and the first person is the actor in (a), the under-goer in (b). The actual expression of actor and undergoer is achieved through the affixes glossed SUFF in (7.13), *-ā-* in (a) and *-ekw* in (b). Assuming an inherent lexical-content hierarchy of $2 > 1 > 21 > 3PROX > 3OBV$, these suffixes indicate whether the direction of the action of the verb follows or contravenes the hierarchy. For example, a second-person argument acting upon a first-person follows the hierarchy; a first-person argument acting on a second-person contravenes it. Thus actions which follow the hierarchy are termed *direct*, those that contravene it, *inverse*. The suffix -*ā*- in (7.13a) indicates that the action of the verb is direct, and therefore the first-person argument must be interpreted as the actor and the third-person as the undergoer. In (7.13b), however, the suffix -*ekw*- signals that the action of the verb is inverse, and accordingly the first-person argument can only be understood as the undergoer, the third-person as the actor. Note that the two types of third-persons are included in this hierarchy, with proximate outranking obviative, so that the action in (7.13b) is direct. If, however, it were the dog that saw the man, then the verb would have to have the inverse marker, as in (7.14).

(7.14) wāpam-ik (< wāpam-ekw-w) nāpēw-∅ atim-wa.
       see-INV-3PROX   man-PROX dog-OBV
       'The dog sees the man.'

Note that in both (7.12b) and (7.14) only the proximate NP is cross-referenced on the verb, and its function, actor or undergoer, is indicated by the direction markers. Even though there is only one third-person affix on the verb, two arguments are definitely signaled by the verb. *Wāpam-* is a member of the transitive animate verb class in Cree, the class of verbs which require an animate actor and undergoer. Accordingly *wāpam-* should be glossed 'someone sees someone/something(animate)' rather than simply 'see', in order to distinguish it from its transitive inanimate counterpart *wāpaht-* 'someone sees something (inanimate)' which can have only an inanimate undergoer. Thus *wāpam-* must involve two animate participants, and if the only person-marking affix on the verb is third person, then the other argument must be third person as well, since all non-third-person arguments are explicitly coded on the verb. (See Wolfart 1978). Since there are two directions and two possible choices for the proximate NP in a transitive clause, any transitive clause has two possible realizations. The other possibilities for (7.12b) and (7.14) are given in (7.15).

(7.15) a. Wāpam-ik   nāpēw-a   atim-∅.
           see-INV-3PROX man-OBV dog-PROX
           'The man sees the dog.'   (= 7.12b)

b. Wāpam-ē-w   nāpēw-a   atim-∅   (= 7.14)
see-DIR-3PROX man-OBV dog-PROX
'The dog sees the man.'

If both the proximate–obviative choices and direction are changed, then the meaning of the sentence (in terms of who does what to whom) is unaffected. If, however, only one of these features is altered, e.g. the choice of the proximate NP as in (7.15b) versus (7.12b), then the meaning of the sentence is entirely different, as a comparison of (7.15b) with (7.12b) and (7.14) with (7.15a) readily demonstrates.

The contrast between proximate and obviative NPs is central to reference tracking in Cree. Unlike PrPs, the proximate NP in Cree is not the preferential controller and target of coreference across clauses; the proximate and obviative NPs are equivalent in this regard.

(7.16) a. Nāpēw-∅   atim-wa   wāpam-ē-w
man-PROX dog-OBV see-DIR-3PROX
ē-sipwehtē-t.
CNJ-leave-3PROX
'The man saw the dog as he [the man] left.'
b. Nāpēw-∅   atim-wa   wāpam-ē-w
man-PROX dog-OBV see-DIR-3PROX
ē-sipwehtē-yit.
CNJ-leave-3OBV
'The man saw the dog as it [the dog] left.'

Each of these sentences consists of a main clause followed by a dependent clause in what Algonquianists call the 'conjunct mode'. Its single argument may be coreferential with either of the main-clause arguments, depending upon whether it is proximate or obviative: if it is proximate, then it is coreferential with the proximate argument of the main clause, *nāpēw* 'man', as in (a), whereas if it is obviative, it is coreferential with the obviative argument in the main clause, *atimwa* 'the dog', as in (b). Thus in order for two arguments to be coreferential they must have the same obviation status.

The working of this system can be illustrated by examining

an excerpt from a Cree text (Bloomfield 1930; repeated in Wolfart & Carroll 1981:103).[3]

(7.17) a. Mēkwa ē-pimohtē-t,   ispatināw
       while   CNJ-walk(AI)-3PROX NI:hill
       wāpaht-am,   ē-āmaciwē-yit
       see(TI)-3PROX CNJ-climb(AI)-3OBV
       ayīsiyiniw-a,   nāpēw-a.
       NP:person-OBV NA:man-OBV
       'As he went along he saw someone climbing a hill, a man.' (Literally: 'he saw a hill on which someone was climbing, a man'.)

     b. Ēkwa   kitāpam-ē-w,   kitāpākan
       and.then observe(TA)-DIR-3PROX NI:spyglass
       ē-kanawāpākanēhikē-yit
       CNJ-look.through.spyglass(AI)-3OBV
       ayīsiyiniw-a   ē-nanātawāpam-ā-yit.
       NA:person-OBV CNJ-look.for(TA)-DIR-3OBV
       'He observed him, watching through a spyglass, this man who was looking for people.'

     c. Kiskēyim-ē-w   ayahciyiniw-a
       know(TA)-DIR-3PROX NA:Blackfoot-OBV
       'He knew him for a Blackfoot.'

     d. Ēkwa   o-paskisikan   pīhtāsō-w;[4]
       and.then 3PROX-NI:gun load(AI)-3PROX
       mōskīstaw-ē-w   ē-pimisini-yit.
       attack(TA)-DIR-3PROX CNJ-lie(AI)-3OBV
       'He loaded his gun and attacked him as he [the Blackfoot] lay on the ground.'

     e. Ēkwa   ē-ki-kiskēyiht-ahk   awa
       and.then CNJ-PAST-know(TI)-3PROX this
       ayahciyiniw-∅   nēhiyaw-a
       NA:Blackfoot-PROX NA:Cree-OBV
       ē-mōskīsta-iko-t,   tapasi-w;
       CNJ-attack(TA)-INV-3PROX flee(AI)-3PROX
       ē-sakā-yik   kotēskamō-w.
       CNJ-bush(II)-3OBV hide(AI)-3PROX
       'When the Blackfoot perceived that a Cree was attacking him, he fled; he hid in the bushes.' (Literally: 'there being bushes, he hid'.)

> f. Ēkosi   pāskisw-ē-w   nēhiyaw-∅
>   so.then shoot(TA)-DIR-3PROX NA-Cree-PROX
>   'The Cree tried to shoot him.'

This story is about Sweet Grass, a legendary Cree chief. When (7.17a) occurs in the text, he is already established as the topic of the discourse and is therefore the proximate NP. This sentence introduces the second major participant in the story, which is treated as the obviative third person. The last verb in (7.17b) is particularly interesting; it has the conjunct-mode direct marker -ā- but the third-person argument coded on the transitive animate verb is obviative. Because proximate NPs outrank obviative NPs and because the actor is direct, the undergoer cannot be Sweet Grass, the proximate topic. The only thing an obviative actor with a direct verb can act on is another obviative NP, and consequently the only possible undergoer is another, as yet unmentioned obviative argument; this is reflected in the translation by the non-specific object *people*. These topic relations are maintained through the first four lines. In (7.17d) the interpretation of the dependent clause *ē-pimisiniyit* parallels that of the dependent clause in (7.16b). There are no explicit morphological or syntactic devices to signal a change in the choice of the proximate NP. Rather, the full NP is repeated in its new status to signal the change. Thus in (7.17e) *ayahciyinw* 'Blackfoot' is repeated in proximate form and *nēhiyaw* 'Cree', which refers to Sweet Grass, also appears in the sentence in obviative form, reinforcing that the shift has occurred. Note that *mōskīsta-* 'attack' now takes the inverse marker because of the change in the obviation status of the participants. The topicality of the Blackfoot is short-lived, however, as in the very next sentence the Cree again assumes proximate status, and here too it is indicated through the repetition of the full NP in its new status.

This Cree discourse system is quite different from that of Yimas, and yet they are both based on tracking participants in distinct third-person categories, Yimas having considerably more than Cree. Other American Indian languages with 'fourth-person' systems include Eskimo (Woodbury 1975, T. Payne 1980) and Navajo (Saville-Troike & McCreedy 1979).

7.3 Switch-reference systems

Fourth-person systems are an interesting transition point between gender systems and another type of morphological reference-tracking system, the switch-reference system. In gender systems nouns are assigned to classes on the basis of inherent features, and a particular NP is tracked through a discourse by virtue of its association with its class. In fourth-person systems NPs are assigned to categories by virtue of their relative salience. A given NP may change its person category in the discourse depending on what other NP types are associated with it. Switch-reference systems are like fourth-person systems in that the NPs are evaluated with regard to their relative salience, but they differ from fourth-person systems in that the NPs are not assigned to different categories for morphological encodings. There is no categorization of nouns in switch-reference systems, rather the morphology simply indicates whether the most salient NP in one junct is co-referential or not with the most salient NP of another junct. This is signaled by a system of verbal morphology which indicates whether this salient NP has the same referent or a different referent from the most salient NP of the other junct. This controlling and target NP is, of course, the pivot of the switch-reference mechanism, and these pivots may be semantic or pragmatic, with the SmPs being by far the more predominant (see p. 345ff below).

Switch-reference systems are common among the languages of the world. They are the most common type of reference-tracking system in the languages of New Guinea (Longacre 1972), and are found as well in central and western Australia (P. Austin 1981), northern Asia (Nichols 1979b), and North and South America (Jacobsen 1967, Weber 1980, Levinsohn 1978). They are always associated with verb-final languages. This is sensible in view of the fact that the switch-reference morphemes occur on the verb and anticipate an NP in the next junct. The primary diagnostic feature of switch-reference systems is a distinction in peripheral junctures between dependent and independent verbs. This is indicative of the use of cosubordinate nexus at the peripheral level, as the dependent verbs take their tense and illocutionary force specifications from the independent verb. The simplest type of switch-reference system is one in which the

dependent verb form signals same referent, while different referent requires an independent verb to be used. Siroi (Wells 1979)
of New Guinea is an example of a language of this type. Dependent
verbs consist of the stem plus the dependent-verb marker -*a/mba*
and always indicate same referent. Independent verbs are inflected
for person and number of the actor, as well as tense.

(7.18) Mbanduwaŋ ngur-mba   buk-ng-ina.
        bow   break-DEP throw-CONJUG-3sgPST
        'He broke and threw away the bow.'

The expression of different referent requires two independent
verbs connected by the conjunction *le*.

(7.19) Agaŋ ndende kusna-niŋ-mba   min-na   le
        thing various ask-3plU -DEP be-3sgPSTCONJ-DR
        teg   puro-na.
        fowl arrive-3sgPST
        'She was questioning them and the fowl arrived.'

Siroi exhibits the simplest switch-reference system attested, as
well as, it seems to us, the simplest possible. The next simplest
is one based on the Siroi pattern, but one in which a number
of different morphemes may be added to the dependent verbs,
each signaling a different semantic relation between the junct
containing the dependent verb and that of the independent verb.
Iatmul (Staalsen 1972) and other Ndu family languages of the
Sepik basin in New Guinea belong to this type. Iatmul has a system
of eight different dependent-verb markers which express a variety
of different meanings such as overlap versus non-overlap of the
temporal span of the two verbs. If there is an overlap, there is
specification as to whether the two actions are concurrent or the
first terminates during the course of the second. If there is no
overlap, the dependent verb morphemes may signal whether the
undergoer in the dependent junct is totally affected, partially
affected, or unaffected by the action of the verb. The Iatmul
system also expresses whether the action of the dependent verb
is the cause of the action of the independent verb, and, if not,
whether the event of the dependent verb is durative or momentary.
Consider the following examples:

(7.20) a. Vi-laa   ya-wun.
        see-CAUSAL/NO.OVERLAP   come-1sg
        'After I saw it, I came.'
    b. Vi-sibla
        see-CAUSAL/OVERLAP/CONCURRENT
        ya-wun.
        come-1sg
        'Because I was seeing it, I came.'
    c. Vi-kiva   ya-wun.
        see-NONCAUSAL/DUR come-1sg
        'I chanced to see it as I came.'
    d. Vi-labilaa
        see-CAUSAL/NO.OVERLAP/
                                        ya-wun.
        U.PART.AFFECT come-1sg
        'After I saw some of it, I came.'

Different referents are expressed exactly in the same way as in Siroi, with two independent verbs connected by a conjunction, in this case *ma*.

(7.21) Kla-di   ma ya-di.
        get-3sgM DR come-3sgM
        'He₁ got it and he₂ came.'

Iatmul has a binary sex-based gender distinction in second and third person singular which contributes significantly to referent tracking in these different-referent constructions in texts with multiple animate participants.

The next stage in the elaboration of switch-reference systems is exemplified by languages in which the function of dependent verb forms is extended to indicate different referent, as well as same referent. This is often combined with the expression of the semantic relations between the juncts, so such languages have portmanteau morphemes expressing same or different referents as well as a semantic relation. Barai (Olson 1981) is of this type.

(7.22) a. Bu ire   i-kinu   vua kuae.
        3pl food eat-SIM/SR talk say
        They were eating and talking.'

b. Bu ire   i-ko   no vua kuae.
3pl food eat-S I M/D R 1pl talk say
'While they were eating, we were talking.'

(7.23) a. Fu juare   me-na   fae kira.
3sg garden make-S E Q / S R fence tie
'He made a garden and then tied a fence.'

b. Fu juare   me-mo   fu fae   kira.
3sg garden make-S E Q / D R 3sg fence tie
'He₁ made a garden and then he₂ tied a fence.'

Languages of the Enjan family, as well as those of the Finisterre-Huon group (McElhanon 1973) and others of northeast New Guinea, represent the next stage in the development of switch-reference systems. In these languages the dependent verb for different referent occurs with an affix indicating the person and number of its pivot, while the same-referent dependent verb is not so inflected. Both types of verb forms are dependent because they may not be inflected for tense, etc., as specifications for these come from the independent verb. This is as expected in these peripheral junctures with cosubordinate nexus. Consider these examples from Kewa (Franklin 1971).

(7.24) a. Ní réko-a   ágaa lá-lo.
1sg stand-S E Q/S R talk   say-1sgP R E S
'I stood up and am speaking.'   (= (4.16a))

b. Ní réka-no   ágaa lá-a.
1sg stand-1sgD R talk say-3sgP S T
'I stood up and he talked.'   (= (4.16c))

c. Nipú réko-na   ágaa lá-ma.
3sg   stand-3sgD R talk say-1plP S T
'He stood up and we talked.'

Sentence (7.24a) is an example of a sentence in which the pivots have the same referent, and the dependent verb occurs only with the same-referent suffix. It has no morpheme indicating the person and number of its actor; that is specified by the following independent verb. Examples (7.24b–c) are of sentences in which the pivots of the juncts have different referents. This is signaled by a set of suffixes on the dependent verb which indicate the person and number of its pivot. Dependent verbs suffixed in this way always indicate that the pivot of the next junct has a different referent.

The most elaborate switch-reference systems known are found in the languages of the Eastern Highlands of Papua New Guinea. The pattern of verb chaining and the switch-reference system is extremely prominent in these languages, and the corresponding verbal morphology is luxuriantly developed. Fore (Scott 1978) is typical of the Eastern Highlands languages. Fore extends the pattern found in Kewa of marking the person and number of the pivot on the dependent verb to verbs signaling same referent. Same-referent verbs in Fore occur with either of two linkage markers *-ki* or *-nta* plus a suffix indicating the person and number of the pivot, which, of course, will be the same as that of the next verb. Consider these examples:

(7.25) a. Mae-ma-ki-na   kana-y-e.
        get-SEQ-LINK-3sgA come-3sgA-DECL
        'He gets it and then comes.'
    b. Mae-ʔte-ki-ʔta   kana-ʔku-un-e.
        get-SIM-LINK-1plA come-FUT-1plA-DECL
        'We shall get it and come.'

In these examples the suffixes *-na* '3sg' and *-ʔta* '1pl' indicate the pivot of both the dependent and the independent verbs, as this is a same referent form.

Different-referent verbs are rather more complicated. As in Kewa, all different-referent dependent verbs occur with a suffix which indicates the person and number of their pivot, but in Fore these are portmanteau with an indication of tense, specifying the tense of the dependent verb as past, present, or future. This suffix is followed by the linker *-ki*, which is then followed by a suffix which indicates the person and number of the pivot of the next verb. These are the so-called 'anticipatory subject' morphemes and are of the same form as the pivot person/number suffixes in the same-referent verbs. We can summarize the structure of the Fore different-referent dependent verb as:

(7.26) stem + p/n of pivot/rel tense + *ki* + p/n of pivot of next verb.

The following examples illustrate this structure:

(7.27)   a.   Kana-a:-ki-ta
              come-3sgPRES/DIFF-LINK-1dlA
              a-ka-us-e.
              3sgU-see-1dlA-DECL
              'He comes and we both see it.'
         b.   Kana-uˀ-ki-na
              come-2sgPST/DIFF-LINK-3sgA
              a-ka-ˀta-y-e.
              3sgU-see-PST-3sgA-DECL
              'You came and he saw it.'
         c.   Kana-isi-ki-nisi
              come-3dlFUT/DIFF-LINK-2dlA
              a-ka-ˀkubu-a:s-e.
              3sgU-see-FUT-2dlA-DECL
              'They(2) will come and you(2) will see it.'
         d.   Kana-a:-ki-ni   ka-ka-i-ki-na
              come-2sgFUT-LINK-3plA 2sgU-see-3plFUT-
                          u-wai-mu-ˀkubu-a:n-e.
              LINK-2sgA say-3plU-give-FUT-2sgA-DECL
              'When you come and they see you, you shall tell
              (it) to them.'

Example (7.27d) illustrates two different-referent dependent
verbs followed by an independent verb. The pivot changes from
second singular to third plural and then back to second singular.
    To this point we have been talking about switch-reference
systems as monitoring same versus different referent without
being explicit about what NPs are (in fact) being monitored. If
we consider (7.27d) again we see that the core arguments for the
verbs are second singular and third plural. The first verb 'come'
is an active intransitive with a second-singular actor. It is followed
by the transitive perception verb 'see' with a third-plural actor
and a second-singular undergoer. As the verb 'come' takes the
different-referent inflection pattern, it is clear that what the
switch-reference system is monitoring in this case is the non-
coreference of the actors of the two verbs, and it ignores the coreference of the actor of the first verb with the undergoer of the
second. The second dependent verb 'see' and the independent

verb 'tell' have the same core participants realized by inflections on the verb, a second singular and a third plural. However, they function in different roles. The verb 'see' has a third-plural actor and a second-singular actor and a third-plural undergoer. As the dependent verb is a different-referent form, the switch-reference system is monitoring the non-coreference of the actors.

The claim that switch-reference systems monitor sameness or difference of the referents of the actor NP is basically true, but needs to be slightly generalized. The vast majority of languages with switch-reference systems operate on a S/A pivot in which the single argument of an intransitive is the pivot regardless of whether it is an actor or undergoer. Thus S/A is the SmP for most switch-reference systems, as in these Kewa examples (Franklin 1971).

(7.28) a. Nı́ réko-a   ágaa lá-lo.
            1sg stand-SR talk say-1sgPRES   (= 4.16a)
            'I stood up and am speaking.'
        b. Rúdu yo-a   madá   na-ria-a
            short be-SR enough NEG-carry-3sgPST (= 4.16b)
            'It was short and didn't reach.'

In (7.28a) the actor of the first verb and that of the second are coreferential and the dependent verb indicates same referent. In (7.28b) there are two intransitive verbs, the dependent one, a stative, and the independent one, an active verb. The S of 'be short' is an undergoer, but that of 'carry' is an actor. However, this difference is ignored for the purposes of switch-reference; the S's of both verbs are coreferential and the dependent verb is the same-referent form. The use of S/A as the SmP for switch-reference is the pattern for the vast majority of languages which possess this device.

There are, however, a few important exceptions. One exceptional language, Eastern Pomo (McLendon 1978), was discussed in Chapter 4. In this language, the switch-reference system seems to monitor directly the notions of actor and undergoer, and not the more abstract notion of an SmP made up of S/A. See examples in (4.18) and the discussion there.

Another exceptional language is Barai (Olson 1978, 1981). Before discussing Barai in some detail, we need to mention an unusual construction found in many Papuan languages. In these languages, predicates expressing physiological or psychological states are impersonal, with the experiencer being expressed as the undergoer of the verb, as in this Usan example (Reesink 1981).

(7.29) Wo toar   war-a.
      3sg sickness 3sgU.hit-DR
      'The sickness hits him.' = 'He is sick.'

Usan like other Papuan languages allows the undergoer to function as the pivot for these verbs for the switch-reference mechanism.

(7.30) Munon isig eng sarau aib eb-et   migeri
      man   old this work big do-SR exhaustion
      war-a . . .
      3sgU.hit-DR
      'The old man is working hard and he will be exhausted, and . . .'

While Usan would also permit the different-referent marker in (7.30), the important point is that the same-referent form is allowed, which demonstrates that this pivot in this construction may be the undergoer and not the actor. This is presumably due to the higher salience of the animate undergoer.

Barai makes a fundamental division of its transitive predicates into two classes. The first consists of normal transitive verbs in which an initiating controlling actor acts upon an undergoer. The other class is parallel to the Usan example in (7.29). For these verbs, an external stimulus causes a physiological or psychological condition in an animate experiencer. This distinction in verb classes is a fundamental organizing principle of Barai grammar. We will term the first class actor-oriented verbs, and the second, undergoer-oriented. Each of the two verb classes is associated with a different pivot position in the clause. The actor-oriented verbs have the actor as their normal choice for pivot, and this occurs as the leftmost NP. The undergoer-oriented verbs chose as their pivot the animate undergoer, which occurs as the rightmost NP immediately next to the verb. These pivot positions control a number of grammatical features. We illustrate some of these with the actor-oriented verb *kan-* 'hit' and the undergoer-oriented verb

visinam- 'sicken'. First, only the pivot can allow a pronominal copy to follow it.

(7.31) a. E   ije   *bu*   na kan-ie.
           man DEF 3pl 1sg hit-1sg
           'The people (they) hit me.'
       b. *Na e   ije   *bu*   kan-ia.
           1sg man DEF 3pl hit-3pl
           'I hit the people (them).'
(7.32) a. Adame ije   e   n-one   *bu* visinam-ia.
           sickness DEF man 1sg-POSS 3pl sicken-3pl
           'The sickness sickened my people (them).'
       b. *Adame ije   *fu* e   n-one   visinam-ia.
           sickness DEF 3sg man 1sg-POSS sicken-3pl
           'The sickness (it) sickened my people.'

As *kan-* as an actor-oriented verb, the pronominal copy can only
follow the actor, the leftmost NP. So (7.31b) in which it follows
the pre-verbal undergoer is ungrammatical. The verb *visinam-*
'sicken' is undergoer-oriented, and so the pronominal copy must
follow the preverbal undergoer. Sentence (7.32b) is ungrammatical because it follows the actor. A set of modal-like
participles in Barai have exactly the same distribution

(7.33) a. Fu-ka   na kan-ie.
           3sg-INTENS 1sg hit-1sg
           'He really hit me.'
       b. *Fu na-ka   kan-ie.
           3sg 1sg-INTENS hit-1sg
(7.34) a. Ije bu-ka   visinam-ia.
           3sg 3pl-INTENS sicken-3pl
           'It really sickened them.'
       b. *Ije-ka   bu visinam-ia.
           3sg-INTENS 3pl sicken-3pl

as does the contrastive clitic *-re*:

(7.35) a. Fu-re   na' kan-ie.
           3sg-CONTRAST 1sg hit-1sg
           '(It is) he (who) hit me.'

   b. *Fu na-re   kan-ie.
      3sg 1sg-CONTRAST hit-1sg
      '(It is) I (whom) he hit.'

(7.36) a. Ije bu-re   visinam-ia.
            3sg 3pl-CONTRAST sicken-3pl
            '(It was) they (whom) it sickened.'

        b. *Ije-re   bu visinam-ia.
            3sg-CONTRAST 3pl sicken-3pl
            '(It was) it (that) sickened them.'

These data suggest that the actor is the pivot for actor-oriented verbs and the undergoer is the pivot for undergoer-oriented verbs. When we investigate the behavior of the switch-reference morphemes, we find that this is, in fact, the case.

(7.37) a. Fu juare   me-na   fae   kira.
            3sg garden make-SR fence tie
            'He made a garden and tied a fence.'

        b. Na visinam-ie-na do   ije   ised-ie.
            1sg sicken-1sg-SR water DEF displease-1sg
            '(Something) sickens me and the water displeases me.'

        c. Bu ije fie-na   fu oesarad-ia.
            3pl 3sg hear-SR 3sg surprise-3pl
            'They heard it and it surprised them.'

Sentence (7.37a) is a juncture containing two actor-oriented verbs, the actors of which are coreferential. The dependent verb occurs with the same-referent suffix -*na*. Sentence (7.37b) contains two undergoer-oriented verbs, and the undergoers of each are co-referential. The switch-reference monitors the coreference of the undergoer pivots, and the dependent verb is suffixed with -*na* for same referent. In (7.37c) we find an actor-oriented verb with an actor *bu* 'they' as pivot followed by an undergoer-oriented verb with an undergoer, also *bu* 'they', as pivot. As the pivots are co-referential, the dependent verb registers same referent. Clearly, the Barai switch-reference system monitors coreferential pivots, not actors.

While Barai differs from the other languages investigated in that it does not monitor an SmP of S/A, the data presented thus far indicates that the pivot is nonetheless a semantic one. For one class of verbs the pivot is the actor, and for the other, it is the undergoer. It would seem that pivot selection is still predictable entirely in semantic terms, and the Barai pivot would be regarded as a semantic one. But we have not yet presented the entire story. While the actor is indeed the pivot for actor-oriented verbs and the undergoer the pivot for undergoer-oriented verbs, these are only the normal unmarked choices, just as the actor is the unmarked choice for the English PrP. Barai does not possess voice oppositions of the English or Dyirbal type, but it does possess word-order rearrangements which are motivated by pragmatic considerations. Barai has a hierarchy of pivot accessibility determined in part by the information status of the NPs:

(7.38) definite > indefinite/specific > unmarked > indefinite/ nonspecific

If the actor and undergoer of an actor-oriented verb differ as to their information status, the higher will occur in the pivot position; if equal, the actor will occur there.

(7.39) a. E   ije   fu-ka   ama ije   kan-ia.
            man DEF 3sg-INTENS child DEF hit-3pl
            'The man really hit the children.'

        b. Ame ije   bu-ka   e   be   kan-ia.
            child DEF 3pl-INTENS man INDEF hit-3pl
            'Someone really hit the children.'

        c. Are   ije   ine kan-a.
            house DEF tree hit-3sg
            'A/the tree hit the house.'

        d. Are   be   ine kan-a.
            house INDEF/SPEC tree hit-3sg
            'A/the tree hit a certain house.'

In (7.39a) both core NPs are definite, so the actor occupies pivot position. In (7.39b) the actor is indefinite, while the undergoer is definite and outranks the actor on the hierarchy of (7.38). Consequently, the undergoer occupies the leftmost NP position of the pivot in place of the actor. That it is pivot is further demonstrated by the fact that it takes the modal clitic *ka*.

Examples (7.39c–d) further illustrate this point by showing that a definite undergoer and an indefinite, but specific, undergoer outrank an unmarked actor and become the pivot.

Another factor which may cause this altered word order is animacy. If the actor of an actor-oriented verb is inanimate and indefinite, and the undergoer is animate, then the undergoer becomes pivot.

(7.40) a. Na ine   bij-ie.
          1sg stick poke-1sg
          'A stick poked me.'

       b. Fu miane   sak-i.
          3sg firestick bite-3sg
          'A firestick bit him.'

As pragmatic factors play a central role in determining the selection of an NP as pivot in Barai, this strongly indicates that the pivot in Barai is a pragmatic one rather than semantic. This is confirmed by the data from complex sentences, as it is exactly this pragmatically selected pivot NP which is monitored by the switch-reference system.

(7.41) a. Fu miane   sak-i-na   barone.
          3sg firestick bite-3sg-SR die
          'A firestick bit him and he died.'

       b. Miane ije   fu sak-i-mo   fu barone.
          firestick DEF 3sg bite-3sg-DR 3sg die
          'The firestick bit him and he died.'

In both (7.41a–b) the dependent verb has the actor *miane* 'firestick' and the undergoer *fu* '3sg'. But the verb in (7.42a) expresses same referent, while (7.41b) indicates different. The explanation is that the actor in (7.41a) is indefinite and is outranked for pivot status by the animate undergoer, which occurs in the leftmost position prescribed for pivots of actor-oriented verbs. This undergoer-pivot and the pivot of *barone* 'die' are coreferential and so the verb registers same referent. In (7.41b) the actor is definite and must be pivot for this actor-oriented verb. This pivot is not co-referential with the pivot of *barone* 'die' and so the verb is a different-referent form. Other illustrative examples are:

(7.42) a. Na i   me-na ine   bij-ie.
         1sg work do-S R stick poke-1sg
         'I was working and a stick poked me.'

     b. Are   ije   ine kana-mo fu   tuae.
         house D E F tree hit-D R   3sg break
         'A tree hit the house and it [the tree] broke.'

     c. Na e   be   kan-ie-mo fu   ko.
         1sg man I N D E F hit-1sg-D R 3sg run.away
         'Someone hit me and he ran away.'

     d. Kusare ije   na tot-ie-mo   fu saere.
         flower   D E F 1sg escape.memory-1sg-D R 3sg wither
         'The flower escaped my memory and it withered.'

In (7.42a) *na* '1sg' is the actor and pivot of the first verb. The actor of the second verb is *ine* 'stick', but, as it is inanimate, it is outranked for pivot by the animate undergoer *na*. The pivots of the two clauses are coreferential, so the dependent verb signals same referent. In (7.42b) the indefinite actor is outranked for pivot by the definite undergoer. As this is not coreferential with the pivot of *tua* 'break', the verb registers different referent. The same applies to (7.42c), in which an indefinite actor is outranked for pivot by an animate undergoer not coreferential with the pivot of the next verb. So the verbs in both (7.42b and c) signal different referent, even though the actors of the two verbs are co-referential. Finally, in (7.42d) we find an undergoer-oriented verb for which the animate undergoer *na* '1sg' is the pivot. Although the actor is coreferential with the next verb, the undergoer-pivot is not, and therefore, the verb takes the different-referent suffix -*mo*.

These data from Barai leave no doubt that in this language the pivots are pragmatic ones. From a theoretical viewpoint Barai is an important language for three reasons. First, it is a language in which the switch-reference system employs a notion of PrP, rather than the general SmP of S/A. Another case of this type has been reported from Western Australia (Dench 1981). Secondly, Barai demonstrates that the notion of pragmatic pivot is not dependent on the presence of a voice opposition in a language. Although most languages with PrPs have a voice opposition, Barai shows that this is not a necessary condition. All that is necessary is that pragmatic factors enter significantly into the selection of the pivot and potentially allow more than one NP argument of a multi-argument verb to assume this status. Thirdly, Barai shows conclusively that the clause-internal (pragmatic) pivot must be distinguished from the clause-external topic, for it has an additional set of verbal affixes which signal same or different topic independent of the indication of same or different PrP. In both of the sentences in (7.43), a new topic is introduced in the second clause, and this change of topic is expressed by the suffix *-ga* on the medial verb.

(7.43) a. Fu vua kuae-ga   siare   ije,   fu naebe ume.
            3sg talk say-DIFF.TOP betelnut DEF 3sg NEG chew
            'He₁ was talking and, as for betelnut, he₁ did not chew it.'

        b. Fu vua kuae-ko-ga   siare   ije,
            3sg talk say-DIFF.PrP-DIFF.TOP betelnut DEF
            fu naebe ume.
            3sg NEG chew
            'He₁ was talking and, as for betelnut, heⱼ did not chew it.'

In both sentences there is a change of topic, but only in (7.43b) is there a change of PrPs; the PrPs can be coreferential in (7.43a) but not in (7.43b). The same possibilities for same and different PrPs can be found with the same topic suffix *-gana*.

(7.44) a. Ve ije,   fu barone-ko-gana
            time DEF 3sg die-DIFF.PrP-SAME.TOP
            bu Sakarina ij-ia   va.
            3pl   DEF-L   go
            'At the time, he was dying and [at the same time] they were going to Sakarina.'

        b.*Ve ije,   fu barone-ko-gana
            time DEF 3sg die-DIFF.PrP-SAME.TOP
            muramura ije,   bu Sakarina ij-ia   va.
            medicine DEF 3pl   DEF-L   go
            'At the time, he was dying, and [at the same time] as for medicine, they were going to Sakarina.'

        c. ... iro ije   ru-na   e   ije
            yam DEF dig-SAME.PrP person DEF
            ivajuo-nami-ma   are-gana   iro
            share-RECIP-until cease-SAME.TOP yam
            ije   dabe me.
            DEF carry plant

'She dug the yams and shared them with the people until she stopped and she carried the yams and planted them.'

The first two examples in (7.44) illustrate the impossibility of introducing a new topic NP after *-gana*; compare (7.44b) with the explicit new topics in (7.43). Coreference between PrPs over a *-gana* juncture is unaffected by the topic constraint, as both different PrPs (in (7.44a)) and same PrP (in (7.44c)) are compatible with *-gana* as with *-ga* in (7.43). Thus the distinction between topic and PrP comes out clearly in Barai clause linkage, as there are separate systems of affixes to monitor each of them.

It was noted at the outset of this section that an important feature of many switch-reference systems is a distinction between independent and dependent verb forms, the dependent ones carrying the switch-reference markers. While this is a feature of all of the systems discussed so far, it is not a necessary feature. Tonkawa (Hoijer 1949) employs switch-reference morphemes in two distinct types of linkage, only one of which involves a dependent verb form.

(7.45) a. Tekeke?e:k š?a:pa-ta   ke-yaše-w.   (= 6.38)
in.that.bush.hide-SAME 1sgU-watch-IMP
'Hide in that bush and watch me.'

b. Tekeke?e:k š?a:pa-w   ?e:-ta
in.that.bush hide-IMP and-SAME
ke-yaše-w.
1sgU-watch-IMP
'Hide in that bush! And watch me!'

The sentence in (a) is similar to those discussed above in that *š?a:pa-* 'hide' is not inflected as in an independent sentence but rather carries the same-subject suffix *-ta* which links it to the independent verb form *keyašiw* 'watch me'. Hoijer comments that *š?a:pata* 'cannot be used independently' (1949:40). In (b), on the other hand, both verbs are fully inflected and could occur as independent utterances; the switch-reference morpheme appears on the conjunction *?e:-*. Thus (b), unlike (a), does not involve a distinction between independent and dependent verb forms, and consequently these examples illustrate switch-reference marking with two distinct nexus types, cosubordination in (a) and co-ordination in (b). We will discuss the interaction of switch-reference and the other reference-maintenance systems with juncture and nexus categories in 7.5.

7.4 Switch-function systems

In a switch-reference system, a particular syntactic or semantic function is monitored (usually an S/A SmP), and the verbal suffixes signal whether the NP having that function in a particular clause is coreferential or not with the NP having that same function in the following clause, hence the name 'switch reference'. A switch-function system achieves the same end as a switch-reference system, i.e. expressing (co)reference relations across clauses, but it does it in a formally different way. In a switch-function system a particular *participant* is tracked across clauses, and the verbal morphology in each clause signals the semantic function of that participant in that clause. This can be illustrated with some simple examples from English.

(7.46) a. John went to work, and____ talked to his boss and
         did not get a promotion.
      b. John went to work and____ talked to his boss and
         ____ was given a promotion.

John is the participant to be tracked in each sentence; he is the PrP of each clause realized as zero in all non-initial clauses. In (a) he is the actor in all three clauses, since the verbs in the two linked clauses are active voice. Active voice in English is the unmarked voice type, and accordingly it counts as the 'same function' category. In (b), on the other hand, *John* is not the actor in all three clauses; the passive morphology of *give* in the third clause indicates that he is a non-actor. Thus the passive verbal morphology signals a change of semantic function, in this case from actor to undergoer–locative. In English the passive voice is the 'different function' category. In both sentences a single participant is tracked across the three clauses, and the morphology of the verb in each clause signals the semantic function of that participant, hence the name 'switch function'.

These two types of reference-tracking systems are summarized in Table 14.

Table 14 *Switch-reference v. switch-function systems*

	Switch reference	Switch function
Monitored	A syntactic or semantic function	A participant
Signaled	Same or different participant carrying out that function	Same or different semantic function

Both systems achieve the same end but by a different organization of form and function.

Switch-function systems are less common than switch-reference systems, but they seem less exotic because they are found in some Indo-European languages. Unlike switch-reference systems, which may monitor coreference between SmPs, PrPs, or particular semantic relations, these systems always involve PrPs. Dyirbal (Dixon 1972), an Aboriginal language of north Queensland, provides an excellent example of a language which depends primarily on a switch-function system for reference-maintenance in discourse.[5] We discussed voice in Dyirbal in 4.1 and 4.5. Because the undergoer is the unmarked choice for the PrP in a transitive clause, an unmarked verb form indicates that the PrP is S or U, depending on transitivity. The antipassive voice, signaled by -*ŋay*, indicates change of function from S or U to A. Simple examples of the antipassive were presented in (4.13) and (4.83); the following is an excerpt from a text in the Mamu dialect of Dyirbal.

(7.47) a. Bulgan   bayi   wabu-ŋga
         big-ABS NM(I)-ABS bush-L
         waymba-ɲu,
         go.walkabout-TNS
      b. bili-nḍa-ɲu,
         climb.trees-REP-TNS
      c. ḍambun-gu   baɲil-ŋa-ɲu,
         grub.wood-DAT split-ANTI-TNS
      d. ŋuṛba-ɲu;
         return-TNS
      e. garḍa-gayul,
         alright-same
      f. baraymbaray bayi   yanu
         dawn   NM(I)-ABS go

g. ḍambun-gu   baɲil-ŋay-gu.
grub.wood-DAT split-ANTI-PURP
'(a) The big one went walkabout in the bush, (b) climbed many trees, (c) split grub-wood [i.e. wood with grubs in it], and (d) returned to the camp; (e) everything was the same, and (f) the next morning he went (g) to split grub-wood.'

The participant to be monitored in this stretch of discourse is *bulgan bayi* 'the big one', which is introduced in (a). In the first two clauses *bulgan bayi* is the single argument of intransitive verbs, but in (c) it is the actor of the transitive verb *baɲil* 'split'. It cannot therefore be simply omitted as it was in (b), as the resulting sequence *bilinḍaɲu ḍambun baɲin* could not mean 'he climbed many trees and split grub-wood'; the only thing it could possibly mean would be 'he climbed many trees and someone (else) split grub-wood'. Rather, the clause must be antipassivized so that the actor is the potential PrP and can be omitted under coreference with *bulgan bayi* in the previous clauses. The *-ŋay* suffix on the verbs signals 'switch function', i.e. that the participant being tracked functions as actor rather than undergoer of the transitive verb in the clause. The chain of clauses with *bulgan bayi* as a participant is broken in (e), which contains an impersonal expression. The sequence resumes in (f), in which the absolutive case class I noun marker *bayi* is repeated. Clause (g) is a purposive construction with a non-finite verb; because *bulgan bayi* is the actor of *baɲil*, as in (c), the antipassive switch-function form is required. Throughout this short discourse we find the antipassive verb forms indicating that the participant under consideration is the actor in all of the clauses with transitive verbs and thus that a change of semantic function from S to A has occurred across clauses.

The clearest examples of *-ŋay* as a switch-function marker involve pronouns. Dyirbal has split-ergative case marking, with pronouns inflecting on an accusative pattern. Nevertheless, in many instances they behave exactly like ergatively case-marked nouns.

(7.48) a. ŋaḍa   bani-ɲu   balan
isgNOM(S) come-TNS NM(II)-ABS

        ḑugumbil   balga-n.
        woman-ABS hit-TNS
      *'I came and hit the woman.'

    b. ŋaḑa   bani-ɲu   bagun
       1sgNOM(S) come-TNS NM(II)-DAT
       ḑugumbil-gu balgal-ŋa-ɲu.
       woman-DAT hit-ANTI-TNS
       'I came and hit the woman.'

(7.49) a. ŋaḑa   balan   ḑugumbil
       1sgNOM(A) NM(II)-ABS woman-ABS
       balga-n bani-ɲu.
       hit-TNS come-TNS
      * 'I hit the woman and came [here].'

    b. ŋaḑa   bagun   ḑugumbil-gu
       1sgNOM(S) NM(II)-DAT woman-DAT
       balgal-ŋa-ɲu   bani-ɲu.[6]
       hit-ANTI-TNS come-TNS
       'I hit the woman and came [here].'

These examples are similar to those in (4.13) and (4.95); (7.49b) is particularly striking, since the antipassivization of the first clause does not affect the form of the pronoun but does make it the PrP and therewith the 'controller of the deletion' in the second clause. There are cases, however, where pronouns behave differently syntactically from nouns.

(7.50) a. ŋaḑa   bayi   yaɽa
       1sgNOM(A) NM(I)-ABS man-ABS(U)
       balga-n walmbi-n   baygu-n
       hit-TNS lift.up-TNS throw.down-TNS
       ḑilwa-n.
       kick-TNS
       'I hit the man, lifted [him] up, threw [him] down, [and] kicked [him].'

    b. ŋaḑa   bala   yugu
       1sgNOM(A) NM(IV)-ABS stick-ABS(U)
       yuba-n   balan   ḑugumbil
       put.down-TNS NM(II)-ABS woman-ABS(U)
       ḑilwa-n.
       kick-TNS
       'I put down the stick [and] kicked the woman.'

In both of these sentences a pronominal actor is the participant which recurs in zero form in a chain of clauses, something which is not possible with a nominal actor. If the pronominal participant changes function from actor to undergoer or intransitive 'subject', as in (7.49a), then the antipassive switch-function form is required, as in (7.49b); this illustrates clearly the use of the *-ŋay* verb form when the participant being monitored changes its semantic function in a clause chain. Alternatively, an interesting type of switch-reference marker may be used, as in (7.51).

(7.51) a. ŋaḍa   balan   ḍugumbil
         1sgNOM(A) NM(II)-ABS woman-ABS(U)
         balga-n   bani-ŋura.
         hit-TNS come-SUFF
         'I hit the woman and came [here].'
      b. Baŋgul   yaṛa-ŋgu   balan
         NM(I)-ERG man-ERG(A) NM(II)-ABS
         ḍugumbil   balga-n   bani-ŋura.
         woman-ABS(U) hit-TNS come-SUFF
         'The man hit the woman and came [here].'

The *-ŋura* suffix, which occurs only on intransitive verbs, signals that the coreferential NP in the previous clause is not the PrP but rather the other core argument, the actor. In all of the switch-reference systems discussed in the last section, the markers indicate whether an argument in the *following* clause is coreferential with an argument in the clause in which the marker occurs; *-ŋura* on the other hand, is concerned not with possible coreference but rather with the existence of a marked controller of the coreference in the *previous* clause. Hence although *-ŋura* operates in the same functional domain as switch-reference markers, it is nonetheless functionally quite distinct from them.

Dyirbal thus presents the interesting example of a language which makes primary use of a switch-function system for reference-tracking in discourse but which supplements it in two ways, namely, the use of gender-class noun markers for anaphoric reference, as in (7.47f), and *-ŋura*, as in (7.51). Yidiɲ (Dixon 1972) and Bandjalang (Crowley 1978) are two other Australian languages which appear to have switch-function systems.

A number of Mayan languages employ this type of reference-maintenance system, particularly Jacaltec (Datz 1980),[7] Tzutujil (Butler & Peck 1980), and Tzotzil (Haviland 1982; see (4.71)). Even though these languages exhibit ergative case-marking patterns in at least some constructions, the unmarked choice for the PrP in a transitive clause is the actor, and it is the passive rather than antipassive voice which signals switch-function. The following excerpt from a Tzutujil text (Butler & Peck 1980) illustrates this; it concerns a man who was caught stealing corn.

(7.52) a. Toq š-∅-urqax-i
      when PERF-3ABS-arrive-CLASS
      ∅-∅-ko?x-(i)   pa če?.
      PERF-3ABS-put.PASS-(CLASS) in jail
      'When he arrived he was put in jail.'
   b. Xa k'a   či r-kab   q'ix
      the next on   3ERG-second day
      ∅-∅-q'e?t-(i)   cix
      PERF-3ABS-cut.PASS-(CLASS) word
      t-r-ix.
      to-3ERG-back
      'On the next day he was judged.'
   c. In š-∅-u-ya?   t-r-ix
      and PERF-3ABS-3ERG-give to-3ERG-back
      či   ni   arxa? wï?
      that INTENS 3sg   INTENS
      n-∅-alaq'a-n-i   xa xäl.
      PERF-3ABS-arrange-PASS-CLASS the corn
      'And he admitted that he was indeed the one who was stealing the corn.'
   d. Bueno arxa? ∅-∅-lasa-š-i
      well   3sg   PERF-3ABS-declare-PASS-CLASS
      r-multa.
      3ERG-fine
      'Well, he was fined.'
   e. K'ak'arï? pa xuu taq'aq'ix
      then   on one afternoon
      ∅-∅-čomi-š-i   xa xäl

PERF-3ABS-arrange-PASS-CLASS the corn
pa yaʔl   Ø-Ø-r-izaq-x
in net.bag PERF-3ABS-3ERG-carry-CLASS
xa r-alaq'om.
the 3ERG-thief
'Then, one afternoon, the corn was arranged in a net
bag and the thief carried it.'

f. K'ak'arïʔ Ø-Ø-lasa-š-i
then   PERF-3ABS-take.out-PASS-CLASS
pa taq bey
in PL street
Ø-r-ixqa-n   xa xäl.
3ABS-3ERG-carry-STATE the corn
'Then he was taken out into the street, carrying the
corn [to show he was a thief].'

The thief is the primary participant in the text, and in the two
clauses in (a) he is the single argument and therefore pivot of the
intransitive verb -*urqax*- 'arrive' and the passivized transitive verb
-*koʔx*- 'be put'. This is very similar to the English example in
(7.46b). There are no other explicit actors in this whole stretch
of discourse, and the only other pivots are inanimate participants
such as *cix* 'word' in (b) and *xäl* 'corn' in (e). There is an interesting series of clauses in (e) and (f) in which the thief is actor
and pivot in the first, undergoer and pivot in the second, and actor
and pivot again in the third. The passive verbs in (a) and (f) are
analogous to the antipassive verbs in the Dyirbal text in (7.47);
i.e. they allow the primary participant to remain the PrP and
indicate a marked semantic function, actor in Dyirbal and undergoer in Tzutujil. These two text excerpts illustrate well the work-
ings of the switch-function type of reference-tracking system, a
type which appears to be less common than either switch-reference
or gender systems in the world's languages.

7.5 Cooccurrence and interaction

Reference-tracking systems are not an isolated aspect of the
grammar of a language but rather are intimately interwoven into
the morphosyntactic system. Voice oppositions, which have tradi-

tionally been considered part of clause-internal syntax, are a crucial component of switch-function discourse systems and therefore a necessary prerequisite for the existence of such a system in a language. In gender and switch-reference systems, on the other hand, there is no comparable fundamental role for voice oppositions, and consequently languages which make primary use of these systems typically lack voice oppositions. Moreover the existence or lack of a voice opposition in a language is directly related to the existence and type of pivot(s) found in the language. Switch-function systems necessarily involve pragmatic pivots, whereas switch-reference systems usually operate on semantic pivots. Gender systems, as we have seen in the English, Yimas, and Cree examples, do not concentrate on particular syntactic NP types but rather express coreference irrespective of the syntactic or semantic function of the arguments in either clause. Accordingly, we often find that languages which employ gender systems as their primary or exclusive reference-tracking system lack pivots altogether (cf. e.g. Archi in 4.1).

Heath (1975) notes the inverse relation between gender systems and switch-reference. Languages with elaborate gender distinctions lack switch-reference, and languages with switch-reference generally have an undifferentiated third person, often morphologically realized by ∅, especially in the singular. New Guinea languages amply witness this generalization. Elaborate gender languages like Yimas lack switch-reference, and languages with a heavy development of the switch-reference mechanism like Kewa (Franklin 1971) or Fore (Scott 1978) lack gender distinctions for their nouns. There are some interesting intermediate languages which use both systems, with a relatively unelaborate development of each. Alamblak (Bruce 1979) is a good example of this type of language. Alamblak has a simple binary gender distinction of masculine and feminine, which it applies to all its nouns along the semantic base discussed above of sex and shape, although there are some seemingly arbitrary assignments. Alamblak verbs occur with suffixes cross-referencing the gender and number of the core arguments actor and undergoer which are commonly not overt. The gender distinction is only apparent in the singular; it is neutralized in the dual and plural. Clearly, this is a much more restricted gender system than that of Yimas, and the amount of work it could be expected to do in the tracking of referents of NPs in the discourse must be correspondingly reduced. Consequently, it is not surprising to find in Alamblak the simultaneous presence of a switch-reference system, again not overly elaborated. The switch-reference morphemes occur as suffixes to the verbs of dependent clauses, whether subordinate or not. The same-referent suffix *-hatë* occurs on the predicate in place of the cross-referencing suffixes for actor and undergoer, whereas the different-referent suffix *-t* occurs in addition to them.

(7.53) a. Yifem-r fëh-t tu-finah-hatë-ne
            father-M pig-F throw-arrive-SR-SUBD
            ha-nayay-më-r-t.
            CAUSE-come-REMPAST-3MsgA-3FsgU
            'After father shot a pig, he brought it.'
        b. Hi-af-rhwa-t-nëm-e
            give-separate-FUT-DR-1pl-SUBD
            nayay-rah-m.
            come-FUT-3pl
            'When we have given and separated, they will come.'
        c. Frkih-më-t-r-r
            full-REMPAST-DR-3MsgA-3MsgU
            nayay-më-r.
            come-REMPAST-3sgM
            'It [the string bag] was full on him and he came.'

The switch-reference markers might be seen as redundant in examples like (7.53a, b) in which semantic plausibility or the cross-referencing suffixes determine the coreference of NPs, but examples like (7.53c) show the useful function it serves. Both participants, the string bag and the person, are masculine, so the cross-referencing suffixes are not sufficient to determine coreference. But the different-referent suffix *-t* uniquely determines that the string bag was full and it was the man who went. Thus, Alamblak uses both gender and switch reference, each of which compensates for weaknesses in the other system. Gender may not be sufficient to distinguish different actors of the same class, which is then the function of switch reference. But switch reference cannot monitor coreference of undergoer NPs, which function only the Alamblak gender system performs. In fact, it seems that monitoring coreference of undergoer NPs is the forte of the gender systems of both Yimas and Alamblak, Yimas being more developed in this area. But both languages require ancillary systems to monitor coreference of actor NPs: Yimas, a fourth-person system and Alamblak, a switch-reference system. We encountered a similar phenomenon in 4.4 in our discussion of Bantu languages; in situations where all of the participants are members of the same gender class, a passive may be used to keep the primary topical participant in pivot status (see (4.94)).

As we saw in 7.1, English, like Yimas and Alamblak, employs two reference-tracking systems, in this case switch function and gender, but the relation between the two is different in English. The two systems complement each other in Yimas and Alamblak in that each compensates for a limitation in the other. In English, on the other hand, the two systems are complementary in that they occur in different clause-linkage relations: the gender system is used in peripheral coordination and subordination, while the switch-function system is found in peripheral cosubordination and all core junctures. The English sentences in (7.7) illustrate the functioning of the gender system in peripheral subordination, and the following examples involve peripheral coordination.

(7.54) a. Max went over to Mary's house, and she let him watch the Super Bowl on her new color TV.
       b. Anna made a big mess in the living room, and then she headed for the bedroom.

Of the three grammatical reference-monitoring systems, only the gender systems can operate across syntactically unlinked clauses. The three sentences in (7.7) are not syntactically linked but are simply juxtaposed in a particular linear sequence in discourse, and coreference among NPs is expressed by the gender-marked pronouns, just as in the syntactically linked clauses in (7.54). The switch-function system with its restricted zero anaphora is employed in tighter linkage categories than the gender systems, from peripheral cosubordination to core cosubordination.

(7.55) a. Laura talked to Thelma and told her some hot gossip.
                              (Peripheral cosubordination)

  b. Marvin convinced Kevin to go back to school.

(Core coordination)

  c. I regretted losing the election. (Core subordination)

  d. Carl forgot to give the teacher his assignment.

(Core cosubordination)

As we saw in 6.5, the linked cause in (b)-(d) may be passive if it is the undergoer which is coreferential with the controller in the finite clause. There is an important exception to this scheme, namely core subordination with sentential pivots, as in (7.56).

(7.56) a. That Max failed to get into med. school shocked him.

   b. That he failed to get into med. school shocked Max.

Zero anaphora is not possible in this syntactic context, and accordingly the gender system is used. We argued in 6.2.2. that sentential pivots are a highly marked construction, and the fact that they are exceptional with respect to the kind of cross-clause coreference system they require is additional confirmation of their marked status.

  Thus the interaction between gender and switch function in English is quite complex. With respect to coreference between PrPs, the gender system operates in peripheral coordination and subordination, the switch-function system in peripheral co-subordination and all core junctures except core subordination with sentential pivots. If there is no pivot–pivot coreference, then switch function cannot be used, since PrP–PrP coreference is a precondition for its use (see Table 14). The gender system operates under no such limitation, and moreover it is not restricted to pivots. Coreference among non-pivot arguments is expressed solely by means of the gender system.[8] Accordingly, in English gender is the more general system, while switch function is restricted to pivot–pivot coreference in certain tight clause-linkage categories.

  These English facts illustrate one of the claims made in Silverstein (1976b) regarding clause linkage and reference-tracking mechanisms which was discussed briefly in 6.4.4. Assuming the clause–clause logical-relations hierarchy in Figure 14, Silverstein claims that 'if a language uses a special form for co-reference relations over a logical connexion at a certain point, it will use at least that mechanism for everything above, and possibly even more elaborate formal distinctions' (1976b:163). This claim can also be interpreted in terms of the Interclausal Relations Hierarchy (IRH) in Figure 13: if a language uses a particular reference-maintenance system for all linkage types higher in the IRH and may use additional systems as well. English seems to follow these generalizations by using gender-marked pronouns to express coreference between arguments regardless of their syntactic or semantic function in peripheral coordination and subordination. At peripheral cosubordination a split develops, with the gender system handling coreference between non-pivot arguments and the switch-function system of voice and zero anaphora expressing pivot–pivot coreference in junctures from there through core subordination (with the exception of sentential pivots). This may be represented as in Figure 16.

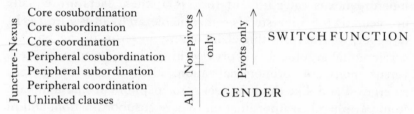

Figure 16 Interaction of clause linkage and reference tracking in English

With respect to the Barai systems of clause linkage and reference tracking, however, these generalizations do not appear to hold. According to Olson (1981), Barai uses a number of different means to express coreference in complex sentences, and they are not distributed along the hierarchy the way the coreference mechanisms in English are. In non-subordinate core junctures, e.g. (5.2a), (5.11) and (6.11), clauses are juxtaposed with no linking morpheme, the coreferential argument in the second junct is omitted, and the controller of the coreference in the first junct is determined according to the principles of control presented in 6.5. In peripheral cosubordination the switch-reference system discussed in 7.3 comes into play (see (7.37)-(7.42)); it involves a number of linkage morphemes expressing both semantic (e.g. temporal sequence) and reference relations between the juncts and zero pronominalization of the coreferential argument in the second junct. There is no switch-reference marking of any kind in peripheral subordinate junctures, and no zero anaphora in the subordinate clause. Finally, in peripheral coordination the switch-topic system operates as in (7.43)-(7.44), with or without switch-reference marking, and there is no zero anaphora. The Barai system is summarized in Figure 17.

Juncture-Nexus	
	Core cosubordination – Juxtaposition w. zero anaphora
	Core subordination – (no zero anaphora)
	Core coordination – Juxtaposition w. zero anaphora
	Peripheral cosubordination – Switch-reference w. zero anaphora
	Peripheral subordination – no switch-reference, no zero anaphora
	Peripheral coordination – Switch-topic (opt. switch-reference), no zero anaphora

Figure 17 Interaction of clause linkage and reference tracking in Barai

Thus Barai does not conform to the claim made in Silverstein (1976b) quoted above when it is interpreted in terms of the juncture–nexus categories of the IRH; these facts are equally problematic for Silverstein's semantic hierarchy in Figure 12. If, however, we interpret this claim simply in terms of the way the coreferential argument is expressed in the linked clause, i.e. zero versus non-zero pronominalization, then a clearer pattern emerges. Barai, like English, uses zero anaphora in clause linkage from peripheral cosubordination to core cosubordination, and in both languages certain types of core subordination are exceptional in not permitting zero anaphora in the subordinate junct. It therefore appears that one cannot claim a strict relationship between juncture–nexus category and type of reference-tracking mechanism but rather only a relationship between the tightness of linkage and the manner of expression of the coreferential argument in the linked junct: the tighter the linkage, the more likely the coreferential argument will be expressed as zero. We see this in both English and Barai which employ zero anaphora in tighter linkages than the ones in which there is no zero anaphora. Exactly where on the IRH a language will start using zero anaphora will vary, but it will always be the case that the linkage types in which zero anaphora is used will be tighter (i.e. higher on the IRH) than those in which it is not.[9]

There is, nevertheless, one generalization which can be made about the interaction of clause linkage and reference-tracking mechanisms. Every language with switch reference which we have investigated employs it in peripheral cosubordinate nexus, and many restrict it to that juncture–nexus type. Moreover switch reference is restricted to peripheral junctures, for the reasons outlined in 7.0. The explanation for this correlation was mentioned at the beginning of 7.3. Switch reference involves a series of dependent but not embedded verbs linked by morphemes expressing referential and possibly semantic relations between the verbs and which depend on the final verb in the chain for the expression of at least one peripheral operator (illocutionary force) and possibly more (usually tense as well). This situation is prototypical cosubordination, hence the repeated cooccurrence of switch reference with peripheral cosubordinate nexus.

There does not seem to be any such strict correlation of a particular clause-linkage type with either gender or switch-function systems. For example, English and German use switch function in peripheral cosubordination (see 6.2.3), but Jacaltec employs it in peripheral coordination. Because it is associated with zero anaphora in English, it operates in core as well as peripheral junctures, and in these core junctures, as noted above, it takes over the expression of pivot–pivot coreference from the gender system. A similar thing happens in Yimas in that in core junctures the coreferential argument in the linked junct is zero (see 7.2). This follows the generalization about zero anaphora proposed above, and so we may conclude that in tighter linkage categories, particularly core junctures, pivot–pivot coreference will involve zero anaphora instead of the gender-marked pronominals of the looser linkage categories.

7.6 Conclusion: from predicate to discourse

This book has addressed the question of what means languages provide to their speakers for keeping track of participants in discourse. In investigating reference-monitoring systems in this chapter we have seen how the functioning of these systems involves all of the aspects of grammar discussed in the previous six chapters. For example, the semantics of verbs in Barai determine the PrP position in the clause, and it is this position which the switch-reference system monitors, a system which operates principally in peripheral cosubordinate nexus. In order to explicate Barai switch-reference, we must rely on the theory of verb semantics in Chapter 2, the concept of (pragmatic) pivot from Chapter 4, and the notions of juncture and nexus from Chapters 5 and 6.

Philippine languages also provide an interesting example of the relationships among the various discourse and morphosyntactic phenomena discussed in this book. We noted in 4.3 (see p. 143) that the focused NP in Tagalog and other Philippine languages appears to have a somewhat different discourse function from the PrP in English, German, and Dyirbal, because the constraint that a definite 'object' (patient or theme) must be in focus overrides all other discourse considerations. This was illustrated in (4.55). This is an interesting constraint, and it raises the question, why the 'object' rather than the actor or one of the other potential arguments? The explanation for it can be found in certain problems in verb semantics discussed in Chapter 2. It was noted in 2.3 (see p. 39) that when the undergoer of an accomplishment verb is an indefinite plural or mass noun, the verb behaves like an activity verb, e.g. *eat a bag of popcorn* (accomplishment) versus *eat popcorn* (activity) (see Dowty 1979:62–5). The referential status of the undergoer is crucially involved in the interpretation of the verb. There is no comparable distinction associated with the referentiality of the actor. Philippine languages generally lack articles, which could code referential status. There are two other possible morphosyntactic means available for expressing the referential status of an NP: demonstratives or a special morphosyntactic status. Demonstratives mark an NP as referential and definite, but they have additional deictic meanings which would render them inappropriate in many contexts. The other option is to develop a special morphosyntactic status in the clause to signal the relevant discourse-referential status. In Philippine languages, as we saw in 4.3, a topicalization construction was incorporated into clause-internal grammar to allow a variety of NPs in the clause to meet syntactic constraints on relativization. Topic NPs, in the sense discussed in 4.2, must be referential and are normally definite, and consequently there developed a clause-internal morphosyntactic status associated with referentiality and definiteness. Since the referentiality status of the undergoer is intimately related to the aspect (in Dowty's sense) of the verb, it needs to be coded, and the morphosyntactic status of clause-internal topic provides a ready means to indicate it. Thus when an undergoer (patient or theme) is definite or referential, the only way to code it unambiguously is to make it the focused NP, hence the constraint. This means there is a potential correlation between the focus form of a verb and its interpretation in terms of the Dowty classification proposed in 2.3.

This correlation is manifested in Sama (Walton 1983), in which many transitive verbs are normally interpreted as accomplishment verbs in undergoer focus, and as activity verbs in actor focus.[10] This is brought out in the interpretation of the aspectual adverbial particles *li'* and *na*.

(7.57) a. Ø-labas   ku   li' huma.
           UF-clean 1sgA   garden(PrP)
           'I'll yet clean the garden.'
       b. N-labas   li' aku   huma.
           AF-clean   1sgPrP garden
           'I'm still cleaning a garden.'

(7.58) a. Ø-b'lli na d'nda   daing   ma   onde'.
           UF-buy woman fish (PrP) OBL child
           'The woman already bought the fish for the child.'
       b. N-b'lli na d'nda   daing ma   onde'.
           AF-buy   woman(PrP) fish   OBL child
           'The woman is now buying fish for the child.'

The difference in interpretation between the sentences in each pair is striking, and the only morphosyntactic difference is the focus of the verb: undergoer focus in (a), actor focus in (b). The particle *li'* seems to have the meaning 'incomplete', and *na* indicates the relationship of the state of the action to the moment of the utterance. Accomplishment verbs typically express a process from the point of view of the resulting state of affairs (the BECOME **predicate'** (...) in the logical structure), whereas activity verbs describe an action in terms of what the participant is doing (see 2.3, Dowty 1979:52–62). Accordingly, with an accomplishment verb, *li'* indicates that the result has not yet come about, as in (7.57a), and with an activity verb it signals that the action is incomplete, i.e. still in progress, as in (7.57b). Similarly, the undergoer-focus verb in (7.58a) is an accomplishment verb which denotes the situation resulting from the woman's buying the fish; hence the interpretation of *na* as 'already', since with respect to the moment of speaking the event of buying has taken place. In (b), on the other hand, the actor-focus verb *m'lli* ($<N + b'lli$) codes the action of buying; and since *na* relates the event to the moment of speaking, it is interpreted as meaning 'now'. The interpretation of these particles highlights the relationship between focus and verbal aspect in Sama.

We have argued that the reason Philippine languages have the constraint that referential and definite 'objects' must be in focus (PrP) is that the referential status of this verbal argument (and no other) is crucial to the aspectual (Dowty) interpretation of the verb, and being in focus is the only universally applicable means of signaling that status. Furthermore, since the referential status coded by being in focus is crucial for the undergoer of an accomplishment verb, there would appear to be connections between 'object' focus and accomplishment semantics, and between actor focus and activity semantics. This was illustrated in the Sama sentences in (7.57)–(7.58). Thus the semantics of the verbal system of Philippine languages cannot be fully analyzed without taking into account the focus system, which is a major part of clause-internal syntax, and the discourse status of a core argument, the undergoer (patient, theme). The phenomena discussed in Chapter 2, verb semantics, are intimately linked to certain syntactic options available inside the clause and to the information structure of discourse.

The converse is true as well: the information structure in a discourse is directly related to verbs and the internal structure of clauses. Hopper (1979a) and Hopper & Thompson (1980) discuss Tagalog narrative discourse, and argue that in the part of the discourse which carries the main story line, i.e. the 'temporal structure which charts the progress of the narrative through time by presenting a series of events which are understood to occur sequentially' (Polanyi-Bowditch 1976:61), 'object'-focus clauses predominate. In the part of the narrative which adds secondary information, i.e. the 'durative/descriptional structure, which provides a spatial, charactrological, and durational context for which the temporal structure marks time and changes of state' (*ibid.*), fewer 'object'-focus forms are found, and actor-focus and other focus types are much more common. Hopper & Thompson attempt to explain this in terms of their notion of transitivity (see Chapter 2, n. 6) by claiming first that transitivity is a discourse-based notion, with high transitivity clauses occurring in the temporal structure of discourse, and low transitivity clauses in the durative/descriptional structure,[11] and second, that Tagalog 'object'-focus constructions are higher in transitivity than actor-focus and oblique-focus constructions (see Hopper & Thompson 1980:280–90).

We asserted in Chapter 2, n. 6 that the transitivity continuum discussed by Hopper & Thompson can be grounded in Dowty's system of verb classification: verbs highest in transitivity are agentive accomplishment verbs, those lowest in transitivity are the various kinds of statives. This interpretation of transitivity in terms of the Dowty classification relates directly to the discourse basis which Hopper & Thompson propose for it. If the temporal structure of narrative discourse consists of a series of sequential events, then the types of verbs most likely to occur in it would be those which denote or describe entire events, and achievement and accomplishment verbs do just that. Similarly, if the durative/descriptive structure of narrative discourse is constituted by clauses which supply information about the location of the events, the characterization of the participants, and secondary events going on independent of and often simultaneous with the main events of the narrative, then the types of verbs which would most likely occur in them would be state and activity verbs. Thus given the characterization of the temporal and durative/descriptional structures in narrative discourse stated above and Dowty's theory of verb semantics, the potential discourse functions of clauses can be predicted: those with achievement and accomplishment verbs will strongly tend to occur in the temporal structure, those with activity and state verbs in the durative/descriptive structure. Furthermore, when the syntactic and semantic features which underlie the Dowty classification are examined (see Tables 1, 3), most of the major transitivity features discussed by Hopper & Thompson fall out. Telicity is a feature of achievement and accomplishment verbs and not of activity and state verbs. Likewise the former verbs tend to be punctual, the latter do not. Volitionality is a feature of both activity and accomplishment verbs, and the potency of the actor is higher in accomplishment verbs because it, unlike the actors of other types of verbs, brings about changes of state or location of another participant. The status of this other participant, the 'object' or undergoer, is related to two other very important transitivity features: the affectedness of the 'object' and its individuation. The high degree of affectedness of the 'object' is expressed directly in the logical structure of accomplishment and achievement verbs, i.e. (... CAUSE) BECOME **predicate**′ (...) in which the change of state or location is explicit. Indeed, achievement and accomplishment verbs are the non-stative verbs which have fully affected patient arguments. The objects of activity verbs are never patients (see 2.5). The individuation of the 'object' is very important, because as we noted above and in 2.3, accomplishment verbs with non-individuated undergoers behave like activity verbs, and conversely some basic activity verbs behave like accomplishment verbs with the addition of a highly indivi-duated object or goal, e.g. *walk* (activity) versus *walk to the store* (accomplishment). Hence highly individuated 'objects' correlate strongly with accomplishment-verb semantics. Thus most of the major transitivity features posited by Hopper & Thompson can be derived from the theory of verb semantics presented in Chapter 2.

The question of the individuatedness of the 'object' brings us back to the question about Tagalog and Philippine languages which motivated this discussion. We argued above that the explanation for the constraint in Philippine languages that a referential and usually definite undergoer must be in focus lies in the fact that focus status is the only means available for signaling the referential status of the verbal argument most crucially in-volved in the semantic interpretation of the aspect (in Dowty's sense) of the verb. Furthermore, we hypothesized that there should be links between 'object'-focus constructions and accomplishment-verb semantics and between actor-focus con-structions and activity-verb semantics; this was illustrated in Sama in (7.57)–(7.58). We can now see why 'object'-focus con-structions predominate in the temporal structure of narrative dis-course in Tagalog: they are the form with which accomplishment verb semantics are associated, and, as we argued above, accomplishment verbs express 'a process that leads up to a well-

defined terminal point beyond which the process cannot continue'
(Comrie 1976a:45); consequently, clauses containing these verbs
are best suited to code the series of discrete sequential actions
or events which constitute the temporal structure of narrative discourse. This explains the correlation between clauses with high
transitivity and the temporal structure of narrative discourse discussed in Hopper & Thompson (1980) and Hopper (1979a), and
it emphasizes the point made above that discourse, clause
structure, and verb semantics are all intimately interwoven. The
same is true with respect to the operators which modify the various
layers of the clause; it is not just the peripheral operators like
illocutionary force and tense which have important functions in
discourse. Aspect, the innermost operator modifying the nucleus,
has been argued to have discourse significance along the lines discussed above with respect to verb classes. Hopper (1979a,b)
shows that the perfective aspect is the primary aspectual category
found in the temporal structure of narrative discourse in a number
of languages, and imperfective aspect is primary in durational/
descriptive structure (see also the papers in Hopper (ed.) 1982).[12]
We argued in Chapter 1 that a language cannot be fully understood without reference to its communicative functions, and these
interactions between verb semantics, aspect, clause-internal
morphosyntax, and discourse structure demonstrate this clearly.

With respect to the reference-tracking systems discussed in this
chapter, we can likewise see the interplay of interclausal and intraclausal syntax. In particular, if we look at the languages which
make primary use of each of the three systems of reference
maintenance we find that the clause-internal morphosyntax of the
languages in each group is for the most part very similar, and
that each group is strikingly different from the other. Languages
which use a gender system for the coding of coreference do not
restrict it to one particular NP type but rather use it for all core
arguments and possibly peripheral arguments as well. These
languages often lack pivots altogether. In 4.1 we showed that Archi
lacks syntactic pivots, and it uses a gender system (see (4.19)–
(4.20)). There is little evidence for syntactic pivots in Cree as well,
and all of these languages lack voice oppositions of any kind. The
only languages we know of which have an elaborate gender system
and a productive foregrounding passive construction are

Chichewa and other Bantu languages, but, as we saw in 4.4, the passive may serve to signal coreference if all of the major participants fall into the same gender class. The rudimentary switch-reference system in Alamblak has the same function. Switch-reference languages, on the other hand, normally have pivots (Eastern Pomo does not; see p. 120), and the pivots are, with at least one major exception (Barai), semantic rather than pragmatic. Moreover, these languages usually lack foregrounding passives and antipassives; some of them do have backgrounding passives and mediopassives, e.g. Choctaw, Ulcha. As in gender languages, there are very few options for altering the internal structure of the clause. Finally, all switch-function languages have pragmatic pivots and foregrounding passive or antipassive constructions. The syntactic status of verbal arguments may vary according to the demands of discourse. Each of these clusters of morphosyntactic phenomena is not accidental, and throughout this book we have attempted to show how and why they cooccur as they do.

Languages are *systems*, not random collections of grammatical constructions. When we explore them from the perspective of how they achieve a certain communicative end, we see their systematic nature most clearly. In seeking to elucidate the notion of 'possible human language', it is not enough for linguists to simply present inventories of rules and constraints. We must strive to account for 'possible human linguistic systems' and to answer questions about why language X has such and such constructions while language Y has a different constellation of forms in some functional domain, rather than about simply what constructions there are.

We have made a few first steps in this direction in this book by exploring the interaction of clause-internal and cross-clause syntax with reference maintenance in discourse. Further work will no doubt yield even deeper insights and more precise generalizations along with the continuing refinement of the conceptual tools of Role and Reference Grammar, which have molded the insights and analyses presented herein.

Notes

Chapter 1

1 See Foley & Van Valin (1977), (in press); Foley (1976), (1980a); Van Valin (1977a,b), (1980a,b,c), (1981a), (1983), (in press); Foley & Olson (in press); Olson (1978), (1981); Walton (1983).

2 Because we are trying to characterize general orientations rather than particular theories, the generalizations may not be accurate with respect to each claim of a given theory in each camp; this does not, however, invalidate the discussion.

3 The speciousness of this argument is revealed when one considers that in current theory (Chomsky 1980a, 1981a,b,c) it is recognized that there are languages which lack a transformational component and hence structure-dependent rules; see the discussion of non-configurational languages in 1.2. Because not all languages have such rules, the language learner must induce from experience whether they are found in the language or not, and therefore this principle cannot be considered a precondition to language acquisition. Building complex models of innate linguistic principles based on this kind of argument is like building a house on a sand dune, because it is crucially dependent on the current state of linguistic and psychological knowledge. It is an empirical question whether all languages have structure-dependent rules; in 1975 it appeared that they did, but in 1983 it is clear that they do not. Therefore the argument that this principle must be universal and therefore innate because of the poverty of the stimulus was plausible in 1975 but is not in 1983, and the reason for this is that linguists' knowledge about the world's languages has increased. It is a logical error to ground an argument that something is a *necessary* feature of the innate cognitive structure of human beings on *contingent* facts.

4 Chomsky claims to be in full agreement with functionalists on this point: 'Surely there are significant connections between structure and function, this is not and has never been in doubt' (1975:56). However, the function which is connected with structure in Chomsky's view is the creative use of language and not communication.

5 See Silverstein (1976a, 1977) and Gumperz (1982) for detailed discussion of how linguistic forms help to create the social and linguistic context in which they occur.

6 There has been something of a division of labor in the study of language

over the last 50 years, with linguists analyzing grammatical structure abstracted away from meaning and use, and anthropologists investigating language use in different societies and cultures without taking into account the grammatical structure of the languages under study. One group tried to analyze form without regard to function, the other function without form (see 1.2). Each group operated under its own set of assumptions which were radically different from and incompatible with those of the other, and consequently any attempt to unite the results obtained in the separate fields would be doomed to failure.

7 In Chomskyan theory internal evidence has a privileged status over external evidence; see the discussion of the argument from the poverty of the stimulus above. See also the papers in Hornstein & Lightfoot, eds., (1981) for arguments for this position, one in which language acquisition is a 'logical' problem rather than a psycholinguistic or neurolinguistic one.

8 Chomsky maintains that the very question of the evolutionary basis of language is illegitimate. The following exchange between Chomsky and S. Harnad at the Conference on the Origins and Evolution of Language illustrates his position.

Harnad: If some rules you have described constitute universal constraints on all languages, yet they are not learned, nor are they somehow logically necessary *a priori*, how did language get that way?

Chomsky: Well, it seems to me that would be like asking the question, how does the heart get that way? I mean, we don't learn to have a heart, we don't learn to have arms rather than wings. What is interesting to me is that the question should be asked. It seems to be a natural question; everyone asks it. And I think we should ask why people ask it. (Chomsky 1976:57)

This refusal to address the evolutionary issue is not a feature of all theories which make strong claims about the innate basis of language. Bickerton (1981) proposes that there are actual linguistic structures which are innate, not just the abstract form of human language; his claims are derived from his study of creole languages. Unlike Chomsky, Bickerton attempts to provide a phylogenetic account of why these particular structures are innate.

9 There has been some confusion on this point in the literature. Munro & Gordon (1982), for example, have construed this to mean that we claim that some languages are deficient communicatively because they do not grammaticalize certain discourse notions the way English and many other languages do. We have made no such claim and in fact have explicitly asserted exactly the opposite: 'all languages can do the same communicative work, regardless of the way syntactic, semantic, and pragmatic factors are treated formally in grammatical systems' (Van Valin & Foley 1980:331). We thus take the position of Boas (1911) and Sapir (1921, 1924, 1933) that 'language is an essentially perfect means of expression and communication among every known people' (Sapir 1933:155).

10 There are a number of other functional theories which fall within the framework outlined in this section. Dik's theory of functional grammar (1978)

shares with RRG all of the major theoretical assumptions and goals but differs markedly from it in terms of theoretical constructs, analytic methodology, and analyses of specific phenomena, e.g. ergativity, Philippine focus systems. No comparison of RRG with Halliday's current theory will be possible until Halliday (in press) appears. Givón (1979) does not present a functional theory *per se* but rather functionally oriented analyses of a variety of linguistic issues; see Van Valin (1981b) for a detailed discussion of Givón's position. Kuno (1980) presents his functional syntax as a component to be added to a theory of grammar which complements existing theories, even the extended standard theory (see 1980:118). It is therefore not clear where Kuno's work belongs, since it seems to make most of the assumptions about language that generative grammar does but seeks to add a layer of pragmatically oriented analysis on top of the standard generative type of analysis.

11 Examples of formal universals are well known in the literature. For some examples of functional universals, see Silverstein (1976b, 1980b, 1981), Heath (1975, 1978), and Givón (1979, 1981).

12 The head noun in a Lakhota relative clause is always marked by *wã* 'a'; its true definiteness status is signaled by the article and demonstrative at the end of the relative clause. *Taku* means 'what' in a question and 'something' in a non-question.

    (i) Hokšila ki taku   čhĩ.
         boy   the WH/something 3sg-want
         'The boy wants something.'

    (ii) Hokšila ki taku   čhĩ   he.
         boy   the WH/something 3sg-want Q
         'What does the boy want?'

Chapter 2

1 A couple of terminological points are in order here. Dowty uses the term 'aspect' in two different senses. One refers to the inherent features of the meaning of a predicate which underlies its classification in the scheme in (2.12), which has been labelled *Aktionsart* by some scholars, e.g. Klein (1974). The other refers to the temporal grammatical category which is subdivided into notions like perfective, imperfective, iterative, etc. (cf. Dowty 1979:52; see also Comrie 1976a:6). In this passage he is using 'aspectual' in the first sense. The term 'logical structure' denotes the representation of the semantic structure of the predicate; we will employ it in this sense. In his discussion of lexical decomposition, Dowty presents logical structures in two forms: in a simple first-order logic and in the intensional logic of Montague's PTQ (Montague 1974). Since logical structures presented in the first form are likely to be intelligible to most readers while those in the second are not, we we will make use only of the first-order logic representations. Readers interested in the intensional logical representations are referred to chapters 4 and 7 in Dowty (1979).

2 In these representations of the logical structures of these verbs, **verb**′ stands

for the constant in Montague's intensional logic corresponding to the English word 'verb'. See Dowty, Wall & Peters (1981:192).

3 These representations are intended to capture one specific meaning of each of these verbs. For example, *realize* can have at least two meanings, as exemplified in (i).

(i) a. Archie suddenly realized who the murderer was.

b. I have always realized that an academic career would be difficult.

Realize is an achievement verb only in (ia), and the logical structure BECOME **know'** (x,y) would be relevant only to it. In (ib) *realize* has a stative meaning very similar to *know* and would have a simple stative predicate as its logical structure. Taking both sentences in (i) into account, we could say that the logical structure of *realize* is (BECOME) **know'** (x,y), since it can occur both as a state and achievement verb.

4 Dowty also gives truth conditions for BECOME in terms of an interval-based temporal logic; see 1979:139-45.

5 Dowty gives the model-theoretic definition of CAUSE on p. 109.

6 Hopper & Thompson (1980) discuss 'transitivity' as a complex notion composed of a number of interacting features, most of which have figured in this discussion in some form: participants (two versus one), kinesis (action versus non-action), aspect (telic versus atelic), volitionality (volitional versus non-volitional), agency (high potency of actor versus low potency), affectedness of object (totally affected versus not affected), and individuation of object (highly individuated versus non-individuated); see 1980: 252–3. Clauses which have more of the positive features are higher in transitivity than those with fewer positive features. The verb classes in Table 3 may be ranked in terms of their transitivity along the following continuum:

$$\xleftarrow{\quad 1(a,b) \qquad 2(a,b) \qquad 3 \qquad 4 \qquad 5 \qquad 7 \qquad 6,8 \quad}\rightarrow$$

LOW   Transitivity   HIGH

Not surprisingly, stative verbs rank lowest in transitivity, agentive accomplishment verbs the highest. Thus Dowty's verb classification can be interpreted as providing the basis for a classification of verbs in terms of transitivity in Hopper & Thompson's sense.

7 The Lakhota orthography is that used in Van Valin (1977a); all symbols have their standard phonetic value, and *h* after a stop or affricate indicates aspiration. Several morphophonemic alternations occur in the data. First, the final [a] of many verbs changes to [e] under certain conditions, e.g. *t'a* 'die', *ni-t'e* 'you are dead, dying'; the conditions relevant to the discussion are (i) when the verb is phrase final in an utterance, and (ii) when the causative auxiliary -*ya* is suffixed to it (see Boas & Deloria 1939:29–33). The continuitive suffix -*hã* changes to -*he* under these same conditions, but for clarity of presentation it will be represented as -*hã* in (2.17). Secondly, there is a consonantal alternation in some C_1VC_2V neutral verbs such that when -*ya* 'causative' is added, the final vowel drops and C_2 changes its voicing such that voiced C becomes voiceless and vice versa, e.g. *puza* 'dry', *pus-ya* 'cause to be dry', *sapa* 'black', *sab-ya* 'blacken'. Thirdly, in C_1VC_2V neutral verbs with [č] as

C_2, the addition of *-ya* causes the final vowel to drop and [č] to become [l], e.g. *šiča* 'bad', *šil-ya* cause to be bad'.

8 Whether *uya*, *ableza*, and *iyeya* are truly achievement predicates can only be established by means of the syntactic and semantic tests given in Tables 1 and 3. For the purposes of outlining the morphological treatment of these predicate classes in Lakhota, however, the uncertainty with respect to these verbs is not a serious problem because the point here is that achievement predicates, unlike the other three types, are not characterized in a consistent way morphologically. Regardless of whether these three verbs turn out ultimately to be true achievement predicates, the basic point about this class holds.

9 In Fillmorean case grammar 'patient' subsumes both patient and theme relations, while in the Gruber–Jackendoff system of thematic relations, the term 'theme' is used for both. We will see that there are strong grounds for distinguishing locational from condition states.

10 Noun phrases receive complex representations in Montague's intensional logic. Since the semantic issues which motivate these representations are not directly relevant to this discussion, we will employ English noun phrases for simplicity of presentation.

11 This analysis of perception verbs is based on the Western scientific view of the nature of perception, and it is quite conceivable that in languages spoken by members of cultures with a radically different concept of perception this analysis would be inappropriate. The adequacy of this representation is an empirical question, as much with respect to English *see* as to Lakhota *wãyãka*, Dyirbal *buṛan*, and Russian *videt'*. This kind of cultural variation is even more pronounced with respect to cognition verbs, and accordingly our discussion of them is subject to the same qualification.

12 The qualification of n. 11 is particularly relevant here. Indeed, many philosophers, e.g. Wittgenstein, have argued that the western conception of cognition is in fact derived from such linguistic metaphors. Boas (1911) called this process 'secondary reasoning and reinterpretation'; see Silverstein (1979) for detailed discussion. Of course, if our conception of knowing and the mind is derived from linguistic metaphor and usage, then linguistic data such as these provides evidence for the semantic structure of verbs like *know* and *believe* in English.

13 This connective would be equivalent to von Wright's *T* operator 'and next' discussed by Dowty (1979:74–5).

14 This logical structure represents the minimal structure necessary to derive the semantic role relations of the arguments. The addition of DO operators over the two φ CAUSE ψ logical structures would further specify the intentionality of the actions, as in (2.38), but they would have no effect on the interpretation of the semantic relations of the arguments. Accordingly we will overtly indicate the full range of DO operators only when it is relevant to the discussion, in order to avoid overly cumbersome logical structures.

15 The inherent lexical content of NPs is involved in the opposition between agent and effector, as only animate arguments can be agents and therefore

inanimate arguments must be effectors. However, there are cases of animate effectors, as in (2.33a) and (2.38a), so that this contrast cannot be reduced to one involving inherent lexical content alone.

16 All discussions of this phenomenon have concentrated on examples like (2.49a) and (2.50a) with indefinite-plural or mass-noun undergoers. The result of this is that in the (a) sentences in (2.49) and (2.50) *load* and *spray* are behaving like activity verbs, while in the (b) examples they are accomplishment verbs; see 2.3. In this discussion we will use examples with definite undergoers so that the verbs under consideration have the same logical structure in all cases.

17 This formulation was originally suggested to us by David Wilkins (personal communication).

18 This 'focusing' of NPs in the Tagalog clause will be discussed in detail in 4.3.

19 The differentiation of locative relations into source, goal, and positional locative is very common in the world's languages. We will discuss this elaboration in English in our discussion of English prepositions in 3.3.1.

20 The *N* in *maN*– is a morphophonemic symbol subject to the following rules. If the initial consonant of the stem is voiceless, the *N* and the consonant are replaced by the nasal homorganic to the consonant. Thus *maN* + *sakit* 'sick' becomes *manakit* 'injure'. If the initial consonant is voiced, it remains unchanged, but the *N* is realized as the homorganic nasal to the consonant: *maN* + *gulo* 'trouble' becomes *manggulo* 'make trouble'. Finally, in other cases, the *N* is realized as [ŋ]: *maN* + *isda* 'fish' becomes *mangisda* 'catch fish'.

21 Two points need to be made about these examples. First, in terms of this logical structure *kutsilyo* 'knife' is a theme, but because it occurs in the first argument of CAUSE, it is interpreted as an effector–theme, since it is part of the causing event. Secondly, another reading for 'a man got cut on the knife' would be that the knife was stationary and the hand or finger came in contact with it. Such an interpretation would be expressed by the following logical structure:

[BECOME **be-at**′ (lalake, kutsilyo)] CAUSE [BECOME **cut**′ (lalake)]

This specifies that it is the *lalake* 'man' which moves and comes into contact with the knife. In this logical structure, *lalake* is a theme–patient, *kutsilyo* a (effector–) locative. In (2.77) and this logical structure, the argument which functions as the patient in the second argument of CAUSE will be the undergoer, the other the actor.

22 This is not the case in all Philippine languages. In Sama of Pangutaran (spoken on a group of islands south of Mindanao) there is an undergoer macrorole similar to that found in English, as the following examples illustrate (Walton 1983).

(i) a. N-b'lli aku   taumpa ma   si Andi.
       AF-buy1sg(F) shoe   OBL PN Andy
       'I bought some shoes for Andy.'

   b. Ø-b'lli   ku   taumpa ma   si Andi.

U F-buy 1sg(A) shoe(F) O B L P N Andy
'I bought the shoes for Andy.'
(ii) a. *N-b'lli-an* aku ' si   Andi taumpa.
A F-buy-L 1sg(F) P N Andy shoe
'I bought Andy some shoes.'
  b. Ø-b'lli-*an* ku   si   Andi taumpa.
U F-buy-L 1sg(A) P N Andy shoe(s)
'I bought Andy some shoes.'

(*N-* in these examples is a morphophoneme which assimilates to the initial segment of the stem following the pattern in n. 20.) The sentences in (i) exemplify actor- and undergoer–focus forms of *b'lli* 'buy'; note the lack of prepositional case-marking particles for actor and undergoer and the oblique preposition *ma* marking the beneficiary *si Andi*. The evidence for undergoer in Sama is in (ii), in which the beneficiary *si Andi* is not longer oblique but has displaced *taumpa* 'shoe(s)' as undergoer. There is no comparable derived non-focused status in Tagalog. This change in the status of the beneficiary is similar to 'dative shift' in English, which involves a marked undergoer choice, and the English glosses reflect this. That -*an* marks locative undergoer rather than locative focus can be seen in (iia) in which the verb also takes the *N-* actor-focus prefix, indicating that it is actor focus rather than locative focus. When *si Andi* is in focus in (iib), the verb takes the same Ø-prefix as in (ib) when *taumpa* 'shoe(s)' is the undergoer in focus. Despite the lack of a particle analogous to Tagalog *ang* in Sama, it is unambiguous that *si Andi* and not *taumpa* is in focus in (iib) because of the indefinite interpretation of *taumpa*; if it were in focus as in (ib), then it would have to be interpreted as definite (see 4.3). Thus in Sama -*an* indicates a derived undergoer choice, in this case beneficiary, and not locative focus, since -*an* may occur on an actor-focus verb, as in (iia) in which it signals the presence of a non-oblique beneficiary. It appears, then, that Sama, unlike Tagalog, has a notion of undergoer distinct from the semantic case-role of patient.

Chapter 3

1 These terms are in quotes to indicate that they are not part of the theoretical inventory of RRG; see chapter 4, Foley & Van Valin (1977), Van Valin & Foley (1980), Van Valin (1977b, 1981a) for discussions of the RRG view of grammatical relations.
2 Ditransitive verbs require this to be reformulated in terms of marked and unmarked undergoer assignments; cf. below, n. 3.
3 The most obvious apparent counterexample to this claim is *put*, which seems to have three obligatory arguments.
  (i) a. Merle put the tobacco in the drawer.
    b. *Merle put the tobacco.
However, there are instances in which *put* occurs with just an actor and an undergoer.

(ii) a. Merle put the tobacco away.

   b. Merle put the tobacco down.

Moreover, this adverbial element may occur either before or after the under-goer, just as with a typical verb–particle combination like *look up*.

(iii) a. Merle put away the tobacco.

   b. Merle put down the tobacco.

(iv) a. Zeke looked the number up.

   b. Zeke looked up the number.

These facts suggest that *put* in (i) is not a different verb from the one in (ii) and (iii) but rather that it is a verb which obligatorily takes an adverbial particle analogous to *look up*. Hence the verb in (i), (ii), and (iii) is not *put* but *put* PARTICLE. The crucial difference between *put* PARTICLE and *look up* is the range of elements which appear as the particle: not only may adverbs like *down* and *away* occur with *put* but also prepositions such as *in*, *on*, and *under*. Thus we may represent *put* as in (v).

(v)
$$\text{put} \quad \begin{array}{l} ^b \\ ^c \\ ^j \\ ^h \\ ^c \\ ^e \end{array} \left[\begin{array}{l} \text{away} \\ \text{down} \\ \text{up} \\ \text{in} \\ \text{on} \\ \text{under} \end{array} \right] \begin{array}{l} ^h \\ ^c \\ ^e \\ ^b \\ ^c \\ ^i \end{array}$$

Naturally, *in*, *on* and the other prepositions require NP objects, while adverbials like *away* and *down* do not. The occurrence of the NP object blocks the movement of the particle–prepositional phrase.

(vi) *Merle put in the drawer the tobacco. (cf. (i)).

No special constraint is needed to rule out such sentences, since the word-order template in (3.1) specifies that no prepositional phrase may occur between the nucleus and the undergoer. Thus we may conclude that *put* is really *put* PARTICLE which has only two core arguments. Its only idio-syncrasy is that it allows locative prepositions to occur as the particle in addition to locative adverbs, and these locative prepositions must have NP objects, yielding sentences like (ia).

4 We say 'non-undergoer' rather than 'non-"direct object"' here because it is undergoer and not 'direct object' \ ch is the relevant relation, as the sentences in (i) show.

(i) a. The wall was hit with the cane by the man.

   b. Hay was loaded on the truck by Bill.

   c. The pool was drained of its water by John.

   d. The award was presented to Bert Newton by the compere.

The same preposition assignments occur, as one would expect, in passive as in active sentences. Hence undergoer, rather than 'direct object' is the relevant notion.

5 We are using '(locative-)goal' and '(locative-)source' in the senses that they have been used by Fillmore, Gruber, Jackendoff, and others. We will give them a precise characterization below in our discussion of the prepositions *to* and *from*.

6 As noted in 2.3, activity verbs with a definite goal, as in (3.13), behave like accomplishment verbs, hence the complex logical structure in (3.14); see Dowty (1979:60–1).

7 The ∅ in this logical structure means that that argument of the predicate is unspecified. In (3.17) there is no mention of whom the wine and cheese are served to.

8 There has been some dispute in the literature as to whether it is possible to identify the controller in a Dyirbal reflexive construction. See Van Valin (1977b) for evidence that it is in fact the actor, the normal ergative NP, which controls reflexivization in Dyirbal.

9 R. M. W. Dixon (personal communiciation) has reported that all examples of relative clauses modifying locative NPs which he has collected involve inner locatives.

10 There is in fact a third coding possibility which is similar to (3.60a) except that the recipient is expressed as the possessor of the undergoer–theme and is in the genitive case. See Dixon (1972:300).

11 The instrumentive and comitative markers are both -*ma(l)*, but Dixon argues that they should be considered distinct affixes; see Dixon (1972:96–8).

12 There is semantically based variation in the coding of causees with both intransitive and transitive verbs. While most languages with this type of causative construction treat the causee of an intransitive verb as a direct object, Japanese (Shibatani 1973) and Hungarian (Hetzron 1976) present an interesting variation in the case marking of intransitive causees.

(i) a. Taroo ga Ziroo o   ik-ase-ta.
               ACC go-CAUSE-PAST
          'Taro caused Jiro to go', or 'Taro made Jiro go.'

   b. Taroo ga Ziroo ni   ik-ase-ta.
               DAT go-CAUSE-PAST
          'Taro caused Jiro to go', or 'Taro let/had Jiro go.'

The particle *o* in (ia) is normally used in Japanese to mark undergoer, while *ni* in (ib) occurs with goals and the agent of a passive construction. There is an important semantic difference between these two sentences. In (ia) with *o* the causee does not perform the action voluntarily and is being forced by the causer. In (ib) with *ni*, on the other hand, the causee performs the action voluntarily at the suggestion or instruction of the causer. There is a similar distribution in Hungarian which is signaled by accusative versus instrumental case marking on the causee.

(ii) a. Köhögtettem   a   gyereket.
     cough-CAUSE-1sg the boy-ACC
     'I made the boy cough.'

   b. Köhögtettem   a   gyerekkel.
     cough-CAUSE-1sg the boy-INST
     'I had the boy cough (by asking him to do so).'

The semantic contrast between (iia-b) is parallel to that between (ia-b). In the (a)-sentence the causee is not coughing volitionally; Hetzron comments that 'he is induced to do so by, say, the causer blowing cigarette smoke in his face' (1976:394). In the (b)-sentence the causee coughs voluntarily after being asked to do so by the causer. In both Hungarian and Japanese accusative marking of the causee correlates with a lack of control and volition on its part, while dative or instrument (i.e. non-accusative-marking) signals a causee which is a volitional controller of an action.

A number of languages exhibit the same sort of variation in the case marking of causees of transitive verbs. In some languages, e.g. German and Bolivian Quechua, the contrast is like that of Hungarian between accusative and instrumental case marking, whereas in others it is between dative and instrumental marking, e.g. French and Kannada.

(iii) a. Hans ließ   die   Sekratärin den   Brief   (German)
          CAUSE the-ACC secretary the-ACC letter
      abtippen.
      type
      'Hans made the secretary type the letter.'

   b. Hans ließ   den   Brief von der   Sekratärin abtippen.
          CAUSE the-ACC letter by the-DAT secretary   type
      'Hans had/let the secretary type the letter.'

(iv) a. Nuqa   Fan-ta   rumi-ta   apa-či-ni   (Bolivian Quenchua)
      1sg-NOM Juan-ACC rock-ACC carry-CAUSE-1sg
      'I made Juan carry the rock.'

   b. Nuqa   Fan-wan   rumi-ta   apa-či-ni
      1sg-NOM Juan-INST rock-ACC carry-CAUSE-1sg
      'I had Juan carry the rock.'

(v) a. J'ai fait   nettoyer   les toilettes au général.   (French)
      1sg-have made.clean-INF the toilets to the general
      'I made the general clean the toilets.'

   b. J'ai fait nettoyer   les toilettes par le général.
      1sg-have.made. clean-INF the toilets by the general
      'I had the general clean the toilets.'

(vi) a. Avanu   nanage   tīyannu   kudisidanu.   (Kannada)
      3sg-NOM 1sg-DAT tea-ACC drink-CAUSE-PAST
      'He made me drink tea.'

   b. Avanu   nanninda   tīyannu   kudisidanu.
      3sg-NOM 1sg-INST tea-ACC drink-CAUSE-PAST
      'He had/let me drink tea.'

(Bolivian Quechua data are from Bills *et al.* 1969, French from Hyman & Zimmer 1976, and Kannada from Cole 1983.) In German and Quechua the accusative case marks a non-volitional causee, as indicated by the translation with English *make*. The instrumental case in Quechua and the use of *von* 'by' (in this instance) plus dative in German indicates that the causee is a volitional controller of an action. The same distinction is signaled by the contrast between dative and instrumental/agentive marking in French and Kannada. Other languages which exhibit this kind of semantically based variation in the case marking of the causee of transitive verbs include Hindi (Saksena 1980), Sanskrit (Comrie 1976b), and Dutch (Comrie 1976b).

Comrie (1981) attempts to deal with variation of this kind by proposing a control hierarchy of instrumental > dative > accusative, where instrumental case-marked NPs coding causees are highest in control and accusative the lowest (pp. 174–6). This control hierarchy can be derived from Figure 1, since instrumental case normally codes effectors, dative locative (-goal)s, and accusative patients or themes. These are ranked with respect to their control potential, i.e. their proximity to agent on the hierarchy, exactly the same way as in Comrie's hierarchy, and consequently Figure 1 can be taken as the basis of this case-control hierarchy.

13 English causative constructions like *I made John leave, Mary let Bill buy her a hat*, and *Louise had Fred wash her car* involve the joining of two cores, not two nuclei (see 6.2.1, 6.4); the verbs in these constructions do not therefore form a complex nucleus analogous to *faire courir* in (3.64a). Accordingly, the case-marking rules discussed in 3.3.1 apply to each core separately and not to the complex core as a whole (see 6.5). The claims discussed in 3.4, both Comrie's and those of RRG, apply only to causatives which involve a complex nucleus and one set of core arguments.

Chapter 4

1 Not all languages are as straightforward as English in having the same pivot for all of the major syntactic constructions; for example, Jacaltec, a Mayan language, has *four* distinct syntactic pivots (see Van Valin 1981a for detailed discussion).

2 'Pragmatic pivot' is equivalent to the term 'pragmatic peak' used in Van Valin (1977a,b), (1980a,b), and (1981a), and Van Valin & Foley (1980), and to the term 'referential peak' used in Foley & Van Valin (1977).

3 Munro & Gordon (1982) have argued that case marking in western Muskogean languages is not controlled by such a semantic hierarchy. They claim first of all that in Chickasaw, a close relative of Choctaw, verbal case marking cannot be stated in terms of semantic relations such as agent and patient, because there is some variation in the interpretation of the affixes (pp. 84–7). For example, the actor affix occurs with verbs with volitional agents, some perception and cognitive verbs, e.g. *pisa* 'see' as in (4.14c), *ithaana* 'know', and with non-volitional verbs, e.g. *habina* 'get (as a present), receive'. This variation in the interpretation of the actor affix is cited as evidence that there is no strict semantic basis for verbal case marking in these languages. However, the claim here and in Heath (1977) is that these affixes code the more general category of actor [our term] (as well as undergoer and locative) in which such variation is not surprising; indeed we saw a great deal of it in 2.2 and 2.7. D. Payne (1982) presents an analysis of Chickasaw verbal

morphology which defends the basic premise of Heath's analysis, which is that there is a hierarchy of semantic relations underlying the verbal case marking. Munro & Gordon also question that pivot marking is controlled by this hierarchy, but end up concluding that it is, with the qualification that certain idiosyncratic facts about a few verbs must be taken into account (p. 101). See also Heath (1983a).

4   There is a second subject selection hierarchy which applies only in possessive constructions, according to Heath (1977). There is no verb 'have' in Choctaw and Chickasaw, and possessive predicates are derived by means of a construction in which the erstwhile possessor of the 'subject' of an intransitive verb is a verbal argument cross-referenced on the verb by a dative affix. (Chickasaw examples from Munro & Gordon 1982.)

(i)   a.   Jan ipashi'-at   tapa.
           Jan hair-PVT be.cut
           'Jan's hair was cut.'

      b.   Jan-at   ipashi'(-at)   in-tapa.
           Jan-PVT hair(-PVT) 3DAT-be.cut
           'Jan got a haircut.'

(ii) a.   Dan i-holisso-at   wayya'a.
           Dan 3DAT-book-PVT be.located.INAN
           'Dan's book is there.'

      b.   Dan-at   holisso(-at)   i-wayya'a.
           Dan-PVT book(-PVT) 3DAT-be.located.INAN
           'Dan has a book.'

The interesting thing about this construction is that there are now *two* 'subjects' in the clause, both of which may be marked by *at*. In the (b) examples, the possessed NP cannot be marked by $\tilde{a}$:, the oblique marker (cf. (4.14)). Thus there must be a second subject-selection rule in Choctaw and Chickasaw which allows the erstwhile possessor NP in the (b) examples to receive 'subject' marking. There is a clear semantic motivation for this construction; note the meaning difference between the (a) and (b) examples in each pair. Heath (1983a) describes the meaning of this construction in terms of the expression of 'proprietary interest' on the part of the possessor-'subject'.

5   In the possessive constructions described in n. 4 there are two NPs which may be marked by *at*, and in Choctaw either of them may be monitored by the switch-reference system (Heath 1977, 1983a; Davies 1980). In Chickasaw, on the other hand, only the possessor-'subject' may control switch reference (Munro & Gordon 1982).

6   Languages like Choctaw which lack PrPs have not syntacticized the discourse status of NP(s) in their clause-internal grammar. Consequently they employ a variety of other means of discourse organization, e.g. switch reference (see 7.3), and of expressing the discourse status of NPs, e.g. topicalization,

and various morphological means such as topic markers, e.g. *wa* in Japanese, and complex article systems (see McClaran & Herrod 1977). See Van Valin & Foley (1980) for further discussion.

7 Munro & Gordon (1982) criticize this topology and the classification of Choctaw as role dominated, and attempt to show that Chickasaw does have a pragmatic peak (pivot) on the basis of two sets of facts. First, they argue that topicalization and contrastive NPs marked by the article *ako* are 'genuine "pragmatic peaks"' (p. 107) because they are in some way marked as being particularly salient. However, simply being marked as salient in some way does not make an NP a PrP, since, as we have argued in this section, the PrP is a particular syntactic status which is defined in terms of the syntactic constructions in a language and which is correlated with certain types of discourse salience. In 4.2 we show that topics are quite distinct from PrPs, both syntactically and pragmatically, and a morphological marker of contrastiveness which can be attached to any noun in a sentence regardless of its syntactic status has nothing to do with pivots, semantic or pragmatic, in the sense discussed in this section, or with the notion of pragmatic peak as developed in Van Valin (1980b) and Van Valin & Foley (1980). These phenomena in no way demonstrate the existence of a PrP in Choctaw or Chickasaw. Their second argument concerns the possessive construction discussed in nn. 4 and 5. They argue that this is a relation-changing, subject-creating rule which has 'pragmatic effect'; accordingly the *at*-marked NP in these languages must be considered a PrP, and consequently Choctaw and Chickasaw cannot be role dominated. There are several serious flaws in this argument. First, any movement of NPs or other elements in a clause may have 'pragmatic effect', and therefore an alternation does not motivate the existence of a PrP in a language simply because it has 'pragmatic effect'. Rather, the construction must involve the syntacticization of discourse coreference relations and other types of discourse topicality. There is no evidence that this construction is used to meet syntactic constraints on coreference in a way analogous to the English passive or the Dyirbal antipassive. Second, the main motivation for this construction appears to be semantic, rather than pragmatic; in n. 4 it was pointed out that Heath (1983a) argues that it expresses 'proprietory interest' on the part of the possessor-'subject'. It was also noted that the pairs of sentences in (i) and (ii) in n. 4 differ significantly in meaning, and Munro & Gordon comment 'many pairs of sentences related by [the rules relating (ia) to (ib)] show significant changes in meaning' (p. 98). The rule of adding a dative argument to intransitive verbs, which is involved in this construction, is also used to derive transitive from intransitive verbs, e.g. *kaniya* 'go away (somewhere)' becomes 'lose', *ala* 'arrive' becomes 'give birth to' (p. 99). Thus this construction has a primarily semantic motivation, and provides no evidence for a PrP in Choctaw and Chickasaw.

Finally, consider the typological classification of these languages if we accept Munro & Gordon's arguments that the *at* phrases in (i) and (ii) in n. 4 are PrPs. We have emphasized throughout 4.1 that pivots, both semantic and pragmatic, are defined in terms of syntactic constructions. The construction in question involves only *intransitive* verbs; it cannot have a transitive verb. Munro & Gordon state that 'almost any [dative] argument of an originally intransitive verb may become subject if no other argument is overtly marked on that verb' (p. 99). Thus the pivot-defining construction is restricted to unaffixed root or derived intransitive verbs. This means that this construction can never occur in a simple transitive clause like (4.14c), even if the 'subject' is a possessive NP like those in (ia) and (iia) in n. 4. Since this construction defines the purported PrP in the language, sentences like (4.14c) must be considered PrP-less; they have only an SmP as defined by the semantic role hierarchy proposed in Heath (1977) and D. Payne (1982). The only PrP in the language is found in constructions like (i) and (ii) in n. 4. This analysis would mean that Choctaw and Chickasaw are somewhat like Tagalog in having both a PrP and an SmP. When these two languages are compared with the other languages with a PrP discussed in 4.1, it is immediately apparent that Choctaw and Chickasaw are radically different from English and Dyirbal. In these two languages clauses with a PrP accept all types of verbs, regardless of transitivity, and in transitive clauses more than one kind of argument may function as the PrP in order to meet coreference constraints in a number of constructions. The PrP in Choctaw and Chickasaw has no such function, and it is absent in transitive clauses, in which the SmP predominates. Moreover, even in the clauses in which it occurs, the purported PrP does not have any privileged discourse status, because as noted in n. 5 the SmP can still control switch-reference marking in Choctaw. Thus the derived possessor–'subject' in this construction lacks all of the primary properties associated with PrPs in other languages. Hence, even if Munro & Gordon's argument about the possessive construction is accepted in full, it does not change the classification of the language as role dominated, since the SmP is the dominant pivot in the language. As we will see in 4.4, in all other languages which have both an SmP and a PrP, the PrP is unambiguously the dominant pivot in the sense that the majority of syntactic constructions involve it rather than the SmP. Thus Choctaw and Chickasaw must be analyzed as role-dominated languages.

8 Perlmutter (1982) proposes *five* distinct notions of subject within relational grammar and asserts that monostratal theories of grammar, i.e. theories that propose only one level of syntactic analysis such as RRG, cannot in principle express these notions and are therefore empirically inadequate. However, all five of these notions are expressible within RRG (which is not to say that the phenomena which Perlmutter claims motivate these notions would receive the same analysis in RRG).

Perlmutter (1982)	RRG
Final 1	Pivot
Initial 1	Actor
1	either
Acting 1	Actor + Non-core argument
Working 1	Actor + Core argument

These last two kinds of 'subjects' seem rather odd, and Perlmutter presents no strong evidence that notions like 'acting 1' or 'working 1' express any significant generalization and are anything other than an *ad hoc* grouping of relations. Furthermore, he argues against theories positing semantic roles by claiming that they cannot provide unified accounts of, e.g. verb agreement and passivization, because of the wide variety of semantic roles that can be 'subject', 'object', etc. Again this argument has no force with respect to RRG, since, as we noted in 2.1 (see p. 31) the notions of actor and undergoer permit simplified characterizations of such phenomena. Thus, Perlmutter's two main arguments against monostratal syntactic theories do not hold with regard to RRG.

9 Each of the different PTCs has its own distinctive intonation contour; see Prince (1981a) for detailed discussion.

10 See Prince (1981b) for a discussion of given-new information in discourse.

11 There are two other PTCs that we have not discussed: focus movement, e.g. *five dollars this one cost*, and Yiddish movement, e.g. *a sportscar he wants!*; see Prince (1981a) for detailed discussion.

12 In 2.7 we said that *ng* is the case marker for actors, patients, and themes, and *sa* for locatives. Looking at (4.46d), for example, it seems odd to say that *ng* has any real case-marking function, since all three non-focused NPs are marked by it; it in no way signals the semantic function of any of these NPs, nor does it seem to distinguish the NPs from each other. If it is a case marker, then all three of the nouns must be considered to be in the same case. A plausible interpretation of its function in such a sentence is that it simply marks these three NPs as *non-pivot core arguments*. If *ng* marks core arguments, then *sa* must mark peripheral arguments, most of which are some type of locative. Indirect evidence in favor of this analysis comes from Sama, in which core arguments are unmarked and peripheral arguments marked by a variety of prepositions (examples from Walton 1983).

(i) Ø-b'lli   d'nda taumpa ma   onde'.
    UF-buy   woman shoe(s) OBL child
    'The woman bought the shoes for the child.'

(ii) N-b'lli   d'nda taumpa ma   onde'.
    AF-buy   woman shoe(s) OBL child
    'The woman bought some shoes for the child.'

Both *d'nda* 'woman' and *taumpa* 'shoe(s)' are core arguments and unmarked; *taumpa* is in focus in (i), *d'nda* in (ii). *Onde'* 'child' is a peripheral benefactive marked by *ma*. The Sama Ø ~ oblique opposition corresponds to the Tagalog *ng* ~ *sa* opposition (although Tagalog has an explicit focus marker which Sama lacks), and in both languages the content of the opposition is core versus peripheral arguments.

13 Schachter (1977) presents a very similar example as ungrammatical.

(i) *Gusto ni   Juang   suri-in   ng doktor.
    want   PN/A Juan-LIG examine-OFA doctor
    'Juan wants to be examined by the doctor.'

This example differs from (4.54) only in terms of the 'object'-focus affix on the embedded verb; in Cena's example it is *ma-* (see Table 5), while in Schachter's it is *-in*. This sentence is grammatical if the focus pronoun *siya* '3sg' is included in the embedded clause. It appears that the situation in Tagalog regarding equi-NP-deletion is far from clear-cut.

14 These active verbs are all prefixed with *meN-*, which undergoes assimilation with the following stop and, if the following stop is voiceless as in (4.66), undergoes further cluster simplification to the plain nasal. Thus*meN-kirim* becomes *mengirim*.

15 The function of *-kan* in Indonesian is very similar to that of *-an* in Sama; cf. 2.7, n. 22.

16 This is true in other Mayan languages as well, e.g. Tzutujil (Butler & Peck 1980), and Jacaltec (Datz 1980); see 7.4.

17 An important distinction which cross-cuts these categories is that between lexical and transformational (syntactic) passives proposed in Wasow (1977). Many of the backgrounding passives appear to be lexical, especially Choctaw, Chichewa, Spanish, and German (*sein-* passive). On the other hand, all of the foregrounding passives appear to be syntactic. It is not clear whether the backgrounding passives of the Ute and Nanai type are syntactic or lexical, but the Dutch impersonal passive appears to be syntactic.

18 Failure to treat these two functions as independent has led to quite a bit of controversy within relational grammar with respect to the 'true nature' of passivization. Perlmutter & Postal (1977) argue that promotion is primary, with demotion a side effect, whereas Keenan (1975) and Comrie (1977) view demotion as basic and promotion as an optional side effect. The data examined in this section show that these two functions must be treated as independent of each other, and thus arguments regarding the primacy of one or the other will always be inconclusive.

19 It must be noted that Hopper & Thompson's example of a foregrounding passive in Swahili comes from a detective novel, a piece which is an explicit imitation of an English and European literary genre. It is not surprising that this construction would occur in such a text, since they occur in the model which the Swahili writer is attempting to imitate. A demonstration of the generality of this construction would have to involve examples from a traditional narrative, since here influences from European languages could be ruled out or at least minimized. It would not be unreasonable to speculate that foregrounding examples such as (4.82) would be found primarily if not exclusively in European-derived spoken and written genres.

20 Givón (1981) outlines a typological scheme for the analysis of passive constructions cross-linguistically which is similar in many respects to the one developed here. The syntactic properties which he considers to be typologically most significant are the following (p. 168):

(i) The degree to which the new (non-agent) topic of the passive clause assumes the characteristic case-marking properties of the subject/agent of the active clause.

(ii) The degree to which the identity of the subject/agent of the active clause is suppressed in the passive clause.

(iii) The degree to which the passive clause retains semantic and syntactic characteristics of 'activeness' or 'transitivity'.

(iv) The degree to which the various non-subject/agent arguments of the active clause can become the topic/subject of the passive clause.

All of these properties have played a role in the discussion and analysis of passives in this section; (iii) and (iv) are not explicitly represented in Table 6. Givón claims that all passives can be ranked on a single continuum with the Ute at one end and English on the other, but this seems extremely problematic given the great variety of passive constructions, in both structural and functional terms, surveyed in this chapter.

21 All of the languages discussed so far which have PrP also have a foregrounding passive or antipassive construction. However, such constructions are *not* a necessary prerequisite for the existence of a PrP in a language; Barai (Olson 1978, 1981) has no formal passive or antipassive construction and yet definitely has a PrP (see 7.3 for a detailed presentation of the Barai facts). This is an important point, because it relates directly to a major misunderstanding of the role-dominated versus reference-dominated typology discussed in 4.1. Munro & Gordon (1982) misinterpret this typology as follows: 'Thus it seems that the division of the world's languages into reference- and role-dominated types is really a division into languages with and without productive passives' (p. 104). There is no basis for such an interpretation of this typology in Van Valin (1980b) and Van Valin & Foley (1980), the papers on RRG cited by Munro & Gordon. Indeed, Van Valin (1980b:325) explicitly mentions Barai as a language which is reference-dominated but which lacks a foregrounding passive or antipassive construction. In addition, several languages which have productive voice oppositions, e.g. Chinookan and Basque, are discussed and analyzed as role-dominated. We have seen more examples which contradict Munro & Gordon in this chapter, Chichewa and its productive passive being the prime case in point. Thus although the vast majority of reference-dominated languages have foregrounding passive or antipassive constructions, they are not a necessary precondition for the existence of a PrP in a language.

22 By 'explicitly specified' we mean only arguments that occur as variables or constants in the logical structure and not argument positions which are not filled. For example, given the sentence in (i) and the logical structures in (ii), only (iia) could be the logical structure of (i) because of the completeness constraint.

(i) John loaded the truck.

(ii) a. $[DO(John,[\textbf{do}' (John)])] CAUSE [BECOME \textbf{be-at}' (\emptyset, truck)]$

b. $[DO(John,[\textbf{do}' (John)])] CAUSE [BECOME \textbf{be-at}' (boxes, truck)]$

This constraint rules out (iib) as the logical structure for (i) because the argument *boxes* is not expressed in (i).

Chapter 5

1 For detailed arguments against a derivational source of serial-verb constructions from underlying structures consisting of conjoined clauses, see Foley & Olson (in press) and Schachter (1974).

2 It must be emphasized that this is not a claim that languages always order tense and aspect morphemes this way; rather, it is a claim that if there is a definable ordering relation between tense and aspect morphemes with respect to the nucleus, then the ordering will be TNS–ASP–NUCL or NUCL–ASP–TNS. There are, no doubt, languages in which tense and aspect morphemes are not ordered with respect to each other. Suppose, for example, that a language had tense as a prefix and aspect as a suffix, i.e. TNS–NUCL–ASP, as in, e.g. Chinookan languages (Silverstein 1974). In such a case it would be impossible to argue that aspect is closer to the nucleus or that tense is. Such a case would not be a counterexample to our claim, because no ordering relation can be defined. Our claim applies only where there exists a definable ordering relation between tense and aspect morphemes with respect to the nucleus.

3 In this diagram constituents are enclosed in square brackets; operators are in parentheses and capitalized.

4 There appear to be languages in which directional markers function as core rather than nuclear operators. In Jacaltec (Craig 1979b) there is a set of reduced intransitive verbs which serve as directional markers. With intransitive verbs, they specify the direction of the motion of the S with respect to the speaker.

(i) a. X-∅-ah-toj   naj   swi' te'   ñah.
       PST-3ABS-ascend-away.from.speaker CL/he top CL/the house
       'He climbed on top of the house (away from where I stand).'
    b. X-∅-ah-tij   ix   y-ul   ha'
       PST-3ABS-ascend-toward.speaker CL/she 3ERG-in CL/the
       ha'.
       water
       'She came out of the water (here, where I stand).'

Transitive verbs take two directional markers, the first expressing the direction of the motion of the undergoer, the second the orientation of that motion with respect to the actor.

(ii) a. Xc-in   ha-ten-ic-toj   y-ul   carro.
        PST-1sgABS 2sgERG-move-in-away.from.actor 3ERG-in truck
        'You pushed me into the truck.'

     b. Xc-in   ha-ten-il-tij   y-ul   carro.
        PST-1sgABS 2sgERG-move-out-toward.actor 3ERG-in truck
        'You pulled me out of the truck.'

Because these directionals specify the direction of motion and orientation of core arguments, they must be considered core operators.

5 We are grateful to Johanna Nichols for bringing Tesnière's claim to our attention.

6 Note that this sentence cannot be ruled out in terms of the much-discussed inability of modals to occur after *to*, since there is no modal in the sentence, unlike (5.96a–b).

7 This utterance was recorded in Houston, Texas, in December 1981.

Chapter 6

1 The fourth possibility, + embedded − dependent, does not occur, as there are no constructions in which one clause is embedded in another but is totally independent of it in terms of constituents and operators. Such a construction would seem to be inherently inconsistent and hence impossible.

2 We are grateful to Charles Fillmore for bringing this example to our attention.

3 Olson (1981:312) proposes a hierarchy identical to this one ('The Dependency Hierarchy') on the basis of Barai clause-linkage facts alone. Nuclear subordination has been omitted because of its non-occurrence.

4 A syntactic bondedness hierarchy for NPs has been proposed in Foley (1980).

(i) Article + Noun   Strongest
    Deictic + Noun
    Interrogatives + Noun
    Quantifiers/indefinites + Noun
    Adjectives + Noun
    Participle + Noun
    Relative clause + Noun
    Clause + Noun   Weakest

This hierarchy captures the variable strength of the syntactic link between nouns and their adjuncts. 'Clause + Noun' at the bottom includes both complex NPs such as (ii) and the Yimas construction in (iii) which is widely used among Papuan languages for direct discourse and cognition verb complements.

(ii)   Max refuses to believe the claim that his wife saw a UFO.

(iii) a. Pia-mpu-kra-i   'ipa patn   wu-k'.
       words-3plA-1plU-say 1pl betelnut get-IRR
       'They said to us, "we want to get betelnut".'

     b. Pia-ka-kasapal   patn   na-mpu-w-t.
       words-1sgA-forget betelnut 3sgU-3plA-get-PERF
       'I forgot that they got betelnut.'

The noun in the complex NP in the Yimas examples is obligatorily incorporated into the verbal complex.

5 In discussing the Quechua data we have used the name of the constructions rather than clause–linkage categories, because there are not enough data in the source cited to allow determination of the relevant categories by means of the tests presented in 6.2.

6 The nature of the temporal prefixes on Jacaltec verbs is a controversial question. Day (1973) analyzes $x(c)$- and ch-/$\ddot{x}$- as signaling past and non-past tense, respectively, whereas Craig (1977) labels them completive and non-completive aspect, respectively. The distinction between tense and aspect is not significant for theories such as transformational grammar and its offshoots, but it is of fundamental importance for the RRG theories of the layered structure of the clause and clause linkage. Consequently, it is necessary to establish just exactly what these prefixes express. The characterizations which Craig gives for these two 'aspects' suggest strongly that they are in fact tenses. With respect to the 'completive aspect', she says that it 'is used for actions that took place in the past, and as the name indicates, are completed' (1977:59). Whether or not an action is completed is independent of the relationship of the time of the action to the time of the speech event (see 5.3), as illustrated by the English present, past, and future perfect tense–aspect combinations. Since Craig explicitly links this form to past events, we must assume that there is at least some past-tense component to its meaning. Conclusive proof that it is in fact a past tense rather than any kind of completive aspect category comes from the San Marcos dialect of Jacaltec which 'further distinguishes in the completive aspect between recent past and remote past. Thus, recent past is indicated by *ma*- as in: *ma* xa slotij "had already just eaten", *ma* hin ha engañar "you have just fooled me." Remote past is indicated by *x*- as in *x*initoj "brought", *x*to "went"' (Craig 1978:195). This distinction between recent and remote past has solely to do with the temporal relationship between the action and the speech event and not with the internal temporal nature of the action. Hence these are tense and not aspect categories, and accordingly $x(c)$- in Jacaltec must be considered a tense marker. The other category signaled by ch-/$\ddot{x}$- is thoroughly compatible with a non-past tense interpretation, since it encompasses the following range of meanings: present, narrative present, habitual present, present perfect and future (Craig 1977:60–2). As we will see in this section, there is overwhelming syntactic evidence in support of the analysis of these prefixes as tense rather than aspect markers.

7 For detailed discussion, see Craig (1977), Chapter 9.

8 For detailed discussion, see Craig (1977), Chapter 5.

9 The negative morpheme in Jacaltec has two forms, *mat* with untensed verbs (i.e. stative verbs) and *mach* with finite verbs.

10 We are concerned only with the deletion of the 'subject' [S,A] noun classifiers, as it is much more restricted that the deletion of classifiers with other arguments.

11 The 'infinitive' marker in these examples is the future–irrealis suffix. Day (1973:38) reports that bilingual Jacaltec speakers consider verb forms with it to be the equivalent of Spanish infinitives. It is clear from examples like

(6.77a,b) that the suffix has neither future nor irrealis meaning in this construction.

12 These structures are given in terms of the layered structure of the clause. Since English is a configurational language, phrase-structure categories would be added in a more detailed analysis. The relation between clause layers and phrase structure categories is a complex and indirect one, as there are no constituent units which correspond to the various layers, aside from V = nucleus. A full explication of this relationship is beyond the scope of this brief discussion.

13 *Have* in Core$_2$ is an aspectual operator and technically not a constituent of the nucleus (see 5.3). However, for simplicity of presentation we will treat it as part of the nucleus, analogous to the status of tense-bearing *be* (which is also an operator) in Core$_1$.

14 Although we could put inner-periphery brackets in every example we will do so only where an inner-peripheral argument actually appears, in order to keep the labeled bracketing as simple and perspicuous as possible. The existence of an inner peripheral argument (the passive actor) in these constructions does not undermine their status as core junctures, since it is a core argument which is shared by the two clauses, and they share all higher-level operators.

15 Thus we treat *Helen* as the syntactic object of *believe, contra* Chomsky (1973, 1980a, 1981a,b,c). See 6.2.1 and references cited there for arguments supporting this analysis.

Chapter 7

1 See Heath (1983b) for a discussion of Nunggubuyu (Australia); see 4.4, example (4.93) for a discussion of Chichewa (Bantu); see Wise (1971) for a detailed analysis of Nomatsiguenga (Arawakan; Peru); see 4.1, examples (4.19)–(4.20) for examples from Archi, a Daghestani language of the Caucasus (Kibrik 1979a,b).

2 This phenomenon is found in more familiar languages such as German, where the definite article may be substituted for a personal pronoun in order to specify that it is the last mentioned element in the particular gender class which is referred to (example from Charles Fillmore, personal communication).

(i) Er   hielt in der   behandshuhten Rechten
   3sg-NOM held in the-F/DAT gloved   right(hand)
   einen   Revolver, und trug   inder   Linken   einen
   a-M/ACC revolver   and carried in the-F/DAT left(hand) a-M/ACC
   Koffer. Den   stellte er auf den   Tresor.
   suitcase the-M/ACC placed 3sg on the-M/ACC safe
   'He held in his gloved right hand a revolver and carried in his left hand a suitcase. He placed it [the suitcase] on the safe.'

Den unambiguously refers to the last mentioned masculine noun, *Koffer* 'suitcase'. If *ihn* '3sgM/ACC' had occurred in its place, then the second sentence would be ambiguous, since both *Revolver* and *Koffer* are masculine singular.

3 In the text verbs are glossed with respect to their membership in one of the four Cree verb classes:

(1) Animate intransitive (A I): single argument must be animate.
(2) Inanimate intransitive (I I): single argument must be inanimate.
(3) Transitive animate (T A): undergoer must be animate.
(4) Transitive inanimate (T I): undergoer must be inanimate.

The animacy of nouns will be indicated as follows: NA 'noun animate' and NI 'noun inanimate'. The punctuation is that of Wolfart & Carroll (1981).

4 'Transitivity' in the above classification is based on the morphological inflectional possibilities rather than the semantics of the verb. There are formally animate intransitive verbs which have two arguments; this verb seems to be one such verb. See Wolfart (1973:39).

5 Silverstein (1976b) calls the Dyirbal system 'switch reference' because of its functional similarity to switch-reference systems of the type discussed in 7.3. We agree with Silverstein that the two kinds of reference-maintenance systems carry out the same function, but we differentiate them in terms of the formal means used to achieve their common communicative end.

6 There is another way to modify this sentence to yield this meaning which will be discussed below.

7 In 4.5 we discussed the foregrounding antipassive in Jacaltec (see (4.114)-(4.115)), which is involved in the clefting, questioning, and relativizing of actors. Since these constructions have definite discourse-pragmatic functions, their S/U pivot is a PrP. However, in narrative discourse the pivot for cross-clause coreference is S/A (Datz 1980, Van Valin 1981a), which is also a PrP. Thus Jacaltec appears to have two PrPs which are defined by two different sets of discourse-motivated constructions. This does not mean, however, that there are two PrPs in every clause in Jacaltec, because clefts, WH-questions, and relative clauses would not be part of a series of same PrP clauses of the type exemplified in (7.52).

8 This is true also in Jacaltec and Dyirbal, and it may well be a significant generalization that languages which use a switch-function system for pivot–pivot coreference typically also have a gender system to handle both pivot–pivot non-coreference and coreference among non-pivot arguments.

9 We are grateful to Michael Silverstein for emphasizing this point to us.

10 We have used Sama rather than Tagalog examples because the relationship between focus type and verb aspect (in Dowty's sense) is much more perspicuous. Tagalog has extensive aspectual inflection which Sama lacks, in addition to focus marking, and since Tagalog verbs carry both inherent and inflectional aspect, it is much more difficult to isolate the relationship between focus and inherent aspect.

11 Hopper (1979a) and Hopper & Thompson (1980) use the term 'foreground'

to refer to temporal structure, and 'background' to durational/descriptive structure. Since 'foregrounding' and 'backgrounding' were used in Chapter 4 in a different sense, we will not use these terms in this context in order to avoid confusion.

12 This finding is not surprising, since perfective aspect codes completed actions and events and imperfective incomplete events and actions, and the former fit more naturally into the temporal structure of narrative, the latter into durational/descriptive structure.

References

ABBREVIATIONS

BLS   Proceedings of the n Annual Meeting of the Berkeley Linguistics Society.
      Berkeley: University of California.
CLS   Papers from the n Regional Meeting of the Chicago Linguistic Society.
      Chicago: University of Chicago.
IJAL International Journal of American Linguistics
Lg   Language
LI   Linguistic Inquiry
PL   Pacific Linguistics. Canberra: Linguistic Circle of Canberra.
SAL   Studies in African Linguistics
SL   Studies in Language

Aissen, Judith 1974. Verb raising. LI 5:325–66.

Anderson, Stephen. 1971. On the role of deep structure in semantic interpretation. Foundations of Language 6:197–219.

Andrews, Avery. In press. The major functions of the noun phrase. T. Shopen, ed. In press. Syntactic Typology and Linguistic Description, vol. 1. Cambridge: Cambridge University Press.

Austin, J. L. 1962. How to do Things with Words. Cambridge, Mass.: Harvard University Press.

Austin, Peter. 1981. Switch-reference in Australia. Lg 57:309–34.

Bach, Emmon. 1977. Review of Postal 1974. Lg 53:621–54.

Bamgbose, A. 1974. On serial verbs and verbal status. Journal of West African Languages 9:17–48.

Bauman, James & Joel Sherzer, eds. 1974. Explorations in the Ethnography of Speaking. Cambridge: Cambridge University Press.

Bell, Sarah. 1976. Cebuano subjects in two frameworks. MIT dissertation.

Bellert, Irene. 1977. On semantic and distributional properties of sentential adverbs. LI 8:337–50.

Berlin, Brent & Paul Kay. 1969. Basic Color Terms. Berkeley: University of California Press.

Bickerton, Derek. 1974. Creolization, linguistic universals, natural semantax, and the brain. University of Hawaii Working Papers in Linguistics 6(3): 124–41.

——. 1981. Roots of Language. Ann Arbor: Karoma.

Bills, Garland, Bernardo Vallejo C. & Rudolph Troike. 1969. An Introduction to

Spoken Bolivian Quechua. Austin: University of Texas Press.

Bloomfield, Leonard. 1917. *Tagalog Texts with Grammatical Analysis*. Urbana: University of Illinois.

——. 1926. A set of postulates for the science of language. *Lg* 2:153–64.

——. 1930. *Sacred Stories of the Sweet Grass Cree*. Bulletin 60, Anthropological series 11. Ottawa: National Museum of Canada.

——. 1933. *Language*. New York: Henry Holt.

——. 1936. Language or ideas? *Lg* 12:89–95.

——. 1962. *The Menomini Language*. New Haven: Yale University Press.

Boas, Franz. 1911. Introduction. *Handbook of American Indian Languages*, pp. 1–83. Bureau of American Ethnology Bulletin 40, pt 1. Washington, D.C.

Boas, Franz & Ella Deloria. 1939. *Dakota Grammar*. Memoirs of the National Academy of Sciences. vol. 23, no. 2.

Brettschneider, G. 1979. Typological characteristics of Basque. Plank, ed., pp. 371–84.

Bromley, H. Myron. 1981. *A Grammar of Lower Grand Valley Dani*. PL C-63.

Brown, Penelope & Stephen Levinson. 1978. Universals of language usage: politeness phenomena. E. Goody, ed., *Questions and Politeness*, pp. 56–289. Cambridge: Cambridge University Press.

Bruce, L. 1979. A grammar of Alamblak (Papua New Guinea). Australian National University dissertation.

Buck, Carl Darling. 1933. *Comparative Grammar of Greek and Latin*. Chicago: University of Chicago Press.

Buechel, Eugene. 1970. *Lakota–English Dictionary*. Pine Ridge, SD: Red Cloud Indian School.

Bull, W. E. 1960. *Time, Tense and the Verb: a Study in Theoretical and Applied Linguistics with Special Reference to Spanish*. University of California publications in linguistics 19. Berkeley.

Butler, James & Charles Peck. 1980. The uses of passive, antipassive, and absolutive verbs in Tzutujil of San Pedro la Laguna. *Journal of Mayan Linguistics* 2(1):40–52.

Bybee, Joan. 1983. Diagrammatic iconicity in stem-inflection relations. Paper presented at the Conference on Iconicity, Stanford University.

Catford, Ian. 1975. Ergativity in Caucasian languages. *North Eastern Linguistic Society Papers* 6:37–48.

Cena, R. 1979. Patient primacy in Tagalog. Unpublished ms., University of Hawaii.

Chafe, Wallace. 1972. *Meaning and the Structure of Language*. Chicago: University of Chicago Press.

——. 1976. Givenness, contrastiveness, definiteness, subjects, topics, and point of view. Li, ed., pp. 25–55.

Chomsky, Noam. 1957. *Syntactic Structures*. The Hague: Mouton.

——. 1965. *Aspects of the Theory of Syntax*. Cambridge, Mass. MIT Press.

——. 1973. Conditions on transformations. Chomsky 1977, pp. 81–160.

——. 1975. *Reflections on Language*. New York: Pantheon.

——. 1976. On the nature of language. S. Harnad et al., eds., *Origins and Evolution of Language and Speech*, 46–57. Annals of the New York Academy of Sciences v. 280.

——. 1977. *Essays on Form and Interpretation*. New York: North-Holland.

——. 1980a. On binding. *LI* 11:1–46.

——. 1980b. *Rules and Representations* New York: Columbia University Press.

——. 1981a. On the representation of form and function. *The Linguistic Review* 1:3–40.

——. 1981b. Principles and parameters in syntactic theory. Hornstein & Lightfoot, eds., 32–75.

——. 1981c. *Lectures on Government and Binding*. Dordrecht: Foris.

——. 1981d. Markedness and core grammar. A. Belletti *et al.*, eds., *Theory of Markedness in Generative Grammar*, 123–46. Pisa: Scuola Normale Superiore.

Clark, M. 1978. *Coverbs and Case in Vietnamese*. *PL* B-48.

Cole, Peter. 1983. The grammatical role of the causee in universal grammar. *IJAL* 49:115–33.

Cole, Peter & Gabriella Hermon. 1981. Subjecthood and islandhood: evidence from Quechua. *LI* 12:1–30.

Cole, Peter & Jerry Morgan, eds. 1975. *Speech Acts* (Syntax & semantics 3). New York: Academic Press.

Cole, Peter, & Jerrold Sadock, eds. 1977. *Grammatical Relations*. (Syntax & semantics 8). New York: Academic Press.

Comrie, Bernard. 1976a. *Aspect*. Cambridge: Cambridge University Press.

——. 1976b. The syntax of causative constructions: cross-language similarities and divergences. Shibatani, ed., pp. 261–312.

——. 1977. In defense of spontaneous demotion: the impersonal passive. Cole & Sadock, eds., pp. 47–58.

——. 1978. Ergativity. W. Lehmann, ed., *Syntactic Typology*, pp. 329–94. Austin: Texas Press.

——. 1981. *Language Universals and Linguistic Typology*. Chicago: University of Chicago Press.

Craig, Colette. 1977. *The Structure of Jacaltec*. Austin: Texas Press.

——. 1978. The rabbit and the coyote. W. Bright, ed., *Coyote Stories*, pp. 184–97. IJAL Native American Text Series Monographs 1. Chicago: University of Chicago Press.

——. 1979a. The antipassive and Jacaltec. L. Martin, ed., *Papers in Mayan Linguistics 2*, pp. 139–64. Columbia, Mo: Lucas Bros. Publishers.

——. 1979b. Jacaltec: field work in Guatemala. T. Shopen, ed., *Languages and Their Speakers*, pp. 3–57. Cambridge. Mass.: Winthrop.

Cresswell, M. 1978. Prepositions and points of view. *Linguistics and Philosophy* 2:1–41.

Crowley, Terry. 1978. *The Middle Clarence Dialects of Bandjalang*. Canberra: Australian Institute of Aboriginal Studies.

Datz, Margaret. 1980. Jacaltec syntactic structures and the demands of discourse. Univ. of Colorado dissertation.

Davies, W. 1980. Choctaw subjects and multiple levels of syntax. T. Hoekstra *et al.*, eds., *Perspectives on Functional Grammar*, pp. 235–71. Dordrecht: Foris.

Day, Christopher. 1973. *The Jacaltec Language*. Bloomington: Indiana University Press.

Dayley, Jon. 1981. Voice and ergativity in Mayan languages. *Journal of Mayan Linguistics* 2(2):3–82.

De Guzman, V. 1983. Ergative analysis for Philippine languages. Paper presented at the Third Eastern Conference on Austronesian Languages, Ohio University.

Dench, Alan. 1981. Passive and switch reference in Martuthunira. Paper presented at the Australian Linguistic Society annual meeting.

Dik, Simon. 1978. *Functional Grammar*. Amsterdam: North-Holland.

Dixon, R. M. W. 1972. *The Dyirbal Language of North Queensland*. Cambridge: Cambridge University Press.

——. 1977. *A Grammar of Yidiɲ*. Cambridge: Cambridge University Press.

——. 1979a. Ergativity. *Lg* 55:59–138.

——. 1979b. Corrections and comments concerning Heath's 'Is Dyirbal ergative?' *Linguistics* 17:1003–15.

Dowty, David. 1979. *Word Meaning and Montague Grammar*. Dordrecht: Reidel.

Dowty, David, Robert Wall, & Stanley Peters. 1981. *Introduction to Montague Semantics*. Dordrecht: Reidel.

Duranti, Alessandro. 1981. The *fono*: a Samoan speech event. University of Southern California dissertation.

Durie, Mark. 1981. Verbal agreement in Acehnese. Paper presented at the Australian Linguistic Society annual meeting.

Emonds, Joseph. 1976. *A Transformational Approach to English Syntax*. New York: Academic Press.

Fillmore, Charles. 1968. The case for case. E. Bach & R. Harms, eds., *Universals in Linguistic Theory*, pp. 1–88. New York: Holt, Rinehart & Winston.

——. 1971. Santa Cruz lectures on deixis. Indiana University Linguistics Club. Bloomington, Indiana.

——. 1977. The case for case reopened. Cole & Sadock, eds., pp. 59–81.

Firbas, Jan. 1966. Non-thematic subjects in contemporary English. *Travaux linguistiques de Prague* 2:239–56.

Foley, William A. 1976. Comparative syntax in Austronesian. University of California, Berkeley dissertation.

——. 1980a. Functional grammar and cultural anthropology. *Canberra Anthropology* 3:67–85.

——. 1980b. Toward a universal typology of the noun phrase. *SL* 4:171–200.

Foley, William A. & Michael L. Olson. In press. Clausehood and verb serialization. To appear in Nichols & Woodbury, eds.

Foley, William A. & Robert D. Van Valin, Jr. 1977. On the viability of the notion of 'subject' in universal grammar. *BLS* 3:293–320.

——. In press. Information packaging in the clause. T. Shopen, ed., *Syntactic Typology and Linguistic Description*, vol. 1, in press. Cambridge: Cambridge University Press.

Foreman, V. 1974. *A Grammar of Yessan–Mayo*. Summer Institute of Linguistics: Language data, Asian–Pacific series 4. Santa Ana, California.

Franklin, Karl. 1971. *A Grammar of Kewa, New Guinea*. *PL* C-16.

Friedrich, Paul. 1974. *On Aspect Theory and Homeric Aspect*. *IJAL* memoir 28. Chicago: University of Chicago Press.

Gazdar, G., G. Pullum, & I. Sag. 1982. Auxiliaries and related phenomena in a restrictive theory of grammar. *Lg* 58:591–638.

Gerdts, Donna. 1983. Antipassives and causatives in Ilokano: evidence for an ergative analysis. Paper presented at the Third Eastern Conference on Austronesian languages, Ohio University.

Givón, Talmy, ed. 1979. *Discourse and Syntax* (Syntax & semantics 12). New York: Academic Press.

——. 1979. *On Understanding Grammar*. New York: Academic Press.

——. 1980. The binding hierarchy and the typology of complements. *SL* 4:333–77.

——. 1981. Typology and functional domains. *SL* 5:163–93.

Grice, H. P. 1975. Logic and conversation. Cole & Morgan, eds., pp. 41–58.

Gruber, Jeffrey. 1965. Studies in lexical relations. MIT. Dissertation.

Gumperz, John. 1971. *Language in Social Groups*. Stanford: Stanford University Press.

——. 1982. *Discourse Strategies*. Cambridge: Cambridge University Press.

Gumperz, John, & Dell Hymes, eds. 1972. *Directions in Sociolinguistics*. New York: Holt, Rinehart & Winston.

Haas, Mary. 1940. *Tunica. Handbook of American Indian Languages*, vol. 4. New York: J. J. Augustin.

Hale, Kenneth. 1973. Person marking in Walbiri. S. Anderson & P. Kiparsky, eds., *A Festschrift for Morris Halle*, pp. 308–44. New York: Holt, Rinehart & Winston.

——. 1979. On the position of Walbiri in a typology of the base. Unpublished ms., MIT. Cambridge, Mass.

Hall, Barbara. 1965. Subject and object in modern English. MIT dissertation.

Halliday, M. A. K. 1967. Notes on transitivity and theme in English. *Journal of Linguistics* 3:37–81, 199–244.

——. 1973. *Explorations in the Functions of Language*. New York: Elsevier.

——. 1976. Functions and universals of language. G. Kress, ed., *Halliday: System and Function in Language*, pp. 26–31. Oxford: Oxford University Press.

——. in press. *A Short Introduction to Functional Grammar*. London: Edward Arnold.

Harbert, Wayne. 1977. Clause union and German accusative plus infinitive constructions. Cole & Sadock, eds., pp. 121–49.

Haviland, John. 1979. Guugu Yimidhirr. R. M. W. Dixon & B. Blake, eds., *Handbook of Australian Languages*, vol. 1, pp. 27–180. Canberra: Australian National University Press.

——. 1982. *Sk'op sotz'leb: El Tzotzil de San Lorenzo Zinacantan*. Mexico City: Centro de Estudios Mayas.

Heath, Jeffrey. 1975. Some functional relationships in grammar. *Lg* 51:89–104.

——. 1977. Choctaw cases. *BLS* 3:204–13.

——. 1978. Functional universals. *BLS* 4:86–95.

——. 1979. Is Dyirbal ergative? *Linguistics* 17:401–63.

——. 1983a. Choctaw/Chickasaw morphosyntax: review of a pseudocontroversy. Unpublished ms., Harvard University.

——. 1983b. Reference tracking in Nunggubuyu. J. Haiman & P. Munro, eds., *Switch-Reference and Universal Grammar*. pp. 129–49. Amsterdam: John Benjamins.

Hetzron, Robert. 1976. On the Hungarian causative verb and its syntax. Shibatani, ed., pp. 371–98.

Hewer, P. 1976. A lexical approach to clause series in Kasem. *Linguistics* 171:19–34.

Hinds, John, ed. 1978. *Anaphora in Discourse* (Current inquiry into language and linguistics 22). Edmonton, Al: Linguistic Research Inc.

——. 1978. Anaphora in Japanese conversation. Hinds, ed., pp. 139–79.

Hofmann, T. 1976. Past tense replacements and the modal system. J. McCawley, ed., *Notes from the Linguistic Underground* (Syntax & semantics 7), pp. 85–100. New York: Academic Press.

Hoijer, Harry. 1949. Tonkawa syntactic suffixes and anaphoric particles. *Southwestern Journal of Anthropology* 5:37–55.

Hope, Edward. 1974. *The Deep Syntax of Lisu Sentences*. *PL* B-34.

Hopper, Paul. 1979a. Aspect and forgrounding in discourse. Givón, ed., pp. 312–41.

——. 1979b. Some observations on the typology of focus and aspect in narrative language. *SL* 3:37–64.

——, ed. 1982. *Tense-Aspect: Between Semantics and Pragmatics*. Amsterdam: John Benjamins.

Hopper, Paul & Sandra A. Thompson. 1980. Transitivity in grammar and discourse. *Lg* 56:251–99.

——. 1982. The 'passive' in universal grammar: a discourse perspective. Paper presented at the Conference on Language Universals and Second Language Acquisition, University of Southern California.

Hornstein, Norbert & David Lightfoot, eds. 1981. *Explanation in Linguistics*. London: Longman.

——. 1981. Introduction. Hornstein & Lightfoot, eds., pp. 9–13.

Huang, C. T. James. 1981. Move WH in a language without WH movement. *The Linguistic Review* 1:369–416.

Hudson, Joyce. 1976. *The Core of Walmatjari Grammar*. Canberra: Australian Institute of Aboriginal Studies.

Hyman, Larry & Karl Zimmer. 1976. Embedded topic in French. Li, ed., pp. 189–211.

Hymes, Dell. 1971. On communicative competence. J. Pride & J. Holmes, eds., *Sociolinguistics*, pp. 269–93. Harmondsworth: Penguin.

——. 1974. *Foundations in Sociolinguistics*. Philadelphia: University of Pennsylvania Press.

Jackendoff, Ray. 1972. *Semantic Interpretation in Generative Grammar.* Cambridge, Mass.: MIT Press.

——. 1976. Toward an explanatory semantic representation. *LI* 7:89–150.

——. 1977. *X-bar Syntax.* Cambridge, Mass.: MIT Press.

Jacobsen, William H., Jr. 1967. Switch-reference in Hokan-Coahuiltecan. D. Hymes & W. Bittle, eds., *Studies in Southwestern Ethnolinguistics*, pp. 238–63. The Hague: Mouton.

Jakobson, Roman. 1971. Shifters, verbal categories, and the Russian verb. R. Jakobson, *Selected Writings*, vol. 2, pp. 130–47. The Hague: Mouton.

Jesperson, Otto. 1924. *The Philosophy of Grammar.* New York: Norton.

Johnson, David. 1977. On relational constraints on grammars. Cole & Sadock, eds., pp. 151–78.

Kac, Michael. 1980. Corepresentational grammar. Moravcsik & Wirth, eds., pp. 97–116.

Keenan, Edward. 1975. Some universals of passive in relational grammar. *CLS* 11:340–52.

——. 1976a. Remarkable subjects in Malagasy. Li, ed., pp. 247–301.

——. 1976b. Towards a universal definition of 'subject'. Li, ed., pp. 303–333.

Keenan, Edward & Bernard Comrie. 1977. Noun phrase accessibility and universal grammar. *LI* 8:63–99.

Keenan, Elinor & Bambi Schieffelin. 1976. Foregrounding referents: a reconsideration of left-dislocation in discourse. *BLS* 2:240–57.

Kibrik, A. E. 1979a. Canonical ergativity and Daghestan languages. Plank, ed., pp. 61–78.

——. 1979b. *Materialy k tipologii èrgativnosti.* IRJa AN SSSR, Problemnaja gruppa po èksperimental'noj i prikladnoj lingvistiki, Predvaritel'nye publikacii, pp. 126–7, Moscow: IRJa AN SSSR.

Kimenyi, A. 1980. *A Relational Grammar of Kinyarwanda.* University of California publications in linguistics 91. Berkeley.

Kirsner, Robert. 1976. On the subjectless 'pseudo-passive' in standard Dutch and the semantics of background agents. Li, ed., pp. 385–415.

Klein, H. G. 1974. *Tempus, Aspekt, Aktionsart.* Tübingen: Niemeyer.

Kuno, Susumu. 1973. *The Structure of the Japanese Language.* Cambridge, Mass.: MIT Press.

——. 1976. Subject, theme, and the speaker's empathy–a reexamination of relativization phenomena. Li, ed., pp. 417–44.

——. 1980. Functional syntax. Moravcsik & Wirth, eds., pp. 117–35.

Kuryłowicz, Jerzy. 1946. Ergativnost' i stadial'nost' v jazyke. *Izv. Akad. Nauk SSSR* 5:387–93.

——. 1964. *The Inflectional Categories of Indo-European.* Heidelberg: Winter.

Labov, William. 1972. *Sociolinguistic Patterns.* Philadelphia: University of Pennsylvania Press.

Larsen, Thomas & William Norman. 1979. Correlates of ergativity in Mayan grammar. Plank, ed., pp. 347–70.

Levinsohn, Stephen. 1978. Participant reference in Inga narrative discourse. Hinds, ed., pp. 68–135.

Li, Charles, ed. 1976. *Subject and Topic*. New York: Academic Press.

Li, Charles & Sandra A. Thompson. 1976. Subject and topic: a new typology of language. Li, ed., pp. 457–89.

——. 1979. Third-person pronouns and zero anaphora in Chinese discourse. Givón, ed., pp. 311–35.

Lightfoot, David. 1980. Trace theory and explanation. Moravcsik & Wirth, eds., pp. 137–66.

Longacre, Robert. 1972. *Hierarchy and Universality of Discourse Constituents in New Guinea Languages*. Washington, DC: Georgetown University Press.

Lord, Carol. 1973. Serial verbs in translation. *SAL* 4:269–96.

——. 1974. Causative constructions in Yoruba. *SAL* supplement 5: 195–206.

——. 1975. Igbo verb compounds and the lexicon. *SAL* 6:23–48.

Lyons, John. 1968. *Introduction to Theoretical Linguistics*. Cambridge: Cambridge University Press.

——. 1977. *Semantics*. Cambridge: Cambridge University Press.

Macken, Marlys & Charles Ferguson. In press. Cognitive aspects of phonological development: models, evidence, and issues. K. Nelson, ed., in press. *Children's Language*, vol. 4. New York: Gardner Press.

Macnamara, John. 1972. Cognitive basis of language learning in infants. *Psychological Review* 79:1–13.

Martinet, Andre. 1964. *Elements of General Linguistics*. Chicago: University of Chicago Press.

Matisoff, James. 1972. *The Grammar of Lahu*. University of California publications in linguistics 75. Berkeley.

McCawley, James. 1971. Tense and time reference in English. C. Fillmore & T. Langendoen, eds., *Studies in Linguistic Semantics*, pp. 97–113. New York: Holt, Rinehart & Winston.

——. 1981. Notes on the English present perfect. *Australian Journal of Linguistics* 1:81–90.

McClaran, Marlys & Gene Herrod. 1977. Choctaw 'articles' in discourse. *BLS* 3:214–22.

McElhanon, K. 1973. *Towards a Typology of the Finisterre–Huon Languages*. *PL* B-22.

McKay, K. L. 1977. *Greek Grammar for Students*. Canberra: Australian National University, Department of Classics.

McLendon, Sally. 1978. Ergativity, case, and transitivity in Eastern Pomo. *IJAL* 44:1–9.

Merlan, Francesca. In press. Split-intransitivity: functional oppositions in intransitive inflection. To appear in Nichols & Woodbury, eds.

Montague, Richard. 1974. The proper treatment of quantification in ordinary English. J. Hintikka *et al.*, eds., *Approaches to Natural Language*. Dordrecht: Reidel.

Moravcsik, Edith & Jessica Wirth, eds. 1980. *Current Approaches to Syntax* (Syntax & semantics 13). New York: Academic Press.

Munro, P., ed. 1980. *Studies of Switch-Reference*. UCLA Papers in syntax 8. Los Angeles.

Munro, P. & L. Gordon. 1982. Syntactic relations in western Muskogean. *Lg* 58:81–115.

Nichols, Johanna. 1979a. The meeting of East and West: confrontation and convergence in contemporary linguistics. *BLS* 5:261–76.

——. 1979b. Syntax and pragmatics in Manchu–Tungus languages. P. Clyne, *et al.*, eds., *The Elements: a Parasession on Linguistic Units and Levels*, pp. 420–8. Chicago: CLS.

——. 1980. Control and ergativity in Chechen. *CLS* 16:259–68.

Nichols, Johanna & Anthony Woodbury, eds. In press. *Grammar Inside and Outside the Clause*. Cambridge: Cambridge University Press.

Nicklas, T. Dale. 1974. The elements of Choctaw. University of Michigan dissertation.

Noonan, Michael & Edith Bavin-Woock. 1978. The passive analog in Lango. *BLS* 4:128–39.

——. 1981. Parataxis in Lango. *SAL* 12:45–70.

Olson, Michael L. 1978. Switch-reference in Barai. *BLS* 4:140–57.

——. 1981. Barai clause junctures: toward a functional theory of interclausal relations. Australian National University dissertation.

Osborne, C. R. 1974. *The Tiwi Language*. Canberra: Australian Institute of Aboriginal Studies.

Parke, Aubrey. 1981. Some aspects of Fijian grammar. Australian National University M.A. thesis.

Payne, Doris. 1980. Switch-reference in Chickasaw. Munro, ed., pp. 89–118.

——. 1982. Chickasaw agreement morphology: a functional explanation. P. Hopper & S. A. Thompson, eds., *Studies in Transitivity* (Syntax & semantics 15), pp. 351–78. New York: Academic Press.

Payne, Thomas. 1980. Who's kissing who? The fourth person in Yup'ik Eskimo. Munro, ed., pp. 65–88.

——. 1982. Role and reference related subject properties and ergativity in Yup'ik Eskimo and Tagalog. *SL* 6:75–106.

Perlmutter, David. 1971. *Deep and Surface Structure Constraints in Syntax*. New York: Holt, Rinehart & Winston.

——. 1980. Relational grammar. Moravcsik & Wirth, eds., pp. 195–229.

——. 1982. Syntactic representation, syntactic levels, and the notion of subject. P. Jacobson & G. Pullum, eds., *The Nature of Syntactic Representation*, pp. 283–340. Dordrecht: Reidel.

Perlmutter, David & Paul Postal. 1977. Toward a universal characterization of passivization. *BLS* 3:394–417.

Pike, Kenneth, 1967. Grammar as wave. *Georgetown University Monographs on Language and Linguistics* 20:1–14. Washington, DC: Georgetown University Press.

Pike, Kenneth L. & Evelyn G. Pike. 1982. *Grammatical Analysis* (2nd edn). Arlington, Texas: Summer Institute of Linguistics.

Plank, Frans, ed. 1979. *Ergativity: Toward a Theory of Grammatical Relations*. London: Academic Press.

Polanyi-Bowditch, Livia. 1976. Why the whats are when: mutually contextualizing realms of narrative. *BLS* 2:58–77.

Postal, Paul. 1974. *On Raising*. Cambridge, Mass. MIT Press.

Prince, Ellen. 1981a. Topicalization, focus-movement, and Yiddish-movement: a pragmatic differentiation. *BLS* 7:249–64.

———. 1981b. Toward a taxonomy of given-new information. P. Cole, ed., *Radical Pragmatics*, pp. 223–55. New York: Academic Press.

———. 1982. A comparison of topicalization and left-dislocation in discourse. Paper presented at the Linguistic Society of America annual meeting.

Radford, Andrew. 1981. *Transformational Syntax*. Cambridge: Cambridge University Press.

Reesink, G. 1981. Switch reference and topicality hierarchies. Unpublished ms., Summer Institute of Linguistics, Papua New Guinea.

Rosenbaum, Peter. 1967. *The Grammar of English Predicate Complement Constructions*. Cambridge, Mass.: MIT Press.

Ross, John. 1967. Constraints on variables in syntax. MIT dissertation.

———. 1970. On declarative sentences. R. Jacobs & P. Rosenbaum, eds., *Readings in English Transformational Grammar*, pp. 222–72. Waltham, Mass.: Ginn.

———. 1972. Act. D. Davidson & G. Harman, eds., *Semantics of Natural Language*, pp. 70–126. Dordrecht: Reidel.

———. 1973. Nouniness. O. Fujimura, ed., *Three Dimensions of Linguistic Theory*, pp. 137–258. Tokyo: The TEC Co.

Sadock, Jerrold. 1980. Noun incorporation in Greenlandic. *Lg* 56:300–19.

Saksena, A. 1980. The affected agent. *Lg* 56:812–26.

Sankoff, Gillian. 1980. *The Social Life of Language*. Philadelphia: University of Pennsylvania Press.

Sapir, Edward. 1921. *Language*. New York: Harcourt, Brace.

———. 1924. The grammarian and his language. *American Mercury* 1:149–55.

———. 1933. Language. *Encyclopaedia of the Social Sciences* 9:155–69. New York: Macmillan.

Saville-Troike, Muriel & Lynn McCreedy. 1979. Topic prominence in Navajo. Paper presented at the Linguistic Society of America annual meeting.

Schachter, Paul. 1973. Focus and relativization. *Lg* 49:19–46.

———. 1974. A non-transformational account of serial verbs. *SAL* supplement 5:253–70.

———. 1976. The subject in Philippine languages: topic, actor, actor–topic, or none of the above. Li, ed., pp. 491–518.

———. 1977. Reference-related and role-related properties of subjects. Cole & Sadock, eds., pp. 279–306.

———. 1980. Explaining auxiliary order. Indiana University Linguistics Club. Bloomington, Indiana.

Schachter, Paul & Fe Otanes. 1972. *Tagalog Reference Grammar*. Berkeley: University of California Press.

Schreiber, Peter. 1972. Style disjuncts and the performative analysis. *LI* 3:321–48.

Scott, Graham. 1978. *The Fore language of Papua New Guinea. PL* B-47.

Searle, John. 1969. *Speech Acts*. Cambridge: Cambridge University Press.

——. 1975. A taxonomy of illocutionary acts. K. Gunderson, ed., *Language, Mind, and Knowledge*, pp. 344–69. Minneapolis: University of Minnesota Press.

Shibatani, Masayoshi. 1973. Semantics of Japanese causativization. *Foundations of Language* 9:327–73.

——, ed. 1976. *The Grammar of Causative Constructions* (Syntax & semantics 6). New York: Academic Press.

Silverstein, Michael. 1974. *Dialectal Developments in Chinookan Tense-Aspect Systems. An Areal-Historical Analysis. IJAL* memoir 29.

——. 1976a. Shifters, linguistic categories, and cultural description. K. Basso & H. Selby, eds., *Meaning in Anthropology*, pp. 11–56. Albuquerque: University of New Mexico Press.

——. 1976b. Hierarchy of features and ergativity. R. M. W. Dixon, ed., *Grammatical Categories in Australian Languages*, pp. 112–71. Canberra: Australian Institute of Aboriginal Studies.

——. 1977. Cultural prerequisites to grammatical analysis. M. Saville-Troike, ed., *Linguistics and Anthropology*, pp. 139–51. Washington, DC: Georgetown University Press.

——. 1978. Deixis and deducibility in a Wasco-Wishnam passive of evidence. *BLS 4:238–53.*

——. 1979. Language structure and linguistic ideology. P. Clyne *et al.*, eds., *The Elements. A Parasession on Linguistic Units and Levels*, pp. 193–247. Chicago: CLS.

——. 1980a. The three faces of function: preliminaries to a psychology of language. Unpublished ms., University of Chicago.

——. 1980b. Of nominatives and datives: universal grammar from the bottom up. Unpublished ms., University of Chicago. Chicago.

——. 1981. Case marking and the nature of language. *Australian Journal of Linguistics* 1:227–46.

Staalsen, P. 1972. Clause relationships in Iatmul. *Papers in New Guinea Linguistics* 15:45–69. *PL* A-31.

Stahlke, H. 1970. Serial verbs. *SAL* 1:60–99.

Terkel, Studs. 1974. *Working*. New York: Avon Books.

Tesnière, Lucien. 1939. Théorie structurale des temps composés. *Mélanges Bally*, pp. 153–83. Geneva: Georg.

Thompson, Sandra A. 1973. Resultative verb compounds in Mandarin: a case for lexical rules. *Lg* 49:361–79.

Traugott, Elizabeth. 1972. *The History of English Syntax*. New York: Holt, Rinehart & Winston.

Trithart, Lee. 1979. Topicality: an alternative to the relational view of the Bantu passive. *SAL* 10:1–30.

Van Leynseele, H. 1975. Restrictions on serial verbs in Anyi. *Journal of West African Languages* 16:189–218.

Van Valin, Robert D., Jr. 1977a Aspects of Lakhota syntax. University of California, Berkeley, dissertation.

——. 1977b. Ergativity and the universality of subjects. *CLS* 13:689–706.

——. 1980a. Reply to Sadock. M. Kac, ed., *Current Syntactic Theories. Discussion Papers from the 1979 Milwaukee Syntax Conference*, pp. 7–13. Indiana University Linguistics Club. Bloomington, Indiana.

——. 1980b. On the distribution of passive and antipassive constructions in universal grammar. *Lingua* 50:303–27.

——. 1980c. Meaning and interpretation. *Journal of Pragmatics* 4:213–31.

——. 1981a. Grammatical relations in ergative languages. *SL* 5:361–94.

——. 1981b. Toward understanding grammar: form, function, evolution. *Lingua* 54:47–85.

——. 1983. Pragmatics, ergativity, and grammatical relations. *Journal of Pragmatics* 7:63–88.

——. In press. Case marking and the structure of the Lakhota clause. To appear in Nichols & Woodbury, eds.

Van Valin, Robert D., Jr & William A. Foley. 1980. Role and reference grammar. Moravcsik & Wirth, eds., pp. 329–52.

Vendler, Zeno. 1967. *Philosophy in Linguistics*. Ithaca: Cornell University Press.

Walton, Charles. 1983. Sama verbal semantics: classification, derivation, and inflection. Temple University M.A. thesis.

Wasow, Thomas. 1977. Transformations and the lexicon. P. Culicover *et al.*, eds., *Formal Syntax*, pp. 327–60. New York: Academic Press.

Watkins, Mark. 1937. *A Grammar of Chichewa. Language* dissertation 24. Philadelphia: Linguistic Society of America.

Weber, David. 1980. Switch-reference: Quechua. Munro, ed., pp. 48–64.

Wells, M. 1979. Siroi grammar. *PL* B-51.

Wenger, James. 1982. Some universals of honorific language with special reference to Japanese. University of Arizona, dissertation.

Whorf, B.L. 1956. Some verbal categories in Hopi. J. Carroll, ed., *Language, Thought, and Reality*, pp. 112–24. Cambridge, Mass.: MIT Press.

Wierzbicka, Anna. 1980. *Lingua Mentalis*. Sydney: Academic Press.

Wise, Mary Ruth. 1971. *Identification of Participants in Discourse*. Summer Institute of Linguistics publications in Linguistics 28. Norman, Oklahoma.

Wolfart, H. C. 1973. *Plains Cree: a Grammatical Study*. Transactions of the American Philosophical Society 63, pt 5. Philadelphia: American Philosophical Society.

——. 1978. How many obviatives: sense and reference in a Cree verb paradigm. E. D. Cook & J. Kaye, eds., *Linguistic Studies of Native Canada*, pp. 255–72. Vancouver: University of British Columbia Press.

Wolfart, H. C. & J. Carroll. 1981. *Meet Cree*, 2nd ed. Lincoln: University of Nebraska Press.

Woodbury, Anthony. 1975. Ergativity of grammatical processes. University of Chicago Master's essay.

——. 1977. Greenlandic Eskimo, ergativity, and relational grammar. Cole & Sadock, eds., pp. 307–36.

Zubin, David. 1979. Discourse function of morphology: the focus system in German. Givón, ed., pp. 469–504.

Zwicky, Arnold. 1971. In a manner of speaking. *LI* 2:223–33.

Topics index

Languages index